BHATKHANDE'S CONTRIBUTION TO MUSIC
A Historical Perspective

BHATKHANDE'S CONTRIBUTION TO MUSIC
A Historical Perspective

SOBHANA NAYAR

www.popularprakashan.com

Published by
Harsha Bhatkal
for Popular Prakashan Pvt. Ltd.
301, Mahalaxmi Chambers, 22 Bhulabhai Desai Marg
Mumbai - 400 026, India

ISBN 978-81-7154-323-6
(3374)

Printed In India
By Sai Printo Pack Pvt. Ltd., New Delhi 110 020

To the late Shri S.K. Dutt
my revered
'Master Moshai'
who initiated me to
Bhatkhande's work

Foreword

The contribution of Pandit Vishnu Narayan Bhatkhande to the renaissance and reinstallation of Hindustani Music is revolutionising and epoch-making.

Towards the closing decades of the nineteenth century the Hindustani musical scene had touched a veritable low from the social, cultural and educational points of view. The social status and prestige of the musician had gone down. Learning and appreciation of music was taboo and prohibited as an undesirable activity among the middle classes of the cultured intelligentsia. The rich heritage of music had become scattered and fragmented among the narrow circles of the *Gharana* votaries and had become their guarded secret. The hiatus between the theory and practice had widened. There was total lack of material on music pertaining to its theory and history on the one hand and its performance and practice on the other. Without a body of systematised and extensive knowledge properly recorded, no art or discipline can claim a high artistic and academic status; nor can its pursuit in a tangible scholastic pattern be possible.

However, this chaotic condition proved to be darkness before the dawn. The latter half of the nineteenth century was a period of an all-round awakening and resurgence in the history of India. An awareness of India's multidimensional national heritage was growing. Not only in the political and social fields, but also in the scientific, spiritual and cultural spheres, including music, great thinkers and dynamic personalities started making their appearance. The field of music was illumined by the indomitable two-some of Vishnu Narayan Bhatkhande and Vishnu Digambar Paluskar.

The extraordinary genius of Bhatkhande, combined with rare qualities like profound scholarship and discursive brilliance, incisive and extensive vision, tactful and persuasive handling of persons including musicians, was totally harnessed in the service of music. This was a dedicated soul wedded to music.

The vast literature on music created by Bhatkhande runs into seven to eight thousand pages. The valued complex includes a sound and systematised grammar and theory of the present day Hindustani music, hundreds of traditional compositions embodying the *raga* forms, a detailed analysis thereof imparting an historical perspective and deliberations and guidelines for investigation and research. Indeed, it forms a solid bed-rock, a nucleus open-ended, looking ahead, and leading into the future.

Bhatkhande died in the year 1936 at the age of seventy six, leaving a rich legacy for the art and science of music to flourish upon. Today, music is an honourable pursuit patronised and encouraged both as a creative art as well as a discipline for academic studies and research in the highest seats of learning like the Universities.

We are, as it were, in an age of musical explosion. It is desirable and worth-while at this stage, fifty years after his death, to explore into the inspiring life of Bhatkhande who made this explosion possible; to make a critical study of his work and contribution and place these in the perspective obtaining today.

This precisely is the subject of the present work entitled *Bhatkhande's Contribution to Music: A Historical Perspective* by Sobhana Nayar. Based on her doctoral thesis the work encompasses all the relevant aspects of Bhatkhande's life and work. For instance, the socio-cultural environment in which he was born and grew up, the impacts and influences which went into his mental make-up and the formulation of his comprehensive, multidimensional plans for the revival of music have been discussed with a close understanding. Being a research project, the extensive material collected by itself is of value. A critical analysis and evaluation of Bhatkhande's writings and compositions has been carried out with competence and artistic insight. There is a probe into the newly arisen problems and a pointer to the future possibilities.

Dr. Sobhana Nayar's life-long pursuit of music as a performing art and her continued study of its theory have stood her in good stead in writing this book. *Bhatkhande's Contribution to Music: A Historical Perspective* by Dr. Sobhana Nayar is a welcome addition to the growing literature in English on Indian music. I do hope that the work will be of stimulative interest and value to students, teachers and scholars of Indian music at the higher levels of learning whether at home or abroad.

S. MUTATKAR
Producer (Emeritus), A.I.R./T.V.

Acknowledgement

My most grateful thanks are due to my teacher, the late Shri S.K. Dutt, the renowned *sitar* player and scholar, who was a disciple of Shri Vishnu Narayan Bhatkhande and a product of Marris College of Lucknow. He initiated me into the work and life of Bhatkhande. Through Shri S.K. Dutt I had the privilege of coming in contact with the late Pandit Ratanjankar, the great protagonist of Bhatkhande. My thanks are due to him for inspiring me further into the study of Bhatkhande's contribution to music and also to the late Shri N.N. Shukla, a noted musicologist and the Chief Producer of Music, A.I.R., for fruitful discussions about the subject. I offer special thanks to Dr. Mrs. Sumati Mutatkar, a noted performing artist and scholar, who finally helped me to decide to choose the study of Bhatkhande as the subject of my research for the Ph.D. and ably guided me in conducting it. My thanks are also due to the Sangeet Natak Academy and the Delhi University for making available to me their library facilities.

SOBHANA NAYAR

New Delhi
August, 1989

Introduction

The Theme and its Choice

Through my training in music in one of the institutions established by Bhatkhande, I came in contact with his modern method of music education as well as the music literature written by him. I also came across many musicians and students, belonging to the same and allied institutions. I found most of them, after completing their course, plunging into the battle of life. I also found that they regarded Bhatkhande as a myth or a legend. On the other hand, the traditional *ustad*s, the torch-bearers of the famous *gharana*s, with whom also I came in contact, many of them regarded Bhatkhande as an upstart and a pretender to the knowledge of music. It was my impression that none of these categories had the least comprehension of the total magnitude of the work done by him. Nor did they have any understanding of his work from the historical, social and cultural perspective. Therefore, I was curious to learn more about the man who received such wide acclaim on the one hand and such contemptuous criticism on the other. After studying his work thoroughly, I felt amazed at its vastness and thoroughness, its logic and objectivity, its imagination and creativity. I was much impressed by his poetic genius, touched by his enormous suffering and sacrifice for the great cause he espoused and overwhelmed by the rare traits of his character, his humility and humour, his intelligence and scholarship and, above all, his ability to take praise and blame in a spirit of complete detachment. I was amazed at the vastness and multidimensional character of Bhatkhande's monumental achievements which shows what a single individual can do, given the necessary competence, imagination, dedication and inspiration.

I felt provoked to delve deeper and understand more thoroughly such an outstanding personality, evaluate his outstanding contribution and also to get a balanced critical view of this highly controversial figure. I felt that it was necessary to consolidate, serialise and analyse his contribution in the field of music and define the herculean task he performed to resuscitate, revive and systematise a noble art which had reached the lowest depth of degradation at that time. In this exploration, I was further encouraged and inspired by my guide, Dr. Sumati Mutatkar, the Dean of the Faculty of Music, University of Delhi.

This is how I took up *Bhatkhande's Contribution to Music: A Critical Appreciation* as the subject of my thesis for Ph.D. on which the present book is largely based.

The Methodology and Design

The major ingredients of the methodology used are as follows:

(a) As one of the important aims of Bhatkhande was to link the past and the present in an evolutionary process and to bridge the various gaps that had grown between the different periods of history and thereby to preserve and digest for the present, what was still relevant in the past, a significant strand of the methodology has been the historical. Even though Bhatkhande ultimately reached the conclusion that most of the gaps between the past and the present were unbridgeable, his was the most serious and formidable attempt to understand our glorious heritage.

(b) As every revolutionary both draws upon his milieu as well as transforms it, the study of the age of Bhatkhande--in its total social, political and cultural aspects, its decadence and inspiration--formed an important part of the study. This multidimensional approach was also important in view of the inevitable interaction of the various social, economic and cultural forces of which music is, perhaps, the most important manifestation.

(c) The most dynamic element which transforms an age is the personality of the man of destiny. Hence the study of the mental make-up of Bhatkhande became an important element of the method adopted to understand the theme.

(d) In the formation of every personality there are certain individuals who make a significant contribution and hence deserve careful identification and special treatment. Such an attempt in regard to Bhatkhande's contemporaries, therefore, formed an important ingredient of the study.

(e) To understand the magnitude and importance of Bhatkhande's work it is necessary to know the state of music as existed in his time. Therefore in the second chapter the condition of music has been dealt with as regards its practice and training therein as well as the life-style and character of its propagators.

(f) The quality of his contribution in regard to the different areas of present day music has been analysed and discussed elaborately in separate chapters while his books have been particularly reviewed and his masterly composition of songs has been analysed from different angles.

(g) To complete the study in the concluding chapter a synoptic view of Bhatkhande's life and work has been indicated and scope of further research is also added.

(h) In the evaluation of Bhatkhande's work both secondary and primary data have been used. The primary data has been provided by the books, written by Bhatkhande himself, translations of *granthas*, books on the theory of music, collection of his own musical compositions, collection of the traditional compositions etc.

   The secondary data was provided by the opinions expressed on Bhatkhande's work by his contemporaries and successors, some of whom the author had the privilege of knowing personally. I also had the privilege of studying in one of the best institutions that Bhatkhande set up--the Marris College, Lucknow. I was also helped through my formal and informal contacts with the music world for more than 30 years in which Bhatkhande, being one of the stalwarts, could not but be discussed.

(i) As the contribution of Bhatkhande to the revival and rejuvenation of music was many-sided and at the same time deep, the technique used has been both analytical and synthetic. His contribution in each field has been analysed in depth and yet the various activities have been shown acting and interacting, and in inter-relationship.

Review of Existing Literature

Looking for books on Bhatkhande, one finds that the books written on him are few and far between. They give only a part picture of Bhatkhande's work or personality, dwelling on one or two dimensions only. The existing literature is either adulatory or over-critical. It is the need of the day, however, to have a well-balanced critical evaluation of Bhatkhande's work and personality. The value of the existing literature to the research-scholar is, therefore, limited and he has primarily to rely on the primary data presented by Bhatkhande's own books. The most valuable books on Bhatkhande are:

1. *Pandit Bhatkhande* by S. N. Ratanjankar. Published by the National Book Trust.
2. *Bhatkhande Smriti Grantha.* Published by Indira Kala Sangeet Vishvavidyalaya, Khairagarh.

A Hope

I hope this modest attempt of mine will give at least a peep into the great saga of Bhatkhande's endeavour and achievements. The book also aims at serving -- in however limited a way -- both the students in the universities, by collecting widely scattered material and presenting it in perspective, and the research workers. It also aspires to present music as an important component of the social, economic, political and cultural spectrum of national life, acting and interacting with the other components, and thereby bring out the importance of an inter-disciplinary approach. I hope, through this study, I will be able to discharge, at least to some extent, the deep debt of gratitude that I owe to music for enriching and brightening my life.

SOBHANA NAYAR

Contents

PART THREE

THE PARTING MILIEU

PART I

THE PARAMETERS

1

The Age of Bhatkhande

Every man of Destiny, while he alters the course of history, is himself its product. As a matter of fact, his capacity to give a determined push to his age arises from the fact that he vivifies and articulates the still vague, inaudible and inarticulate stirrings of his age which immediately draws to him, in some apparently inexplicable way, the mass of his people. So with Bhatkhande. He brought about a revolutionary change in Hindustani classical music. It was never the same after Bhatkhande--quantitatively or qualitatively. Music is, however, not an isolated phenomenon. It interacts with and shares the pulsation of every band of the socio-cultural spectrum. From ancient times it was at the heart of Indian culture. The very name Bharata is explained by some scholars as consisting of the three ingredients of music Bha=*bhava* (feeling, mood) + Ra=*raga* (composition) + Ta=*tala* (beat or the rhythmic pattern). Music is both the expression and architect of India's deeper consciousness. From ancient times to Bhatkhande's age it changed and developed with changes in the social, cultural and political situation, while carrying within its womb the heritage of the past. It is, therefore, impossible to study and understand Hindustani classical music except in its total socio-cultural context in an historical perspective. It was especially so with Bhatkhande who bestrode the gap of centuries, trying to link both the past and the present, with a dedication and capacity rarely to be met with.

I

HERITAGE OF THE ANCIENT PAST

Indian civilization is one of the most ancient civilizations. The excavations of Harappa and Mohenjodaro bear ample testimony to this fact. It is recognised that by the third and fourth millennium B. C. the Indian civilization was ahead of other existing advanced civilizations of the world. Explorations by archaeologists have uncovered, in a fine state of preservation, "great cities and industries, comfortable homes and luxuries, ranging from bathrooms to statuary and jewelry."[1] Even at this early period she had an elaborate drainage system which speaks of a social condition "superior to that prevailing in contemporary Babylonia and Egypt."[2]

The culture of music was not lagging behind as appears from the 'diggings of Mohenjodaro and Harappa mounds.' Among the 'valuable things' found were "musical instruments, like crude type flutes, lutes or *veena* with seven strings, different kinds of drums and a bronze dancing girl. The 'veena with seven strings' proves that the musical sense of the Indus Valley people was very keen and artistic."[3]

From the days of the Buddha, the sixth century B. C., through the times of Ashoka down to the sixteenth century, India was as advanced as the West in crafts, commerce, industry and agriculture, education and civil government, religion, philosophy, music and many branches of science and learning. In many respects she was even more advanced. A rich literature on music existed from the period of A. D. 200. In the sixteenth century Vijayanagar--with its legendary wealth, art and culture--flourished in South India and under Akbar Fatehpur Sikri and Agra dazzled the traveller from afar. The marvellous architecture of Shahjahan's time followed. This was the golden age in regard to the culture of music, architecture, painting, sculpture etc. The firmament of music was glowing with the galaxy of talented artists and creative exponents like Baiju Bawara, Nayaka Gopal, Amir Khusrau, Raja Man, Swami Haridas Goswami and their worthy successors.

With Aurangzeb, however, the decline began of art and culture because of his antipathy towards these and after him there were fifty years of widespread fighting and confusion in the country. Most of the kings who succeeded Aurangzeb were weak and were interested only in enjoying themselves. "During the time of Shah Alam II (eighteenth century A.D.), the last titular Mughal Emperor of Delhi, the glorious musical tradition of the Delhi Court came to an end. Muslim and Hindu *ustad*s of Delhi, Agra and adjacent places dispersed all over Northern India."[4] After this period the English established their rule in this country.

II

THE ENGLISH CONQUEST AND ITS IMPACT

When the Europeans established their power in this country in the eighteenth century, India was still culturally rich and economically prosperous. She was, however, politically disorganised and militarily weak and was passing through a phase of social decay. Her rulers, who were petty kings, nobles and princes, were busy in internecine strife. They, with their antiquated outlook, proved no match for the foreigners who came "armed with the latest European artillery and morals."[5] And so a country with an ancient culture and civilization went under the onslaught of an invader who was culturally, and also in several other respects, her inferior. The musicians, who depended upon the nobility and the native princes, were suddenly uprooted. They were forced to take shelter in different durbars of the smaller states of Rajputana, Awadh, Betiya, Rewa, Gwalior, Bengal etc.

The British systematically annexed the territories belonging to the small kings and nawabs as the first step towards subjugation of the whole country.

Mysore was conquered from Tipu Sultan in 1799. Two years later, Karnatak was annexed and Awadh was forced to cede a part of its territory to the British. Slowly and steadily the other princely states were annexed under one pretext or the other. Lord Dalhousie completed the work that Lord Wellesly had begun by annexing the territory of any Indian ruler, who died without leaving a direct heir. Before the nineteenth century was half through, the Maratha Confederacy's power was broken (1818), Sind was seized (1843), the Sikh state was liquidated and Punjab was annexed (1849). Burma was conquered in 1852 and in 1856 Awadh was taken over. As early as 1764 the last Mughal ruler of Bengal was deposed. The Mughal emperor at Delhi was reduced to a mere shadow. The British had their grip firm on the soil of India.

Effect of Foreign Rule

An inevitable consequence of foreign rule is the deterioration of national character and culture. India had been conquered before by Mughals, Pathans, Hunas etc. Some of them plundered, looted and destroyed the country and left it leaving behind a trail of devastation. But she recovered from these shocks. Mughals and Pathans settled in this country and made India their home, thus making for a fusion of cultures. Under British rule, however, India for the first time was enslaved and became an appendage of another country. The result was that she was drained dry.

Economic Condition

The British came to this country to amass wealth and pursued beyond human imagination a ruthless policy to extort money as taxes from the masses. Unlike the other plunderers -- the Shakas and the Hunas etc. -- whose plundering activity was temporary and short-lived, the British remained in this country to exploit its rich resources and carry the wealth home. India was bled white.

The last Mughal ruler of Bengal, as stated, was deposed in 1764 and within thirty years the British rulers raised from the same territory a revenue three and a quarter times of the previous figure. Allahabad and some other rich districts, ceded to the British in 1862, met with the same fate. "Every effort, lawful and unlawful, was made to get the utmost out of the wretched peasantry, who were subjected to torture -- in some instances, cruel and revolting beyond all description... Numbers abandoned their homes and fled into the neighbouring Native States. Large tracts of land were thrown out of cultivation and in some districts no more than a third of the cultivable area remained in occupation."[6]

In 1770 a terrible famine carried off ten million people -- one third of the entire population of Bengal. Yet the revenue was collected fully by adding 10 per cent "by which the living made good revenue losses which were owing to other tax payers having been so unpatriotic as to die."[7]

Wherever the British power spread, the above conditions followed and the longer it continued, the worse became the plight of the peasantry and the general poverty of the people. In a *Minute* dated 18th September, 1789, Lord Cornwallis reported:-- "I may safely assert that one third of the company's territory in Hindustan is now a jungle inhabited only by wild beasts."[8]

Administration

Not only this, even the person and property of a citizen were completely insecure. Daring dacoities were committed in broad daylight in large towns and centres of trade. "A monstrous and disorganised state of society, in consequence, existed under the eye. of the supreme British authorities and almost at the very seat of the Government."[9] Although special magistrates under European superintendents were appointed and armed with special powers to put down robbery the situation became worse as people were not willing to come forward as witnesses. Witnesses were consequently dragged from their homes until the people considered it one of the severest punishments to be cited as witnesses. The informers or 'Goendas' engaged by the British often led to the arrest and punishment of innocent people. "Dacoity itself, dreadful as it is, cannot be compared in its quantum of mischief to what was produced by this horrid system."[10]

The Moral Drain and the Educational and Cultural Assault

The worst sufferers, however, were the country's morale, education and culture. The British, in order to strengthen their grip on this country, reserved all the high offices for their countrymen. They pursued a policy of discrimination in every field and consequently a moral drain ensued. Except for the petty clerks or others of similar subordinate positions, India's talented natives were not allowed to gain, retain and develop experience and knowledge of statesmanship, of administration, and of high scientific and learned professions. The English, who were in charge of the senior positions where this experience and knowledge could be gained, at the end of their career returned to England and carried these intellectual and moral assets with them. All the talent and nobility of intellect and soul, which nature gives to every country, thus became to India a lost treasure.

Music also felt the impact of these impoverishing forces. The conqueror's race, proud and arrogant as it was, naturally did not respect the traditional heritage of art and music of our country. The greatest casualty of foreign invasion was that of our heritage of art and culture. In 1824 Elphinstone, the Governor of Bombay, wrote that the English people had "dried up the fountains of native talent, and that from the nature of our (*their*) conquests, not only all encouragement to the advancement of knowledge is (*was*) withdrawn, but even the actual learning of the nation is (*was*) likely to be lost and the production of the former genius to be forgotten."[11]

The British regime not only dealt a death blow to indigenous learning and culture, even elementary education was also made by it to decline. Before British rule India had its indigenous system of education which brought elementary education within the reach of even the poorest. The Mughal rulers had recognised the duty of the state to spread education and encourage learning. The learned and the scholars were held in high esteem and the Emperor's court was well-known for having a galaxy of talent. When the British came they annexed all the free lands given to the *pathashalas*, *maktabs* and *madarsas* for the increase of revenues. The East India Company pursued a policy of not educating the native for fear of losing their grip on the country. "It was our policy in those days," wrote Kaye in his *Life of Metcalfe*, "to keep the Indians in the profoundest possible state of barbarism and darkness, and every attempt to diffuse the light of knowledge among the people...was vehemently opposed..."[12]

Some measure of English education, however, indirectly seeped in, because of the need to train a sufficient number of low paid clerks to run the administration. The Christian missionary too entered the field of education primarily for the spread of the Gospel.

The question soon arose whether education in India should be given through the medium of the Indian languages or through English. The supporters of the former view were known as 'Orientalists' and of the latter view as 'Anglicists.' In 1835, the Orientalists in a royal battle with the Anglicists were routed and Macaulay introduced his scheme of imparting education on Western lines with English as the medium. Macaulay believed that "a single shelf of a good European library was worth the whole native literature of India and Arabia."[13]

He looked upon the languages and literature of the East as a 'diseased limb' which he proposed to cut off. "The aim of English education," stated Macaulay, "should be to create a class of persons, Indian in blood and colour and English in tastes, in opinions, in morals, in intellect."

This came to be known as the filteration theory. What English education actually achieved was to denationalise, de-Indianise the educated people and turn them into 'imitation Europeans.' Those who came under its influence lost their moorings and were lost to themselves and to the country.

In the words of Lord Ronaldshay, one time Governor of Bengal, "By the middle of the nineteenth century a period of intellectual anarchy had set in, which swept the rising generation before it like a craft which had snapped its mooring."[14]

Westernism became the fashion of the day -- and westernism demanded of its votaries that they should cry down the civilization of their own country. The more ardent was this admiration for everything Western, the more vehement became their denunciation of everything Eastern. Ancient learning was despised, ancient customs and traditions were thrust aside, and ancient religion was decried as an outworn superstition. The ancient foundations upon which the complex structure of Hindu society had been built were undermined and the new generation of non-believers of everything Indian found little enough with which to underpin the edifice, which they were so recklessly depriving of its own foundations.

Learning of Sanskrit, Persian and Arabic came to be regarded as barbarous, unwholesome and unfashionable. Use of the mothertongue was looked down upon as undignified and a sign of backwardness. Western food, dress and way of living were adopted by the educated youth who copied Western manners and speech. As a result they became strangers in their own land and were alienated by their habits, language and way of thinking from the mass of the people. Michael Madhusudan Dutt, the famous Bengali poet, boasted that he "even dreamed in English."[15]

As the educated Indians reacted against their own past in the aforesaid manner they were also gripped by religious scepticism which "ate its way into the moral fibre of young Bengal with all the virulence of a corroding acid. Irreverence, indiscipline and dissipation became the fashion among the educated youth."[16]

A well-known Bengali landlord, philanthropist and educationist, Babu Raj Narayan Basu of the nineteenth century, who was the grandfather of Shri Aurobindo Ghosh, on the mother's side, described in his autobiography how in his days blind copying of English vices was regarded as fashionable including the habit of drinking wine.[17] Intemperate drinking, licentiousness of thought, taste and character were rampant. Infidelity, indifference to religion and point-blank atheism were unblushingly professed.[18] It is an old observation that he who loses his liberty loses half his virtue. This is true of nations as well as of individuals.

The invasion of culture was accentuated by the English missionaries sent by England to work against the religious beliefs of the natives. Bengal society received a rude shock when a number of young men of outstanding ability and character, of a missionary college in Calcutta and coming from some of the highest Hindu families, were converted to Christianity. It was a reasonable guess by Macaulay that 'enlightenment' would kill Hinduism and bring in Christianity. For a while it looked as if Bengal, led by its young intelligentsia, was at the start of a mass movement into Christianity.[19] History records that it could not materialise for the reason that great men were born to inspire the new generation to reverse the trend. When the condition was at its darkest a great upheaval came in the form of revolt by which the British were forced to change their policy.

III

THE GREAT REVOLT

For a century the people suffered in silence but as the expression of general discontent arose, they ultimately stood against the British in armed violence and thus came the Great Revolt of 1857. The reason on the surface was the refusal of Indian sepoys at Meerut to handle cartridges greased with the animal fat forbidden by their religions. But the real cause lay much deeper. It was to register their protest against the repressive policy of their conquerors that the Indian sepoys turned their guns on their masters. This great uprising was fomented by the discontented masses and the deposed rulers of the princely States, which helped to turn it into a revolutionary war. But in military efficiency the mutineers were no match for the British. By the autumn of 1858 the rising was crushed and its leaders were killed. Not only this, the Mughal Emperor, Bahadur Shah II, was deposed and deported to Rangoon where he died in prison. His heir and three of his sons were shot by a British military officer and their dead bodies were dragged through the streets of Delhi in full public view. Thus the era of the once prosperous Mughal rule came to an end. Also came to an end a prosperous era of art and music patronised by them.

Following the suppression of the 1857 rising, a bill was introduced in the British Parliament for the abolition of the East India Company's rule and for direct assumption by the Crown of the responsibility for governing India.

When the Crown took over from the Company, British India was less than one-half of what it became later. The expansion of British territory after the Crown took over was continued by absorbing more and more territories represented by Indian and the border States.

British regime was distinguished from all other previous regimes by the fact that the British never settled down in India. They never made India their home. They came as foreigners and stayed as foreigners till the very last. On the other hand, India's other conquerors -- Pathans, Mughals and others -- made India their home and the culture of these foreigners had a great impact on the existing literary, musical and artistic field of our country. Wrote Edmund Burke: "The Asiatic Conquerors very soon abated of their ferocity, because they made the conquered country their own. They rose or fell with the rise and fall of the territory they lived in... With many disorders and with few political checks upon power nature had still fair play, the sources of acquisition were not dried up, and therefore the trade, the manufacture, and the commerce of the country flourished... But under the British Government all these orders were reversed."[20]

As stated earlier, the 1857 rising was ruthlessly suppressed and those who had taken part in it were liquidated most cruelly for establishing the prestige and power of the British. Not only that, to make another rising impossible, the whole of British India was disarmed. The British engaged themselves in re-establishing their rule firmly in this land and outwardly India appeared to be in peace.

The British now cultivated the elements which belonged to the feudal class, represented by those of the Princely order and the landlords, who had prevented the people under them to join the revolt. For strengthening and consolidating the British rule, the Zamindari System was introduced. With this a new class of landlords came into being pampered by the British who resorted to a life of luxury and entertainment at the cost of the mass of the people who were the tax-payers.

IV

THE RENAISSANCE

It appears that the Indian rising of 1857 had been no more than a desperate plunge into a mass holocaust by the dispossessed class. It is said that suffering by itself has no regenerative power. But in case of India, beneath the surface stagnation, there still rolled deeply the placid waters of life. Defeated, crushed and humiliated, she, with her rich cultural past and unbroken spiritual tradition, fell back upon the silent inner reservoir of vitality for a renewal of her strength. In less than thirty years, after the great revolt had been ruthlessly put down, she was once again heading for a national resurgence which gathered volume till she was a free country.

Prof. Arnold Toyenbee, in one of his lectures on India, spoke of the "contemplative way, of the creative withdrawal into the spirit without which man may not live." "This was", he observed, "the Buddha's way." Two thousand years after, it became the way of India's redemption also. With her vitality at a low ebb and a creeping paralysis coming over her, India in her bondage found the means of her national regeneration in her introversion where, in the words of Romain Rolland, "the fire of her threatened life had taken refuge." The resulting inner transformation manifested itself in a sudden burst of renaissance in the latter half of the nineteenth century in all walks of her national life--religion, culture, art, science, music, literature, social reform and political activity. It taught us to take pride in our old values and explained our ancient heritage in a new perspective. Music, being one of the most important components of our culture, was remodelled and recast.

The Indian firmament at this time glowed with a host of luminaries, which included orientalists like Rajendralal Mitra and R.G. Bhandarkar; scientists like J.C. Bose and P.C. Ray; artists like

Abanindranath Tagore and Gaganendranath Tagore, the founders of the Bengal School of Art in the North, and Ravi Verma in the South; scholars like Krishna Mohan Banerji, who edited the first Bengali Encyclopaedia in 13 volumes in 1851; and a host of poets, playwrights, artists and prose writers. Pandit Vishnu Narayan Bhatkhande and Pandit Vishnu Digambar Paluskar, whose names were connected with the reviving and revitalising of music ever afterwards, were also products of this age. Ishwarchandra Vidyasagar (1820-1891), the kind-hearted agnostic, humanitarian, educationist and social reformer, took up the work of social reform where Raja Rammohun Roy had left it. His name will for ever be remembered for strongly advocating the cause of widow remarriage. Michael Madhusudan Dutt (1824-73), the Christian poet and the author of the celebrated epic poem *Meghanada Vadha* created blank verse in Bengali; Dinabandhu Mitra (1829-74) made history in the indigo cultivators' revolt by his sensational play *Nil Darpan* and Girish Chandra Ghosh, the bohemian actor-manager-playwright, transmuted into a devotee by the alchemy of Ramakrishna Paramahansa, made the Bengali theatre into a great living force for forty years.

Foremost among the prose writers was Bankim Chandra Chatterji, popularly known as the Walter Scott of Bengal. Father of modern Bengali prose and creator of the historical novel, he led the revolt against the craze that had seized the Indian educated youth as a result of their Western education to copy English manners, dress and ways of living and to hold in contempt their mothertongue. He also revolted against the classical tradition of the Bengali writers, and by turning popular Bengali into the medium of literary expression made Bengali literature the heritage of the millions instead of being the cherished possession of the learned few.

Another bright luminary was Rabindranath Tagore. He put India on the map by attaining world-wide fame as a thinker, philosopher, poet, artist and man of letters, and, above all, as the Prophet of Humanity.

Among the Muslims there rose poets like Hali, Ghalib and Iqbal; theological writers and historians of Islam like Amir Ali and Shibli Numani and reformers like Syed Ahmed Khan.

This renaissance was partly the result of the violent political and cultural impact of the West which awakened India to the necessity of putting her own house in order. Partly it was the fruit of cross-fertilisation of the cultures of the East and the West, following the spread of Western education. In the years 1870-80, large numbers of Indians had drunk deep of English political philosophers like Mill, Bentham, Comte, Herbert Spenser and Burke. But essentially it was the result of India's vitality reacting with its native vigour to these external stimuli. No small service in this was rendered by the orientalists, archaeologists, epigraphists and critics like Sir William Jones and Sir Charles Wilkins; Colebrook, Wilson and Muir; Monier-Williams, Paul Deusson and Max Muller; Buhler, Fleet Havell and Ananda Coomaraswamy. They revealed to India the greatness and glory of her treasures of ancient wisdom, architecture and art and made her take pride in her rich heritage.

The Social and Religious Reformers of the Renaissance

The most important person, responsible for the Renaissance was Raja Rammohun Roy (1772-1833) who was responsible for giving it a powerful impetus. The names of reforms and progressive causes with which he was identified is legion. An intellectual giant, Raja Rammohun Roy is remembered as the Father of Modern India, the Prophet of Indian Nationalism and the pioneer of public life in India. Born in the latter half of the eighteenth century, he was a crusader who fought a relentless battle against the evil social customs of his time. Hindu society, then, was full of superstitions, meaningless religious rituals and a host of evil social customs and prejudices. His main contribution was to purify Hindu faith and Hindu society. He displayed his spiritual talent by establishing the *Brahmo Samaj* in 1828 which practised the pure worship of the Eternal, Formless and Omnipresent Being, who is the Author and the Preserver of the Universe. He was the one to bring about the synthesis of the cultures of the East and the West after making a deep study of Christianity, Islam, the Vedas and the Upanishads. He strongly advocated abolishing *sati*, stopping polygamy, introducing remarriage of widows and intercaste marriages, friendship between Hindus and Muslims, education on modern lines, women's education, liberty of thought, legal reforms and political equality. He was the first to recognise that only Devnagari and Hindi, and not English, could be India's *Lingua Franca*. He was a passionate lover of liberty. In 1830 he went to England as the envoy of the Delhi Emperor to represent the latter's grievances to the King of Great Britain. He died in 1833 at Bristol.

Raja Dwarakanath Tagore of Jorasanko, Calcutta, was a close associate of Raja Rammohun Roy in his movement for social reforms and founding of the *Brahmo Samaj*. His son, Maharshi Debendranath Tagore, father of poet Rabindranath Tagore, was initiated in his father's ideology and succeeded Raja Rammohun Roy as the leader of the *Brahmo Samaj*. A deeply religious person, Maharshi Debendranath Tagore was an aristocrat in mind and soul. He slightly differed in religious ideas from the Raja but followed him as a social reformer. He also was out to reform Hinduism so that, purged of its evils, it might re-emerge unified and strengthened to play its rightful role in national regeneration.

Keshab Chandra Sen was the next leader of the *Brahmo Samaj*. He was a keen champion of purging Hinduism of its evils and in the process of doing so he gave *Brahmo Samaj* a doctrine which gave it a marked Christian colouring. But Maharshi Debendranath's knowledge and wisdom saved the Samaj from severing connection completely with Hinduism. Keshab Chandra Sen, however, felt that in regard to social reform the *Brahmo Samaj* could not make much headway. Therefore, to give social reform a push forward, he broke away from the original organisation and founded *Nav Vidhan Samaj*. The influence of Ramakrishna Paramahansa, however, convinced him that the Gods were, at bottom, nothing but the names of different attributes of one God, and idolatry was nothing but the worship of divine attributes. The *Brahmo Samaj* helped to liberalise and rationalise Hinduism and infused social reform into Hindu society. In Gandhiji's words, *Brahmo Samaj* "liberated reason and left room enough for faith."[21] Devotional songs were a part of the Samaj's meetings and some of them were *dhrupad*s sung with *pakhavaj*.

An offshoot of *Brahmo Samaj* was *Prarthana Samaj*. In 1849 an association named *Paramahansa Sabha* was formed in Bombay which had as one of its objectives the breaking down of caste barriers. The association later broke up. But when Keshab Chandra Sen visited Bombay, the earnest members of the aforesaid Sabha gathered together and decided to form a new association for the purpose of introducing reforms such as remarriage of widows, abolition of child-marriage, disapproval of caste and propagation of women's education. *Brahmo Samaj* and the *Prarthana Samaj* were responsible for producing some of the greatest nationalist leaders. The *Brahmo Samaj* produced Surendra Nath Banerji, B.C. Pal, C.R. Das and the Tagores in Bengal; K. Natarajan, Narayan Chandavarkar, Mahadev Govind Ranade and Gopal Krishna Gokhale were the products of *Prarthana Samaj* in Bombay.

In regard to social reform another important movement was launched by Swami Dayanand Saraswati in the North. Born in the year of 1824, his attempt was to revive the pure ancient Vedic faith, culture and institutions. Unlike the *Brahmo Samaj* movement, which believed in borrowing knowledge and wisdom from the West, the *Arya Samaj* revolted against anything Western and propagated the supremacy of the Vedas and the doctrine of *Karma*. He condemned idolatry, animal sacrifice, ancestor worship, pilgrimages, priestcraft and child-marriage. The *Arya Samaj* tried hard to rid Hindu society of its evils by throwing open the ancient spiritual knowledge, confined hitherto to the scriptures written in Sanskrit, to everybody by translating and writing them in the vernacular -- the common language of the people. Their study was previously restricted to the orthodox Brahmins only. In humanitarian service the *Arya Samaj* organised the following activities:-- founding and running of orphanages, widow's homes, workshops for boys and girls and voluntary services at the time of public calamities. Swami Dayanand fought, with a passion seldom equalled, against the various handicaps from which women suffered and the inferior status which custom had assigned to them in society.

At this time a very important international association was founded by Madame Blavatsky and Col. Olcott which was named the Theosophical Society. The word 'Theosophy' is an exact translation of the well-known Sanskrit term *Brahmavidya*, or the knowledge of the Absolute. It symbolised the West turning to the East for knowledge and wisdom. Among the more important of the teachings of the Theosophical Society are the "unity of Godhead, corresponding to the Vedantic conception of the Absolute; the immortality of the soul and the realisation of universal brotherhood."[22] The Theosophical movement was important as it stood as a champion of India's ancient faiths and culture at a time when the Indian intelligentsia had developed a strong inferiority complex. The Theosophical movement helped to restore to them their lost self-respect, pride in themselves -- their traditions and their past -- and to reawaken the urge again to take their place among the great nations of the world. It laboured to popularise in Europe and America a number of the best oriental scriptures like the Upanishads and the *Gita* and taught the Western nations to sympathise with the people of the Orient as their brothers worthy of their respect. The most outstanding figure in this movement was Annie Besant. Sir Valentine Chirol wrote about her:-- "It is surprising that Hindus should turn their back on our civilization when a European of highly trained intellectual power and with an extraordinary gift of eloquence comes and tells them that it is they who possessed the key to supreme wisdom, that their gods, their philosophy, their morality are on a higher plane of thought than the West has ever reached."

Shri Ramakrishna Paramahansa, born in 1836, was the foremost among the religious path-finders of that century. He was an illumined soul which touched the Supreme. His spiritual genius was responsible for showing the light of truth to many who were learned, wise and thinkers of his time. Himself a simple, unlettered plebian soul, a man of the masses and from the masses, having no air and pretensions, he possessed an intuitive burning knowledge of the Absolute and radiated the same. To satisfy the inner quest, people from all walks of life congregated around him. His positive spiritual experience was that realisation is the essence of religion. All disputes, controversies and polemics stop when realisation begins. It is only those who have no religious experience quarrel about the forms of God. To a man, who has realised, all religions are paths leading to the same goal. The society of his time was ridden with factional quarrels of caste, creed and religious belief. Therefore, his teachings held an important place in India's social and national regeneration. He himself had practised all religions -- Hinduism, Islam and Christianity -- and declared that it was the same God towards whom all were travelling -- only they were coming through diverse ways. In his religion there was room for both the formless God and the forms of all gods. He insisted that every man should purge himself of lust and greed before he could do any useful service to the world. He also insisted that unless one had self-realisation, his service to humanity would be devoid of His will and would be the means of pampering the individual ego rather than doing any social service in the real sense of the word. Therefore, social service and striving for self-realisation were complementary to each other.

He was very fond of singing in praise of Goddess *Kali*. His sweet voice and rendering with great feeling and devotion cast a spell on his listeners.

He was the torch-bearer of teachers like Guru Nanak, who said that he was neither Hindu nor Muslim but a worshipper of the Formless one. Preceding Ramakrishna were Muslim saints like Shaikh Mahomed Farid and Mahomed Kazi, who were respected by Hindus and Muslims alike, and Chaitanya Mahaprabhu, who had Muslim disciples as well as Hindu.

Narendra Nath Dutt, later known as Swami Vivekananda, was Shri Ramakrishna Paramahansa's chief disciple and was responsible for translating his masters gospel into action. He was also responsible for interpreting his message to the West. Narendra Nath was the founder of Shri Ramakrishna Mission which even today carries on service to humanity, based on Shri Ramakrishna's principle that nobody can truly serve man unless he sees the God in himself.

In 1863, Narendra Nath was born in a middle class family of Calcutta and in his early youth he became a member of *Sadharan Brahmo Samaj*. Later he came into contact with the great Saint of Dakshineshwar and was completely transformed. He was a singer of *dhrupad* with devotional content which he often sang at the feet of the master.

After the death of his master he took to travelling on foot the entire country from one corner to the other and was overwhelmed by the appalling poverty of the people. His travels also revealed to him the eternal India, with her bewildering diversity of races, cultures and creeds as also the fundamental unity of flesh and spirit beneath that diversity. He went to America to join the Parliament of Religions and to appeal to the West for the means of ameliorating the material condition of India and to propagate the gospel of the Spirit.

His speeches in the West spoke that India must render service true to her own self. The soul of India's national life was religion. Therefore, social reform, politics and education must all draw their vitality from a quickening of the religious spirit. India would be lost if she forgot her spiritual ideal in the pursuit of material progress or power after the manner of the West. India was the proud inheritor of the eternal grand idea of the spiritual oneness of the whole universe, embodied in the *Vedanta*, the one ultimate sanction of all morality, that you and I are not only brothers but that you and I are really one. It should be India's proud privilege to realise this idea and then present it to the world.

The message that Vivekananda delivered on his return from America was one of self-help, unity, uplift of the masses, elevation of the status of women and the need for organisation and remembering the long forgotten truths of the Upanishads so that the Indian masses might realise their own strength and overcome their ignorance and poverty. His idea was to merge into religion the idea of patriotism and service to humanity.

The Nationalist Movement

Along with the movement for reforming religious and social customs the nationalist movement also gained momentum as people were exasperated by the British policy of discrimination, subjugation and humiliation.

Observes Wilhelm Dibelius:-- "There are two possible solutions to the relations between the ruler and the ruled. One is assimilation of the ruled to their conquerors, the other is paternalistic promotion of the material welfare of the dependent people in every way subject to the maintenance of a sharp line of distinction between two social classes never to be obliterated."[23] The first represented the goal of British statesmanship, the second reflected the outlook of the average Englishman. The conflict between the two concepts created an anomalous situation. A young Indian, who returned after winning the highest academic degree with distinction from Cambridge or Oxford, found that in spite of all his qualifications, all positions were beyond his reach.

To spread education and to de-Indianise Indians universities on modern lines were established in Calcutta, Bombay and Madras in 1858. But Macaulay's filteration theory -- which was an all-out attempt to create a class of people, Indians in blood and colour but English in taste, opinions, morals and intellect -- had by that time worn thin. In nine cases out of ten the educated Indian, instead of becoming a zealous apostle of the new order, became a determined opponent of British rule from the bottom of his heart. Even after the Great Revolt when the British consolidated their position and firmly established themselves as the rulers of this country, the economic drain and the repressive and humiliating policy continued in general which made the educated youth feel the scorching effect of subjugation.   They were in search of some way to release themselves from such repression. It slowly dawned on them that only by the development of their internal strength by mass awakening, organisation and training for political action, could they win back their lost independence. With the access to liberal thought and ideas of Western democracy and freedom, coupled with the historic events like the American War of Independence and the French Revolution, the mind of the educated Indian felt the surge of Indepe ence. All the leaders from Raja Rammohun Roy onwards contributed to it.

Raja Rammohun Roy, Maharshi Debendranath Tagore, Keshab Chandra Sen, Shibnath Shastry and Bepin Chandra Pal became also the prophets of Indian nationalism. Maharshi Debendranath Tagore influenced noble and idealistic people like Babu Raj Narayan Basu (1838-1899), popularly known as Rishi Raj Narayan. Raj Narayan was a teacher and such was the influence of his personality that he moulded the lives and the character of hundreds of youths, who came under his influence. To counter the attack of Westernism and the cultural ill effects of western education and to counteract its denationalising trend, he established a society called *Jatiya Gaurabechchha Sancharini Sabha* (Society for the Propagation of Nationalism). The objects of the proposed society included the physical training of youth, publication of books for diffusion of knowledge about the glories of ancient India, encouraging the study of Sanskrit, making the use exclusively of the mothertongue the rule for every son of the soil, promotion of the study of indigenous medicine and other sciences, and revival of customs and manners and institutions calculated to foster national feelings which would lead to the formation of national character. "India is our motherland," wrote Raj Narayan, "We will serve her even at the cost of our lives."

The years of 1860 and 1861 are notable in Indian history which saw the birth not only of Indian nationalism but also of a galaxy of Indian nation builders -- P.C. Ray, Motilal Nehru, Madan Mohan Malaviya and the poet Rabindranath Tagore.

Around the same time in 1860 was born Vishnu Narayan Bhatkhande in the state of Maharashtra. Like all other branches of culture, art and education, music also reached a stage of degeneration and stagnation with the advent of British rule. It was Bhatkhande, who performed the herculean task of rescuing it from the decadent state and re-establishing it as a major force in our cultural life.

Guided by the above-mentioned luminaries the national movement was gaining momentum in the late 19th century. In 1867 Nabagopal Mitra, the editor of the *National Paper* started by Debendranath, two years earlier, in consultation with Raj Narayan, organised the *Jatiya Mela* (National Conference) for the promotion of unity and self-help among Indians through the cultivation and development of national consciousness. This met annually for twelve years in Calcutta. Scholars used music as a vehicle for the above purpose and the illustrious family members of Maharshi Debendranath composed songs inculcating nationalism. In all sessions national songs were specially composed to be sung. Rabindranath, then fifteen, composed a poem called *Bharat* and also sang other songs of his own.

This *Mela* gave birth to *Jatiya Sabha* (National Society) in 1870. To promote the national spirit and faith in our heritage the *Mela* arranged lectures by competent persons on art, literature, philosophy, science and technology. As envisaged by its founders, within five years its influence transformed the national life of Bengal and the minds of the educated youth felt the tide of denationalisation turned and they awoke to their surroundings.

The pioneer political organisation of India, the British Indian Association--with branches in Madras, Bombay and Calcutta--had been founded between 1851 and 1857. Later the Bengal National League was established jointly by Sisir Kumar Ghosh, the well-known founder-editor of *Amrita Bazar Patrika*, and Ananda Mohan Bose, the first Indian Senior Wrangler of Cambridge University. This body was in its turn superseded by the Indian Association of Calcutta. The Bombay Association was founded in the Western Presidency, largely through the efforts of Dadabhai Naoroji.

In Maharashtra, the *Poona Sarvajanik Sabha* was formed in 1867. The moving spirit behind it was Sita Ram Hari Chiplunkar, the veteran educationist and nationalist of that region, who, with Lokamanya Bal Gangadhar Tilak and Agarkar, became the co-founder of Maharashtra's premier vernacular journals:-- the *Kesari* and the *Mahratta*. The outstanding qualities of the persons inspiring patriotism and nationalism were nobility, idealism, vision and capacity to inspire others. They realised that before achieving political liberty their countrymen should first attain deliverance from social and spiritual evils. They worked tirelessly in that direction and this infused new life in the politics of the country. Quite a few conscientious Englishmen contributed to the cause of Indian nationalism. These were Cobden, John Bright, Charles Bradlaugh, Henry Fawcett and Gladstone in England, with their outspoken utterances; Sir Henry Cotton in Bengal; Sir William Wedderburn in Bombay; and A.O. Hume in the North-Western Province. They kept alive the spark of hope in the Indian breast when the horizon was the darkest.

In 1883, at the instance of the Indian Association, a national conference was held in Calcutta under the leadership of Surendra Nath Banerji. In the following year the Bengal National League was established under the leadership of Sir Jatindra Mohan Tagore.

In Madras the *Mahajan Sabha* was established early in 1881 under the auspices of the leading public men who had started the premier English daily of South India -- *The Hindu*, with its illustrious editor Subramania Aiyar. Under the impetus of the new movement, the Bombay Presidency Association was started on January 31, 1885 by Phirozeshah Mehta, the Hon. Kashinath Tryambak Telang and the Hon. Badruddin Tyebji. Phirozeshah Mehta was one of the greatest political leaders India has ever seen. He was a born leader of men and the greatest debator that our country ever produced. His courage and independence were unparalleled.

All these organisations preceded the birth of the Indian National Congress. Lord Ripon's regime was liberal in nature. It infused a new hope in the Indian mind for a fruitful nationalist movement in India.

India was now ripe for the establishment of a central organisation for the advancement of nationalism. It is surprising that an Englishman should have been the founder of the Indian National Congress. His name was Allan Octavian Hume (1829-1912) who has gone down in India's modern history as the founder and father of the Indian National Congress -- an institution and a political party to which ultimately the British transferred complete political control. He was one of the few highminded Britishers who worked in India's interest. The Indian National Congress was formed in 1885 after many consultations with Ranade, Naoroji, Bonnerji,

Mehta, Tyebji etc. Had it not been for Hume, an Englishman, being the founder of the Congress, it would have been ruthlessly suppressed by the authorities. He realised that corrupt and oppressive policy of the British had brought the discontent of the people to a level where the possibility of explosion at any moment could not be ruled out. In his famous circular letter addressed to the graduates of the Calcutta University, Hume appealed for "fifty men good and true" to come forward and form a body of founders dedicated to the task of moral, social and political regeneration of the country. His appeal evoked wide response all over the country. As a result the Indian National Union was formed in 1884 whose purpose was to devote itself to social work. In March 1885, the Union held a meeting of representatives from all parts of India. The Union held another meeting at Pune in the Christmas of that year and named this congregation as the Indian National Congress. Later the scene was shifted to Bombay. Seventy-two public men, stalwarts in their fields, from all over the country, participated in the conference.

The first Congress session at Bombay passed nine resolutions and was to be followed by several other sessions in the following years. The fourth session of the Congress was held in Allahabad under the Presidentship of George Yule, a leading merchant of Calcutta, and the fifth in Bombay, with Sir William Wedderburn as President. It was in this year that Gopal Krishna Gokhale joined the Congress. He was an eminent economist, parliamentarian and statesman whose budget speeches are even today studied as classics on the subject. Prominent among the rising stars of this movement were Kashinath Tryambak Telang, Narayan Ganesh Chandavarkar and Dinshah Mehta. Calcutta was represented by W.C. Bonnerji and from Pune there were Gopal Ganesh Agarkar and Vishnu Shastri Chiplunkar. Foremost among the public men was Mahadev Govind Ranade, who contributed to the rise of renascent India. He had not only taken a prominent part in founding the Indian National Congress along with Dadabhai Naoroji, Hume and Wedderburn, but was also a religious reformer, preacher and theologian of great popularity. Social reform was a passion with Ranade. It brought him into conflict with his great contemporary, Bal Gangadhar Tilak. Junior to Ranade by fourteen years and a savant like him, Bal Gangadhar Tilak was the celebrated author of *Gita Rahasya* and a daring man of action.

Between 1894 and 1895 Tilak instituted the Ganapati Festival and the Shivaji Festival in Maharashtra. The object of the latter particularly was to draw the masses into politics. The Shivaji cult caught the imagination of the people in other parts of the country as well. It was propagated by Lala Lajpat Rai in Punjab and Surendra Nath Banerji in Bengal. Tilak will go down to the generations to come as one of the most important makers of modern India, who is rightly called as Lokamanya till today. As the nationalist movement gained momentum in Bengal *'Vande Mataram'* (Hail Mother) became the war cry of the religion of patriotism. The Mother invoked is not an ordinary religious deity but the mother country, not a mere mass of territory but a living entity. Sung for the first time in the Congress by Rabindranath Tagore in 1896, it was only after 1905 that *'Vande Mataram'* became the battle cry of India's freedom struggle.

The Muslim Movement

Along with the surge of religious reform and renaissance in Hinduism there were stirrings among the Muslims also. The most important figure in the reform movement in Islam was Sir Syed Ahmed Khan (1817-1898). The Muslim community, already backward and bitterly repressed by the British Government, took an active part in the 1857 rising and consequently was further repressed and discriminated against in its administrative policy of divide and rule. Sir Syed Ahmed Khan promised loyalty and cooperation to the British regime in his article on the causes of the Mutiny and gained some favours.[34]

In regard to his reform work he established the Mohammedan Anglo-Oriental College at Aligarh where Western knowledge and culture were taught along with the religion of Islam. For modernising Islam he had to face strong opposition from the conservatives but the new middle class rallied round him and gave him full support. In his early years he was anything but communal and kept the door of his Aligarh College open to the believers of all faiths. Members of all communities contributed funds to his college and also sent some students to join it. For his policy and advocacy of loyalty to the British, he was appointed a Member of the Imperial Legislative Council and was awarded the Knighthood being decorated with a K.C.S.I.

Unfortunately, however, towards the end of his life Sir Syed Ahmed Khan adopted the role of a communal political reactionary and began to foster the fear of Hindu domination lest the Muslims should make common cause with the nationalists. In 1885 when the Congress was founded he first ignored and then opposed it. In 1889 he established the Upper India Mohammedan Defence Association to organise the Muslim middle class in opposition to the Congress. So the seed of communalism was sown in India for all time to come.

After Sir Syed Ahmed Khan's death in 1898, his ideas were expanded by a group of Muslim intellectuals whom he had been able to draw to him during his lifetime. The Anglo-Oriental Mohammedan College at Aligarh became the stronghold of the pro-British, politically conscious Muslim section and a hotbed of promotion of communalism among the Muslims. This tradition was carried on by his successors. Ultimately it was Aga Khan who was responsible for asking for separate electorates and for founding the Muslim League, which was instrumental in bringing about the division of the country in 1947.

Development of Swadeshi Movement

Bengal was partitioned in 1905 and national resentment took the form of boycott of British goods in *Swadeshi*. At first the concept of *Swadeshi* was confined to the revival of Indian industries only. But it gradually expanded till it became one with every phase of national life. The *Swadeshi* movement thus came to include moral and social reform, spiritual uplift and industrial, cultural and political revival of the country.

On August 7, 1905 the leaders of Bengal assembled in a public meeting at the Calcutta Town Hall under the presidency of Maharaja Manindra Chandra Nandy of Cossimbazar, and resolved to declare a general boycott of British goods as a practical protest against the proposed Partition.

October 16, 1906, the day when the Partition of Bengal was effected, was observed in both parts of Bengal as a day of mourning. Wearing black badges on their arms as a sign of mourning people paraded the streets bareheaded and barefooted, singing patriotic songs and rent the sky with shouts of *"Vande Mataram"*. From Calcutta the boycott and the *Swadeshi* movement spread like wild-

fire all over the province and also outside the province. The more
the authorities tried to suppress it by force the greater was the
outburst. At this time Aurobindo Ghosh flung himself into this
movement and organised *Sabha*s, *Samitis Akharas* and *Ashram*s
everywhere to promote the nationalist feeling. Aurobindo Ghosh
was a first class honours graduate from Cambridge. He gave up
his lucrative job with the Maharaja of Baroda and dedicated himself
to the service of the motherland. Later he migrated to Pondicherry
and renounced the world and came to be known as Shri Aurobindo.

Every mass movement throws up its own leaders. The leadership
of the new movement was symbolised by the Bal, Pal and Lal
trio -- Bal Gangadhar Tilak in Maharashtra, Bepin Chandra Pal
in Bengal and Lala Lajpat Rai in the Punjab. Pal was the
theoretician of the new nationalism, Lal the symbol of its
masculinity and courage and Bal its heart and soul.

The year 1907 was marked by a fervid implementation of the
three-fold programme of boycott, *Swadeshi* and national education.
In the north, Punjab became the storm centre. The whole country
was in a state of ferment. Driven to desperation by the orgy of
repression, a section of Nationalists declared that "force must be
faced with force." So a cult of 'terrorists' came into existence
who resorted to guerilla warfare against the authorities. Barindra
Kumar Ghosh, Aurobindo's brother, and Bhupendranath Dutt, a
brother of Swami Vivekananda, became the leaders of this cult.

So among the nationalists grew up two groups--extremists and
moderates. The terrorist interlude had left the Congress divided
and the masses demoralised. The country's leaders were either
in prison or in exile. The man who brought together the various
forces in the situation in a dynamic amalgam to forge an invincible
movement which forced the British to cede independence was
Mohandas Karamchand Gandhi (1869-1948). Born in 1869 in
Porbandar, a small state of Kathiawar, he was destined to become
the Father of the Nation of independent India. As he grew up
he came in touch with the liberal Christian ideas and the teachings
of Tolstoy. He stirred the Indian masses to their depths and led
the national movement for 28 years. Although he was a Bar-at-
Law, he chose a life of self-imposed poverty, as he wanted to
identify himself with the poverty-stricken masses. His ideas, which
he turned into a system, were ethical and spiritual as well as
practical and political. At the heart of his ideas lay the doctrine

of non-violence or *ahimsa*.   For, violence was the   expression of
unreason and hate, the antithesis of love; and love was the essence
of the spirit that permeates the universe.   Gandhi disciplined his
various ideas for political action through appropriate techniques
of mass organisation which resulted in freedom from the mighty
British Empire on which 'the sun never set.' The weapon of non-
violence that he forged had and has global significance in the
context of nuclear weapons and the   complete annihilation that
stares humanity in the face.   It was in the early twentieth century
under Mahatma Gandhi's leadership that India was moving towards
developing a rich composite civilization based on mutual understanding and respect, and a zest for higher values of life and love
of peace and harmony.   The ground for it had been well-prepared
by a galaxy of dedicated leaders who had stirred the imagination
of young India and awakened in her a new spirit which gave a
new life and dimension to social and religious reform, educational
activity and   nationalism.

This was a great and dynamic age, bubbling with the upsurge
of a new vitality in all walks of life, when the nation was stirred
to its depths by great men and great movements in rich abundance,
which re-established its contact with its source of spiritual strength,
its rich and dynamic past, to meet contemporary challenge. Vishnu
Narayan Bhatkhande was a product of this age. As a part of
the multi-dimensional revolution in all spheres he spearheaded a
revolution in the field of music.   His life and contribution had
all the characteristics of the dynamic age he represented which
brought a total change in the existing method of teaching, theory
and practice of music of North India. It was largely due to his
effort that music was once again recognised as an essential part
of our national culture and education. It was he, who, with his
undaunted endeavour, revived and re-established its past glory.

References

1.   Durant, Will : *The Case for India*, p.5
2.   Marshall, Sir John : 'The Prehistoric Civilization of the Indus', *Illustrated London News* (Jan. 7, 1928). Quoted by Will Durant in 'The Story of Civilization,' p.395
3.   Projnanananda, Swami : *Historical Development of Indian Music*, Chap.3, p.60
4.   Ibid., Chap.1, p.17
5.   Durant, Will : *The Case for India*, p.8

6.   *Bombay Administration Report of 1872-73*, p.41
7.   Thompson, E. & Garatt, G.T. : *Rise and Fulfilment of British Rule in India*, p.110
8.   Lord Cornwallis's *Minute*, dated Sept. 18, 1789
9.   *East India Papers* (1820), Vol. II, p.70
10. Ibid.
11. Forest's *Selections from the Minutes and other Official Writings of the Hon. Mount Stuart Elphinstone (1884)*, p.102
12. Kaye : *Life of Metcalfe*, pp. 247-'8
13. Ronaldshay, Earl of, The : *The Heart of Aryavarta* (1927), p.20
14. Ibid., p.45
15. Ibid., pp.61-'2
16. Ibid., p.46
17. Basu, Raj Narayan : *Sakal and Ekal*
18. Ibid., p.47
19. Thompson, E. & Garatt, G.T. : *Rise and Fulfilment of British Rule in India*, p.310
20. Edmund Burke's Speech, quoted by Romesh Dutt : *The Economic History of India under Early British Rule*, pp.49-50
21. Gandhi, M.K. : 'Brahmo Samaj's Contribution to Hinduism,'*Young India* (Aug. 30, 1928), p.291
22. Sharma, D.S. : 'Studies in the Renaissance of Hinduism,' p.225. Quotation taken from *Ancient Wisdom*, p.37
23. Dibelius, Wilhelm : *England*, p.61
24. Smith, Wilfred Cantwell : *Modern Islam in India* (1943), pp.19-20

2

The State of Contemporary Music

The Requisite Climate

Culture of music and art depends largely on the socio-economic conditions of the country. For music, art and literature can only thrive in an atmosphere of peace, religious tolerance and affluence. Their development also depends on the encouraging policy pursued by the rulers of the country. There was a very rich and progressive cultural life flourishing in our land during the pre-British period.

In the courts of Ashoka, Vikramaditya, Bhoja and other Hindu kings -- as also in the courts of Akbar, Shahjahan and other Mughal emperors -- the outstanding artists and thinkers of that period congregated. Music was cultured and nourished in their respective courts in an atmosphere of internal peace and security. The proverbial Tansen adorned the court of Akbar whose reign is known as the golden period in the history of art and music.

Pages of history reveal that in ancient India, during the reign of the Mauryas (600 B.C.), the Kushanas (A.D. 120-162) and Harshavardhan (A.D. 600-647), the life of the people was peaceful, prosperous, and the trade between India and the West was booming. The king was the protector of the life and property of the people. How the administration ably discharged this divine responsibility is narrated by Megasthenes and Chanakya during the time of Chandragupta.

When the Mughals came, they brought their culture and religion which they implanted in this country. They were also able administrators who set up their administrative machinery in a way that crime was controlled and the rule of law established. They placed the welfare of the people as the goal of their administration so that justice could reach down to the lowest stratum of society. The government was benevolent. It built irrigation canals and wells and looked after the maintenance of the schools, hospitals, gardens, temples etc. It was a tradition that the king looked after the welfare of the people and the people in return gave their loyal services to their master.

Period of General Decadence

At the end of the eighteenth century and the beginning of the nineteenth, the Mughal rule weakened and the country was torn asunder with internecine strife. Consequently music and art suffered a setback in an atmosphere of insecurity. The state of affairs worsened when the British came and liquidated the Mughal Emperors. They were not interested in the welfare of the people, leave alone the art, music and culture of this country. They were only keen to amass wealth from the rich fertile land of India. So the economic condition which was already deteriorating, when the Hindu and Muslim rulers of the country engaged themselves in the struggle for power, became much worse under the British.

We have already discussed in the previous chapter that the policy of the British was to push up Westernism and cry down the civilization of this country. The ancient learning was despised, ancient customs and traditions were set aside and ancient religion was decried as an outworn superstition. Our great heritage of philosophy, Sanskrit literature and music was thrown aside.

In the annals of the Hindustani classical music and also the other forms of art and education, it was the most critical period. It was a time when economically India was impoverished and hunger-stricken; socially she was full of inferiority complex and meaningless prejudices; and, culturally, she was badly shaken under the weight of an imposed foreign culture. It was a time when alongwith other forms of art, music lost its intellectual growth.

Henry Louis Vivian Derozio, a half-cast Portuguese, a free thinker and poet, styled by his admirers as the Byron of Bengal, became the centre of a cult of Young Bengal. He wrote the following poem which clearly indicates the condition of the country in his time:

"My country! In the days of glory past,
A beauteous halo circled round thy brow
And worshipped as a deity thou wast
Where is that glory, where that reverence past
The eagle pinion is clamped down at last
And grovelling in the lowly dust art thou!
Thy minstrel hath no wreath to weave for thee
Save the sad story of thy misery!
Well let me dive into the depth of time
And bring from out of the ages that have rolled
A few small fragments of those wrecks sublime
Which human eye may never more behold;
And let the guerdon of my labour be,
My fallen country! One kind wish for thee."[1]

It was a state of general decadence, ruinous economic conditions, maladministration and anti-Indian policy of the rulers that resulted in the Great Revolt. But after the storm that swept over and convulsed the whole of Northern and Central India in 1857 the British reversed their previous attitude towards the Indian States, which, in Lord Canning's words, had during the rising "served as break waters through the storm which would otherwise have swept over us in one great wave." It is true that if some of the states had not assisted the British in quelling the Mutiny, history would have been written differently. Therefore, the British wanted to rely more on these states and changed their attitude in their favour.

The survival of these States served one useful purpose. They provided a sanctuary for indigenous talent when it was progressively being squeezed out of British India. Some of India's foremost statesmen, including Dadabhai Naoroji and Phirozeshah Mehta, found scope for their genius in the Indian States, and nationalists and revolutionaries of the calibre of Aurobindo Ghosh found asylum there when they were barred from all opportunities in British India. The economic condition and the treatment of the people were far better in the Native States.

They also provided sanctuary for the cream of musicians who for many generations were patronised and sheltered by the Muslim rulers. Swami Projnanananda is of the opinion that in fact the musicians had lost the royal patronage right from the time of Shah Alam II. "Shah Alam was a man of weak personality and when on the 12th August, 1765, he granted by a *firman* the Diwani of Bengal, Bihar and Orissa to the East India Company, he became only the titular Mughal Emperor living under the protection of the British. It was, therefore, impossible for him to carry on the musical legacy of his glorious predecessors. The noted musicians, who belonged mostly to the Tansen School, began to leave Delhi, and sought refuge in different Durbars of Muslim Nawabs and Hindu Kings and Zamindars of Awadh, Betiya, Rewa and other places. It is said that some of the descendants of Tansen went eastward, and the Seni *ustad*s, belonging to Tansen's line of disciples, went to different parts of Rajputana. The British Raj was not interested in preserving the traditional culture of Indian music, and so they were indifferent to patronising the musicians. Many of the *ustad*s took shelter in the Durbar of the King of Banaras, and some of them came to Bengal, and settled in Krishnanagar, Vishnupur, Murshidabad and other places."[2]

The result of this was two-fold. On the one hand, music was forced to decentralise itself and was propagated in different places of our country, bringing itself in touch with a much larger populace; on the other hand, because of the scattering of talent the musicians lost the stimulating effect of the concentration of talent. The musicians, in order to earn their livelihood, tried to cater to the tastes of their masters, often low and connected with base thoughts and desires. It also gave rise to different *gharanas*, developing rivalry, quarrels and jealousies. But, on the positive side, the most significant contribution of the *gharanas* was the evolution of different beautiful styles, or modes of rendering, by the talented artists of the different families.

Social Censorship

The Zamindari system or landlordism was established in this country by the British for the purpose of raising taxes in the easiest possible way. This system created a class of people who resorted to a life of luxury and mostly debauchery. These self-styled moneyed aristocrats were fed by the poor farmers and workers, who bore the brunt of the payment of heavy taxes. These Zamindars reared and patronised the musicians and music as a part of their amorous life. Wine, music and vice were closely connected and music was used for exciting sensual desire. Therefore, the musicians who took shelter with these aristocrats had to cater to their cheap tastes except in a few cases where their master was a knowledgeable person, having regard for Classical music.

To earn their livelihood, a class of songsters and songstresses came up, fostered by the low tastes of this nobility. They were naturally looked down upon by society. In the literature of this age one finds many descriptions of singing girls who were often prostitutes and they were brought for festivities to entertain the guests. At such performances children and ladies were not allowed.

In the latter half of the nineteenth century and thereafter music and vice were closely connected. The result was that to an educated mind with puritanical values, music meant a straight road to immoral and sinful living. Culture of music meant giving up decent life and resorting to a life of sensuality. Our great heritage of music and its purpose of elevating and uplifting the soul was lost and forgotten. Lost was the idea that music was born in the hermit's hut, round the sacrificial fire (Yajnakunda) and was reared in the temple. Lost were the ideas about the divinity, the spiritualism and the aesthetics in music as expounded by our old masters like Bharata, Kohala, Narada and others. In the words of His Highness Maharaja Vijay Devji of Dharamapur, "Let us visualise the times...with which Pandit Vishnu Narayan Bhatkhande's name remains immortally associated. When Pandit Bhatkhande began and subsequently resolved to translate his love for Hindustani music into a continued, unwearied, day to day programme of service, he had to confront social, intellectual and finally, professional prejudices."[3] The general idea was that "Music was not the correct thing for a respectable man. For women, music was to be not even thought of. Such was the pious horror which music seemed to arouse"[4] at that time.

Again, the same writer says about the social censorship and repression of music of that age : "The intellectual community, composed mostly of lawyers, doctors and administrators, found itself under a lop-sided system of education which served only to segregate music from life and accentuate the intellectual prejudices against it. Puritanism which had exhausted its stern anathemas in the West found strange roots and strength in this country. In no other country in the world, not even in the country from which we have borrowed our system of education, music finds its place so low, so contemptuously neglected, as in this country. Nowhere in the West were the young natural instincts for music so completely repressed, censored and banned as they happened to be in this country. Music had literally become the direct Harijan child in the 'reformed' community of those whose learning was, obviously, lop-sided and whose puritanism ended with the repression of one of the noblest of gifts of art to mankind."

Vishnu Narayan Bhatkhande could not escape, in his early years, the social taboo connected with music. Bhatkhande, who "imbibed the fragrance of music deeply enough from the beginning," in his young age, was an important figure as a flute player and singer in the festivals of *Ramnavami, Janmashtami, Diwali*, etc. in his locality. "The parents as was the custom of those days felt worried, thinking that the boy would be lost in music and would turn a vagabond."[5] The parents never intended, nor did they ever expect, their son to distinguish himself in or become a great rejuvenator of Hindustani Music."[6]

Loss of Theoretical Base

In the ancient period the theory of music was formulated and enriched by the celebrated masters like Muni Bharata, Kohala, Yastika, Kashyapa, Matanga, Parshvadeva, Sharngadeva, Vidyaranya etc. It is presumed that the practising artists of that period were also well versed in theory. When the Muslims came to rule this country, the expert musicians, who accompanied them, also settled in this country. The existing Classical music had a happy fusion with theirs and a rich type of Classical music emerged. It is well-known that a genius like Amir Khusrau contributed greatly to the evolution of the rich individual style of North Indian Classical music. On the other hand, however, Classical music gradually lost contact with the *granthas* as the new-comers were not conversant with the Sanskrit language. They were mainly performers and their patrons were the Nawabs or the Kings who were themselves well versed in practical music. After the Mughal rule was liquidated their patrons changed. Consequently they had to change their pattern and attitude to music. They were orthodox in outlook and had contempt for text or written music. Young Bhatkhande, when he came into contact with the Classical music of his time and heard and learnt from the stalwarts of music, noticed the gap between the knowledge and the written text of the old masters, and expressed this view in one of his writings : "Everywhere we are told that in the North music prospered during the time of the Mughal Emperors. This may be true. I doubt, however, that there were any persons, in those times, who had read the ancient Sanskrit works on music. None of the great *nayaka*s such as Nayaka Gopal, Baiju, Dhondi, Haridas etc. appears to have written any work on music. Their compositions also do not convince us of any depth of learning. In the old Imperial days they might have made a name by their practical performances and by talks, here and there, on the theory of music. But I have not come across a single record to show that even one of the *nayaka*s had studied the *grantha*s like *Sangeet Ratnakar*. They themselves have not written any work on music. Why should it be so? Their compositions, even in the most authoritative versions, are full of bare references to elementary technical terms, such as *Sapta Sur, Teen Grama, Ikayees, Moorchhana, Bara-Vikrita, Bayees-Shruti, Ga-maka*s such as *Urapa and Tirupa Laga, Dant, Arohi, Avarohi, Astayee, Sanchari, Swara-Beore,* etc. I do not see any deep study in it. The *nayaka*s lived just 400 years ago. They could have put their knowledge of the theory of music in writing. They must have at least heard the names of *Ratnakar* and other works. It appears to me that these *nayaka*s must have been practical experts like those of our own days, though of a much higher order and calibre."[7]

Therefore, from the 13th century onwards, till the latter half of the nineteenth century, the practical musicians, a large majority of whom were Muslims, had no knowledge of the old texts of their theories. They only practised and demonstrated the *ragas*, composed songs in them and sang them according to the traditions of their *gharana*s (families or traditions) handed down from father to son or from teacher to pupil. Very few attempts were made to write books on the theory of music which changed greatly during the Muslim rule, especially in the North.

The condition of the theoretical part of music at that time and its connection with the old literature is apparent from another writing by Bhatkhande : "It is a general notion among people that our Hindu music is an ancient and very important branch of knowledge. It is not intended here to turn down this notion as erroneous. It will never be fitting to say so. We have before us quite a large number of names of the Sanskrit texts of music and some of them are even available for our study. But the question that arises in our minds is: 'Is there any connection between the theories of these texts and the art that we consider today as music?' We may have read the *granthas* and even understood them, and yet, if there is no connection between the music propounded in the *granthas* and the music which is in practice today, i.e., if the music which is in vogue today is entirely different from that explained in the *granthas* then why bother to study the *granthas?* Such a question was put to me by many people. It must be admitted that it is difficult to give a satisfactory answer. Can we say that we sing the music that has been explained in *Ratnakar, Darpan, Raga Vibodha, Parijat,* etc. following their rules? Just because the names of the notes or the names (only) of the *ragas* given in the *granthas* are still in vogue, can we claim that we sing the ancient music? The descriptions of the *ragas* as given in the *granthas* do not fit in with their forms as they are today. If, on the other hand, we try to sing the *ragas* according to their descriptions in the *granthas,* some of them will not appeal to us; to some, we shall give fresh names. If such is the state of affairs, why study the *granthas* and why call that person who has studied the *granthas* a learned scholar of music? What is the use of such a musicologist for the modern form of music? Such questions do face us. Do they not? And if so, what reply could we give to them? The ten types of *ragas* as given in *Ratnakar* may be explained with their names and detailed rules, but can we find even a single scholar who will be able to sing these and reconcile them with at least some of the *ragas* now in vogue? What is then the use of these *granthas?* Why not, some people will say, take up the music that is in vogue today itself independently, study the forms it has developed through the past ages and write a separate independent work on modern music?"[8]

The Development of Gharana System

In fact in his time music was kept alive by a handful of musicians.

At the beginning of the British rule the gifted musicians who were patronised by the Mughal rulers were scattered and took shelter in the different native states of the North. In course of time Rajas, Nawabs and Princes of these small states treated the musicians of their courts as objects of their entertainment, often of personal pleasure. Not only that, they considered the musicians as their personal property and did not allow them to move out from their protective custody. Therefore, the musicians got isolated from the mainstream of life as well as from their fellow musicians. This, on the one hand, narrowed down their concept of music and made them conservative and self-centred; but, on the other hand, this isolation proved a boon by making them practise their own art rigorously and relentlessly to perfection and as a result thereof individual styles evolved in their modes of rendering. This fervent effort to perfect their modes of singing gave birth to *gharanedar gayaki* in course of time due to the contributions of individual geniuses. This rigid adherence to one's own style became an addiction and an obsession and the style assumed the status of a *gharana*, or a style of singing peculiar to a particular family, where it was carried on faithfully for at least three successive generations, from father to son or from *guru* to *shishya*. In fact, *Khayal gayaki* got its sharply defined identity at this time, breaking away from its initial mode of rendering which was very much akin to its predecessor, *dhrupad*. At the time of Bhatkhande five or six *gharana*s dominated the realm of music.

Whatever might be its effect in polishing the *gharanedar gayaki*, it hampered the growth of music and brought it into a blind alley for the following reasons. Firstly, as the *gharanedar ustad* taught only persons belonging to a very limited circle, many persons with creative ability, who would have otherwise learnt from him and in turn enriched the art, were denied this opportunity. Secondly, after an outstanding individual genius had established a *gharanedar gayaki*, those who followed him were not allowed the slightest deviation from it and so were unable to apply their creative ability to the further development of the style. And the law of life is that what does not grow stagnates. Thirdly, the exact imitation of the master was insisted upon even when the voice characteristics of the artists made that impossible. This could only result in caricature unfair to the artists. Fourthly, this insistence on exact imitation prevented music from responding to the changing environment, so essential for a living art. There was no rational approach and, therefore, no intellectual grasp of intellectual handling of *ragas* at the time of demonstration. So each *ustad* was a tradition by himself and established his own school of music or *gharana*. Sometimes the form of a particular *raga* used to be different in different *gharanas* and in some instance, the same combination of notes used to be named differently by different *gharanas*, each claiming authenticity for its own practice.

Often there were quarrels among the followers of the different *gharanas* and abuses were freely hur'ed to the utter disgust of all music lovers. Classical music lost i'٫ dignity and became a subject of ridicule by educated and intelligent people. Misunderstanding and ignorance reigned supreme and to them were added professional prejudices. The *ustads* were obsessed with the idea that music was a treasure and it should be preserved and accumulated in his own family and given only to his own family members or close relatives. The question of talent, which is a gift of God and can be had by an outsider also, did not come in for any consideration. Pandit Ratanjankar said: "The musicians were brought up with the old idea that music is a precious treasure which should be locked up and not given excepting to a few chosen students."[9] How personal conceits had their play in the name of *gharana* will be clear from the Presidential address of the Raja of Dharampur Vijay Devji, as late as in the year 1936: "My friend, Sir Sultan Ahmed, in a recent article in *Calcutta Review*, has pointed out with great force the problem which touches the Muslim musicians of India. Music and literature, for a number of years, have been segregated and, as he points out, the lamentable consequence of this divorce was the springing up of various schools and musical families with their own ways of singing and notions (rather than first-hand knowledge) of the theory, and their own ideas and memories (naturally different views differing by lapse of time and distance of places of abode even among the followers of the identical distant ancestor or preceptor). The result is that at present musicians even of the Northern School differ violently from one another in the musical features of many *ragas* and *raginis*, each citing the name of his *ustad* as the authority. And very few even know the names of the written and published books on the theory of our music."[10]

One can well imagine the plight of a student of music in those days.   The *gurus* and *ustad*s were illiterate and incapable of explaining anything objectively.   Each *ustad* claimed to be the descendant of a great master of the middle ages and was full of anecdotes of musical miracles by his ancestors.

Young Bhatkhande, when he attempted to rationalise the system of music, was baffled by the stories of miracles: "The legends-- stone being melted by music, deers being attracted and weaving garlands, the rains coming down by singing of *Malhar* in Akbar's time, lamps being lit by *raga Deepak* etc. -- are all right as symbolic praises of music. But I am not prepared to accept them as facts. Until I see with my own eyes, such miracles happening again, I shall always be telling my friends and pupils that these are imaginary and probably imagery of poetry. My friends argue that sound is a strange phenomenon. Certain peculiar passages of music may be capable of producing supernatural miracles. They say that we are ignorant, today, of the decadence of music and hence such miracles today do not take place. I am afraid now-a-days we shall not be satisfied by such arguments."[11]

Music Lessons

It is interesting to note how a student of music used to get his lessons. A student of music at the time of Bhatkhande had to be wedded to a *gharana* and tied to a particular *guru*. The *guru* demanded complete surrender of the pupil in regard to all material and immaterial things. Often a learner had to do a menial work in the *guru*'s house in return for his music lessons which also depended upon the whims of the *guru*. The system of training was oral, and in an oral system some additions and alterations were inevitable. There was no trace of any type of a notation system. The *ustad*s had an abhorrence of written music. Whatever the *ustad* or the teacher said was the final word about the structure of a *raga*. It was considered rudeness and impertinence to ask questions about the formation of a *raga* or its individual character. The invariable answer would have been : "My *guru* sang like this" or "My father taught me like this." And the pupils were forced to believe that this was the only authentic form and had to accept his lessons as gospel truth. He had no scope for comparing, contrasting or creating something new. Whatever was old was gold and whatever was new or a deviation was destructive -- that was the training students of music used to receive.

However, the *guru shishya parampara* or the handing down of knowledge from teacher to pupil had one advantage that the pupil used to have enough opportunity to listen to his *guru* as he used to live in intimacy with him. Music is an art which is learnt best by listening. Thakur Jaidev Singh is of the opinion that, "these advantages were, however, counterbalanced by many disadvantages. The teacher usually did not impart the secrets of his art to everybody. His pupils consisted of three categories: (1) *Khasul-Khasa*, (2) *Khasa*, and (3) *Gandabandha*. The *Khasul-Khasa* teaching, in which the teacher imparted all his knowledge without concealing anything, was meant only for the sons of the teacher. The *Khasa taleem* or teaching was meant only for very closely related pupils. In this the teacher did not impart all his knowledge. He imparted only about three-fourths of his art, one-fourth being reserved for his sons. The *Gandabandha taleem* was meant for those whom the teacher had accepted as his pupils by a formal ceremony. In this, the teacher imparted only about fifty per cent of what he knew."[12]

Even a *gandabandha shagird* was not accepted easily. Sometimes one had to wait for an indefinite period if he was lucky enough not to be rejected straight away. The pupil belonging to this category was a victim of whimsical and irregular hours of teaching by the *guru* against which he was in no position to protest. The result was that a considerable precious time was wasted to receive even elementary knowledge. Needless to say, he received no training in the theory of music. If he were an intelligent person with educational background he would perhaps try to enrich his theoretical knowledge from the books which were scanty and not easily available. The pupil of this category had to do the entire household chores in the name of service to the *guru* and, therefore, he could hardly get any time for practice.

The results of all these factors were disastrous. The intelligentsia of this country lost interest in this great art for lack of understanding, for factional quarrels among its propagators and the social stigma and vices connected with it. Further, as a profession it was regarded as lewd and useless. The necessary rapport between the listener and the performer was missing. But as poet Tagore said : "Song cannot be sung alone, it is meant for the two, one sings loudly while the other sings silently." When the listener is not trained, music is lost in the wilderness. The apathy of the educated class accentuated the pathetic degeneration of the musical art.

Harbinger of a New Dawn

It was, however, the darkness before the dawn. The answer to all the challenges had already been forged by a person who was born in Maharashtra in a Brahmin family in the year of 1860. His name was Vishnu Narayan Bhatkhande who rescued music from its present degenerated state due to the destructive forces of foreign rule and the neglect of the educated classes. His unremitting toil was responsible for re-establishing music as a classical art and a part of our education and culture. In one of his writings in the year 1918 he said : "Now the all-round awakening in India is clamouring for it. There should be the revival of the most delightful of the fine arts as it is the foremost need of the time. Every self-respecting nation considers music as one of the most necessary social accomplishments."[13]

Through painstaking research he collected the data of the present day music and created a vast literature which included a sound and systematic grammar and theory of current music.

During his research work he discovered the following artists who, under the banner of *gharanas*, kept the flickering lamp of music burning and with their assiduous practice became finished artists: Nazir Khan, Anjanibai Malpekar, Anant Manohar Joshi, Arthubuwa Apte (of Maharashtra; died towards the end of the 19th century), Abdul Karim Khan, Aman Ali Khan (Bijnaur, Muradabad), Shamir Khan (court musician of Indore and father of Amir Khan), Alladiya Khan (born in 1855; learnt music from his uncle Doulat Khan, state musician of Kolhapur; died on 16th March, 1946), Alabande Khan (death 1923; *dhrupad* singer; state musician of Alwar; father of Nasiruddin Khan and Rahimuddin Khan Dagar), Aditya Ramji (of Saurashtra; born in 1872; died in 1936), Omkar Nath Thakur, Inayat Hussain Khan (born in 1843; learnt from Bahadur Hussain Khan of Rampur *dhrupad, dhamar, khayal, tappa, thumari,* etc.; died in 1919; pupils -- Mushtaq Hussain Khan, Fida Hussain Khan, Haider Hussain Khan etc.), Tanras Khan (Delhi), Eknath Pandit (born in 1870 in Gwalior; died in 1917), Khurshid Ali Khan (pupil of Sadik Ali Khan; born in 1855 at Lucknow; died in 1950), Ganapati Buwa (helped Bhatkhande in writing *Kramik Pustak Malika;* born in 1882; pupil of Balkrishna Buwa, Maharashtra; died in 1927), Ganesh Ramchandra Behre Buwa (Maharashtra; born in 1890), Gopeshwar Banerji (born in 1878; *dhrupad, dhamar, tappa*), Fida Hussain Khan (1883-1948), Chhote Mohammed Khan (eldest son of Hardu Khan; died in 1874), Bande Ali Khan (*Beenkar*), Pannalal Bajpayee (*Sitar*), Tanras Khan, Rahimat Khan and Mohammed Khan (sons of Haddu Khan), Nissar Hussain Khan (Vocalist, Gwalior; 1844-1913), Naththan Khan (Vocalist, 1840-1900), Ali Hussain Khan and Faiyaz Khan (Vocalists, *Khayaliyas*), Zakiruddin Khan of Udaipur (Vocalist and expert in *alapa*), Naththan Khan (of Agra; 1840-1900; father of Vilayat Hussain Khan), Balkrishna Buwa Ichalkaranjikar (Kolhapur; 1849-1926), Wahid Khan (Kolhapur; died in 1948), Sadik Ali Khan (*Been*), Wazir Khan (Rampur; 1860-1927), Muhammed Ali Khan (*Rabab*; 1834-1927), Bundu Khan (1880-1895), Bahadur Hussain Khan (Senia *gharana, Sursingar* etc.), Badal Khan (*Sarangi*), Amir Khan (*Sitar,* Rampur), and others. It is noteworthy that the above list includes 2 or 3 musicians of eminence from each *gharana*. These musicians were demonstrators of high calibre and it were they who with their hard work, devotion and egoism saved music from extinction.

References

1.   Basu, Raj Narayan : *Sakal and Ekal*, p.56
2.   Projnanananda, Swami : *Historical Development of Indian Music*, p.204
3.   *Bhatkhande Smriti Grantha*, p.222
4.   Ibid.
5.   Ratanjankar, Pandit S.N. : *Pandit Bhatkhande*, p.3
6.   Ibid., p.2
7.   Ibid., pp.52-'3
8.   Ibid., pp.15-'7
9.   Ibid., p.56
10.   *Presidential Address of H.H. Maharaja Shri Vijay Devji of Dharampur*, Sangeet Natak Academy, p.4
11.   Ratanjankar, Pandit S.N.: *Pandit Bhatkhande*, pp.53-'4
12.   Singh, Thakur Jaidev : 'Guru Shishya Parampara,' *Lipika*, Vol.2, pp.32-'3
13.   *Bhatkhande Smriti Grantha*, p.418

3
Bhatkhande's Special Mental Make-up

Anyone who turns over the pages of *Hindustani Sangeet Paddhati* (*Kramik Pustak Malika*) comes across on the very first page itself the photograph of a man bearing the stamp of an outstanding personality. The very first look impresses one with the man's poise and dignity. The countenance bears the stamp of authority and mellowed wisdom that inspire confidence. The eyes hold and haunt and look into the depth of one's being with a clear steady gaze. The chin is firm but not aggressive. The tightly compressed lips, slightly stretched in a smile, proclaim a man of strong feelings, determination and a sense of humour. This outstanding portrait – wearing a cap, a coat and a *dhoti* – is that of Vishnu Narayan Bhatkhande.

This analysis of his portrait brings out the main traits of his character. These traits enabled him to establish his place in history as an epoch-making national figure in the world of Hindustani music. He also stands out as a symbol of our culture. Writes Shrikrishna Ratanjankar, his chief disciple, that, whoever met Bhatkhande even at his age of sixty, was struck by his radiant appearance the glow of which was the radiance of a spiritually illumined soul. He had a broad forehead, shining eyes, fair complexion, broad chest, long hands and feet and a straight nose–giving the impression of a handsome and extraordinarily brilliant person.[1]

His Birth

Vishnu was born in the Bombay Presidency (Maharashtra) in a Brahmin family in the year of 1860 on August 10, a holy day, being *Janmashtami*, the birthday of Lord Krishna.

Bombay is known for its great men born at the turn of the century, who revitalised the Indian nation in all walks of life. Its Malabar Hill stands at the edge of the rippled waters of the sea frilled by a wide border of sand. A tiny temple of Shiva emerges from this sandy foot-hill called 'Walukeshwar'-- the Lord of the Sand. The family of Vishnu, who migrated from a village called Nagaon in Konkan, settled in this sleepy village of Walukeshwar against the backdrop of hills overlooking the sea. "They were simple folk, living a modest life. They were far from affluent."[2]

Bhatkhande was the second among the three brothers and two sisters and was fondly called Anna. His elder brother, Appa, worked in the Police Department and died young. His younger brother, Haribhau, was fond of music and used to play *dilruba*. He was an employee of a bank. His father, a *munim* to a rich *seth*, was a lover of music and played *swarmandal* in his leisure time.

His Inborn Artistic Talent

Vishnu was a born musician. As soon as he was out of the cradle, he started singing, inspired by his mother, nursery songs. While studying in a Marathi Primary School, he was a much sought after child singer who could reproduce all the songs he had heard from his mother. He fared much better than the other boys of his class in reciting poems in tune or singing *geets* and *bhajans*. He won prizes in school for his melodious voice.

The South is famous even today for propitiating her deities by dance, drama and music on religious festivals. So, as was the custom, on the holy days of *Ramnavami, Janmashtami, Diwali* and *Holi*, special music programmes were arranged in Walukeshwar by the Marwaris, Gosais and Gujaratis. Young Vishnu, who had taken to flute playing in addition to singing, was very much in demand for such programmes. It was the beginning of a great career which later rejuvenated and illuminated the entire degenerated musical set up of the early 20th century.

His Qualities of Leadership

A leader requires to have initiative and the capacity to command, to create a team spirit among the followers, to inspire confidence and evoke loyalty. He displayed qualities of leadership right from his school days and as he grew up they flowered into full bloom and enabled him to fulfil his mission of reconstruction work in the field of music.

After completing his study in the Marathi Primary School, Vishnu was admitted to the Elphinstone High School, Bombay. As a school boy he was fair complexioned, tall and lively. Even at that age he was an accepted leader of his school-mates who thronged round him, loved him and followed his lead. In every school there are some mischievous boys who always harass their younger and weaker fellows. In Vishnu's school there was no dearth of such boys. But the weaker ones thronged round Vishnu who punished the evil-doers and was dreaded by them.

Leadership was a born quality in him, which was the cause of his success in later years when as a reformer in the domain of music he brought round an *ustad* of a renowned *gharana* to toe his line of thinking. Comments His Highness Maharaja Vijay Devji of Dharampur : "...Vishnu Bhatkhande found it very difficult to win over the prejudices of those who could not see the relation between singing and books and instruments, between theory and practice of music. But he did finally win them over. Such was the persuasive tenacity of the man, whom in annoyance they began to tease and subsequently not a few of them in admiration honoured as *Panditji*."[3]

The veteran musician of Pune, Ramkrishnabuwa Vaze, accepted, with humility, that although initially he was opposed to the idea of the notation system as propagated by Bhatkhande in Classical music he ultimately accepted it and adopted it with great admiration for Panditji. In later years when he organised music conferences, on an All India basis, which were joined by the stalwarts of that time, 'his personality reigned supreme'.

His capacity for initiative is undisputed. He trod the forbidden ground of the world of music and gave it a new vitality and status.

Later, when his movement gained momentum he inspired a team of workers to serve his cause. They followed his lead and dedicated themselves to his task. The veteran musicians like Shankarrao Karnad, Rajabhaiya Poochhwale and Thakur Nawab Ali had deep respect for him and his work. Scholars like Kashinath Shastri, Appa Tulsi, Brij Kishan Kaul, Rai Umanath Bali were influenced by him and served his cause. They accepted him as their undisputed leader and were fully and steadily loyal to him. Their admiration for him was so great that even after his death his followers served his cause with the same intensity and followed his line with the same sincerity.

His Early Training

In his college days, side by side with his studies, he took to *sitar* playing. There was one Gopal Giri in Vishnu's locality who used to play *sitar*. Through him Vishnu was introduced to Vallabhdas Damulji who was not only a *sitar* player but a *been* player as well. Vallabhdas was a well-to-do man but he had lost his eyesight. Therefore, he decided to dedicate his life to music. As asked by him Vishnu used to visit his house at late hours every night. "Knowing that his parents would object to this, Vishnu managed to go to Vallabhdas without their knowledge. Vishnu was much impressed by the art of playing *sitar* and *been* by Vallabhdas and having passed all the tests of patience and service, as was the custom of those days, he started learning the instruments."[4]

With his aptitude and talent he made great progress within a short time and "became a reputed *sitar* player in Bombay."[5] He was a sought after artist at musical soirees held occasionally where he also gave demonstration without the knowledge of his parents. But the secret could not be kept for long. Ratanjankar records in *Bhatkhande Smriti Grantha* that in a private *mehfil*, where Vishnu was to play *sitar*, his father was also invited. Thus father and son came face to face. The father's surprise knew no bounds to find in his son a finished artist, appreciated by others. Vishnu's father's reaction was two-fold: on the one hand he felt elated at his son's success as a musician, who made such progress stealthily practising his instrument, and on the other his culture of music filled him with worries about his future. For it was the belief of the day that music 'was an occupation fit only for the idlers and good for nothing and pursued by the illiterates.' The parents' worry was dispelled when Vishnu passed the Matriculation examination in 1880 and entered college. Along with music his studies also progressed well. Vishnu passed his B.A. in 1885, LL.B. in 1887 and later started his professional career as a lawyer, specialising in Criminal Law and the Act of Evidence. In 1884 he joined the Gayan Uttejak Mandali established by the Parsee Community for propagating Classical music. Here he had both the opportunities of listening and learning. This Mandali used to invite *ustad*s to perform their art from all over the country.

His Power of Discovering Method in Music

Thus Bhatkhande got the advantage of listening to the performances of great artists like Tanras Khan, Inayat Hussain Khan, Naththan Khan, Ali Hussain Khan Beenkar and his maternal uncle Vilayat Hussain. He also got the opportunity of listening to Mohammed Khan and Rahimat Khan, sons of the great Haddu Khan, and also to the performance of Nazir Khan, the leading *sarangi* player of his time. But listening was not mere entertainment or satisfaction of the aesthetic sense for Bhatkhande. His analytical mind and native intelligence discovered a system in the demonstrations of the current musicians, though they were neither aware of any theory or rules and regulations of the note movement underlying them nor were they conscious of the theory's historical evolution. They only reproduced the art which they learnt from their teachers orally. In their art, underneath the apparent incoherent system, there was a flow of method which was the basis of the modern Hindustani music. This discovery inspired the receptive mind of Bhatkhande to form an idea of this scientific background which the demonstrators themselves were incapable of realising. "On this basis Bhatkhande started thinking and building up a fully systematised classification of the Indian melodies."[6]

His Inquisitiveness and Exploring Capacity

In his formative period he toured extensively to study the ancient *granthas* available in the libraries of the Native States for the purpose of consolidating the available knowledge of the evolution and practice of Hindustani music. His tours, undertaken at different periods, covered Madras, Tanjore, Ettayapuram, Madura, Ramnad,

Rameshwaram, Trivandrum, Trichinapally, Mysore and Bangalore. He also visited Gujarat and toured Surat, Broach, Baroda, Navsari, Ahmedabad, Rajkot, Wankaner, Jamnagar, Junagarh and Bhavnagar. Subsequently, he visited Hyderabad, Shikarpur and other places in Sind, Kutch and Multan. Some years later he visited Nagpur, Calcutta, Jagannath Puri, Vizianagaram, Deccan and Hyderabad. This tour was followed by his visits to Allahabad, Banaras, Gaya, Mathura, Lucknow, Agra, Delhi, Jaipur, Jodhpur, Bikaner, Udaipur and Rampur.

The information gathered during his extensive tours was scrutinised, compared and analysed against the form of music of the day which Bhatkhande had heard and learnt. Knowledge thus digested and assimilated was later responsible for his writing the invaluable theoretical works which are now cherished by all music lovers.

Bhatkhande realised that there had been a great deal of transformation in the practical shape of music and, therefore, a completely new systematisation and classification was necessary to put the existing system, underlying Hindustani music, on a sound footing.

Further Study and Collection of Compositions

To dig deep into the world of music Bhatkhande started learning from various *ustads*. He felt that the traditional compositions were the source from which the form and structure of a *raga* could be evolved. In the absence of a theory and a notation system these compositions were the only material on which one had to rely for the *chalan* or the movement of a *raga*. Bhatkhande learnt about 300 *dhrupad*s from Raojibuwa who was a pupil of Zainalabuddeen Khan of Hyderabad. Bhatkhande also collected a good number of *khayal*s from Ali Hussain Khan and his maternal uncle, Vilayat Hussain, both of whom were also in the service of the Gayan Uttejak Mandali. His most important teacher was Muhammed Ali Khan of Jaipur known as 'Kothiwal'. His son Ashiq Ali Khan, who was in dire need of money then, was engaged by him to teach him valuable compositions belonging to the Jaipur *gharana*. Not only did Bhatkhande learn them to perfection with dexterity but also took them down with notation and *tala* marks. It was the beginning of a life of continuous learning which blossomed into the original unprecedented work on the theory of music of the modern age.

In later years he published, to serve as textbooks, his *Kramik Pustak Malika* in six parts, containing about 1000 compositions. They were the result of the knowledge thus gathered throughout his life of learning.

He had an insatiable thirst for collecting traditional compositions belonging to all branches of Classical music for which not infrequently he had to suffer humiliation, refusal and rudeness. His collection from Gwalior *gharana* included a large number of *dhrupads*, *horis* and *khayals* from Eknath Pandit, known as Maoo Pandit. He also learnt many compositions belonging to the famous Senia *gharana* of Rampur which included a large number of *dhrupads*, *horis* etc. How he used tact, suffered humiliation, spent money and used persuasion to collect the compositions from the hereditary musicians, who guarded them as sacred treasure, is brought out in interesting episodes.

His Capacity to Perform

He was not an ordinary compiler of musical compositions from the traditional *ustads*. He was also an expert in singing and a full-fledged artist. As he dedicated himself to the task of recasting music into a systematic theory, he never demonstrated his art to earn fame and money. There is ample testimony of his singing capacity. M.K. Samanta writes in *Bhatkhande Smriti Grantha* that he heard Bhatkhande singing *alapa* of *Darbari* which touched three *saptaks* and which was rendered artistically.[7]

We find in the writings of Vishnu Shamrao Atre that he heard him sing 22 *shrutis* one after the other and that Bhatkhande was fond of singing *dhamars*, *dwigun* and *chowgun* with the help of beats by hand.[8]

Balaji Shridhar Pathak, of Allahabad, who had the opportunity of learning from Bhatkhande, recalls that his voice was very sweet and deep. He was more fond of *dhrupad* than *khayal*. He was well versed in singing *alapa* of *dhrupad* and was fond of elaborating it in the lower octave. He used to sing *khayal's* *sthayi* and *antara* melodiously and preferred elaboration in the *dhrupad* style. He disliked the volley of *tanas*.[9]

His Intelligence and Memory

His intelligence and retentive momory was remarkable. In the task of giving music the status of an academic subject the way he scrutinised each composition that he collected, the way he noted down the *tala* and *sur* with ease with the help of a simple notation system which he himself evolved, the way he studied and scanned the old *granthas* for useful material, and the way he reasoned about the current theory in his works bear ample proof of a razor sharp intellect and extraordinary memory. Much later, when Bhatkhande was at the helm of affairs of the Madhav Sangeet Mahavidyalaya, Gwalior, recalls Balaji Shridhar Pathak about the prolific memory of Bhatkhande who happened to be a teacher when Balaji was a student there. At times when Bhatkhande used to talk about a book or about an artist, he easily remembered the dates and the details in a way as if he had read them only yesterday. Once he ordered Balaji to procure a monthly magazine from the library giving him the dates etc. Balaji was surprised to learn that the particular magazine Bhatkhande had noticed was being read by a co-passenger in the train three years earlier.[10]

Bhatkhande, who had such a gift of memory, got on well with his study as a student in the school and learnt the subjects like English, History, etc. with little effort.

His Knowledge of Languages

Bhatkhande was well versed in different languages. This proved very useful in studying and writing books on music. During his study tours he studied all the old available music literature in Sanskrit, Marathi and Gujarati and jotted down the important points therein. He had a profound knowledge of Sanskrit which in later years flowered into two unique books of theory namely *Shrimallakshya Sangeetam* and *Abhinava Raga Manjari*. He was also well versed in Hindi and Marathi and could well express himself in English. His unique series on theory, namely, *Hindustani Sangeet Paddhati*, was written in Marathi in four parts. His three informative papers in English, later published as books, were of invaluable quality and were the first of their kind. His innumerable articles in both the languages are also praiseworthy.

His Disposition

Young Bhatkhande was witty and always cheerful. As he could

not afford to go to school by a conveyance—a distance of five to six miles—he walked with others and his witty talks kept his companions cheerful, making them forget the boredom of a long walk. This quality of sociability he retained to his last day. Perhaps this quality alone attracted several learned intelligent and dedicated people who contributed greatly to his research work.

In his reminiscences Balaji Shridhar Pathak recalls that Bhatkhande had an inimitable way all his own to relate and describe things. He had a "sincere, simple and happy disposition, somewhat of a shy nature."[11]

His Shrewdness

He was determined to weed out any obstacles to achieve his goal of collecting materials and compositions from the musicians, *ustad*s, theoreticians and Pandits. The musicians and Pandits were vain and egoistic, unwilling to part with their knowledge. Therefore, he had to fight their prejudices, hypocrisy and arrogance, not to speak of their ignorance. He shrewdly overcame all these difficulties. His main armour against all these was utter humility mixed with courtesy and self-respect. Sometimes he had to stoop down or had to be comical or humorous to overcome their prejudices and suspicion of new ideas. It is relevant to mention a few interesting episodes displaying his presence of mind and shrewdness to assess the situation. They are related by Ratanjankar, his very close and favourite pupil, in his book *Pandit Bhatkhande*. During his early formative period when he was toying with the idea of forming a theory of the current Hindustani music and was in search of good compositions, he was introduced to Ashiq Ali Khan, the son of Muhammed Ali Khan of Jaipur. He was in possession of the priceless compositions of his *gharana* which was nicknamed as 'Kothiwal' or the 'House of Songs'. As Ashiq Ali Khan was in great financial need, he agreed to teach Bhatkhande these compositions for remuneration. Bhatkhande not only learnt them by heart but also wrote them down in notation from which he could reproduce them immediately. He also recorded the compositions sung by Ashiq Ali on phonographic discs. It was a time when the music teachers or the *guru*s belonging to the family of singers did not allow the pupil to record their music in any form. Therefore, this type of learning was resented by the music world and soon Muhammed Ali, father of Ashiq Ali, was informed. He lost no time in reaching Bombay and when he found that the valuable compositions of his *gharana* were thus given away to Bhatkhande, he was furious. Bhatkhande managed this situation by surrendering himself to the old *Ustad* as his pupil and pacified him by profuse apologies. The *Ustad's* anger was assuaged and he accepted Bhatkhande as his pupil. This relationship he retained till his last day.

The second important episode relates to his collection of compositions belonging to Rampur *gharana.* Nawab Hamid Ali Khan, himself a knowledgeable musician, was the ruler of Rampur who had Ustad Wazir Khan, the descendant of Mian Tansen of mythical fame and the doyen of the classical artists of his time, in his employ as a court musician. As Bhatkhande's movement had gained momentum he aspired to collect the priceless compositions belonging to the Tansen *gharana* from Ustad Wazir Khan. Knowing fully well that direct approach to the *ustad* would meet only with blunt refusal, on account of the conservatism in teaching practised in those days, he devised a roundabout way to attain his objective. Through a common friend he got himself introduced to the Nawab and ceremoniously became his pupil. After learning from the Nawab for some time he requested him to introduce him to Ustad Wazir Khan for the purpose of learning compositions. The Nawab appreciated his purpose of such collection and complied with his request. Wazir Khan could not brush aside the request of his patron. Therefore, Bhatkhande was able to collect a large number of *khandani bandish*s from this *gharana.* The way he tackled egoistic Pandits in his study tours was remarkable.

Writes Chinchore in *Bhatkhande Smriti Grantha* that Bhatkhande had an extraordinary intelligence – almost an intuitive power to judge a man. When he was entrusted with the work of developing music in the States of Gwalior and Baroda, he himself went there and measured everyone's capacity with his wisdom.[12] He judged the traits and quality of character of an individual so accurately that he discarded people who suffered from false vanity and useless ego and cunning and opportunistic attitude. He picked up people who were dedicated to music and entrusted work to them. One such classic example was when he chose Rajabhaiya Poochhwale as his close associate for reorganisation of music. Rajabhaiya, who was branded as a mere harmonium player by the other musicians, proved himself worthy of being his associate in every respect. This quality of sound judgement of men was mainly responsible for pushing forward his great task.

His Quality of Humility

Bhatkhande was a man of extraordinary humility. About the quality of humility in a man Gandhiji holds: "Service without humility is selfishness and egoism." This saying fits in exactly with the nature of Bhatkhande. With his monumental scholarship he was a model of sweetness, softness and humility. It was this basic quality which, combined with others, enabled him to render the great service to posterity in regard to a fully systematised musical theory of the Hindustani Classical music of his time. Recalls Balaji Shridhar Pathak that when he approached Bhatkhande to learn vocal music Bhatkhande refused on the ground that he himself was not a singer.[13] It appears so unusual in today's context when one frequently comes across a musician of poor knowledge whose sole professional capital is egoism, vanity and self-advertisement.

Such was his humility that he used even to order the people who served him in a sweet and soft way. Anything he uttered was uttered quietly. Wrote Balaji Shridhar Pathak that he never found him getting angry. Even during fiery discussions on music, where differences of opinion occurred, he tried to press his point of view with patience and a smile.

Sometimes some of the orthodox type of musicians used to use harsh language against his publishing the *gharanedar cheej* in notation. Even then he used to protest softly and patiently. His extraordinary humility never offended the challenging vain *ustad*s. M.K. Samanta writes that Bhatkhande used to take notice of everybody's point of view, even though the other party was nothing more than a beginner in music. He had an extremely considerate and sweet nature. It was nothing but humility that prompted him to write his compositions under the pseudonym of 'Chatur Pandit'.[14] These compositions as they stand now are an invaluable treasure both from the point of poetic and technical quality. He wrote his books in the name of Vishnu Sharma which are now cherished by all the music lovers and referred to as the authentic books on the theory of Hindustani Classical music. These books and the compositions therein bear the stamp of his great knowledge, hard labour and poetic imagination. The use of pseudonym shows his aversion to self-advertisement and supreme apathy to fame.

His Wit and Humour

Bhatkhande was a man of quick wit and a keen sense of humour. For a few years he practised law and earned enough to support himself for the rest of his life. Later he gave up his profession to devote himself completely to the cause of music. While he practised law he never lost a case and was a successful cross-examiner.

About his sense of humour Balaji Shridhar Pathak quotes an incident. Bhatkhande started having difficulty in hearing but that did not affect his capacity to listen to music. While Bhatkhande was watching a music class being conducted by a Khan Saheb, the latter took Pandit Bhatkhande as a deaf man and continued to teach in his own way. Pandit Bhatkhande was fully aware of the entire situation but in a good humour, pretended to be really a deaf man and later narrated it jokingly.[15] His wit was displayed when he functioned as a teacher.

Chinchore has narrated Bhatkhande's witty method of selection of boys for enrolment in the music school. He used to keep a long whistle with him which when elongated used to give high notes and low notes when shortened. When the students came for admission, they were made to stand in a row and asked to reproduce at least three notes of different pitches produced by Bhatkhande's whistle. By this process he used to measure quickly the potentiality of a student.[16]

N.L. Gune quotes an instance of his extraordinary wit to explain the theory of music to the students. About the division of *tala* in *teentala* having 16 *matras*, he asked: "Children! Tell me if you have four rooms and if you have 16 guests to accommodate what would be the number you would put in one room."[17] The answer would be identical with the division of *tala* in a *teentala*.

His Poetic Genius

His poetic genius is unparalleled in the history of music. When he was a lawyer, he used to rhyme the dry definitions of law in small couplets. Shrikrishna Ratanjankar writes in his book *Pandit Bhatkhande:* – "He conducted law classes in Bombay for a few years. He composed little verses on the clauses of the Evidence Act, set them to music and taught them in the classes."[18] Later his poetic genius flowered into a great composer in the field of Classical music. His books on theory of music, viz., *Shrimallakshya Sangeetam* and *Abhinava Raga Manjari*, written in crisp Sanskrit couplets, bore ample proof of his genius and were highly acclaimed by scholars. His mammoth compositions cover a wide range of moods, themes, *ragas, talas* and types. His *khayals, dhrupads, saadras, lakshan geets, sargams* (note patterns) written in beautiful chaste Hindi, but with a tinge of Braj Bhasha, are a class by themselves. Even in rare *talas* his compositions are amazingly lucid and compact. Apart from his other contributions his name should be immortal even for his contribution as a composer. He has left a huge treasure for posterity. This has been discussed elaborately in a separate chapter.

As a Teacher

All these traits of his character were displayed fully in his personality as a teacher which was a unique example of its kind. It was he who introduced the modern scientific method of teaching music for a group of students based on notation. This was unprecedented in history. Ramchandra Madhab Agnihotri points out that his method of teaching was unique. In the beginning he would explain all the peculiarities of a *raga* according to the Shastras. Then he would explain the characteristics of the allied *ragas* in such minute detail that the students grasped it intellectually and consequently felt confident. He would take the combination of *Sā* and *Ma* and go on explaining the subtle usage of the above combination in different *ragas* along with the *kan*. He would then draw endless illustrations. He would sometimes sing twenty-two *shrutis* in a *saptak* and he would also explain which one of them would be used in which *raga*.[19] When the order of the day was that a music student had to serve the music teacher for years and bear humiliation and insults in return for which he was taught only superficially, Bhatkhande created a revolution by explaining and teaching a *raga* scientifically and rationally. Unlike the *gharanedar* professionals he was ever ready to teach anybody who was a willing learner.

M.K. Samanta recalls an incident when a friend of his from Madras, who was not a singer, visited Bhatkhande who was charmed by the former's untrained sweet voice. Immediately he asked Ratanjankar, who was his favourite student, to teach M.K. Samanta's friend some *bandish* in *Bhairavi* and *tappa* in *Khamaj*. To teach without reservation was really a revolution in the world of music coaching at that time. Many celebrated singers who were once his pupils remember his intelligent, easy and quick method of teaching. M.K. Samanta recalls that at the time of teaching a *raga*, Bhatkhande would explain all about the theory of the *raga* before he would teach singing. Not only that, he would explain all other allied *ragas* and their points of similarity in such clear and detailed way that it was stamped for ever on the mind of the student.

Again, writes Balaji Shridhar Pathak that Panditji's bass voice was very sweet and deep. While teaching he would explain how to break the words of a song while developing it along with note patterns. He also used to teach the importance of pronunciation and enunciation of a particular *raga*. His method of imparting knowledge was novel and interesting. He would himself sing *sthayi* and *antara* in such a way that the *raga*'s form was immediately established and imprinted on the mind of his students for ever.[20]

At his instance, the Madhav Rao Scindia School was established in Gwalior. His students, who are even now living, recall how affectionate he was to them. Narrates Bala Sahib Poochhwale, the son of Rajabhaiya Poochhwale, the celebrated singer of Gwalior and Bhatkhande's right hand man for propagating his new method of music, that such was Panditji's affection for him that he used to keep sweets for him out of his own share.

His personality was so attractive to his pupils that they eagerly awaited his arrival and enjoyed his presence. When he visited the music school in Gwalior for conducting the examination, his first duty was to dispel the fear of the examination from the minds of the students. "For this purpose he used to personally meet the students before the examination and used to minimise the fear of the examination by informal discussion about music."[21]

N.L. Gune writes in *Bhatkhande Smriti Grantha* that as an examiner he used to measure the knowledge of a pupil very cleverly.

In this his legal mind worked. Rai Umanath Bali writes, "He stayed with me for one month... He not only taught me vocal music in detail but every day he used to give me lectures for about two hours about the theory of music."[22] P.N.Chinchore has written that at the instance of Bhatkhande a music school was opened in Gwalior where the students were taught through the new method introduced by him. The impact of his personality was so deep that the teacher and the students used to forget themselves in music practice day and night. He also felt concerned about the students who duly passed the music examination from the school. He took interest in rehabilitating them so that they could keep up their music practice. His affectionate nature, extraordinary devotion to music and his simple habits created such an impression that his mere look at the students would fill them with unspeakable joy and this all encouraged and inspired his students.

It was his legal mind which worked when he tried to evaluate a musician. The musicians used to come to him with the purpose of testing his knowledge and defeating him. But at the end they had to accept him as a great scholar and a master theoretician.[23]

His Faith in God and Simplicity in Life

He was basically a soft-hearted imaginative man with great devotion and faith in God. He was born and brought up in an atmosphere of faith in God. His father was a great devotee of Lord Krishna and was worshipper of the deity Dattatreya whom he established in his house and served him daily with great devotion. Bhatkhande's mother was equally devotional in temperament. She observed all the prevalent religious rites neglecting her comforts. Thus Bhatkhande imbibed a deep faith in God from his childhood. Later he became a devotee of Lord Shiva and was seen often with a rosary in his hand remembering the Lord's name. In his personal letters to his pupils he mentioned and prayed to Lord Shiva to help him to fulfil his great task of the revival of music. In fact his attitude to life was one of renunciation and dedication to God. Although he loved to look at this world in its beauty and diversity, he never forgot its short-lived nature and had an eye on realising the unity underlying this diversity. His conception of the Universe was that it was the manifestation of the Eternal Formless One — an idea which pervades his poetic compositions in music.

He was an example of asceticism, reducing his worldly needs to the minimum. His living, eating and other habits were simple. Like a saint he was averse to staying at one place and was fond of travelling. He had no greed for money. He was offered a salary of Rs. 600/- per month and a free bungalow by the Gwalior Government but he refused. He gave up his lucrative practice of law and sustained himself with the paltry sum of money he had collected. He took a vow not to accept a penny in the reconstruction work of music and he adhered to it. At the end one can rightly say that to rescue music from its then existing decadent state and re-establish it as a major force in the country's cultural life was a herculean task for which every inch of Bhatkhande seemed to have been carefully prepared by Destiny.

References

1. Ratanjankar, Pandit S.N. : 'Jeevan Charitra', *Bhatkhande Smriti Grantha*, p.1
2. Ratanjankar, Pandit S.N. : *Pandit Bhatkhande*, p.2
3. *Bhatkhande Smriti Grantha*, p.283
4. Ratanjankar, Pandit S.N. : *Pandit Bhatkhande*, P.5
5. Ibid., p.6
6. Ibid., p.9
7. *Bhatkhande Smriti Grantha*, p.315
8. Ibid., p.309
9. Ibid., pp.296 and 303
10. Ibid., p.303
11. Ibid., p.301
12. Ibid., p.81
13. Ibid., p.297
14. Ibid., p.314
15. Ibid., p.301
16. Chinchore, P. N. : *Bhatkhande Smriti Grantha*, op. cit., p.83
17. *Bhatkhande Smriti Grantha*, p.290
18. Ratanjankar, Pandit S.N. : *Pandit Bhatkhande*, p.10
19. *Bhatkhande Smriti Grantha*, p.319
20. Ibid., pp. 296-'7
21. Bala Saheb Poochhwale : *Bhatkhande Smriti Grantha*, op. cit., p.316
22. *Bhatkhande Smriti Grantha*, p.276
23. Chinchore, P. N. : *Bhatkhande Smriti Grantha*, op. cit., p.90

PART II

HIS CONTRIBUTION

4

The Framework and the Perspective

When an art drifts -- having no system, no method and no connecting link with the past -- it becomes like a boat without a rudder which capsises in mid-stream when the flood comes. Reviewing the entire scene from the socio-political and economic perspectives we can state in short that in the last half of the nineteenth century the condition of North Indian Classical music was similar to such a rudderless boat which had lost its old moorings and had not yet found new ones. To describe it more clearly, it had lost all contacts with the *granthas* written by the old masters like Bharata, Kohala, Narada etc. and yet had not evolved any new methodology and science as a base for learning and teaching. For its survival, it needed a rational, integrated theory of music which would be intellectually satisfying. It also needed a scientific, modern approach and treatment as other subjects of study like Law, Languages, Economics, History, Philosophy etc. For only the intelligentsia and the educated class of our country could preserve and develop our musical heritage and save it from extinction. The condition of music in the late nineteenth century was deplorable, being totally in the hands of the illiterate musicians. Although there were some practical stalwarts, the availability of study materials was a cipher compared to the other modern subjects. The elite of that period felt disgusted at the *gharanedar* quarrels, exploitation of the students, and the egoism and lowly living style of the musicians. Consequently, the educated society did not think music worthy of being included and introduced as a subject in schools and colleges. The general attitude was to despise it as unnecessary, superfluous and vulgar.

Only a handful of musicians kept practical music alive in the native courts and only the fortunate few, having an entry there, could enjoy their performance. The treatment of these musicians by their patron Nawabs, Rajas and Chieftains was far from edifying. They were often not treated or respected as scholars in subjects like History, Law, Languages etc. They were looked upon as means of satisfying the whims and varying tastes of this self-styled aristocracy. Sometimes the masters became the pupils of their protege musicians, thus boosting their vanity. Yet the nineteenth century produced some great practical stalwarts like Haddu Khan, Hassu Khan, Muhammed Ali and others. With their assiduous practice they kept up the glorious tradition of music.

It was the most critical phase in the annals of Hindustani music. Everywhere a shadow of gloom was cast on its future. For a century national life had been deteriorating. There was a void and degeneration in all walks of life -- artistic, literary, philosophical and political. But India is known for its gyrostatic quality, and when her talent seems to be at its lowest ebb she recovers in surprising abundance. Soon a period of Renaissance ensued when great ideas loomed on the horizon and men of destiny were born to revitalise, reorganise and reorient art, politics and social customs. This Renaissance has already been discussed in detail.

Each age has its great men and just as a particular period creates them they also give shape to that period and build it up beautifully with their own contributions. Bhatkhande was one of such men to whom destiny assigned the great task of revitalising, systematising and uplifting music from its decadent state. But before he could act as a versatile architect of Hindustani Classical music he had to pass through a long and arduous formative period through which he thoroughly prepared himself to accomplish this great task. His formative period comprises:

1. Listening and Learning,
2. Study Tours, and
3. Collection of Compositions.

Listening and Learning

Bhatkhande started singing since he was out of the cradle. He was a popular singer during the annual festivals in his locality at his birth-place. In his early youth he became a flute player and learnt *sitar* from Shri Vallabhdas Damulji who was the pupil of the renowned *sitar* and *been* player Jeevanlal Maharaj. Under his guidance Bhatkhande established himself as a reputed *sitar* player in Bombay. He kept up his studies along with music and having passed his B.A. and Law, he started practising in Bombay. In 1884 he joined the Gayan Uttejak Mandali established and run by the Parsee community of Bombay. The main aim and object of this association was to give the public an opportunity to hear and enjoy the Classical music of the renowned music artists. The influx of musicians into Bombay may be attributed to the 1857 Mutiny when the British massacred the princes and the nobility who took part in it. The princes who escaped their wrath suffered monetarily and their protege musicians were uprooted. Most of them came to Bombay to earn through their performances. Bhatkhande thus came into contact with the cream of the musicians and had the opportunity to listen to their masterly demonstrations. Many of the chips of the old block were still alive. Famous artists from Delhi, Lucknow, Agra, Jaipur, Gwalior, Patiala, Baroda, Hyderabad etc. came to Bombay to demonstrate their skill. Some of the important names were Naththan Khan of Agra, Bande Ali Khan (*Beenkar*), Pannalal Bajpayee (*Sitar* player), Rahimat Khan of Gwalior, Balkrishna Buwa, Tanras Khan, Ali Hussain and his brother Fateh Ali, Hyder Khan, Banne Khan etc. The people of Bombay were thrilled to hear such masters but among them Bhatkhande was the only one for whom listening was not the purpose of gratifying his aesthetic sense only, or a pastime or mere entertainment. Listening to the best performances of the *ustads* of his time opened a new vista before his eyes. His well-developed mind, trained in modern methodology and having the capacity of scrutiny and synthesis, pondered over these performances and detected a method, a system and a science underlying them. While he tried to argue logically and enquire the fundamentals of the *ragas*, he realised that the artists were themselves ignorant and had no understanding of their art. They were completely incapable of any coherent explanation of the process of rendering and developing a *raga* — its framework, its salient features, the points of similarity and dissimilarity with other *ragas*, and the typical phrases used etc. One reason for this was that the *ragas* of Hindustani Classical music were learnt, practised and performed in the traditional way in which lessons were imparted orally and no questions were allowed to be asked or answered. The question of explaining anything rationally never came in. The *guru shishya parampara* method was followed in teaching which largely depended on the whims of the *ustad*. Bhatkhande became painfully conscious of the reality of the situation. Years of absence of any scientific study and training in the theory of music had left the performers ignorant of it. It had lowered the position of music in the world of knowledge and learning and had reduced it to the position of a mere medium of entertainment, often cheap. Therefore, unlike subjects like History, Philosophy etc. — where there is no dearth of research workers, students, critics and writers, with modern and logical approach — music had none. It became stagnant. Observing the above fact, he wrote in Marathi: "To learn the great art of music or, in other words, to learn the system of *raga* and *ragini* in our music is the main object. That society today is ignorant of music is not true. Classical music is well-known to the public. But the rules and regulations, i.e., scientific knowledge, is nowhere near, as it should be. My desire in music is that the present day *raga*s and *ragini*s should be classified nicely and the rules they observe should be clearly indicated. That our music does not enjoy these coveted qualities is well-known to everybody. By saying this it is not meant that whatever the musicians sing or play are without any system or irregular.The crux of the argument is that the artists have never made an attempt to place it properly before others."

To delve deep into the world of music he started learning it to have the real feel of it. He started intitially his music lessons from the *ustad*s of the Mandali. The Gayan Uttejak Mandali, apart from arranging musical soirees, engaged *ustads* for imparting lessons to the persons interested in learning Classical music. One such *ustad* was Raojibuwa Belbagkar. Buwa was a *dhrupad* singer and a pupil of Ustad Jainullah Khan of Hyderabad (Deccan).[1] Bhatkhande learnt by heart at least 300 *dhrupad*s from Buwa. There was another musician employed by this Mandali whose name was Ustad Ali Hussain *Khayalia*. From him and also from his maternal uncle, whose name was Vilayat Hussain Khan, Bhatkhande learnt about 110-125 *khayal*s. He learnt with care the compositions of *khayal* and *dhrupad* in the traditional way, as was in vogue at the time, and practised them with the greatest care. He discovered that at least 75 *ragas*, which were widely and frequently demonstrated, were performed in the same way by the various North Indian Schools (*Gharanas*) all over the country. His learning of music further convinced him of the necessity of formulating an integrated theory of music to preserve our musical heritage. He felt that the basic principles of a *raga* should be clearly enunciated to ensure that its individuality was properly brought out. An art which had grown and languished could not be recovered unless it was reconstructed. For this an all out movement—a new approach, a new realisation, a new conception was necessary to build a rapport with the art lovers. Desperately he tried to find a way to convince and inspire our countrymen to be aware of our musical heritage and the necessity of its revival.

In this, initially, he was greatly inspired by a book called *History of Music* written by Dr. Burn. While the English were ruling this country, Bombay society had many enlightened people with modern thoughts and ideas and its library was full of modern subjects. Bhatkhande came across there many books on European music written by foreign scholars. He was much impressed by their way of dealing with music as a subject of analysis and study. The broad-mindedness in accepting new ideas, capacity for collecting evidence and using it as rational argument for establishing a theory displayed in these books influenced him greatly. *History of Music* by Dr. Burn had all the qualities mentioned above and, in addition to that, very logically the writer had tried to establish a relationship between European and the Greek music. Bhatkhande aspired to do similar work on our Classical music. But the stumbling blocks were many. The ancient *granthas* were not easily available and even if they were there was nobody to explain the theories contained therein, in the context of the present. There was no dearth of pandits who had profound knowledge of Sanskrit but they had no idea of the grammar of music (*Sangeet Shastra*). Bhatkhande used to fret often by saying that how useful it would have been if one could trace the development of music from the date of *Samaveda* to the 20th century.

Not being cowed down by these obstacles Bhatkhande kept on collecting data both by learning from the *ustad*s of Gayan Uttejak Mandali and discussing with them the theoretical part of it. He started collecting whatever material he could lay his hands on. He was also able to collect some material on the theoretical aspects of Classical music from his friends who belonged to the Gujarati, Parsee and Maharashtrian communities. Though the knowledge and information gathered in this way were often incomplete and haphazard, he recorded and stored them like a precious possession and analysed and compared them carefully. If the material thus collected appeared rational he recorded it as an established fact, and if he felt it was illogical, he jotted it down to be discussed, clarified and later accepted or rejected.

In addition to this he studied and scanned all the available books on music in Bombay. Simultaneously he collected hundreds of musical compositions from the *ustad*s. He studied, analysed and scrutinised the musical part of these compositions with great care and formed an outline of the rules and framework of *raga*s from them.

In this way, in Bombay alone, he collected plenty of material for research and made a plan for constructing the theory of music. The scholars and music lovers of Bombay were impressed by his plans, but Bhatkhande was not satisfied with his research material obtained from Bombay only. He was keen to study the old *grantha*s and analyse and compare their *Swaradhyaya and Ragadhyaya* chapters with the present day forms of *raga*s. So he decided to go for a study tour to all the corners of the country and explore the theoretical literature in the libraries of the native states and also the practical knowledge of the living *ustad*s. Another purpose of his study tours was to establish a link between the past and the present forms of the classical art. How deeply he felt the need of it Pandit Ratanjankar quotes, his own words, in his book *Pandit Bhatkhande:* "It is a general notion among people that our Hindu music is an ancient and very important branch of knowledge. It is not intended here to turn down this notion as erroneous. It will never be fitting to say so. We have before us quite a large number of the Sanskrit texts on music and some of them are even available for our study. But the question that arises in our mind is: Is there any connection between the theories of those texts and the art that we consider today as music? We may have read the *grantha*s and even understood them, and yet, if there is no connection between the music propounded in the *grantha*s and the music which is in practice today, i.e., if the music which is in vogue today is entirely different from that explained in the *grantha*s, why bother to study the *grantha*s? Such a question was put to me by many people. It must be admitted that it is difficult to give a satisfactory answer. Can we say that we sing the music that has been explained in *Ratnakar, Darpana, Raga Vibodha, Parijat* etc., following their rules ? Just because the names of the notes or the names (only of the *raga*s) given in the *grantha*s are still in vogue, can we claim that we sing the ancient music? The descriptions of the *raga*s as given in the *grantha*s do not fit in with their forms as they are today. If, on the other hand, we try to sing the *raga*s according to their descriptions in the *grantha*s, some of them will not appeal to us, to some, we shall give fresh names. If such is the state of affairs, why study the *grantha*s and why call that person who has studied the *grantha*s a learned scholar of music? Such questions do face us. Do they not and if so, what reply could we give to them? The ten types of *raga*s as given in *Ratnakar* may be explained with their names and detailed rules, but can we find even a single scholar who will be able to sing these and reconcile them with at least some of the *raga*s now in vogue? What is then the use of these *grantha*s? Why not, some people will say, take up the music that is in vogue today itself independently, study the forms it has developed through the past ages and write a separate independent work on modern music..........I am going to visit all the (musically) important towns. I am going to find out the texts which lend the Shastrik authority to the music in vogue there and see if they have any link with ancient works like *Ratnakar.* If I am able to do so, I shall consider it a useful service to music."[2]

Study Tours

Bhatkhande's wife and infant daughter died a premature death. This bereavement further pushed him towards the cause and service of music with rare devotion, love, and sacrifice. In 1910 he gave up his legal practice and dedicated himself entirely to the great cause of formulating the theory of music. In Bombay, he was connected with the Sukthankar family with many ties since a long time. In fact he was appointed as a trustee to look after the property of Mrs. Sukthankar, the widowed daughter of a Bombay Lawyer. So, when Mrs. Sukthankar went on religious trips to the different parts of the country and requested Bhatkhande to accompany her, by careful planning he turned them into study tours.

First Study Tour : Ratanjankar, in his book entitled *Pandit Bhatkhande,*describes his study tours to the North, South, East and the West. "In his first tour to the South, Bhatkhande visited Madras, Tanjore, Madura, Ettayapuram, Bangalore, Trivandrum and Mysore. He met musicians and musicologists of these places and also visited the public libraries. At Ettayapuram he met Shri Subram Dixitar, a descendant of Govind Dixitar, and Venkatamakhi, the author of the work *Chaturdandi Prakashika.* He acquired from him the manuscript of *Chaturdandi Prakashika.* He got some useful information from Subram Dixitar also along with Ramamatya's *Swaramelakalanidhi.* Tulajendra's *Sangeetsaramrit* and another work by name *Raga Lakshana* was copied out for him by the librarians. On return to Bombay he got all these works printed and published and made them available to the public at a nominal price of 4 to 8 annas per copy."[3]

Second Study Tour : The places he visited during his second tour, to the East, undertaken in 1907, were Nagpur, Calcutta, Jagannath Puri, Vijayanagar and Hyderabad. As usual he met all the important and renowned musicians and musicologists to gather information. He formed great friendship with Raja Sourendra Mohan Tagore of Calcutta, a well-known scholar in the field and exchanged with him views on this subject. The mutual regard between them continued till the end and they kept on exchanging their views through letters. Raja Tagore held Bhatkhande in great esteem for his deep study of the *granthas.* The Raja, after discussion with Bhatkhande, revised his ideas about some of the contents of the *granthas,* for he thought that the interpretation given by Bhatkhande was more authentic than his own. Later, a journey was undertaken to Jagannath Puri from where a visit to Vijayanagar followed. Here also he met some knowledgeable people and also visited the library of the Maharaja. The last place visited in the Eastern tour was Hyderabad. At Hyderabad he met Kashinath Sastri Appa Tulsi who played a key role in his work of formulating the theory of modern Classical music by writing several books on the definition of *ragas* on the line of Bhatkhande's theory. He also met a number of professional musicians of Tanras Khan's family, Ghulam Ghore, Umrao Khan, Abdul Karim Khan, Muhammed Siddiqui and the *dhrupad* singer Murad Khan.

Third Study Tour : The places visited during the last tour of research in the Northern part of the country in 1908-1909 were Jabalpur, Allahabad, Banaras, Agra, Delhi, Mathura, Jaipur, Bikaner and Udaipur. Everywhere he met some people reputed for their scholarship in music — such as Peetamlal Gosai of Allahabad, Ganeshi Lal of Mathura and Pannalal Goswami of Delhi--and heard a number of *ustad*s--particularly Zakiruddin Khan and his brother Ala Bande Khan at Udaipur. He was much impressed by the style of their *alapa*, the praise of which he had heard from Wadilal Shivram—later a pupil and an ardent admirer of Bhatkhande — who was under the training of Zakiruddin Khan at Udaipur. At Allahabad he also met Pandit Shri Krishna Joshi, through whose efforts he got a copy of Lochan's *Raga Tarangini*. Towards the West he visited Kathiawar, Surat, Broach, Baroda, Navsari, Ahmedabad, Rajkot, Wankaner, Jamnagar, Junagarh, Bhavnagar etc. and explored the literature on music at all these places.

His Manner of Collecting Information

It is interesting to note the words of Chinchore in *Bhatkhande Smriti Grantha* in regard to the manner in which Bhatkhande used to collect information and knowledge in his study tours. He noticed that the scholars, practitioners, critics and learners were sheltered and patronised by the rich in the big cities. When he visited a place he had the list of the artists there ready with him, the information of which he collected from his friends. For the purpose of visiting the libraries of that place and to have himself introduced he carried several introductory letters with him from his Gujarati, Marathi and Parsee friends. Whatever knowledge he could collect from a particular place, based on that he would prepare a list of hundreds of important and controversial questions and facts and alway; carried them with him to discuss the problems posed therein with knowledgeable persons. In these discussions many doubts were removed. Sometimes new ideas emerged which he noted down. Where the problems remained unresolved, he put down his own tentative conclusions to be checked with well-informed people. It was his daily routine to inform his friends and pupils by letters about the knowledge thus gathered.

When he reached a new place during a tour he would visit the music lovers, the theoreticians and the practical musicians and also the people who patronised them. Without meeting such people and discussing with them about music and musical problems and thereafter meditating on and revolving these discussions in his mind, he would not move to another place. Collection of important books on music, reading of rare books in the library and copying the rare manuscripts with his own hand or buying them outright were parts of a continuous process with him. What would be the next day's programme of work was prepared by him in advance, and he stuck to it with rare devotion—as one reads the religious scriptures. People used to be surprised at his eagerness to know even seemingly insignificant facts and to solve the problems of music which in those days was a neglected and despised subject. "Some people took him as an idler who had enough time and money on hand to waste them on useless questions and enquiry."[4]

The Books He Studied

During his tours he studied all the books available in the libraries of the places he visited. He studied in Sanskrit:– (1) *Naradi Shiksha,* (2) *Manduki Shiksha,* (3) Bharata's *Natyashastra,* (4) *Sangeet Ratnakar,* (5) *Sangeet Darpan,* (6) *Raga Vibodha* and (7) *Sangeet Parijat.* These were the only old books available at that time. English books were only useful for the science of sound. The available books were written by Feston Willard and Chintuswami Mudaliar. They, however, discussed only about English music. In Bengali, there were books written by Sourindra Mohan Tagore and Krishnadhan Bannerji. No books were available in Marathi. In Hindi, there were *Radhagovinda Sangeetsar* and the translation of *Sangeet Darpan.* In Gujarati, Aditram and Dadabhai Dalpatram's books were available. It is already mentioned that he availed of the manuscript of *Chaturdandi Prakashika* as also of *Swaramelakalanidhi, Sangeetsaramrit, Raga Lakshana* and *Raga Tarangini.*

His Findings

After reading all these books he reached the conclusion that the present day music had outgrown the old system greatly and new books about the new system needed to be written.

Another thing he noticed was that in the absence of any written theory or notation of music the prevalent similar *ragas* or *bandishs* with individuals in different parts of the country differed in form and language.

After these study tours and after having collected and arranged the material and data from the ancient *granthas* and discussions with scholars, he realised, with great disappointment, that the problems he faced in the study of the old texts remained unsolved due to the lack of understanding he encountered in regard to the correct interpretation of the sayings of Bharata and Sharngadeva on the fundamental principles of music of the ancient period. He was keen to find out some link between the ancient systems of *Grama Moorchhana, Jati Raga* etc. as described by Bharata and Sharngadeva with the *raga ragini* or the *Mela Raga* system of the later age. In this regard a ray of hope appeared at the time of discussion with Subram Dixitar of Ettayapuram but ultimately no appreciable results emerged. In fact, he was not able to meet anyone in the whole of India who could throw light on these questions.

He always had with him an elaborate questionnaire on these points and used to discuss it with the musicologists and musicians he met on his tours. In the 2nd part of *Hindustani Sangeet Paddhati* he has recorded these questionnaires on page 351. The questionnaires reveal his deep thinking on the subject and his insatiable curiosity about the ancient theory of music. These questionnaires are also a proof of his desire for enriching his knowledge from well-informed sources instead of arriving quickly at his own interpretations.

Thus not being satisfied with the facts available to link up the system of music of the pre-*Ratnakar* period with the later one, he engaged himself in the work of reorganisation and resystematisation of music, that was current in his own time, on the basis of the theory derived from the traditional compositions of music, as elaborated and demonstrated by recognised *ustads*. For the gap of centuries had made current practice divorced from the theory depicted in the *granthas*.

In this regard he writes (in Marathi): "It is an accepted fact that our music is an ancient art. It is also accepted that we can avail of the ancient *granthas* depicting music then prevalent. But it is erroneous to say that the form of our present day music follows the pattern of the ancient music. However, to some extent, we can apply the theory of our old music to the present one. With the passage of time the attitude of the public mind has changed and the form of a *raga* has deviated from its old structure. For the sake of argument, however, we can say that the method of constructing a *raga* is ancient."

Collection of Compositions

With the resolve to reconstruct the theory of music of his time, he set himself to analysing and scrutinising the compositions he had collected so far from the *ustad*s of the Mandali as well as from other sources. He realised that in the absence of written theory and notation, only the traditional compositions contained the vital essentials of the *ragas*, handed down from father to son and from guru to pupil *(guru shishya parampara)*. Therefore, he decided to approach the famous *gharana*s of that period in order to collect more of the precious and pure traditional compositions. His most important collection was from Ashiq Ali and Ustad Muhammed Ali, known as 'Kothiwal', belonging to Jaipur *gharana*.

In his early days, when he was a member of the Gayan Uttejak Mandali, and was in search of a *gharanedar* musician as a teacher, he came across Ashiq Ali, the son of Ustad Muhammed Ali. Bhatkhande engaged Ashiq Ali as his teacher in exchange of money and reached Muhammed Ali, the veteran *Ustad,* through him. He accepted Muhammed Ali as his *guru* and learnt from him the highly stylised form of *khayal* compositions of Jaipur which, with his *guru*'s permission, he published in the *Kramik Pustak Malika* series. His relationship with Muhammed Ali, his *guru*, remained cordial ever after.

Later he composed many *lakshan geet*s on the model of the compositions which he collected from Muhammed Ali and Ashiq Ali. These *lakshan geet*s were acclaimed and approved by the *Ustad* himself.

His next step was to approach the Gwalior *gharana* for collection of compositions. His earlier teachers, connected with the Gayan Uttejak Mandali, belonged to this *gharana*. Therefore, from the beginning he was well-acquainted with the compositions of this *gharana* and the style of singing them. Later he collected a good number of *dhrupad*s, *hori*s and *khayal*s from Eknath Pandit known as Maoo Pandit. The other sources of this *gharana* from whom he collected hundreds of compositions were Raojibuwa Belbagkar, Ganapatibuwa Milbarikar and Rajabhaiya Poochhwale.

Lastly, he approached Rampur *gharana*, which held an important position in the world of music known as Senia *gharana*, named after Tansen of proverbial fame. Ustad Wazir Khan, a descendant from Mian Tansen's daughter's line, was the court musician of Nawab Hamid Ali Khan of Rampur and was the inheritor of the priceless compositions dating back to the time of Tansen. Bhatkhande realised that approaching Wazir Khan directly for learning would be a futile attempt, as the *gharanedar ustad*s were conservative and averse to parting with their knowledge. Thereupon he cleverly decided to reach the *Ustad* through the Nawab Sahib. For that purpose, it was necessary to have proper introduction to reach the Nawab Sahib who was himself a knowledgeable musician and a pupil of Ustad Wazir Khan. Raja Nawab Ali, Talukdar of Akbarpur, a great connoisseur of music, was responsible for introducing and presenting the credentials of Bhatkhande to the Nawab Sahib. It was Bhatkhande's capability and winning power that convinced the Nawab of his wisdom and sincerity of purpose. The Nawab accepted Bhatkhande as his pupil (*gandabandha shagird*) and after sometime, being requested by Bhatkhande, sent him to Ustad Wazir Khan for learning. The *Ustad* could not disobey the Nawab, who was his patron, and was obliged to accept Bhatkhande as his pupil. Thus he was able to learn the priceless traditional compositions of Rampur *gharana* in the form of *dhrupad, dhamar, khayal* etc. He also collected a good number of *hori*s and *dhrupad*s from Muhammed Ali Khan of Giddhaur, who was also a court musician of Rampur. These compositions were later published by him in the *Kramik Pustak Malika* series to be learnt by all music lovers of all times to come. It is relevant to mention that collection of traditional compositions, belonging to all branches of Classical music, was a practice which he carried on throughout his life. In Rampur he had the opportunity of forming friendship with two expert musicians belonging to the princely states—Raja Nawab Ali and Chhamman Sahib which proved very fruitful for giving momentum to Bhatkhande's movement. This will be narrated in detail in the next chapter.

After having involved himself deeply with the Classical music of his time, Bhatkhande came to the conclusion that though current music was not the same as music described in the *grantha*s, it was not loose and disjointed. As a dynamic art, it had grown and changed with the environment. The need of the day, therefore, was to look at music from a new perspective. So he set himself tirelessly to formulate a new theory of current music. He felt the need to reconcile the existing conflicts, bridge the differences and tie up the loose threads to give it symmetry and form. His insight and long research found expression in his manifold and unique contributions. These may be categorised as follows:

1. Collecting the Scattered Treasure.
2. Providing the Theoretical Framework.
3. Establishing the Academic Status and Methodology of Music.
4. As a Composer.
5. Music Conference as a Tool and Strategy.
6. Forming a Notation System.
7. Overcoming Social Taboos.

These are discussed in the subsequent chapters.

References

1. Ratanjankar, Pandit S.N. : *Bhatkhande Smriti Grantha*, p.9
2. Ratanjankar, Pandit S.N. : *Pandit Bhatkhande*, pp.15-'7
3. Ibid., p.18
4. Chinchore, P.N. : 'Sangeet Uddharak Bhatkhande', *Bhatkhande Smriti Grantha*, op.cit., pp.57-'8

5

Collecting the Scattered Treasure

The foundation of the great work of Bhatkhande lies in the huge collection of the traditional compositions for which he spared no pain and effort.

When he resolved to formulate the theory of music based on the current practice of Classical music his first step was to collect the traditional compositions known as *bandish* or *cheej* in musical terminology. He wanted to extract from them the model of the form of a *raga*. The reason for their use for this purpose can be ascertained from certain historical facts and their social impact which are repeated hereafter for easy comprehension.

The Muslim invaders conquered and settled down as the rulers of the northern part of our country from the 11th century onwards. The existing artists could not adjust themselves to the changed political and cultural milieu. Therefore, they either became non-entities or went underground. The mighty stream of art and music reached its lowest ebb. But state of affairs did not last long. From the 13th century onwards the Muslim rulers -- Allauddin and Jalaluddin Khilji -- encouraged the musicians who, in their turn, slowly brought in a new type of music which was a happy fusion of the Hindu and the Muslim traditions. This type of blended music drifted away from the Sanskrit *granthas* and, as centuries advanced, it fell into the hands of the hereditary illiterate professionals. The method of training was oral under *guru shishya parampara* and consequently the forms of the *ragas* and their modes of rendering underwent considerable change. It was obvious that the *ragas* that were played and sung in Bhatkhande's time had developed forms which were very different from that described in the *granthas*. Thus to learn or understand the changed new forms of the *ragas* one had to depend upon the practical demonstration of the traditional compositions.

While Bhatkhande was a member of the Gayan Uttejak Mandali he listened to the practical demonstration of the *ustads* intently and discovered that the note formation of the compositions contained a well-organised system from which the rules and regulations of the *ragas* could be derived. In fact the basis of extempore elaboration in note pattern and rhythm which is a unique characteristic of our Classical music was woven round the framework of the compositions. Bhatkhande wanted to systematise the theory of *ragas* keeping in view the demonstration of the *ustads* as models. Therefore, it was necessary to collect the traditional music compositions to get a correct idea of the forms of the *ragas* that were in vogue. His work of collection of compositions began from the time when he was a member of the Gayan Uttejak Mandali of Bombay. Here he came into contact with several reputed musicians who were either in the employ of the said Mandali or were invited by it to demonstrate.

Bhatkhande learnt about 300 *dhrupads* from Raoji Buwa and collected a good number of *khayals* from Ali Hussain Khan and his maternal uncle Vilayat Hussain. These musicians were employed by the Gayan Uttejak Mandali. It was his continuous endeavour to collect any good composition from any *ustad* he came across.

Not being satisfied with stray collections, he decided to approach the *gharanedar ustads*, as the Classical music in those days was confined to a few families who reared up their own family members as their descendants and the future musicians of the country. Each such family or *gharana* developed its own style of rendering or *gayaki* and refined it to a high degree of excellence. The *gharana* was often known by the name of the place to which the family belonged.

The Development of Gharana System

The growth of the *gharana* system may be attributed to the following causes. After the death of Aurangzeb, gifted musicians all over the North got absorbed in the different native states. The rulers of these states engaged them as their court musicians and did not allow them to move out of their protective custody. The musicians, therefore, got confined in the various courts purely for the personal entertainment of the Princes, Rajas and Nawabs; and so lived in forced segregation from their fellow musicians and knowledgeable people. As a result they could not exchange views with them and widen their musical concepts nor could they be inspired by outside forces. Though this isolation narrowed their outlook, it had a very happy consequence. They diligently practised, with unremitting effort, what they knew and perfected their own style of rendering, developing greater and greater refinements and subtleties. In this regard an individual genius of a particular family, or a school of musicians contributed greatly to developing a particular style. This stylised singing tradition was carried down from father to son for at least three successive generations before establishing its credentials as a *gharana*. In the latter half of the 18th century Hindustani Classical music was thus enriched by *gharanedar gayaki* created by six or seven musical families of the North. These *gharana*s developed some very imaginative and intricate compositions, truly representing all the characteristics of a *raga*, in all branches of Classical music, especially in *dhrupad*, *dhamar* and *khayal*, which were handed down from father to son, generation after generation.

As stated earlier, the musicians from the time of the Mughals lost touch with the *granthas* and due to the absence of any written theory of music and notation, the musicians of Bhatkhande's time had to depend upon the note formation of the traditional compositions especially of *dhrupads* and *dhamars*. For, they contained the vital essentials of a *raga*. These are the number of notes it employs, the order of the notes in ascension and descension, its typical phrases, with special emphasis on a particular note, and also the subsidiary notes. They also demonstrated the discarded notes and the place of pauses. In fact, the proper presentation of an authentic and typical composition immediately established the technical character and spirit of a *raga*. Let us quote an instance.

This is a traditional composition in *raga Bhairava*, *Chautal*, with the name of Tansen mentioned in the last stanza. It is taken from *Kramik Pustak Malika*, part 2, page 217, Hindi Edition:

Sthayi

ग	म	प	–	नि	–	–	प	सा	नि	म
S	ब	न	S	घ़	S	S	यो	स	सा	न
३		४		छा		०		र	घ़	०
				×				घ़	०	प
ग	म	प	–	नि	–	–	प	S	प	घ
S	ब	न	S	घ़	S	S	यो	र	०	०
३		४		छा		०			ग	ग
३ म				× प				–	प	प
S ऱे	ग	म	प	मप	म	ग	म	S	द़ू	म(ग
३	बे	ली	S	माँS)	धो	S	भ	र	०	मS)
		४		× नि.		०				०
सा	ग	–	सा	सा	नि.	नि.	सा	रे़े	सा	सा ति
प्र	रे़े	S	स	ब	धा़रे	न	ब	ब	न	०
३	का	४		×		०		र		प
रे़े	ग	प	प	म	–	ग	म	रे़े	–	ग
ब्य	रे़े	S	ग	ल	S	S	S	S	S	म
३		४		×		०		र		S
सा	म	गु	प						नि.	०
घ	न	S ब)	न						सा	सा
३		४							यो़,	स
									०	०

On analysis of the notes and the *swara sangati* (grouping of notes) of this *dhrupad* we find that the pauses are pronounced in *komal dha* and *shuddha ma*. On the fourth, fifth and the sixth line of the *swara sangati* of *ga ma* to *komal re* is taken more than once. So we can deduce from this composition that the above-mentioned note combination should be the peculiar feature and characteristic movement of *raga Bhairava*.

The Importance of a Composition

The descendants of Tansen, who gave up vocal music and took to the playing of *rabab* and *veena*, had to learn as a rule the traditional *dhrupad*s and *dhamar*s in order to understand the correct form of the *raga*s. They did not read the *grantha*s nor did they study the theory of music; all the theory they knew was the *dhrupad*s and *dhamar*s. It was an accepted fact that the traditional compositions were very important to reveal the correct form of a *raga*. In regard to *khayal*, the compositions of Sadarang and Adarang had the same status as the *dhrupad*s and *dhamar*s. In fact, the *khayal*s composed by Sadarang and Adarang were composed on the models of the *dhrupad*s and *dhamar*s in the matter of purity, that is, the authenticity of the *raga* form. Important and distinctive passages of a *raga* were linked up in cadence with the musical effect in them so that a full and complete recital of the text placed before the listeners gave a full idea of the *raga* and also established the possibilities of expanding the cadences in the extempore improvisation. In reality along with the *dhrupad*s and *dhamar*s a large number of these *vilambit khayal*s have served as the basis for framing and prescribing the rules of the *raga*'s form -- the *aroha avaroha*s, the *vadi samvadi*s, the *swara sangati*s, the *pakad* (catch phrases) etc.

For example, here is a popular *vilambit khayal* of *Multani* by Sadarang. *Multani Trital Vilambit* :(*Kramik Pustak Malika*, 4th part, p. 772, Hindi Edition) :

Sthayi

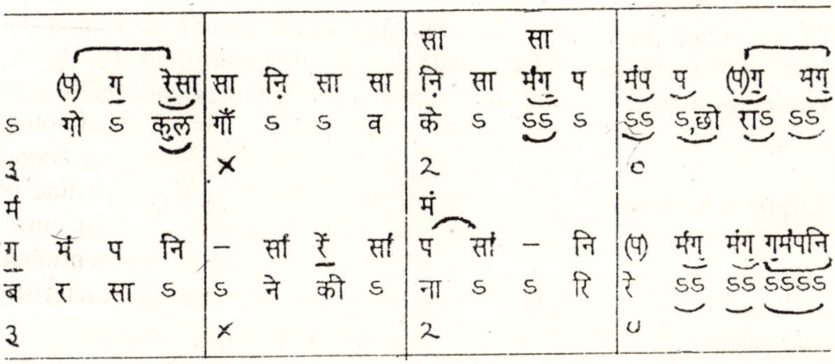

(प)	ग	रे॑	सा॑	सा	नि॒	सा	सा	नि॒	सा	मँग॑	प	मं॑प	प	(प)ग॒	मग॑
ऽ	गो॑	ऽ	कुल	गाँ	ऽ	ऽ	व	के	ऽ	ऽऽ	ऽ	ऽऽ	ऽ,छो	रा॒ऽ	ऽऽ
३ मं				×				२				०			
ग	मं॑	प	नि	–	सां	रें॑	सां	प	सां	–	नि	(प)	मंग॑	मंग	गमंपनि
ब	र	सा	ऽ	ऽ	ने	की	ऽ	ना	ऽ	ऽ	रि	रे	ऽऽ	ऽऽ	ऽऽऽऽ
३				×				२				∪			

Antara

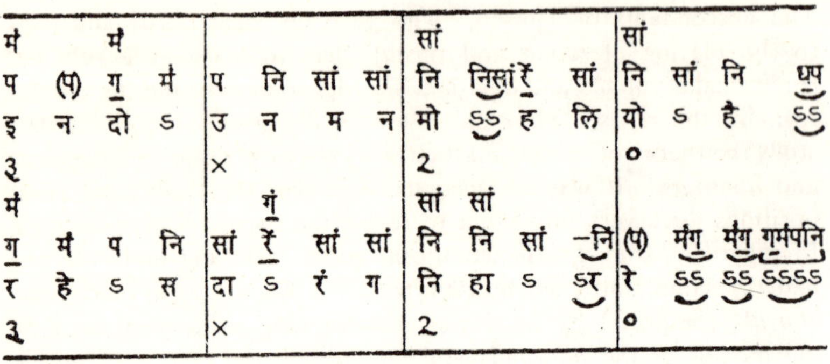

मं प इ ३	(ए) न	गॗ दो	मं ऽ	प उ ×	नि न	सां म	सां न	सां नि मो 2	निसांरैं ऽऽ	सां ह	सां लि	सां नि यो o	सां ऽ	नि है	धप ऽऽ
मं गॗ र ३	मं है	प ऽ	नि स	गुं सां दा ×	रैं ऽ	सां रं	सां ग	सां नि नि 2	सां नि हा	सां ऽ	-नि ऽर	(ए) रे o	मॆंगॗ ऽऽ	मॆंगॗ ऽऽ	गॗमॆपनि ऽऽऽऽ

The note combinations, the *meend*, the pauses as given here are accepted as the characteristic feature of *raga Multani*. Realising the value of such compositions, Bhatkhande started collecting authentic compositions covering all branches of Classical music.

Having collected them from the celebrated musicians like Naththan Khan, Ali Hussain Khan etc., he, while being a member of the Gayan Uttejak Mandali, approached the *gharanedar ustads* for further collections.

Overcoming Difficulties in Collection

But it was an extremely difficult task. The musicians had a narrow outlook and they were unwilling to part with their compositions which they learnt and preserved as a sacred treasure through generations. According to them, Bhatkhande was not born in a musician's family and so had no right to learn music. In learning, in those days, clan and caste played an important role. To surmount these obstacles Bhatkhande had to devise many novel methods and there are many anecdotes connected with them.

Jaipur Gharana

His most important source of collections was from Ashiq Ali, son of Ustad Muhammed Ali, of Jaipur. Jaipur *gharana* was very well-known and Ustad Muhammed Ali was its greatest exponent. He had such a rich repertoire of classical compositions in different *ragas* that he was called the 'Kothiwal' or the 'Master of the House' (of songs). How Bhatkhande came into contact with Ashiq Ali and his celebrated father is told by S. N. Ratanjankar in *Bhatkhande Smriti Grantha*, page 16.

Ustad Nazir Khan, an employee of the Gayan Uttejak Mandali, was living in Bhendibazar, Bombay, where Muhammed Khan, the eldest son of the famous vocalist Naththan Khan, also lived. Although Muhammed Khan possessed a good number of traditional compositions he was reluctant to teach them to outsiders. One day when he was strolling along with Wadilalji, a pupil and admirer of Bhatkhande, Muhammed Khan pointed towards a man to Wadilalji and mentioned him as belonging to a famous *gharana*, having in its possession innumerable traditional compositions. Being requested by Wadilalji, Muhammed Khan introduced him to this man who was Ustad Ashiq Ali Khan, son of the veteran Ustad Muhammed Ali Khan of Jaipur. It was Wadilalji who introduced Ustad Ashiq Ali to Bhatkhande for the purpose of the latter's collection ·work of compositions. Bhatkhande was greatly impressed by his knowledge when he demonstrated at least five or six *cheejs* or compositions of each *raga*. Bhatkhande immediately engaged him to teach him on attractive terms. As Ashiq Ali was passing through a financial crisis, he readily agreed.

Bhatkhande's method of learning the compositions was unique. Not being satisfied by learning them orally and practising them in front of the *ustad* only he wrote them down in notation. In order to perfect the notation, he reproduced the notations in practical demonstration and gave them final shape only when this process was approved by Ustad Ashiq Ali. This way he took utmost care to record these compositions without the least distortion. In those days it was a practice unheard of. He created a revolution by writing Classical music into note patterns.

As for centuries, the method of learning music was not only oral, but also based on long association of the teacher and the pupil. The pupil had to serve the *guru* for years, and in return he used to get music lessons according to his whims and choice. There was nothing systematic in that training and no record was kept in writing. So, no wonder that the way Bhatkhande learnt music from Ashiq Ali created a commotion and resentment among the artists' circle. The result was that the musicians of that time started condemning this type of teaching and learning. Very soon report reached Ustad Muhammed Ali Khan, the father of Ashiq Ali, that Bhatkhande was squeezing out all the musical knowledge of Ashiq Ali. He was furious and immediately rushed to Bombay from Jaipur. As stated earlier, in the meantime, Bhatkhande had not only learnt by heart 250 *cheej*s from Ashiq Ali within two to three months but also written them down with notation. On top of that he also recorded them down in phonographic discs. As soon as Muhammed Ali reached Bombay he immediately visited Bhatkhande along with Ashiq Ali and asked Bhatkhande to sing those compositions which he had learnt from Ashiq Ali.

Bhatkhande thereupon, with sincerity, presented all the compositions he had learnt, singing from the notations. Even he played the phonographic records for him. The result was that Muhammed Ali became white with rage and started abusing and rebuking his son for parting with their own valuable *bandish* to a stranger.

Now Bhatkhande played the key role in pacifying him and made him understand the purpose of such collections and its necessity for the purpose of revival of music. Ultimately he succeeded in pacifying him by self-surrender and offering himself as his pupil. With all this Muhammed Ali Khan's anger vanished and he saw Bhatkhande's endeavour in the right perspective. He admitted that he had never thought or dreamt of written music, for their own training and practice had remained oral only. He also admitted that the same *cheej*s varied from *gharana* to *gharana*. But he was pleased that Bhatkhande reproduced their *cheej*s exactly in its pure form. As a result, he was pleased with Bhatkhande and accepted him as his pupil. Now Bhatkhande got the opportunity of learning from him directly for which he served him with great care and affection. Bhatkhande was able to collect about three hundred *cheej*s of Manarang *gharana* of Jaipur from Ashiq Ali and Muhammed Ali. He not only wrote them down in notation but also had them recorded in discs. He also learnt a few uncommon *ragas* and *Kayada*.

Bhatkhande felt greatly elated and his self-confidence increased after learning these compositions. He started composing *lakshan geets* on the model of the compositions which he collected from Muhammed Ali and Ashiq Ali of Jaipur.

The *lakshan geets* contained the description of the essentials of a *raga* set in that particular *raga* and filled in a variety of *tala*s. That from the traditional composition he could compose identical compositions (melodically) explaining the essentials of a *raga* shows Bhatkhande's acute power of analysis, and assimilation. The *lakshan geets* composed by Bhatkhande were duly approved by Muhammed Ali who became greatly pleased with his effort.

Bhatkhande recorded on gramophone the voice of Muhammed Ali and Ashiq Ali singing *khayal*. Unfortunately, these records were spoilt being kept negligently. Otherwise they could have been a great treasure for the music lovers of posterity.

His relationship with Muhammed Ali as the *guru* remained cordial ever after. Bhatkhande openly acknowledged him as his *guru* and composed several songs praising him and subtly indicating their relationship. As for example:

"सोहनी को चतुर सुनाय

हररंग को मन रिझाय ।"

नाचत चतुर कान, हरख भरो हररंग ।

Here 'Chatur' stands for Bhatkhande himself and 'Hararang' stands for his *guru* Muhammed Ali of Jaipur. These songs also indicate that Muhammed Ali not only supported his cause, but also encouraged him to compose *khayal*s and *lakshan geets*. Thus Bhatkhande was able to collect about three hundred *cheej*s of Manarang *gharana* of Jaipur from Ashiq Ali and his father Ustad Muhammed Ali. He not only wrote them in notation but also recorded them in discs.

Bhatkhande's collection from this *gharana* comprised of *vilambit* and *drut khayal*s, both in common and uncommon *raga*s. He also collected *sargam* or note names in rhythm and some *kayada*.

Collection from Gwalior Gharana

Another important source of his collection of compositions was the

Gwalior *gharana*. Haddu Khan, Hassu Khan and Naththu Khan, the three musician brothers were responsible for bringing into prominence this famous *gharana*. They were court musicians during the reign of Daulat Rao Scindia of Gwalior in the early 19th century. All the three brothers were not only excellent singers but equally good teachers. They left behind several first-rate performers to carry on their tradition and style of singing. They in their turn produced many excellent classical musicians, including Vishnu Digambar Paluskar who was another towering pioneer in the revival of music in the nineteenth century.

Gwalior is a place where Tansen, the great musician, was born and where his grave exists being regarded as sacred by all the music lovers of today.

Bhatkhande's early teachers who were the musicians employed in the Gayan Uttejak Mandali of Bombay belonged to Gwalior *gharana*. Therefore, from the beginning he was well-acquainted with the singing style of this *gharana* and was much impressed by its *gayaki*.

Later, he collected a good number of *dhrupad*s, *hori*s and *khayal*s from Eknath Pandit, known as Maoo Pandit. He was the younger brother of Shankarrao Pandit, the famous *khayal*-singer of Gwalior.

The other stalwarts of Gwalior *gharana* from whom he collected hundreds of compositions or *bandish*s were Raojibuwa Belbagkar and Ganapatibuwa Milbarikar. Rajabhaiya Poochhwale also belonged to this *gharana* whom Bhatkhande held in great esteem for his knowledge and cultured disposition. Bhatkhande regarded him as the true representative of his *gharana*, as his singing was the most authentic reproduction in form and style of Gwalior *gharana*. Bhatkhande's collection from this *gharana* comprised of hundreds of *dhrupad*s, *dhamar*s, *khayal*s and *tarana*s.

Rampur Gharana

After having collected the compositions of Jaipur and Gwalior, Bhatkhande wanted to collect the compositions from Rampur also. It was a fact that Rampur had the richest and the purest collection of classical compositions from the period of Tansen, the proverbial musician.

This *gharana* held an important position in the world of music and was well-known as Senia *gharana*, a name derived from

Tansen of mythical fame. At that time Ustad Wazir Khan, who was a direct descendant of Tansen in his daughter's line, was shining like a luminous star in the *firmament* of music. He was a great .*been* player and was the court musician of the State of Rampur in the employ of Hamid Ali, the Nawab of Rampur. Bhatkhande was greatly impressed by the beauty and intricacy of the compositions of this *gharana* and aspired to learn them and use them for the purpose of his research work.

But it was an impossible task as the order of the day was to guard one's own musical knowledge zealously and never to allow it to be learnt by the outsiders at any cost. Each *gharanedar ustad* was proud of his *gayaki* and hereditary coaching. It can be well .imagined that Wazir Khan, the doyen of the *gharanedar ustads* by virtue of his connections with Mian Tansen, would possess all the pride and conservatism of that age and would be least willing to part with his knowledge. The disqualification of Bhatkhande, according to them, was that he could not claim to have the family background of musicians. On the contrary his origin was from an educated Brahmin family. Nor was he initiated in the traditional way of learning music from the beginning.

Realising all this, Bhatkhande did not think it wise to approach Wazir Khan directly, thinking that it would be a futile attempt. Usually in such circumstances a normal prospective student would try to serve his *guru* in many ways to attract his attention and sympathy, in return, perhaps, to get only rebuffs. But Bhatkhande, being a shrewd man of the world and having assessed the situation, resorted to a novel method to become a pupil of Wazir Khan. He resolved to reach Ustad Wazir Khan through the Nawab of Rampur.

Nawab of Rampur

Hamid Ali, the Nawab of Rampur, was a learned musician and a great patron of music. He gave shelter in his court to a few gifted musicians of his time. Apart from Ustad Wazir Khan, there was another knowledgeable musician in the court whose name was Muhammed Ali of Giddhaur. He was an excellent *rabab* player and had a good stock of *dhrupads*, *dhamars* etc. The Nawab was a pupil of the above-.mentioned musicians. His cousin, Chhamman Sahib, also learnt music from these *ustads*. Saadat Ali Khan, the Prince of Bilsi and popularly known as Chhamman Sahib, was also a great connoisseur of music and an expert *sursingar* player.

Bhatkhande was introduced to the Nawab of Rampur by Raja Nawab Ali, the Taluqdar of Akbarpur, U. P. and Kale Nazir Khan, a musician in his employ.

Raja Nawab Ali and Kale Nazir Khan

Raja Nawab Ali was a musician of repute and an expert harmonium player which he learnt from the late Ganapatrao Bhaiya, a famous princely harmonium player of Gwalior. Nawab Ali also could sing traditional songs in a very attractive style.

Raja Nawab Ali heard the reputation of Bhatkhande and his systematic work on music based on deep study and research. He resolved to gather first-hand information about this and for this purpose sent Kale Nazir Khan down to Bombay. Kale Nazir Khan was highly impressed by Bhatkhande's knowledge, study and research work. He learnt a number of *lakshan geet*s from Bhatkhande and in return taught Bhatkhande a number of his own compositions. Raja Nawab Ali was much impressed when he learnt all about Bhatkhande from Kale Nazir Khan and started corresponding with him. The intimacy grew through letters and in the year 1912 Raja Nawab Ali came down to Bombay to meet Bhatkhande personally.

He got himself acquainted with Bhatkhande's idea of the theory of modern Hindustani music and became his great admirer and friend. Their alliance proved highly productive and with his help and encouragement Bhatkhande's work gained momentum. It was a mutual inspiration for both of them. Being inspired by Bhatkhande, Nawab Ali started writing a series of books on music called *Marif-un-Naghmat*.

In the first part of this series he explained in Urdu Bhatkhande's outline of musical theory. In his books, alongside his own and other compositions, he inserted a large number of Bhatkhande's *lakshan geet*s. In the preface he expressed his deep gratitude and respect in very clear words. In the chapters on *Swaradhyaya* and *Ragadhyaya* he got the consent and affirmation of Bhatkhande.

Raja Nawab Ali was a regular visitor at Rampur where Nazir Khan was also engaged as a court musician later. Nawab Hamid Ali Khan heard a lot of praise of Bhatkhande from both Nawab

Ali and Nazir Khan who demonstrated a number of *lakshan geets* composed by Bhatkhande. The Nawab had already heard Bhatkhande's reputation as a scholar, musician and theoretician. Therefore, his regard for and inquisitiveness about Bhatkhande increased further and he invited him to visit Rampur.

Bhatkhande readily accepted his invitation and on reaching Rampur he became closely acquainted with the Nawab. Acquaintance within no time developed into a great friendship. Needless to say that the basis of the friendship was their common interest in music. Nawab Sahib was a knowledgeable musician and Bhatkhande was already in possession of many authentic compositions out of which he derived the theory underlying them. They exchanged notes about the theory and practice of music in which the court musicians of the Nawab also joined. As the traditional musicians of those days were orthodox, not to speak of the Rampur musicians who hailed from the family of Mian Tansen, there was some opposition to Bhatkhande's reasoning but later he could convince them by practical demonstration of the soundness of the theories he had propounded and proved that the *alapa*s and development of *raga* expositions which Ustad Wazir Khan was playing on his *been* were exactly according to the rules that he had written and there was no difference between them. The formation of notation and theory and their importance were also discussed. Ultimately the Nawab Sahib was converted to Bhatkhande's ideas and asked him to stay on at Rampur for some time and honoured him by bestowing on him the membership of the Durbar. It was no mean achievement of Bhatkhande and a proof of his deep knowledge, power of reasoning and talent for demonstration that he could convert a sophisticated learned musician like Nawab Sahib to his own ideas. Bhatkhande thereafter lost no time in enrolling himself as a formal student (*gandabandha shagird*) of Nawab Hamid Ali Khan of Rampur. As stated earlier the Nawab was well-known as a knowledgeable musician and a pupil of Wazir Khan. But it was not a priviledge for Bhatkhande only, the Nawab also felt proud to have him as his pupil as by that time Bhatkhande's reputation had spread far and wide as a scholar musician.

Having learnt from him for a considerable period, Bhatkhande requested the Nawab to introduce him to Ustad Wazir Khan so that he could learn more of the priceless compositions of Tansen *gharana*. As Wazir Khan was in the employment of the Nawab, he had no other way but to accept Bhatkhande as his pupil. Bhatkhande thus learnt and collected the compositions of *dhrupad, dhamar* and *saadra* belonging to the Rampur *gharana*. These were the priceless compositions belonging to the great Senia *gharana* which Bhatkhande published in his *Kramik Pustak Malika* series with notations. By virtue of being the pupil of the Nawab he could claim being the pupil of Rampur *gharana*. Bhatkhande also impressed upon the Nawab his keenness to record by notation the rich compositions of the Rampur tradition. The Nawab readily complied with his request and ordered Ustad Wazir Khan to teach Bhatkhande whatever he wanted.

Raja Nawab Ali's whole-hearted cooperation helped Bhatkhande greatly to collect the huge number of compositions from the *ustads*. With Nawab Ali's cooperation subsequently he could successfully establish and run the All India Music Association and establish Marris College of Music at Lucknow.

Raja Nawab Ali's close friend, Rai Umanath Bali, used to talk about the friendship of Raja Nawab Ali and Bhatkhande. It was so selfless and sincere that the credit of writing the book *Marif-un-Naghmat* was attributed to Bhatkhande by Raja Nawab Ali.

It was the result of Bhatkhande's winning power and wisdom that the sacred and secret compositions of Tansen *gharana* were collected and written down in notation for all to understand and profit by. The public started respecting the compositions belonging to the Tansen family and the monopoly of musical compositions was eliminated for ever. Today we all are the owners of this great heritage.

Chhamman Sahib

In Rampur Bhatkhande also formed friendship with the prince of Bilsi--Saadat Ali Khan Bahadur--a cousin of the Nawab of Rampur, popularly known as Chhamman Sahib. He also had the opportunity of learning music from Ustads Wazir Khan and Muhammed Ali Khan of Giddhaur and was regarded as a reputed musician. Chhamman Sahib developed great admiration and respect for Bhatkhande's research work. In fact he became a pillar of strength to Bhatkhande's work for the revival of music. He was a resident of Rampur and was accepted in the household of the Nawab as a family member. Both Bhatkhande and Chhamman Sahib discovered in each other a catholic mind and great devotion for music. Chhamman Sahib immediately enrolled himself in Bhatkhande's movement for the revival of music and rendered him all help in regard to his collection of compositions. Both Bhatkhande's and Chhamman Sahib's opinion about the theory and practice of music were so identical that they appeared to be uttered by one and the same person. Their friendship was unique in nature and the common point of their unity was music.

The writer of *Marif-un-Naghmat* (written in the year 1924), Thakur Nawab Ali, mentioned a *dhrupad* (page 55) in *Bihag* where as composers both Chhamman Sahib's and Bhatkhande's names were mentioned. It is obvious that this *dhrupad* was composed jointly by both these scholars:

"जो लों मारतंड, चंद्र सोहे असमान मांहि
शीश सेस भू अचल बनी रहे ।
जो लों गंगा जमना की धार धरो मंडल में
जो लों कैलास में कुबेर सो धनी रहे ।।
जो लों छीर सागर, उजागर जहां बीच
जो लों विष्णु–चक्र असुरन पर गनी रहे !
सादत के प्रभु रसिक श्री नवाब बहादुर
जो तो लों जग रावरी सो कीरत बनी रहे ।।"

In the last line Chhamman Sahib mentioned his own name, Saadat, and praised his master the Nawab Hamid Ali Khan of Rampur. In the third line suggestively he mentioned *Vishnu Chakra* which indicated Bhatkhande and his movement in regard to the revival of music. Vishnu was the first name of Bhatkhande and the *chakra* is connected with the killings of demons by God Vishnu in Hindu mythology. In the same line it is also suggested that the opposition in regard to Bhatkhande's movement may be totally eliminated.

This *dhrupad* was published in *Hindustani Sangeet Paddhati, Kramik Pustak Malika*, 3rd part (page 219 of the Hindi Edition) after a few changes of words. The composition of a song done jointly indicates the merging of the best of Gwalior style with that of Rampur as Bhatkhande, who had initial training from Gwalior *gharana*, blended its style with Chhamman Sahib's who belonged to Rampur *gharana*. It is noteworthy that the name of neither of them appeared as the composer, nor was it possible to ascertain which line was composed by whom.

Another happy blending of Rampur and Gwalior type of singing was done by Bhatkhande in consultation with Chhamman Sahib in regard to *raga Bihag*. The gliding movement of *ni pa* and *ga sā* belonging to Rampur was introduced into *Bihag* demonstrated in Gwalior and *ma pa dha mā pa ma, ma ga ma ga* phrase belonging to Gwalior was introduced into Rampur. Bhatkhande included this blended *Bihag* in his *Lakshya Sangeet*. Thus Bhatkhande's dream of giving Classical music a universal form was realised in which Chhamman Sahib was the guiding spirit.

Chhamman Sahib also assisted Bhatkhande in formulating the theory from the compositions he collected. A consensus was worked out regarding the controversial form of *Malhar, Sarang, Todi, Bilawal* and *Kanhara* in the All India Conferences, and a standard form was established of each of these *raga*s with the help of Chhamman Sahib in consultation with other stalwarts.

The association of these two scholars paved the way for a new era in the field of Hindustani music in those days of factional and *gharanedar* quarrels.

In the Delhi All India Music Conference, the proposal for establishing a Central National Academy of Music was discussed but for the sudden premature death of Chhamman Sahib at the age of forty-four Bhatkhande's plans were shattered to pieces and no proper music institution could be founded at Rampur.

Analysis and Processing of the Compositions

In this way Bhatkhande was able to collect hundreds of compositions from Jaipur, Gwalior and Rampur *gharana*s. He had also in his possession a number of phonographic records sung by the *ustad*s. For years his colleagues and associates listened to them repeatedly and noted down their exact note formation. After the notations were done, they were duly signed by the persons who had done them. All this material Bhatkhande arranged methodically and systematically for comparison, analysis and scrutiny. Bhatkhande was in the habit of always noting down the compositions in notation and also his comments underneath after his own analysis. In *Bhatkhande Smriti Grantha* (p.164) a few uncorrected compositions, collected by Bhatkhande, are published with footnotes and his comments.

These comments are interesting as he discovered that the last part of the *vilambit khayal*, which he recorded in notation, was not in conformity with the note movement of the first part of the song. It was his artistic sensibility, knowledge of Classical music along with a keen sense of proportion which enabled him to discover such discrepancies. Needless to say that this type of compositions needed corrections. It was evident that oral form of training through generations brought some distortions in the compositions both in regard to the classical tune and words. Therefore, it was necessary to correct and standardize them and make them flawless before they could be   published

Not depending entirely on his own judgement Bhatkhande placed all his collections in front of Eknath Pandit and Rajabhaiya to correct them from the angle of language and classical melody. It has already been stated that Bhatkhande held in great esteem Rajabhaiya, who was the torch-bearer of the tradition of Naththan Peerbaksh. Rajabhaiya's singing strictly adhered to his traditional training. He also had in his possession a large number of compositions belonging to his *gharana*. Bhatkhande regarded him as the most methodical and cultured musician among others while he was despised as a mere harmonium player by his fellow musicians. Rajabhaiya also reciprocated with great admiration and deep regard for Bhatkhande resulting in a lifelong friendship. Not only that, all these feelings culminated in the complete surrender of his artistic self to Bhatkhande, accepting him as his *guru*.

Both Rajabhaiya and Bhatkhande agreed that many compositions appeared incorrect in regard to language and classical form. Therefore, in the year 1922, Bhatkhande arranged a seminar at Hardwar to arrive at a consensus about the different versions of *bandish* (*Khandani cheejs*). With the help of Madhav Rao Scindia, the Ruler of Gwalior, who was a great patron and admirer of Bhatkhande's movement, Rajabhaiya and seven or eight other musicians reached Hardwar along with their papers.

Every musical composition has two aspects -- poetry and melody. Each one is the vehicle of the other. Each one is important from the point of view of Classical music. Yet every singer need not necessarily be a linguist, nor should every linguist understand the classical melody. For the purpose of correction of the language part of the compositions Bhatkhande invited *Shastris*, *Pandits*, *Maulavis* and other scholars who had real regard for the traditional music and its compositions together in that seminar. These scholars examined the language part of the compositions and with proper editing made them suitable for learning by the students of music. Correction was mainly done where the words were illegible, meaningless and vulgar.

Now it was necessary to study the traditional compositions in order to have a picture of the form of the *ragas* in which they were set. For this he greatly relied on two scholars -- Eknath Pandit and Rajabhaiya Poochhwale. Rajabhaiya did a marvellous job in classifying the compositions *raga*-wise so that the movement and note formation of a *raga* could be derived from them. After the compositions were compared and corrected melodically by the above-mentioned scholars, Bhatkhande got them approved by the other stalwarts of music before he approved them finally for teaching and publishing. For correcting them melodically and clearing them of the deviations which had crept in due to the oral training Bhatkhande admirably put forth his arguments and convinced the above-mentioned scholars.

To get the consensus on the controversial points of the form of a *raga* he arranged several conferences and made the musicians of different schools sit on the same platform and agree to a common rule for learning.

The Benefit of Collection

In this fashion Bhatkhande collected all the best compositions belonging to those different sources and the study and analysis of these helped him to form the theory of current Classical music which he wrote and published in the form of four volumes of books namely *Hindustani Sangeet Paddhati.*

When he felt that he had obtained the accurate and complete form of the *ragas* collected from these compositions he published them for the students of music in the *Kramik Pustak Malika* series in 6 parts. Thousands of compositions were included in them divided *raga*-wise and without the names of the *gharanas* to which they belonged.

It was a revolutionary idea for the prosperity of music to make it free from the fetters of the *gharana* system. When it was the order of the day that music and knowledge were guarded like a valuable treasure and a person possessing it made much of it in money and pride, Bhatkhande distributed his carefully and pain-fully earned knowledge to the people for all time to come.

The Criticism

Some of the modern musicologists have criticised Bhatkhande for not publishing the names of the *gharana*s from which he obtained the compositions. But the reason for this was that Bhatkhande was keen to keep the future generations and the students of music away from the stifling atmosphere and factional quarrels of the *gharana* system. He launched a crusade against the narrow-mindedness, false vanity and whimsical and conservative training in music prevalent at the time. For, every renowned musician of his time created an impenetrable wall of vanity of *khandani* atmosphere, establishing self-made laws. The quarrel of *gharana*s reached a stage when it was openly declared that Rampur had no connection with Gwalior in music and nor had Gwalior anything common with Jaipur. Consequently, it was expected that a pupil would stick to his own *gharana* only and under no circumstances would be singing compositions of any other *gharana* even though they may be valuable. The compositions and the *raga*s bore the stamp of *gharana*s and as a result the musicians became sworn enemies of each other and there were frantic attempts to run down one another. In the domain of *Khayal* one section of musicians used to run down the compositions of Sadarang and Adarang branding them as fit only for being sung by beggar boys. It is said that Niamat Khan (Sadarang) taught, for experimental purposes, two beggar boys the *khayal*s he composed for the first time.

In regard to the teaching of music the poison of narrow-mindedness spread its vicious effect to such an extent that at the time of imparting lessons *doodh-khoon ke rishte* (milk-blood rela-tionships) used to be taken into account when choosing pupils even though they may be lacking talent and aptitude. Even among the family members the son's family had to have and retain only a particular type of coaching and the daughter's family had to have something separate. The result was that a musician died with his treasure of knowledge not allowing it to be bestowed on the right person having proper intelligence and artistic bent of mind.

Bhatkhande realised that all this lowered the status of music in the academic world. Therefore, he despised the lables of *gharana*s being stuck to the compositions as that invariably led to quarrels for supremacy among them. For this reason, he decided to publish the compositions he collected without the names of the *gharanas* attached to them and left the future generations to appreciate their beauty aesthetically.   Drawing   inspiration   from   Bhatkhande, Rajabhaiya, Chhamman Sahib and Thakur Nawab Ali composed songs without their names stamped on them. Bhatkhande also believed in the merging of styles. He believed that if the *khayals* of Jaipur, for example, were accepted in Gwalior with respect then the status of music would go up in the eyes of everybody. It would not only carry universal respect but would also arouse the spirit of national integration. Guided by this idea he wanted to merge the style of Jaipur, Gwalior and Rampur and present to the future generations what was aesthetically satisfying and ·sublime in music.

6
Providing the Theoretical Framework

I

INTRODUCTION

It was Bhatkhande's earnest desire, right from the early age of his training, to formulate a well-reasoned and easily intelligible systematic theory of the current practice of music. He wrote several articles where he gave vent to his deep feelings about the necessity of such formulation. Let us quote from one of these:

"The best way to begin the work of regeneration is to recognise the present Hindustani practice of music and to establish the same on a scientific and sound basis, that is to support it by a good, well-reasoned and easily intelligible theory. Theory is rightly described as the backbone of practice, and when that perishes, the practice gradually begins to degenerate. This means that the time has now arrived when the educated classes should take up the subject in hand earnestly and proceed to give it its due position and importance."[1]

He despised the fanciful stories in the name of theory which were in vogue. He was desperately trying to find out the correct knowledge and information about the *shastra* of music. He said:

"We live now in an age of science and technology. There is no place for such notions unless proved by practical demonstrations today. Some of my friends tell me that Theosophy can explain these mysteries. Out of respect for them and their views I keep quiet. My views are meant for my readers. If they are proved wrong by demonstration, I shall be glad. Should the state of musicology be so poor even in North India where the Art has had a glorious history? I have given vent to these musings, appalled by this poverty of correct knowledge and information. North India, the home of the great super masters of music, has guarded very little knowledge of it today. The *nayak*s flourished just four centuries ago. Today no trace of any written record of their services in the cause of music is available. Their very descendants know little and can read less. There is not a single instance of a *nayak* having been well versed in Sanskrit. Agra is a town which was dear to the heart of Emperor Akbar. Today, the only music we hear there is that sung by the dancing girls and their *sarangi* players. One feels very much discouraged indeed when one looks at the picture. I do not think that any of the *nayak*s had studied *Ratnakar* and other *granthas*. Probably such study was not current during the time of the Mughal Emperors. According to the general practice of music in those days, musicians like Tansen and others were practical musicians of a very high order, but they were not required to study the texts in Sanskrit. We should make a thorough research and investigate objectively these legendary stories concerning music of those days."[2]

His reasons for formulating and writing a theory of the current practice of Classical music could be broadly classified as follows:

1. It would bring the subject of Music at par with other subjects of study where there is no dearth of scientific and rational data.
2. It would enable the provision of collective training in music.
3. It would provide the educated and cultured people an easy and intelligent understanding of Music as a subject of study.
4. Practical knowledge of music could only thrive when it has its roots in a scientific and systematic theory.
5. Only a sound base of theory could preserve music from undue distortions which would be inevitable in the absence of a theoretical background.

With this idea, in addition to learning and listening to Classical music and collection of compositions from early times, he travelled through the entire country with the mentality of a student desirous to learn and collect valuable materials. His main object in studying the old literature about music and its theory was to establish a link between the ancient and the current practice. He also wanted to understand music in an historical perspective to study the evolution of music through the ages till the present time.

Therefore, while touring the different cities, he made a deep study of all the available Sanskrit *granthas* and lived in continuous association of the musicians, always comparing and evaluating his notes and knowledge. He did not hesitate even to declare himself a pupil of any *ustad* where he felt that such gesture would benefit him with further information. Alongside, he continuously collected thousands of compositions and studied them thoroughly from the musical point of view.

Armed with vast knowledge and experience, having thousands of compositions and data in his possession, and endowed with an analytical and artistic mind, he set out to write the theory of the current form of Hindustani Classical music. His contribution in coordinating and systematising the existing practice of music may be seen in the form of several invaluable books which bore proof of his life-long research. These books on the theory of music are authoritative sources of knowledge for all time to come. He arrived at the conclusion that music, as it was then practised, had very much changed in its form from what was described in the ancient texts. He worked hard to reaffirm what he found rational in the ancient texts and readjust the past theory to the new realities. He frankly acknowledged where he failed to decipher the ambiguous ideas of the ancient books. He did not forcibly try to amalgamate the present and the past system.

II

BOOKS HE WROTE

The books he wrote on the theory of music are   listed below:
1. *Shrimallakshya Sangeetam* (in Sanskrit).
2. *Abhinava Raga Manjari* (in Sanskrit).
3. *Abhinava Tala Manjari* (in Sanskrit).
4. *Hindustani Sangeet Paddhati* (in Marathi).   In 4 volumes. Later translated into Hindi.
5. *Kramik Pustak Malika*. In 6 parts which were meant to be

used as graded textbooks.

6. *A Comparative Study of the Music Systems of the 15th, 16th, 17th and 18th Centuries* (in English).
7. *A Historical Survey of the Music of Upper India* (in English).
8. *Swara Malika.* A small booklet written in Gujarati.
9. *Lakshan Geet Sangraha.* In three parts.
10. *Geet Malika.* The compositions were originally published in 23 monthly issues, each containing 25 to 30 classical compositions of Hindustani music in notation. They were later incorporated in *Kramik Pustak Malika*, mentioned at 5 above.

Apart from these he also wrote a number of articles in many journals and magazines.

'SHRIMALLAKSHYA SANGEETAM'

This book is a treatise on the theory of music. In 1909 he wrote this important book in Sanskrit. The purpose of writing in Sanskrit was that the musicologists of all the corners of this country could read it. The theory of current music was ably described in a condensed form in Sanskrit couplets in the traditional style of Hridayanarayan Dev, an author of the 17th century.

This book contained precisely his theory of modern music in outline which he elaborated in *Hindustani Sangeet Paddhati* and illustrated in *Lakshan Geet Sangraha* and *Kramik Pustak Malika*. While writing *Shrimallakshya Sangeetam* he concentrated especially on the two chapters--one dealing with the *swara*s and the other dealing with the *raga*s. These he defined and explained with great clarity, bringing to bear upon them all the matter in their regard that he had collected during his researches. It was his speciality to explain in very clear and definite terms the subject matter with his own comments written underneath. He introduced himself as 'Bharatpurvakhandanivasi Chatur Pandit' writing ingeniously his pseudonym 'Chatur' as writer and hinting at his surname as Bhatkhande.

He started with the definition of *Sangeet* (pp.2 and 3) and the difference between *Deshi* and *Margi Sangeet* quoting from the following books: *Sangeet Ratnakar, Sangeet Darpan* and *Raga*

Vibodha. After analysing every relevant point he, then, recorded his own comments in beautiful Sanskrit couplets. He declared after analysis that *Sangeet Ratnakar* was the best among the old books. He also described Venkatamakhi's *Chaturdandi Prakashika* as the best exponent of old *raga*s.

About *shruti* (pp.10-17) he quoted and compared Sharngadeva, Kallinath, Bharata and Shingabhupala and ended with a chart of ancient *shruti*s placed on the veena. Then he wrote his own comments on them. He quoted from *Sangeet Ratnakar* and *Sangeet Darpan* the definition of *vikrit swara*s and placed the *swara*s on the *shruti*s according to the ancient and middle age authors. He then prepared charts indicating the place of the various *swara*s according to *Swaramelakalanidhi*, *Raga Vibodha*, *Chaturdandi Prakashika*, *Sangeetsaramrit*, *Raga Tarangini*, *Sangeet Parijat* etc. Then he expounded the place of the *swara*s in modern music in a chart.

He also defined *moorchhana* (page 59), *tana* and *raga* (page 67), 'Daslakshana' of old *raga*s, *vadi*, *samvadi* and *thaat*s and ended with the descriptions of important *raga*s in vogue according to 'Janya Janak Bhava' in the second chapter.

His style of writing is terse and forceful. The Sanskrit couplets are balanced in regard to the use of words. They are expressive and precise. He covered a vast area of ancient and middle age music with clear cut objective and commented on it in a surprisingly precise and logical manner. It is a complete book with the definition of *swara*, *shruti* and *raga* of the ancient and current music. But as it was highly condensed, commentaries to elucidate its meaning was necessary. Hence, as a corollary, he wrote the *Hindustani Sangeet Paddhati* in 4 volumes.

'ABHINAVA RAGA MANJARI'

It is a treatise on the definition of the *raga*s, each being described in one simple *shloka*. It required a great ingenuity and poetic genius to express the intricate rules of a *raga* in a condensed Sanskrit couplet with note names. For example, let us take the definition of *raga Kedar*. It is complete in the following two lines:

समौ मपौ धपौ मश्च पधौ पमौ पमौ रिसौ।
केदारो मोशको रात्या प्रारोहे रिगिदुर्बलः ।।

In the first line note pattern of the *raga* is given. The next line says that the *vadi swara* of *Kedar* is *madhyam*, *Re* and *Ga* are weak in ascension and its singing time is night. All the characteristic features of the *raga* are laid down clearly and thus a complete picture is presented. This book deals with all the *raga*s in vogue, like any other important book on the theory of *raga*s.

'ABHINAVA TALA MANJARI'

Abhinava Tala Manjari deals with *tala*s in Sanskrit couplets.

The fact that he wrote these three books in Sanskrit shows his deep respect for the Indian culture and tradition. He used very simple and direct terms to explain his ideas. This was unlike the traditional *granthas* where by virtue of the ambiguous and difficult terms used the subject matter was made complicated.

'HINDUSTANI SANGEET PADDHATI'

It has already been stated that the four volumes of this were written as a commentary on *Shrimallakshya Sangeetam* and *Abhinava Raga Manjari*. They were originally written in Marathi, Bhatkhande's mother-tongue, and were later translated into Hindi. The reason for writing in Marathi was that it was easier for him to express himself informally and intimately in his own language. Another reason, of course, was to spread his knowledge, which he gained with infinite labour and profound thinking, to lovers of music even with scant education.

These four volumes of *Hindustani Sangeet Paddhati*, which were written between 1910 and 1914, are even now regarded as an authoritative and detailed analytical study of the prevailing 150 *raga*s in vogue. In its entirety it is a vast treatise containing about 3000 pages depicting elaborately the history of Music from the earliest days to the present.

The style of writing is in the form of a dialogue between a student and a teacher. The student, often commonplace and ignorant, puts the question and the answer is given by the teacher satisfying all his queries. Bhatkhande thought it would be the easiest and most intelligible style if this was written in question and answer form between a teacher and a student. This style came handy to him as an outcome of his long-standing experience as a teacher. It is surprising how he brought himself down to the level of a beginner and an ignorant pupil when he put questions on his behalf.

Unlike his other books he wrote these 4 volumes under his pen-name Vishnu Sharma and in the preface he mentioned what painstaking work he had to do to study and collect facts for expounding the theory of modern Music and comparing the same with that of the ancient's.

Apart from the ancient *granthas* which he thought were not very clear in the present day perspective, he consulted for reference and comparison for forming the theory of modern *ragas* and quoted from the following books:

1. *Raga Tarangini*
2. *Hridaya Kautuk*
3. *Hridaya Prakash*
4. *Sangeet Parijat*
5. *Raga Tattva Vibodha*
6. *Sadraga Chandrodaya*
7. *Raga Manjari*
8. *Raga Mala*
9. *Anupa Sangeet Ratnakar*
10. *Anupa Sangeet Vilas*
11. *Anupankush*
12. *Rasa Kaumudi*
13. *Swaramelakalanidhi*
14. *Raga Vibodha*
15. *Chaturdandi Prakashika*
16. *Sangeetsaramrit*
17. *Raga Lakshana*

Among these, the first 12 books belong to the North Indian writers; the rest are by South Indians. He also consulted and mentioned about *Sangeetkalpadrum, Sangeetsar, Geetasutrasar, Radhagovindu Sangeetsar, Naghmate Asafi.* He also had a look at the following books: *Sangeet Narayan, Sangeet Shiromani, Sangeet Chudamani, Sangeet Samayasar, Narad Samhita, Sangeet Vinod, Sangeet Lakhsan Dipika,* etc. But he gave a lot of importance to the above-numbered seventeen books and asked every student to read them.

Contents of 'Hindustani Sangeet Paddhati'

In this book he discussed music on such a broad canvas, drawing references from hundreds of books written by Indian and European scholars, that it is baffling for a reader to fathom the depth of his knowledge. The references and illustrations from 30 Sanskrit *grantha*s belonging to different centuries show the vast compass of his study. This certainly made the task easy for a music student or a musicologist saving him from the laborious task of reading the *grantha*s and collecting the facts and data from them.

In its four volumes every *raga* was treated in detail, with its history, if available, its evolution through the past ages with all the modifications which took place in different periods, its traditional background and development along with its present form in vogue. He supported the definitions with Sanskrit *shloka*s ending with the *alapas* in *sthayi* and *antara* followed by notation of some authoritative traditional compositions.

The First Part

In the first part of *Hindustani Sangeet Paddhati* 45 *ragas* belonging to *Yaman Bilawal* and *Khamaj Thaat* were analysed and discussed. It contained 398 pages (Marathi version). He discussed at length the *raga*s belonging to *Kalyan* or *Yaman Thaat* and further classified them into three groups having common note patterns. Then he discussed 'Thaat Paddhati' and their evolution including Venkatamakhi's theory of 72 'Melakartara'.

After that he took up the *raga*s belonging to *Bilawal Thaat* and discussed in detail each variety of *Bilawal* throwing light on their combined *raga* form.

Then he discussed the *raga*s belonging to *Khamaj Mela*. In between he described the different ancient terms of music drawing references from many ancient *grantha*s and discussed them from historical and modern perspective.

His discussion of *raga*s in all the volumes was unique in nature. The approach was completely intellectual and objective. There was no place for fanciful theory or pseudo-religious explanation. He outlined a *raga* in precise form defining its *aroha avaroha, vadi-samvadi swara, thaat,* singing time, catch phrase and ended with their note patterns.

The most interesting part was their comparison with the allied *raga*s. The discussion is so vivid in description that it is bound to leave its unfailing impression on the reader's mind. There is nothing hazy or confusing about it. He sincerely admitted. where the *raga*'s form was controversial or obsolete. Wherever possible, he connected the *raga* with the ancients and did not hesitate to quote their definition. Sometimes he mentioned an anecdote connected with a particular *raga*, which was amusing and interesting.

Take for instance *raga Malkauns*. It is a popular *raga* and is demonstrated by all modern musicians. When Bhatkhande discussed it he went back to Sharngadeva's *Sangeet Ratnakar* which mentioned this *raga* in the name of *Malavakaushik*. He quoted the Sanskrit *shloka* as reference and established that this *raga* was one of the *grama raga*s of *Sangeet Ratnakar*. Afterwards he came down to *Sangeet Darpan* which mentioned *raga Malavakaushik* where the *aroha avaroha* was not the same as in the modern *Malkauns*. The most interesting fact was that in the above-mentioned book Malavakaushik was described as a deity with red complexion, holding a blood coloured baton and wearing a garland of the skulls of his dead enemies. He quoted the *shloka*s in support of his statement. Again, he mentioned the description of Vyasa in *Ragamala* which depicted *raga Malkauns* as a human being. The *shloka* reads like this -- "He is dark complexioned, wearing yellow coloured robe, the neck is bejewelled and he is surrounded by beautiful women" etc. Apart from this he quoted many *doha*s which described Malkauns as a charming and comfort-loving human being.

The Second Part

In the second part of *Hindustani Sangeet Paddhati* 20 *raga*s belonging to the *Bhairava Thaat* were discussed and analysed drawing references as usual from the ancient *grantha*s wherever possible. In this book he discussed and compared the *swara* and *shruti* of the ancients and the mediaeval age authors. He took into account the opinions quoted in the ancient books like *Naradiya Shiksha,*

Mandukya Shiksha and *Natyashastra*. He analysed also the *swaras* and *shrutis* of the mediaeval age authors like Sharngadeva, Ramamatya, Somnath, Parshvadeva, Pundarik Vitthal, Ahobal etc. In this regard he did not leave out even the European scholars like Parry, Blassemera etc. After a detailed discussion and rational analysis he established the anomaly in the arrangement of *shrutis* to derive the modern *swaras*. Later he gave his own arrangement for establishing the position of the modern *swaras* on the gamut thereby fixing the modern scale of notes. His findings in this regard will be discussed in the next section.

In this part he has mentioned his experiences of meeting several immature musicologists during his study tours. These not only read like amusing anecdotes but also indicate the decadent state of music and musicology of his time. In this part he took *raga Bhairava* and discussed in detail the kinds of *Bhairava* -- *Anand Bhairava*, *Ahir Bhairava*, *Shivamat Bhairava* etc. He also discussed other *ragas* belonging to *Bhairava Thaat*. For example, *Gunakari*, *Jogia*, *Prabhat*, *Saveri*, *Ramkali* etc. In this process of discussion, he mentioned the *shlokas* from the *granthas* about these *ragas* ending with the quotations from his own book, *Abhinava Raga Manjari*, which establishes their present form.

This part of *Hindustani Sangeet Paddhati* contains about 500 pages (Marathi version).

The Third Part

In the third part 25 *ragas* belonging to *Purvi* and *Marwa Thaats* were discussed. In between discussion, he also analysed the *granthas* and some contemporary books along with some theories of South Indian music. The most interesting feature of this part is his discussion and camparison of the identical and allied (*samaprakritik* and *samaakritik* respectively) *ragas*. As for example, he compared and noted the point of differences between *Bhairava* and *Shri* (page 21 of Part 3, *Hindustani Sangeet Paddhati*), *Purvi* and *Kalingra* (page 30), *Triveni* and *Tanki* (page 240), *Purvi* and *Pooriya Dhanashri*, etc. His analysis was so logical that the reader was able to get a clear picture of each individual *raga* discussed and a learner could never mix up the *ragas* which differed from each other in subtle shade. These masterly analyses are a proof of his amazing capacity for grasping and digesting the subject with a razor sharp intellect.

The Fourth Part

In the fourth part -- which is the largest volume of the series, consisting of 1120 pages (Marathi version) -- he discussed elaborately 35 *ragas* belonging to *Kafi Mela* and some other *ragas*. In this part his discussion and analysis of *ragas* reached a new scholarly height. His discussion was precise and objective, drawing references from the *granthas*, wherever relevant, narrating its different forms and varieties, ultimately ending with its present structure. They showed his depth of scholarship and expanse of study. Take for instance, *raga Darbari Kanhara*. It is a popular *raga* and is sung by almost every artist. While discussing it Bhatkhande defined *Kanhara* in general and named different *Kanhara*s in vogue. Then he defined the forms of *Sorati Kanhara* and *Gara Kanhara*. Then he drew references from the ancient *granthas* and described in nutshell the relevant points from *Nadodadhi*, which was written by Puran Kavi of Jaipur. Then coming down to the modern age he quoted the opinion of some modern scholars like Raja S.M. Tagore. At the end he gave the outline of the present form of *Darbari Kanhara*, with its *sargam* set in *tala* and defined in *shlokas*. Needless to say that all the *ragas* discussed in this volume received similar treatment.

He also discussed 14 *ragas* belonging to *Asavari* and *Bhairavi Mela*. Later, after discussing *Malkauns* he analysed and discussed 3 more *ragas* belonging to *Todi Thaat*.

All these volumes are great in exposition and razor sharp in analysis. These books are still the standard treatises on Hindustani music detailing all the *ragas* with their scientific definitions and historical backgrounds.

'KRAMIK PUSTAK MALIKA'

Kramik Pustak Malika is written in six parts and as a textbook it is meant for teaching in the music classes where the modern method of teaching music, introduced by Bhatkhande, is used. The four parts of this book are taught in 5 years for the Degree course. Another two years cover the other two parts. All these parts deal with the theory of 150 *ragas* grouped *thaat*wise, with introductory chapters on the general theory of music, besides a short description of every *raga*, followed by *swara vistar*. They contain about 1000 traditional compositions besides Bhatkhande's own compositions which are about 300 in notation. They cover all branches of Classical music, viz., *Dhrupad, Dhamar, Bara Khayal, Chhota Khayal, Tarana, Sargam, Lakshan Geet* etc. In the introductory chapters he included the theory of music and some instructions for the students and the teachers.

Each *raga* is dealt with in the following manner -- its form and main features, its *aroha avaroha*, and its historical background, including its different versions written in a condensed and easily intelligible form. Its catch note and *vadi swara* are invariably mentioned. At the end of every part note patterns of all the *ragas* in the form of *vistar* and *tana* are given.

'A COMPARATIVE STUDY OF THE MUSIC SYSTEMS OF THE 15TH, 16TH, 17TH AND 18TH CENTURIES'

This is a very important book written in English, the first of its kind in this century, marked by lucidity, precision and objectivity. The chief object was to place before the readers a comparative analysis of the different Sanskrit works on Indian music written at different periods. This was done precisely so that it should help in the determination of a suitable system for the present day Hindustani music. In dealing with the subject he pinpointed the following details:

1. The name and the place of the author of the work so far as can be traced.
2. The probable date of the work.
3. The explanation of the *shruti*s and *swara*s as explained in the treatise.
4. The *thaat*s if any used for the classification of the *ragas*.
5. The *janya raga*s and their classification under the *thaat*s.
6. General remarks.

He began with discussion about the two important ancient authors, Bharata and Sharngadeva, who belonged to the period prior to the 15th century. The purpose of this, as explained by him, was to present before the public the results of his study of ancient music. While doing this he put two questions which would naturally come into the mind of the reader and endeavoured to answer them. They are:

1. What is the use of paying any attention to the old Sanskrit texts which do not directly relate to the music of the present day?

2. Admitting it to be of any use, what was the best means of studying them?

While discussing the ancients, viz., Bharata and Sharngadeva, he bore in mind as a careful research scholar the following rules:

1. The mind has to be kept entirely free from any preconceived ideas or theories.

2. No statements or assumptions should be made which are not strictly warranted by the text in hand.

3. In the interpretation of ancient texts the directions given by the author himself as a guide for interpretation must be strictly adhered to. It will not be permissible to take as a guide what subsequent writers have said on the subject.

After discussing the ancients he took up the authors belonging to the 15th, 16th, 17th and 18th centuries for analysis. The purpose of studying them he explained in the following lines:-- "Music changed its form at the advent of the Muslim rule. We are now two centuries ahead of that period. Therefore music has further changed. By studying the texts we can restore some *ragas* which are now obsolete. We can correct the method of singing some melodies which are at present incorrectly sung. One can note the principle changes in the name of the *ragas*, *thaats*, and *gamaks*. The substratum of our music is undoubtedly the music of the past. Therefore, a study of the past is essential."

The following books are discussed:

1. *Raga Tarangini*
2. *Hridaya Kautuk*
3. *Sangeet Parijat*
4. *Hridaya Prakash*
5. *Raga Mala*
6. *Raga Manjari*
7. *Nartan Nirnaya*
8. *Raga Tattva Vibodha*
9. *Anupa Sangeet Ratnakar*

10. *Anupa Sangeet Vilas*
11. *Anupankush*
12. *Rasa Kaumudi*
13. *Swaramelakalanidhi*
14. *Raga Vibodha*
15. *Sangeetsaramrit*
16. *Chaturdandi Prakashika*
17. *Raga Lakshana*

The first 12 of the above-mentioned books were written by the North Indian scholars and the rest by the South Indian scholars.

All these books were scattered all over the country. Bhatkhande mentioned in the *Hindustani Sangeet Paddhati* (Ist part, pp.192-195) the names of the music works he came across during his travels.

He discussed and clarified the *shruti, swara, thaat* and *raga* portion of about 16 treatises. He quoted the relevant Sanskrit *shloka*s and noted down his observations in clear words giving his argument in favour or otherwise. For illustration we can quote his analysis of Somnath's work *Raga Vibodha*. It is from page 88 of *A Comparative Study of the Music Systems of the 15th, 16th, 17th and 18th Centuries.*

After ascertaining and discussing the date of Somnath, which he assumed as A.D. 1610, he proceeded to analyse the subject matter of Somnath's *Raga Vibodha* and began with the following words: "The important points in connection with this work for consideration will be:

1. How many out of the 22 *shruti*s did Somnath use as *swara*s in his *raga*s?
2. How did he place his *shuddha* and *vikrit swara*s on the *shruti*s?
3. How many *thaat*s did he use for the classification of his *ragas*?
4. What was the classification of the *janya ragas*?
5. Will any of the *raga* definitions be useful for the Northern musicians?"

By pinpointing the issues discussion was focussed in a definite direction and he proceeded to discuss all the above points quoting Sanskrit *shloka*s from *Raga Vibodha* and later ended it with his own observations. His observations are lucid and precise in nature and markedly intelligible and rational in interpretation. He compared Somnath's *swara*s with those of his predecessors and also discussed their applicability to the present music. For better understanding he gave the *swaras* names of the *melas* of Somnath and his *janya ragas*; thereafter, he ended with these following words: "It is not necessary to discuss the definitions of those derivative *ragas* here. Many of these *ragas* will be found to have retained the major portions of their old forms to this day, and thus the *Raga Vibodha* will be of great importance from the historical point of view to the Northern musicians. The fifth question therefore may be safely answered in the affirmative."

It was Bhatkhande who explained and established that Somnath's standard scale was like the *'Mukhari'* scale of the Karnatak system of music and Ahobal's standard scale was like the *'Kafi'* of the Hindustani system of music. His commentaries on these *granthas* were named *Raga Vibodha Praveshika* and *Parijat Praveshika*.

This is an illustration at random to show the modern rationalistic method and objective approach he adopted to explain the ancient authors to the modern musicians.

Apart from satisfying one's curiosity from the historical angle, Bhatkhande's idea was that the study of the 17 books of the authors belonging to the middle age as mentioned earlier have another very important utility. He found that the subject matter of our present music is of the same nature as that of ancient music. The division and the classification of the subject matter as adopted in those texts could be the base for systematising the present day music. The present condition was a vacuum created by the misrule of the British and the apathy of the educated class. These books could serve as models for the improvement of the present day condition of our music. Therefore, it would not be wrong to say that the study of those books would give a thorough insight into our music as it was and would inspire us constructively to do groundwork for the future.

'A HISTORICAL SURVEY OF THE MUSIC OF UPPER INDIA'

This is a paper in English read by Bhatkhande in the First Conference of Music held at Baroda in 1916. It presented an historical survey of the Music of Upper India. He begins this article with the following words:-- "We are now alive to the fact that no study of the science is complete without the study of the history of that science."

The historical study is interesting and informative. For his work he divided the periods into (i) Hindu Period, (ii) Mohammedan Period, and (iii) British Period. Each period he subdivided as 'earlier' and 'later'. From Bharata and Sharngadeva he discussed datewise all the middle age authors, the books written by them and also the practical musicians like Amir Khusrau, Mian Tansen, Nayak Gopal, Baiju Bawara, Mirabai etc. He came up to Aurangzeb and mentioned the anecdotes connected with him about the burial of music. He mentioned the anomalies of dates and the original names of the authors in a very interesting manner, depicting elaborately the condition of music in each period, sometimes naming the *thaat*, *raga*s or *janya raga*s of the respective periods and comparing them with each other. Coming down to the British Period he recorded the void created by the foreign invasion and mentioned *Naghmate Asafi* (A.D 1813) by Mohammed Reza of Patna which established *Bilawal* scale as *shuddha* scale clearly. He also wrote that there was no evidence to show that a systematic treatise in Sanskrit on the modern Hindustani music was written during the last hundred years.

'SWARA MALIKA'

It is a small booklet. Published in 1907, it was written in Gujarati. It mainly contains notation of *raga*s in *swara*s and *tala*s in set compositions.

'LAKSHAN GEET SANGRAHA'

It contains the description of the *raga*s in vogue, aptly fitted into a poem and set in notation in that very *raga*. The book was produced in three parts.

Old Manuscripts edited by Bhatkhande

1. *Swaramelakalanidhi* by Ramamatya

2. *Chaturdandi Prakashika* by Venkatamakhi
3. *Raga Lakshana*
4. *Raga Tarangini* by Lochan
5. *Raga Tattva Vibodha* by Shrinivas
6. *Sadraga Chandrodaya* by Pundarik Vitthal
7. *Raga Manjari* by Pundarik Vitthal
8. *Raga Mala* by Pundarik Vitthal
9. *Nartan Nirnaya* by Pundarik Vitthal

In the course of his study tours he met Kashinath Sastry Appa Tulsi, and a number of well-known professional musicians at Hyderabad. To Appa Tulsi he explained the outline of the theory of music he had formulated on the basis of the practice in vogue and Appa Tulsi at once took up the ideas and adopted them with enthusiasm. Appa Tulsi composed his own couplets of the definition of the various *ragas* as explained and expounded in the *Shrimallakshya Sangeetam* and wrote these books -- *Sangeet Sudhakar*, *Sangeet Kalpadrumankur* and *Raga Chandrika*. The above-mentioned books were written in Sanskrit and *Raga Chandrikasar* was written in Hindi by him. These books were edited by Bhatkhande and the couplets were quoted by him in the *Kramik Pustak Malika* series as definitions of *ragas*.

About his own books he wrote in *A Historical Survey of the Music of Upper India* the following words which speak for themselves:

"Whoever learns from the *Lakshya Sangeet* and *Hindustani Sangeet Paddhati* teaches himself at least the firm and unshakable foundation of his music and the finishing. The picking up of the graces and beauties is done by merely listening to the singing of excellent practical artists and for this *swaragyana*, practice of *Swara Malika* is necessary, which is the first part of *Kramik Pustak Malika*... The *Lakshya Sangeet* reads like a 'Sutra' book and its object is easy memorisation and the same may be said of the books written by Appa Tulsi. By working out this system it has been given enough stability at a time when its state was getting far from satisfactory."

These books written by Bhatkhande are invariably an invaluable treasure of today. It is ample recognition of his monumental work that every musician and musicologist of today keeps these books with him either for reference or study.

III

PROVIDING A THEORY

For his work he divided music broadly into three categories.
1. *Grantha Sangeet*
2. *Lakshya Sangeet*
3. *Bhavi Sangeet*

1. Grantha Sangeet

It means the books on the theory of music written in the Sanskrit language by the ancient and middle period scholars. While studying and discussing the ancient form of music he took into account the following books:
1. *Naradiya Shiksha*
2. *Natyashastra*
3. *Mandukya Shiksha*
4. *Sangeet Ratnakar*
5. *Sangeet Samayasar*
6. *Sangeet Darpan*
7. *Sadraga Chandrodaya*
8. *Raga Tarangini*
9. *Swaramelakalanidhi*
10. *Raga Vibodha*
11. *Sangeet Parijat*
12. *Anupa Sangeet Vilas*
13. *Anupa Sangeet Ratnakar*
14. *Anupankush*
15. *Chaturdandi Prakashika*
16. *Sangeetsaramrit*

He studied these books, digested and noted the contents for the purpose of deciphering the theory mentioned there with a view to discovering its possible relationship with the present day music. All these books he could not get in any single library. He, therefore, had to visit several libraries and search for them also from other sources throughout the length and breadth of the country. After studying them he further sub-divided them into books belonging to the ancient period and the books belonging to the middle period. Among the ancients he took into account three books which were

available:
1. *Mandukya Shiksha*
2. *Naradiya Shiksha*
3. *Natyashastra*

Although he considered these three books among the most ancient ones but he never claimed his findings as final and foolproof. In *Bhatkhande Sangeet Shastra* (2nd part, page 16) he said with all humility that as far as his knowledge went these were the most ancient *grantha*s available. But this might not be an absolute fact, there could be always scope for more research and new findings. He also stated that it was a difficult task to determine the exact date of these ancient *grantha*s. He did not deem it necessary to spend useless time in ascertaining the period and date of Bharata etc. In this regard it will be relevant to quote from his writings. Addressing a pupil he says:

"भरत आदि का काल निश्चित करने का कार्य हम अपने सिर पर नहीं लेंगे। सम्भवतः इह कार्य करना कठिन भी होगा। कैसी-कैसी कठिनाई उपस्थित होंगी उनका अनुमान तुम्हें संक्षेप में कराये देता हूँ। हमारे किसी वर्तमान विद्वान् का मत है कि भरत तीसरी शताब्दी में हुआ था, और उस समय राग शब्द का प्रचार ही नहीं था। इधर कल्लिनाथ की टीका में राग-स्वरूपों के वर्णन में भरत का आधार लिया हुआ दिखाई देता है। —— ग्रंथकारों ने क्या कहा यह हमारा विषय है। मगर उन्होंने यह कब किस काल में कहा, यह खोजना हमारा विषय नहीं है।"

The Facts He Ascertained from the Ancient Granthas

He emphasised the importance of the *Swaradhyaya* (the chapter dealing with the musical notes) of any book belonging to any century. Therefore, he began analysing the *swarasthana* of the ancients.

By studying and scrutinising these books he found that all the authors had established that the knowledge of the *shruti* and *swara*s were the foundation of all systems of music of our country. It was our ancient method to divide the gamut into twenty-two fine audible sound units named *shruti*s and place the *swara*s on them. While studying *Naradiya Shiksha* and *Mandukya Shiksha*, Bhatkhande was baffled by the ambiguous and mystic language of the *shloka*s defining *shruti* and *swara*. In *Hindustani Sangeet*

Paddhati (2nd part, page 17) he quoted profusely from these two books to show that the position of the *swaras* on the gamut was not indicated clearly. Instead the *shlokas* personified them as deities -- describing their carrier animals of particular species, their particular colours and also the different heavens from which they descended on earth. Sometimes the *swaras* were attributed to have originated from particular parts of the human body. All these had nothing to do with their musical position on the gamut.[3] Having failed to pinpoint the place of the *swaras* of the ancients from such illustrations and descriptions he tried to gather information by meeting and discussing with the Pandits who claimed to have read those books. He met such a Sanskrit scholar who claimed to know the secret of these ancient *granthas*. Bhatkhande faithfully recorded his conversation with this scholar in *Hindustani Sangeet Paddhati*, 2nd part, which is of very amusing character. The Pandit, in the course of their conversation, avoided Bhatkhande's straight questions and gave evasive, non-scientific and spiritualised explanation of the *swarasthanas* of the ancient *granthas*. It was Bhatkhande's attempt to show how the form of music changed and with the gap of centuries the knowledge of the ancients became illegible in terms of present day music.

Bharata and His Method

Among the ancients Bhatkhande found Bharata's *Natyashastra* as the most categorical and elaborate. In fact, the principal writer on Music in the ancient period was Bharata who wrote *Natyashastra* in about A.D. 200. Like his predecessors he divided the gamut into 22 minute audible sound divisions called *shrutis* and placed the *swaras* on them.

It is interesting to note the method of Bharata's determining the sound gap between the *shrutis*. In *Hindustani Sangeet Paddhati* (part 2) Bhatkhande went at length to explain how with the help of the *veena* Bharata fixed his twenty-two *shrutis* and divided them on the seven principal notes. In this process he extensively quoted Sanskrit couplets from the *Natyashastra*.

From his writing we find that Bharata had four *veenas* identical in shape and size, which he tuned uniformly. There were no frets in the *veena* of that time and it contained nine strings. He turned seven strings to the seven principal notes and the other two strings

were tuned to *Antar Gandhar* and *Kakali Nishad* -- two displaced
notes prevalent at his time. He divided the entire gamut into 22
*shruti*s and placed the *swara*s on them in the manner indicated
below:

चतुश्चतुश्चतुश्चैव षड्जमध्यमपंचमाः   ।
द्वेद्वे निषादगांधारौ त्रिस्त्री ऋषभधैवतौ।।

Swara	Shruti
Shadja	4th
Rishabh	7th
Gandhar	9th
Madhyam	13th
Pancham	17th
Dhaivat	20th
Nishad	22nd

This pattern on deriving *swara*s from 22 *shruti*s was later followed
by all other scholars of ancient and the middle period.

One of the *veena*s, tuned in the above-mentioned method, was
called as *achala* or *dhruva veena* of *Shadja grama*. It contained
strings tuned to the seven notes, which were left undisturbed.

The other three *veena*s which were also tuned in the same way
were called *chala veena*s. Now the string tuned to the *Pancham*
of one of the three *chala veena*s was lowered by one *shruti* while
the strings tuned to the other notes, viz., *Shadja*, *Rishabh*, *Gandhar*,
Madhyam, *Dhaivat* and *Nishad* remained undisturbed. The *veena*
with the lowered *Pancham* was now to be called as *Madhyam
grama veena*.

It is obvious that the sound of the *Pancham* of *achala* or *dhruva
veena* and of *Shadja grama* and the sound of the *Pancham* of the
disturbed *chala veena* would be different. According to Bharata
this was the sound gap between the two *shruti*s.

Bharata further instructed that all other notes of the second *chala
veena* might be lowered down by one *shruti* each as follows:

Swara	*Shadja*	*Rishabh*	*Gandhar*	*Madhyam*	*Pancham*	*Dhaivat*	*Nishad*
Shruti Number	3	6	8	12	16	19	21

Bharata further wrote that the *Pancham* of third *chala veena* should again be lowered down compared to the second *chala veena* mentioned above by another *shruti* and in the same way the other six notes should also be lowered down by one *shruti*, so that the notes would be placed as follows:

Swara	*Shadja*	*Rishabh*	*Gandhar*	*Madhyam*	*Pancham*	*Dhaivat*	*Nishad*
Shruti Number	2	5	7	11	15	18	20

Now the *Gandhar* and *Nishad* of last mentioned *chala veena* which are placed on 7th and 20th *shruti*s consecutively would coincide with the *Rishabh* and *Dhaivat* of *dhruva veena* which are placed on 7th and 20th *shruti*s respectively.

The process of deriving the notes of the three *chala veena*s from those of the *achala veena*, described above, is called *Sarana Kriya* and of the *veena*s using for such purpose is named as *Sarana Chatushtaya*.

From this process the following points are apparent:

1. The gaps between the *shruti*s were taken as uniform so that the notes coincide with one another when their pitch was lowered by one *shruti*.

2. The definition of *shruti* did not have any mathematical measurement. The measurement of the sound gap of *shruti* depended on the establishment of the two *Pancham*s of *Shadja grama* and *Madhyam grama* on the two *veena*s.

3. The theory of *Chatushchatushchatushchaiva* was obtained by this method of lowering and coinciding the *shruti*s.

4. One had to depend largely on one's power of hearing to ascertain the fine gap between the two above-mentioned *shruti*s. The capacity, however, differed from individual to individual. It is assumed that the people's ears were trained to catch the difference of the two *Pancham*s of the two *grama*s in the period of Bharata. This is not possible in the present day. Perhaps it would not be wrong to surmise that firstly the *swara*s were established and the imaginary division into *shruti*s was done later.

Bharata's *swara*s on *dhruva veena*, which were called *Shadja grama*, depended on the hearing association of *Sā* and *Pa* and *Sā* and *Ma* relationship. Again, in the absence of a fool-proof definition, it was left to the human power of hearing, which could have been faulty. However, we arrive at the assumed relationship of the *Pa/Sā* which is 3/2, *Ma/Sā* which is 4/3, and *Ga/Sā* which is 5/4. The language of *Natyashastra* was such that the meaning could be stretched to opposite sides also, which made its theory more complicated. It is said:

$$\text{''मुनीनाम् पुनराधानाम् वाचमर्थोऽनुधावति।''}^4$$

Therefore, the confusion remained and, as the centuries advanced, we find that the scholars, although having accepted the theory of Bharata in general, put a question mark in regard to the difference in sound gap between the two *shruti*s.

Let us take the illustration of Matanga's *Brihaddeshi*, a work of A.D 5th century. This is an important book as in it we come across the word '*Raga*' which was slowly coming into vogue. The technical definition of *shruti* was necessary to be deciphered properly on which depended the success of establishing *Shadja grama* and *Madhyam grama*. It appears that the gap between the *shruti*s was even then confusing.

This fact was apparent from his writings (Commentary is made by Shingabhupala):

$$\text{ननु श्रुतेः किम् प्रमाणम् उच्यते। पंचमस्तावद् ग्रामद्वयस्थो लोके प्रसिद्धः}$$
$$\text{तस्योत्कर्षणापकर्षणाभ्याम् मार्दवादायत्तत्वादगमदन्तरम् तत्प्रमाण श्रुतिरिति।}$$

Matanga discussed in detail about the *grama raga*s. When he came to the subject of *shruti* he put the question: What is the measurement of *shruti*? Then, in answer to that, he said:

"Everybody recognises the *Pancham* of *Shadja grama* and *Madhyam grama*. The gap obtained by the difference of the two *Pancham*s of these two above-mentioned *grama*s is the sound measurement of a *shruti*."

From this statement again it is apparent that the ear-training and capacity for differentiating the two *shruti*s, viz., *Pancham* of *Shadja grama* and the *Pancham* of *Madhyam grama*, were very accurate and common in those days.

After Bharata

After Bharata till the 10th century very few worthwhile books were written. Bhatkhande mentioned about *Naradiya Shiksha* and *Sangeet Makarand* written in this period. But these books, while they were largely influenced by Bharata's writing, were also full of fanciful descriptions of *ragas* and *ragini*s depicting them as husband and wife, having a family of offshoot *ragas*. However, descriptions might be considered as the precursor of the classification of *ragas* of later age.

Under the Muslims

In the 11th century the Muslim invaders conquered and settled in North India. The ancient music was subjected to gradual change from that period due to its fusion with the music of the invaders. It definitely started deviating from its root, viz., the *granthas*, as the Muslims were unable to understand Sanskrit. However, under Mulism rule the practical art of music thrived and musicians were provided with the patronage of the rulers.

In the 12th century the muslim rulers were busy fighting and annexing small kingdoms of the Hindu kings and princes. As the condition of the country was full of unrest and insecurity, the culture of music was consequently hampered. The onslaught of the Muslim invaders did not reach South India at that time. Devagiri of the South was flourishing kingdom in the 13th century where Sharngadeva lived as a Court Musician. He wrote a treatise named *Sangeet Ratnakar* which is regarded as an important book on theory by the scholars of all times.

According to Bhatkhande Sharngadeva's writings were more accurate and elaborate in description and definitions of *shruti*s, *swarasthana*s, *grama*, *moorchhana*, *jati* etc. He described the *vikrit* forms of *jati*s as well. In placing the notes on the gamut he followed the method of Bharata and accepted the following facts:

1. The gamut was divided into 22 *shruti*s. In place of Bharata's 'Sarana Chatushtaya' Sharngadeva introduced two *veenas* with 22 strings tuned to 22 *shruti*s respectively.

The *shloka* containing this fact was as follows:

व्यक्तये कुर्महे तासा वीणाद्धे निदर्शनम् ।
द्वे वीणे सदृशे कार्ये यथा नादः समो भवेत् । ।
तयोद्वार्विंशतिस्तंत्रयः प्रत्येक तासु इत्यादि ।

To give practical shape to this process he further instructed that out of the twenty-two wires in the *shruti veena* the first wire should be tuned to the lowest pitch, then the second should be slightly higher and the third and the fourth will also be higher in pitch in the same way and in the same ratio. The supporting *shloka* Bhatkhande has quoted is as follows:

कार्यामिन्द्रतमध्वाना द्वितीयोच्चध्वनिर्मनाक् ।
स्यान्निरन्तरता श्रुत्योर्मध्ये ध्वन्यन्तराश्रुतेः । ।

He also observed that this process of obtaining slightly higher pitch in geometrical progression was established in three registers -- 'Mandra, Madhya and Tara.'

He has discussed this in detail in *Bhatkhande Sangeet Shastra*, 4th part, page 33, Hindi Edition.

2. In *Sangeet Ratnakar* the *swaras* were placed on them after Bharata; namely, *Shadja, Rishabh, Gandhar, Madhyam*; on the 4th *shruti*, the 7th *shruti*, the 9th *shruti*, the 13th *shruti* respectively and so on.

3. The gap between two *shrutis* was accepted as uniform in ascension and descension.

4. The *shuddha swaras* he placed on the last *shruti* like Bharata.

5. His *shuddha swaras* presumably consisted of *komal Ga* and *Ni* resembling our *Kafi Mela*.

The point of his deviation from Bharata was the number of *vikrit* notes obtained from one gamut. The development of the *vikrit* notes and their use during the different periods, as the century advanced, has been discussed on page 122.

After ascertaining the *swaras* and *shrutis* of the ancients, Bhatkhande tried to explore the type of songs existing at that time. At the time of Bharata, *Grama ragas* were prevalent. But at the time of Sharngadeva *Jati gayan* was the principal classical type of songs. Bhatkhande observed that in the seventh chapter of the *swaradhyaya* of the *Sangeet Ratnakar*, written by Sharngadeva, two varieties of *Jatis* were described, viz., *shuddha* and *vikrit*. Under the heading of *Upanga* many *ragas*, whose names we are now acquainted with, were mentioned. Sharngadeva recognised the number of his *Shuddha Jati* as seven. He named them according to the names of the principal seven notes: *Shadji, Arshavi, Gandhari, Madhyama* etc. Sharngadeva further described the rules and signs of *Shuddha Jati* as follows: -- "It should have *Nyasa, Apanyasa, Ansha* and *Graha Swara,* and it should always be *Sampurna,* or employ seven notes in ascension and descension and will never perform *Nyasa* in *Tara Saptak.*" He further described that if the *Nyasa* rule is observed but the other rules are changed than it would change into *Vikrit Jati.* In this way *Shadji Jati* could have fifteen *vikrit* or *sansargaj jati*s and *Arshavi, Gandhari* and other six *Shuddha Jati*s have 23 *vikrit jati*s each. In all 153 *vikrit jati*s were described. Bhatkhande realised that in the context of today's music the *jati*s have no practical relevance. As even now it could not be ascertained what was the exact note pattern of *jati.* Nor is it clear as to what was the *Shuddha* scale of Sharngadeva, or how many strings he used to attach to his *veena* and in which notes he used to tune them. During Bhatkhande's study tour no scholar or musician could throw light on these points.

The Authors of the Middle Period

There was a lot of change in the existing music during the middle period which commences from the 15th century.

The mode of practical music changed inevitably in this century and the scholars experimented with the number of *swara*s both *shuddha* and *vikrit,* obtained from the gamut of the *saptak.* The scholars of this age did not bother much about the gap of the *shruti*s, which remained somewhat vague and imaginary, but attempted to pinpoint the *swara*s on the gamut.

In this regard a revolutionary step was taken by Ahobal in the 17th century. His book *Sangeet Parijat* was an important step forward for scientific and categorical fixture of *swara*s. In this book he introduced the method of placing the notes (*swara*s) on the wire by measuring the length in a very clear manner.

His notes were twelve in number on the gamut. His *shuddha* scale was equivalent to the present day *kafi* scale.

Although like his predecessors he divided the gamut into twenty-two *shruti*s and placed his *swara*s on the last *shruti,* he minimised the importance of *shruti* by comparing the *swara*s and *shruti*s with a snake and his coil which indicated that they were really one but appeared different in their outward forms only, depending on the hearing capacity of a human being:

श्रुतयः स्युः स्वराभिन्ना श्रावणत्वेन हेतुना।
अहिकुण्डलवत्तत्र भेदोक्तिः शास्त्रसम्मता।।
सर्वाच्च श्रुतयस्तत्तद्रागेषु स्वरतौ गताः ।
रागहेतुत्वं एतासां श्रुति संज्ञैव सम्मता।।
(संगीतपारिजात)

Ahobal's method had a great impact on posterity. On his line Hridayanarayan Dev wrote two books on theory -- *Hridaya Kautuk* and *Hridaya Prakash*. Another important writer Bhavabhatta wrote *Anupa Sangeet Vilas*, *Anupankush* and *Anupa Sangeet Ratnakar*.

Coming down to the 18th century we find that Shrinivas' *Raga Tattva Vibodha* was the most important work. He followed the theory of Ahobal and accepted twelve notes in a *gamut* and *Kafi Mela* as the *Shuddha Mela*. It is interesting to note from some of his Sanskrit couplets the position of the notes on the wire.

To establish the *Sa* of *Madhya Saptak* and *Tara Saptak*, Shrinivas said:

पूर्वत्नियोश्चमेर्वोश्च मध्ये ताराकसः स्थितः ।
तदर्धे त्वत्तितारस्य सस्वरस्य स्थितिर्भवेत्।।

Now the next important note *Ma* was established in the following manner:

मध्यस्थानादिमषड्जमारभ्यातारषड्जगम् ।
सूत्रे कुर्यात्तदर्धे तु स्वरं मध्यममाचरेत्।।

Having established the note *Ma*, *Pancham* can be obtained in the following manner:

भागत्रयसमायुक्तं तत्सूत्रं कारितं भवेत् ।
पूर्वभागद्वयादग्रे स्थापनीयोऽथ पंचमः ।।

After obtaining the two important notes on a gamut the rest

were obtained in proportion to these two, which were indicated in the same way.

It is but natural that after the discovery of obtaining the notes from the measurement of the string of the *veena*, the utility of *shrutis* for this purpose became less important. The division of *shrutis* and their numbers existed in theory and their division among the *swaras* remained also merely theoretical.

Vikrit Swaras

In *Sangeet Ratnakar* the displaced or *vikrit swaras* are explained in two ways:

1. When a *swara* leaves its own original *shruti* and either steps down or steps up by one *shruti* from either the preceding or the succeeding *swara* respectively.

2. When a *swara* remains steady in its original position, but as a result of the stepping up or stepping down of the immediate neighbouring *swara* the displacement takes place, it is also called a *vikrit swara*.

To be more specific, according to Sharngadeva *vikrit swaras* are those which when displaced to the higher side or lower side, from their original position, cause either decrease or increase in the number of *shrutis* between them and the neighbouring *swaras*.

It is obvious that all this was explained in the technical terminology of *shruti* which is very different from the terminology of present day music. After having obtained the *shuddha* notes the scholars of the ancient and middle periods experimented with the number of displaced or *vikrit* notes and their positions.

Sharngadeva evolved as many as twelve *vikrit* notes from the gamut apart from the seven *shuddha* notes obtained by the same method as of Bharata. According to him even *Shadja (Sā)* and *Pancham (Pa)* could be displaced from their original *shruti* which is confirmed as *achala swara* or steady note in today's music.

His predecessor Bharata mentioned only two *vikrit swaras*, viz., *Antar Gandhar* and *Kakli Nishad*, which were displaced by two *shrutis* of *Madhyam* and *Shadja* respectively.

It has already been discussed that Bharata's method of adjusting the *veena* of *Madhyam grama* was to lower down

Pancham of *Shadja grama* by one *shruti*. The note thus obtained
by lowering down the *Pancham* of *Shadja grama* could be regarded
as a *vikrit* note in the *Shadja grama* which Bharata failed to
recognise.

As the centuries advanced scholars experimented with the
number of *vikrit* notes and their nomenclature. A particular
vikrit note was placed on a particular *shruti* and its number was
indicated. Later, Lochan of 15th century mentioned in his book
Raga Tarangini as many as eleven *vikrit* notes fixing them on the
following *shrutis*:

Vikrit Swaras		Shruti Number	Shruti Names
Teevratara	*re*	8	*Raudri*
Teevra	*ga*	10	*Vajrika*
Teevratara	*ga*	11	*Prasarini*
Teevratama	*ga*	12	*Priti*
Teevra	*ma*	14	*Kshiti*
Teevratara	*ma*	15	*Raktika*
Teevratama	*ma*	16	*Sandipani*
Teevra	*dha*	21	*Ugra*
Teevra	*ni*	1	*Teevra*
Teevratara	*ni*	2	*Kumudvati*
Teevratama	*ni*	3	*Manda*

Pundarik Vitthal also mentioned about 10 *vikrit* notes, the names
and position of which differ from those of Lochan's:

Vikrit Swaras		Shruti Number
Kaishik	*ni*	1
Kakali	*ni*	2
Laghu	*sā*	3
Teevra	*re*	8
Sadharan	*ga*	10
Antar	*ga*	11
Laghu	*ma*	12
Panchashruti	*ma*	14
Laghu	*pa*	16
Teevra	*dha*	21

In this way Bhavabhatta also mentioned seven *vikrit* notes and their positions. It is obvious that in the absence of any other method of fixing a note on the gamut the notes were mentioned with the help of the technical terminology of the *shruti*.

Ahobal of the mid-Seventeenth century has mentioned eight *vikrit* notes in his *Sangeet Parijat*:

Vikrit Notes		Shruti Number
Purva	*ra*	5
Komal	*re*	6
Purva	*ga*	7
Komal	*ga*	8
Purva	*dha*	18
Komal	*dha*	19
Purva	*ni*	20
Komal	*ni*	21

Since Ahobal was the first to invent the method of placing the notes by measuring the length of the wire in *veena* he did not depend for this purpose on the technical terminology of the *shruti*, but expressed it in terms of measurement.

The number of *vikrit* notes as mentioned above had connection with practical demonstration of the respective periods.

Coming down further to the 18th century we come across a very important book called *Raga Tattva Vibodha* written by Shrinivas. The number of *vikrit* notes shrank to five only in his time. He also placed his notes, both *vikrit* and *shuddha*, by measuring the length of the wire of the *veena* following the method of Ahobal.

All the above-mentioned facts Bhatkhande collected from the *granthas* after having studied them thoroughly.

He discussed the *swaras* and *shrutisthanas* with quotations from the *granthas* in *Hindustani Sangeet Paddhati* (Part II, pp.23-118) and established the following conclusions based on sound and rational analysis:

1. The authors of the ancient times divided the gamut into 22 divisions and placed the *swaras* on them.
2. It was unanimously agreed by the authors of both the ancient and the middle period that the *shrutis* were the smallest unit

of audible musical sound and they were twenty-two in number in a gamut. Out of these *shrutis* seven *shuddha swaras* were obtained by distributing them in the following manner:

Swara	Sā	Re	Ga	Ma	Pa	Dha	Ni
Shruti	4	3	2	4	4	3	2

3. The *swaras* were placed on the last *shruti*.
4. It was a well-established fact that *shrutis* always had musical quality and any one of them could be used as a musical note.
5. In practical music 12 or 14 *shrutis* were used only as *swaras*.
6. This was also apparent that the same *shrutis* which were discarded in a particular *raga* as irrelevant were used as *swaras* in another *raga*.
7. The scholars of different ages had different conceptions of the interval in between two *shrutis* or their positions on the gamut. Every writer tried to explain the relationship of *shrutis* and *swaras* according to their own imagination and capacity. Therefore, it was but natural that there would be differences of opinion among them.
8. The scholars of the ancient period never indicated on which particular point on a particular length of wire the first and the subsequent *shrutis* would be established. Even in Sharngadeva's *Sangeet Ratnakar* where twenty-two strings were attached to a *shruti veena*, tuned to the sound of 22 *shrutis*, he failed to indicate the length of the wires.
9. Bhatkhande quoted from *Sangeet Ratnakar* about the *shruti veena* (*Hindustani Sangeet Paddhati*, 2nd part, p.44), where the *shruti* interval was described *as manak uchcha dhvani*, which means 'slight higher sound', as an unspecified gap which had the scope of varying from individual to individual.
10. It was also not established that the gap between the *shrutis* was uniform.
11. The gap between the *shrutis*, which were imaginary, also varied from time to time with the scholars belonging to the middle age and the ancient times. For example, the scholars of the ancient times -- Bharata etc. -- took the gap between

the *shrutis* as uniform while the scholars of the middle period -- Ahobal etc. -- took the gap of *shrutis* as irregular:

उत्तरोत्तरसंकोचस्त्वाकाशे भवति ध्रुवम् ।
समभागप्रकल्पोऽत्र न साधु मन्यते बुधैः । ।
तस्माद्भागास्तु विषमाः कल्पिता भरतादिभिः ।

(This Bharata, mentioned above in the third line of the Sanskrit text, does not seem to be the author of the *Natyashastra*. This *shloka* was written by Bhavabhatta in his book *Anupa Sangeet Vilas*).

12. The method of fixing the *vikrit* notes of the gamut was also expressed with the help of the technical terminology of *shruti* only.

13. The scholars of different centuries experimented with the number of *vikrit* notes and their nomenclature. Their position in regard to *shruti* varied from time to time.

14. As the measurement and position of the *shrutis* remained vague, consequently the position of the *vikrit swaras* as well as the *shuddha swaras* also remained uncertain. Bhatkhande, while taking into account the *swaras* of Ramamatya, Somnath and Pundarik, also made a chart of their *swaras* on the *shrutis* for comparative study. He also discussed the *swaras* of other scholars prior to Lochan and Ahobal.

15. It appeared that they were unanimous about the position of the following *swaras*:
     1.   *Shuddha*   *Sā*
     2.   *Shuddha*   *Ma*
     3.   *Shuddha*   *Pa*

16. The importance of *shrutis* and *swara* relationship was minimised from the time of Ahobal as the method of obtaining the *swaras* by measuring the length of the string of the *veena* came into vogue. As a result the *swaras* could be more specifically placed on the gamut.

In view of the above findings, Bhatkhande's idea was that it was not possible to ascertain the exact type of music which was prevalent in the ancient period. The reason was that it was not possible to pinpoint the *shrutis* and *swaras* on the gamut. For nowhere was it mentioned that at which point the first *shruti* should be established on a particular length of wire. Therefore, as the *swaras* were dependent on the *shrutis*, in the absence of correct and accurate measurement of the *shrutis*, the position of the *swaras* could not be ascertained. The type of music prevalent in those days, therefore, was invariably difficult to understand whether it was in the form of *jati*, *grama* or *moorchhana*. However, Bhatkhande never ruled out the possibility of more research and finding of more facts. In fact with years of research and analysis Bhatkhande found that there was no evidence of the ancient *swaras* and the form of *ragas* of that period. The modern *swaras* could not be the *swaras* of the ancients and it was obvious that the *ragas* which were created by those *swaras* could not be the same as mentioned in the *granthas*. If a modern *raga* had a name identical with that of the *raga* mentioned in the *granthas*, similarity was in the name only. The changed form of *swaras* was responsible for the modern texture and form of the prevalent *ragas*. Therefore, it would not be correct to claim the modern *ragas* as the continuous form of the ancient *ragas*. In fact, music is a practical subject which depends on the sense of hearing applicable both to the performer and the listener. But while describing this practical subject in writing there should have been some efficient method by which its main structure could be easily understood by future generations. The writings of the ancient scholars sadly lacked in this method. Bhatkhande studied hard but failed to gather the relevant material in regard to the position of *swaras* as sung or played in that period.

The ancient theory of Music as propounded by the ancient scholars could be understood only if it could be explained with practical demonstration. Even with his most strenuous efforts Bhatkhande could not come across anybody who could throw light on the practical music of that period. In the absence of any sound recording or notation system, the practical art of the ancients had completely disappeared. It was difficult to ascertain the actual music of Swami Haridas and Mian Tansen who belonged to the 16th century, not to mention the practical music of Bharata of A.D 2nd century or Sharngadeva of the 13th century.

Bhatkhande rightly claimed that so far nobody could exactly locate the *shuddha thaat* of Bharata and his successors including Sharngadeva. In *Hindustani Sangeet Paddhati* (2nd part, p.24),

Bhatkhande condemned the attitude of the so-called 'Pandits' for giving the reference of the ancient books without having understood them. Some of them were not even conversant with the Sanskrit language. In fact mere mention of these *granthas* was done with the purpose of creating a feeling of awe and reverence among the pupils and the laymen. Therefore, he did not think it worth-while to debate on the *swaras* of *Shadja grama* as propounded by Bharata. He felt that this sort of discussion would not benefit anybody though it could have some historical importance.

However, these ancient *granthas* were useful from the historical point of view and Bhatkhande encouraged the music students to study them thoroughly. He also felt that there was great scope for more research and analysis.

When Bhatkhande wrote the second part of the *Hindustani Sangeet Paddhati* it appears that the musicologists and scholars of that time were discussing and publishing several articles about the *shruti*s and *swara*s of the ancients giving vent to their own ideas and explanation. Bhatkhande refuted all the current practice of explaining the *shruti*s and *swara*s of the ancients on the ground that they were based on presumption and assumption. His idea was that the modern writers, while attempting to decipher the theory of the ancients, should first translate and explain the *shloka*s of the relevant portion and then only they should put forth their argument for accepting or rejecting it.

As some writers of that period endeavoured to compare the *Shruti* theory with the Western system of music, he strongly rejected the theory of explaining 4 *shruti*, 3 *shruti* and 2 *shruti* interval in the light of the Western theory of Major tone, Minor tone and Semitone.

The debate on the *Shruti* theory of the ancients even now continues. There is hardly any seminar or group discussion on music where one or two papers are not invariably read by the scholars on *Shruti*. But the theory remains as baffling as ever. No scholar, so far, could establish an absolute theory which could be accepted by all. Bhatkhande, after studying all the ancient *granthas*, rightly arrived at the conclusion that the present day music had outgrown the old system greatly and new books with new approach were necessary to be written. Therefore while propounding his theory Bhatkhande rightly left out the controversial matter and focussed his attention on the current practice of music.

2. Lakshya Sangeet   (The Current Practice of Music)

After *Raga Tattva Vibodha* there was no worth-while book written on the theory of contemporary music. But music changed inevitably in theory and practice as the years advanced. At the time of Shrinivas North India was full of turmoil because of the factional fight and war between the small states till the British assumed power. Due to their non-patronising and discouraging policy and the consequent general set-back in all spheres of life, music fell into the hands of the illiterate musicians and became devoid of a rational systematic theory which could be studied, analysed and digested by an intelligent, educated and curious student of music. Bhatkhande realised that it was necessary to write the theory of the present day music in modern language instead of looking back and trying to decipher the abstruse theory of the ancients. He has expressed his ideas about this in *Hindustani Sangeet Paddhati* (2nd part, p.10):

"We shall consider it (the music of the ancients) a separate type of music having a different theory. This technique of Classical music was not prevalent in our country at all. Now music is evolved and practised only with both *shuddha* and *vikrit* notes derived from one gamut only. We cannot vouchsafe that if we could revive some of the *raga*s as prevalent in the time of Sharngadeva, we would have accepted his theory of music instead of the present day's music. At present our musicians are completely ignorant about the *jati, moorchhana, grama* etc."

He further adds:-- "Our music changed its form slowly due to various reasons but even now it retains enough facts which can help us to connect it with the music mentioned in the ancient *granthas*. It is understandable that as music changed inevitably due to different circumstances, the writer of the subsequent ages also had to add new facts and figures according to the available material. This is not a surprising fact. With the progress of centuries when the writers could no longer master Sanskrit for writing they started writing in the language in vogue as a natural rule. When the *Deshi* language also became illegible, music fell into the hands of the illiterates and even now it remains in that state. The practical musicians of today have cultured and polished their voice in a whimsical manner and have taken the taste of the public astray with their vocal power. This distorted taste has found its grip strong in holding the society."

Bhatkhande, therefore, decided to present the rules and *shastra* of the Classical music prevalent at his time in a simple and systematic way so that the listeners and the learners both could be benefited from it. The task was not easy. There was a gap of hundred years between him and Shrinivas, and music changed considerably in its natural evolutionary process. The contemporary musicians could not show any light in this regard and failed to link up the present music with the old. Therefore he had to start work from scratch.

His main source of theory was based on the practical demonstration of the musicians of his time of which he had plenty of material in hand in the form of note patterns, compositions and even phonographic records. Although he decided not to spend time and energy in trying to link up current music with the old, yet, wherever possible, he accepted the old system for the purpose of systematising music of his time. In that way he suffered no prejudice either to discard or accept the old theories, partially or fully.

His Swaradhyaya

His first step in this regard was to establish the exact position of the present day *swaras* on the gamut. He accepted the old theory of *shrutis* -- their names (*Manda Chhandovati* etc.), their number (22) in a gamut and their division among the *swaras*:

चतुश्चतुश्चतुश्चैव षड्जमध्यमपंचमाः ।
द्वेद्वे निषादगांधारौ त्रिस्त्री ऋषभधैवतौ ।।

Like the ancient and mediaeval authors he accepted the *shrutis* as microtones, each one placed at a very small but cognisable interval from the other. Twelve out of these -- namely, *shrutis* with nos. 1,3,5,6,8,10,12,14,16,18,19,21 -- are known as *swaras*. They were selected for forming the *ragas*.

In regard to their gaps from one another, both in ascension and descension, he differed from the mediaeval scholars and accepted the ancient scholars' theory that *shrutis* maintained uniform gaps between each other. Unlike the mediaeval and ancient scholars Bhatkhande formulated a very important theory by shifting the place of notes on the *shrutis*. He placed the notes on the first *shruti* as against the earlier practice of placing them on the last *shruti*. According to Bhatkhande the position of the seven notes on the 22 *shrutis* are as follows:

SWARA	*su*	*re*	*ga*	*ma*	*pa*	*dha*	*ni*
SHRUTI	1	5	8	10	14	18	21

The *swaras* thus obtained coincide with the notes belonging to *Bilawal Saptak* of today.

Bilawal Scale

In North India for the purpose of teaching Classical music, the notes of *Bilawal Saptak* are taught in the beginning as the *shuddha swaras*. The *swaras* which are used in *Bilawal Saptak,* either lowered or raised in pitch, are named as *komal* or *teevra* respectively. In fact, *komal* or *teevra* gives indication of the position of a note -- either higher or lower than its original position. *Shadja* and *Pancham* are two steady notes having no distortion or displacement. *Rishabh, Gandhar, Madhyam, Dhaivat* and *Nishad* are accepted as having two forms -- one high and one low. In *Bilawal Saptak,* except *Madhyam,* the other notes are higher than their distorted (*komal*) form. Therefore, they are called either *shuddha* -- Re, Ga, Dha, Ni or *teevra.* In this *saptak Madhyam* is lower than its distorted (*teevra Ma*) form. So it is called *komal* or *shuddha Madhyam. Bilawal* scale was an old scale and was known to all writers of music but it was never recognised as the *shuddha* scale by any of the old Sanskrit writers. It is an established fact that the *shuddha* scale of Bharata and Sharngadeva was not *Bilawal.*

One can be more categorical about the *swaras* of the middle period, viz., Lochan, Hridayanarayan Dev, Ahobal and Shrinivas as they had indicated the places of the *swaras* on the *veena* by measuring the length of the wire. Taking into account the *swaras* by Hridayanarayan Dev, in his book *Hridaya Kautuk,* the *shuddha* scale mentioned by him coincided with our modern *kafi* scale having both *Ga* and *Ni komal.* Later, the *kafi* scale was replaced by *Bilawal* as *shuddha.* This practice has been in vogue for the last two hundred and fifty years. Even in the sixteenth century

Mian Tansen, Swami Haridas and Baiju Bawara composed *dhrupad*s in *Bilawal* as *shuddha* scale. These are available even today. Coming down to the British period, Bhatkhande mentioned *Naghmate Asafi* (A.D. 1813) by Mohammed Reza of Patna which established the *Bilawal* scale as *shuddha* scale clearly.

Maharaja Pratap Singh of Jaipur (1779-1804) wrote *Sangeetsar*. His *shuddha* scale was *Bilawal*. The next important book of the nineteenth century was *Sangeet Ragakalpadruma* by Krishnanand Vyas. His *shuddha* scale was also *Bilawal*.

Bhatkhande had written a scholarly article in *Sangeet Traimasik*, a journal of music published from Lucknow, establishing the above-mentioned facts with proper data. It was Bhatkhande who explained, in terms of *shruti*, the *Bilawal* scale which was regarded as *shuddha* for a number of centuries by merely shifting the *swaras* from the last *shruti* to the first. *Bilawal* scale, therefore, did not have to transgress the universal theory of distributing the *shruti*s on the gamut in the following manner:

चतुश्चतुश्चतुश्चैव षड्जमध्यमपंचमाः ।

It is one of his most important contributions to establish in a rational manner that the *Bilawal thaat* is the *shuddha thaat* and the notes it employed are the *shuddha swara*s. Therefore, it is regarded as the foundation scale of modern Hindustani music.

Not being satisfied by placing the notes of modern music *shruti*wise, Bhatkhande endeavoured to place them by measuring the string of the *veena*. In that process he followed the method of Shrinivas and his measurement. Of course, he compared them also with the notes demonstrated by the musicians of his time. As a result, nomenclature of *Ga* and *Ni* and their position changed from *komal* to *shuddha* in *shuddha* scale. The measurement of the wire and the place of the notes on it, according to Bhatkhande, is as follows:

Sa		-	Full length of the wire sounding between the two bridges.
Re	(Shuddha)	-	8/9
Ga	(Shuddha)	-	4/5 approximately.
Ma	(Shuddha)	-	3/4

Pa	-	2/3
Dha (Shuddha)	-	16/27
Ni (Shuddha)	-	8/15 approximately.
Sā (Tara Saptak)	-	1/2

Bhatkhande accepted the number of *swaras* as twelve, evolved from one gamut only as the practice of *jati* and *moorchhana* had long become obsolete.

He recognised three octaves or registers, namely, *mandra* or lower, *madhya* or normal and *tara* or higher.

Out of the 12 notes of the gamut, seven were recognised as *shuddha* and five *vikrit*. The *swaras* were respectively *Shadja, Komal Rishabh, Shuddha Rishabh, Komal Gandhar, Shuddha Gandhar, Shuddha Madhyam, Teevra Madhyam, Pancham, Komal Dhaivat, Shuddha Dhaivat, Komal Nishad* and *Shuddha Nishad*. So *Shadja* and *Pancham* had no changed form while the rest of the 5 notes had one *vikrit* form each. These *swaras* were written and pronounced in practice in the abbreviated forms, namely, *Sā, Re, Ga, Ma, Pa, Dha, Ni* respectively while their *vikrit* forms mentioned with the names of *Komal* and *Teevra* added to them. It has already been mentioned that *Raga Tattva Vibodha* was a very important book written by Shrinivas in the 19th century where both *vikrit* and *shuddha* notes were placed by measuring the length of the wire of the *veena* following the method of Ahobal.

Bhatkhande accepted the position of the seven *shuddha* notes on the string of the *veena* as mentioned by Shrinivas but differed from him in the placing of some of the *vikrit* notes:

SWARASTHANA OF SHRINIVAS		SWARASTHANA OF BHATKHANDE	
Names of Swaras	**Lengthwise**	**Names of Swaras**	**Lengthwise**
Shadja Shuddha	36 inches	*Shadja*	36 inches
Rishabh Komal	33-1/3 inches	*Rishabh Komal*	34 inches
Rishabh Shuddha	32 inches	*Rishabh Teevra*	32 inches
Gandhar Shuddha	30 inches	*Gandhar Teevra*	28-2/3 inches
Gandhar Teevra	28-2/3 inches	*Gandhar Teevra*	28-2/3 inches

Madhyam Shuddha	27 inches	*Madhyam Komal*	27 inches
Teevratara Madhyam	25-1/9 inches	*Madhyam Teevra*	25-1/2 inches
Pancham Shuddha	24 inches	*Pancham*	24 inches
Dhaivat Komal	22-2/9 inches	*Dhaivat Komal*	22-2/3 inches
Dhaivat Shuddha	21-1/3 inches	*Dhaivat Teevra*	21-1/3 inches
Nishad Shuddha	20 inches	*Nishad Komal*	20 inches
Nishad Teevra	19-1/9 inches	*Nishad Teevra*	19-1/9 inches
Shadja Shuddha (Tara)	18 inches	*Tara Shadja*	18 inches

It is apparent from the chart that Bhatkhande differed from Shrinivas in placing the following notes -- *komal Re, komal Dha* and *teevra Ma*. According to Shrinivas the measurement of *komal Re* on the string on *veena* should be as follows:

भागत्रयोदिते मध्ये मेरोर्ऋषभसंज्ञितात्।
भागद्वयोत्तरं मेरोः कुर्यात् कोमलरिस्वरम्।।

The distance from *Meru* to *teevra* (*shuddha*) *Re* should be divided into three parts. *Komal Re* should be placed after leaving 2 parts from *Meru*. As against this Bhatkhande wrote in his *Abhinava Raga Manjari*:

मध्ये षड्जर्षभकयोः संस्थितः कोमलर्षभः ।
षड्जपंचम भावेन तत्संवादी घ कोमलः ।।

Exactly in the middle of *Sā* and *teevra Re, komal Re* is placed. Therefore, if the length of *Sā* on the wire is 36 inches and *teevra Re* is 32 inches, *komal Re* would be 34 inches. The *komal Re* of Shrinivas is established at 33-1/3 inches.

About *komal Dhaivat* Bhatkhande mentioned in the second line of the above-mentioned couplet that after ascertaining the position of *komal Re*, place *komal Dha* on the basis of *Shadja Pancham Bhava*. About the placing of *komal Dhaivat* on the wire Shrinivas wrote:

भागत्रयान्विते मध्ये पंचमोत्तरषड्जयो : ।
कोमलो धैवतः स्थाप्यः पूर्वभागे विवेकिभिः ।।

The word *vivekibhih* undoubtedly referred to *Shadja Pancham Bhava*. The theory of *Shadja Pancham Bhava* needs further elucidation. For quite some time the relation and distance between *Sā* and *Pa* were the basis for establishing notes both in the *Purvanga* and *Uttaranga*. If *Sā* is taken as placed at 36 inches on the wire, *Pa* would be placed at 24 inches only. The mathematical calculations would be one and a half times. Therefore, if the length of *Sā* is divided by 1-1/2 times then the length of *Pa* is obtained. The scholars were of the opinion that the distance and relation between *Sā* and *Pa* should be maintained in *Ga* and *Ni*, *Re* and *Dha*, both in their *teevra* and *komal* forms. This relationship which is the "Cycle of the Fifth" is mentioned as *Shadja Pancham Bhava* by the scholars. Again:

षड्जपंचम भावेन षड्जे ज्ञेयाः स्वरा बुधैः ।

Again:

स्वरज्ञानविहीनेभ्यो मार्गोऽयं दर्शितो मया ।
स्वरसंवादिता ज्ञानं स्वरस्थापनकारणम् ॥

This is undoubtedly the relation of the fifth, that is the Cycle of the Fifth.

Again Shrinivas says:

सपयो रिधयोश्चैव तथैव गनिषादयोः ।
संवादः संमतो लोके मसयोः स्वरयोर्मिथः ॥

This means that the gap between *Sā* and *Pa* should also be observed between *Re* and *Dha*, *Ga* and *Ni*, -- both in their *shuddha* and *vikrit* forms. In other words, *Dha* should be the *Pancham* of *Re*, similarly *Ni* should be the *Pancham* of *Ga*. Therefore, when *komal Re* was placed it was obvious that according to the *Shadja Pancham Bhava* the length of *komal Dha* should be ascertained by dividing the length of *Re* with 1-1/2 times. So, when Shrinivas placed his *komal Re* at 33-1/2 inches in a 36 inches long wire, his *komal Dha* would come to 22-2/9 inches according to *Shadja Pancham Bhava*. As against this when Bhatkhande placed his *komal Re* at 34 inches his *komal Dha* had to be placed at 22-2/3 inches. It has already been stated that Bhatkhande placed *Madhyam Teevra* at 25-1/2 inches as against 25-1/9 inches position by Srinivas.

The Reason of Deviation

Bhatkhande's deviation from the notes of Shrinivas was based on the practical demonstration by the eminent musicians of his time. He also discussed these controversial points with scholars and artists who were invited from time to time to perform at the *Mandali* and the music conferences arranged by him. One such illustration can be quoted about Ustad Zakiruddin Khan demonstrating the exact position of *Shuddha Rishabh* in the first All India Music Conference held at Baroda in the year 1916. This incident has been narrated by Pandit Ratanjankar in his book *Pandit Bhatkhande* on page 32. He writes:

"Papers on different topics of music were read by scholars of music that came to the Conference from all over India including South India. Mr. K. B. Deval and Mr. E. Clements, ICS, read their papers the main gist of which was that the Major Tone, Minor Tone and Semitone were the same respectively as the four *shruti*, three *shruti* and two *shruti* intervals of the ancient musicologists and accordingly the *Shuddha Rishabh* and *Shuddha Dhaivat*, which were at three *shruti* intervals from *Sā* and *Pa* respectively according to the ancients, were Minor Tones and, therefore, the *Shuddha Rishabh* should be considered to be at a degree lower by one *shruti*, i.e., 10/9 (Minor Tones) than that of *Sā*. Similarly, *Shuddha Dhaivat* too should not be the 9/8 of *Pancham* but at a degree lower by one *shruti*. This proposition was vehemently opposed by many musicologists including the learned Subram Panditar. It was tested also by a practical demonstration by Mr. E. Clements on his *Shruti* Harmonium on the one hand and, on the other, by reproduction of the correct pitch of *Shuddha Rishabh* of Hindustani music by no less a person than Ustad Zakiruddin Khan of Udaipur. Ultimately, Messrs. Clements' and Dewal's theory was not accepted."

Having thus ascertained the position of the *swaras* in modern music Bhatkhande noted them down in terms of vibrations after the modern European music as follows:

Sā	-	240 per second
Komal Re	-	254-2/17
(Shuddha) Teevra Re	-	270
Komal Ga	-	288
(Shuddha) Teevra Ga	-	301-17/43
(Shuddha) Komal Ma	-	320
Teevra Ma	-	338-14/17
Pa	-	360
Komal Dha	-	381-3/17
(Shuddha) Teevra Dha	-	405
Komal Ni	-	432
(Shuddha) Teevra Ni	-	452-4/43
Sā	-	480

After these *swara*s were established in terms of vibrations, it was apparent that some of them differed from the notes universally accepted by European musicians. The differences were in regard to the following *swara*s: *komal Re, teevra Ga, teevra Ma, komal Dha, teevra Dha* and *teevra Ni.* In European music, their vibrations are 256, 300, 337-1/2, 384, 400 and 450 respectively against those of the Indian notes noted above. In Hindustani music the vibrations of the above-mentioned *swara*s are: 254-2/17, 301-17/43, 338-14/17, 381-3/17, 405, 452-4/43.

It is a fact that some *raga*s demand *komal teevra swara*s either higher or lower by one shade than their original position for their successful delineation. For example, the *komal Ga* of *raga Darbari* should be one shade lower than its prescribed form. Similarly, *komal Re* of *raga Marwa* should be a shade higher than its original form. Bhatkhande termed *ati komal* and *teevratara swara*s as ornamental notes and did not indicate their usage in *raga*s either in terms of *shruti,* the length of the wire, or in terms of vibrations.

His idea was that the ornamental notes remained flexible in the process of the delineation of a particular *raga* and could be mastered by the hearing capacity of an artist. In fact for adhering to the rules of a *raga* the *varjya swara* and the *vadi swara* have the maximum importance. It would remain pure as long as it observed the rule of its ascension and descension with the prescribed notes of *komal* and *shuddha* on the gamut. If it is argued that *komal Re* used in a particular *raga* should be *ati komal* it would have no dispute with the main form of the *raga.*

The Rules and Definition of Ragas

Every musicologist has recorded and described music prevalent in his time only. Music being an art created by man can have no fixed and eternal rules and guidelines. The form of music is everchanging, as the human society itself, keeping pace with its habits, customs, fashions and behaviour.

We gather from history that practical music prevalent at the time of Bharata was changed to *Raga Gayan* even at the time of Matanga barely a few centuries after. It kept on changing its form. Sharngadeva of the 13th century mentioned the earlier practised and later obsolete music as *Marga*. Even the notes (*swaras*) kept on changing. At the time of Bharata there were only two *vikrit swaras* in use, while at the time of Sharngadeva their number increased up to twelve. Bharata never accepted *Shadja* to be displaced from its original position, while Sharngadeva's work records that both *Shadja* and *Pancham* could be displaced to a lower position.

After Sharngadeva music went through further changes. *Grama, moorchhana, jati* etc. became obsolete. *Shadja* and *Pancham* became steady and undisplaceable on the gamut. In natural course, the scholars wrote new theories and framed new rules to fall in line with the current practice of music.

Bhatkhande noticed from the writings of the middle age authors, viz., Lochan, Ahobal, Hridayanarayan Dev, Pundarik and Shrinivas that the *ragas* prevalent in their time changed a good deal. In fact, in the writings of the middle age authors, the present day *ragas* were described in a different way. This change could be considered as normal as our customs and culture showed a great deal of change within the last three hundred years. It is, however, necessary to mention, while taking into consideration the evolutionary process of music, that the changes which took place during the centuries are only on the surface. Within its traditional framework music goes on absorbing new modes from the environment and its interaction with the different forces in society. In fact, music has its root deeply embedded in its ancient theory. This is a special character of our music and this particular feature has established an unbroken link between the past and the present. Therefore, one can rightly describe that music has been transformed into its present form through a continuous evolutionary process.

We have already mentioned that within hundred years prior to Bhatkhande no worth-while book was written about the theory of music. Therefore, to fill up the vaccum, Bhatkhande took up on himself this great and painstaking task. The main ideal which goaded him to take up this work was that rational and systematic theory should be established as the backbone of practice. With this idea, he formulated the theory of the current *raga*s as he learned, listened to and analysed them.

To accomplish the task he was guided by the following principles:

"Every writer should describe the *raga*s as explained to him by his own *guru* and his family musicians. Then he should also take into account the different versions of the other schools of music and discuss them with great care. Then he should mention in easy and legible language what had been mentioned in the old *granthas* about these *raga*s. Only then the reader and the learner would have a clear idea about the present and the past form of a *raga*. I have tried this method in my book *Hindustani Sangeet Paddhati*.

"Firstly, I have mentioned the *granthas* belonging to the North and the South, then I have mentioned how those *granthas* have described the *raga*s which are in vogue.

"After that, I have noted down all the details of the *raga*s in the light of *guru parampara* tradition of the present day. I have given the note patterns of those *raga*s and have also mentioned the Sanskrit *shlokas* based on them. I have also assembled many legends and anecdotes connected with these *raga*s as I heard them from the mouth of so many musicians. I cannot say whether the reader will accept my version of this book in toto but it is my duty to let the reader know how hard I had to work to collect the facts to write my books."[5] (Translation mine.)

After having fixed the position of the *shuddha* and *vikrit swaras* on the gamut, Bhatkhande, after much study and scrutiny, set the present day rules of the *raga*s derived from the demonstration of the current musicians. He realised the fact that music was a practical subject where demonstration was the basis of its shape and form. He defined the word *raga* and also laid down the following rules for the formation of a *raga*:

1. A *raga* should evolve from a *thaat*.
2. A *raga* consists of a particular combination of notes.
3. A *raga* also consists of *swara* and *varna*.
4. A *raga* should have pleasing quality.

5. A *raga* should employ minimum five notes both in ascension and descension.

6. A *raga* should have notes in order of ascension and descension -- *aroha* and *avaroha*, otherwise its variety cannot be ascertained.

7. In all *ragas Shadja* or *Sā* is never discarded.

8. A *raga* consists of *vadi* and *samvadi swaras*. These two factors are very important for the formation of a *raga*.

9. *Ragas* have their timings for singing.

10. While defining a *raga* Bhatkhande discussed the definition of the earlier scholars and emphasised the pleasing quality or *ranjakatva* of a *raga* above all others.

11. A *raga* cannot be formed by using less than five notes and having more than seven notes.

12. *Ragas* can be classified broadly under three categories (*Jatis*):
    (a) *Auduva* -- comprising of 5 *swaras*
    (b) *Shadava* -- comprising of 6 *swaras*
    (c) *Sampurna* -- comprising of 7 *swaras*
    Applying these combinations, without taking into account the fact whether a note is *shuddha* or *komal,* out of 7 notes 9 varities can be evolved.

13. In addition to all these rules Bhatkhande identified the catch notes of each *raga* which established its characteristic note movement denoting its identity. In the introductory chapter of each *raga* in the *Kramik Pustak Malika* series he has included these catch notes making it easy to intellectually grasp the minute differences between hundreds of *ragas*. For example:

Kamod	--	Catch notes: *re, pa, ma pa, dha pa, ga ma pa, ga ma re sa*
Kedar	--	Catch notes: *sa ma, ma pa, dha pa ma, pa ma, re sa*
Desh	--	Catch notes: *re, ma pa, ni dha pa, pa dha pa ma, ga re ga sa*
Tilak-Kamod	--	Catch notes: *pa ni sa re ga, sa, re pa ma ga, sa ni*
Bhairava	--	Catch notes: *sa, ga, ma, pa, dha, pa*
Kalingra	--	Catch notes: *dha pa, ga ma ga, ni, sa re ga, ma*

With the formation of these rules Bhatkhande defined a *raga* in clear rational terms. He made successful and conscious effort to break away from all mystic pseudo-religious definitions of a *raga* and brought back in its definition a scientific pattern in line with modern methodology. In this he deviated also from the middle age definition of a *raga:*

रंजयन्ति मनांसीति रागास्ते दशलक्षणाः ।
लक्षणानि दशोक्तानि लक्ष्यन्ते तावदादितः ॥

The ten *lakshanas* of the middle age scholars, viz., *graha, ansha, nyasa, apanyasa, bahutva, alpatva*, etc. became obsolete. So it was necessary to draw up a new definition of a *Raga.*[6]

Classification of Ragas

He minutely studied and analysed all the contemporary *ragas* and found that at most 125 or 150 *ragas* were demonstrated in actual practice. These *ragas* he broadly classified into three groups according to the *shuddha* and *komal swaras* they employed. These groups are as follows:

1. The *ragas* which employ *Re, Dha* and *Ga teevra.*
2. The *ragas* which employ *komal Re* and *Ga Ni teevra.*
3. The *ragas* which employ *Ga* and *Ni komal.*

He observed that there are some *ragas* which stood as exceptions to the above categorisation, but they were not so pronounced that they could be placed in a separate category.

The above-mentioned classification was the base for his further classifying them according to *Janya Janak Mela* and the time of their singing. It was his unique contribution in theory that he classified the *ragas* in vogue, in the following manner, keeping in view the group of *shuddha* and *komal* notes they used:

(A) Under the ten parental scales or *thaats* (*Janak Mela*).
(B) According to the *komal* and *teevra* notes they employed.
(C) According to the time of singing in relation to:
    (C-i) The introduction of *teevra Madhyam;*
    (C-ii) The vadi swara -- the governing or the expressive note of …

(D)   According to the *purvanga* (lower tetrachord) and *uttaranga* (higher tetrachord).

(E)   According to the *ragangas*, such as *Kanhara anga*.

(F)   According to *Rasa* or the Aesthetic Mood.

All these points are given herebelow a detailed description respectively:

(A) Thaats

The classification of *raga*s was in vogue in the ancient music. We find that in ancient *grantha*s six *raga*s were classified as males having their counterpart *ragini*s as their wives. They were further classified under their family names as sons and daughters. In later years the scholars developed a scientific approach and classified the *raga*s under *thaat*s which were called as parental scales or *Janak Mela*. In fact, within the 17th century, the classification of *raga*s under the figurehead of *thaat*s came into vogue as it was apparent from the books of the middle period, viz., *Sangeet Parijat* by Ahobal and *Raga Tattva Vibodha* by Shrinivas. While defining *Mela* Shrinivas said that *raga*s evolve from *thaat*s and *thaat*s could be of three types: *Auduva, Shadava* and *Sampurna*. Although the scholars were in common agreement in the matter of having a group of notes called *thaat*s for evolving *raga*s, they differed in regard to their number. As for example we can quote the number of *thaat*s mentioned in *Raga Vibodha* as 23, in *Swaramelakalanidhi* as 20, and in *Chaturdandi Prakashika* as 19.

The South Indian scholar Venkatamakhi took the help of mathematics and accurately calculated the maximum number of *thaat*s as 72, which could possibly be produced from one gamut[7]. But for practical purposes he selected 19 *thaat*s only. The number of *thaat*s as formulated by Venkatamakhi was accepted by the Southern musicologists but it did not influence the North Indian scholars. While they accepted Venkatamakhi's theory as absolute and foolproof, they realised that so many *thaat*s would only confuse the system of classification of *raga*s under them. Therefore, the North Indian scholars accepted only 32 *thaat*s of Venkatamakhi's 72. For, according to the rule of a *thaat*, no note should be discarded in ascension. This was possible only in 32 *thaat*s according to the concept of

North Indian music.

As for practical purposes Venkatamakhi took 19 *thaats* in use. Bhatkhande accepted 10 *thaats* as the parent scales for the classification of the *ragas* in vogue, thereby ending all experimentation of the middle age authors with their numbers. Bhatkhande also defined clearly the qualities of a *thaat*:

1. Although *thaats* evolve from 12 notes of a gamut but one *thaat* consists of 7 notes only.
2. The 7 notes should be in natural order in ascension.
3. It is not necessary to have both ascending and descending notes (*aroha* and *avaroha*) in a *thaat*. In fact, the notes are only in ascending order.
4. A *thaat* can take the two forms of a note -- *komal* and *teevra* -- side by side.
5. It is not necessary for a *thaat* to have the pleasing quality.
6. For the purpose of identifying a particular *thaat* it is named after an important *raga* which comes under its banner.

These definitions show clearly the difference between a *raga* and its parent scale called *thaat*. These clear cut points help a learner to grasp and conceive the subject matter in an easy and rational manner.

The 10 *thaats* are:-- *Kalyan, Bilawal, Khamaj, Bhairava, Purvi, Marwa, Kafi, Bhairavi, Asavari* and *Todi*.

(B) Komal and Teevra Notes they Employed

After having divided the gamut into 10 parental scales Bhatkhande further subdivided them into 3 classes:--

1. *Thaats* which could produce *ragas* having *Re Dha Ga shuddha: Kalyan, Bilawal* and *Khamaj*.
2. *Thaats* which produce *ragas* with *komal Re* and *shuddha Ga Ni: Bhairava, Purvi* and *Marwa*.
3. *Thaats* which produce *ragas* with *komal Ga* and *Ni: Kafi, Bhairavi, Asavari* and *Todi*.

As *Todi thaat* consists of *komal Ga* and in some varieties of *Todi* also employs *komal Ga* and *komal Ni*, Bhatkhande put it in the third category.

The following is the chart of the 10 *thaat ragas* along with their *shuddha* and *komal* notes:

1. *Bilawal thaat*   --   sa re ga ma pa dha ni
2. *Kalyan* or *Yaman thaat* --   sa re ga ma pa dha ni
3. *Khamaj thaat*   --   sa re ga ma pa dha ni
4. *Bhairava thaat*   --   sa re ga ma pa dha ni
5. *Purvi thaat*   --   sa re ga ma pa dha ni
6. *Marwa thaat*   --   sa re ga ma pa dha ni
7. *Kafi thaat*   --   sa re ga ma pa dha ni
8. *Asavari thaat*   --   sa re ga ma pa dha ni
9. *Bhairavi thaat*   --   sa re ga ma pa dha ni
10. *Todi thaat*   --   sa re ga ma pa dha ni

Ragas were produced out of these *thaats* by

(i)   treating the *thaat* itself in its full content as a *raga*, and
(ii) dropping one or two notes except *Sā* from the scale either in the *aroha* or in the *avaroha* or in both, thus producing *Sampurna*, *Shadava* or *Auduva* varieties of *ragas*.

It will be seen from the above facts that in our music system the *thaats* are named after the principal *ragas* evolved from them and those principal *ragas* are called *Ashraya Ragas*.

Some of the modern scholars have criticised Bhatkhande's method of distributing the current *ragas* under the ten parental scales (*Janya Janak Mela*) as arbitrary and impractical. Among others, we can mention Rabi Ray, the former Dean of the Faculty of Music, Delhi University, who, in his book *Raga Nirnaya* mentioned *raga Bhupali*, *Deshkar* and *Vibhas* as examples of the above-mentioned statement. According to Ray *raga Bhupali*, which has no *Madhyam* or *Nishad* could not rationally be fitted into the *Kalyan thaat*. Similarly *Vibhas* which does not use *Madhyam* and *Nishad* cannot be fitted into *Bhairava thaat*. Similarly, *Deshkar*'s classification under *Bilawal thaat* is another instance of this arbitrary distribution. As against this we can quote Bhatkhande from *Hindustani Sangeet Paddhati*, part 4, page 701. Initially in the first part of *Hindustani Sangeet Paddhati* he analysed and discussed the *ragas* belonging to *Kalyan thaat*. They were as follows:-- *Yaman, Bhupali, Shuddhakalyan, Jaitkalyan, Chandrakant, Malashri, Hindol, Hamir, Kedar, Chhayanat, Kamod, Shyamkalyan* and *Gaudsarang*.

Yamani Bilawal, although having two *Madhyams*, showed more of *Bilawal anga* and is sung in the morning. Therefore it was classified under the *Bilawal thaat*.

He further classified in groups the above-mentioned 13 *ragas* of

Kalyan thaat as follows:

1st Group	2nd Group	3rd Group
1. *Bhupali*	1. *Yaman*	1. *Hamir*
2. *Shuddhakalyan*	2.. *Malashri*	2. *Kedar*
3. *Chandrakant*	3. *Hindol*	3. *Chhayanat*
4. *Jaitkalyan*		4. *Kamod*
		5. *Shyamkalyan*
		6. *Gaudsarang*

The *ragas* belonging to the first group totally discard the note *Madhyam* and if it is taken at all, it is taken in descension only. The *ragas* belonging to the second group take only *teevra Madhyam* while the *ragas* belonging to the third group take two *Madhyams*, viz., *shuddha* or *komal* and *teevra*. Further, *ragas* belonging to the third group take *shuddha Madhyam*, both in ascension and descension, and use *teevra Madhyam* less than the other. Therefore, one argument could be that they should have been assigned to the *Bilawal mela*. But the reason for classifying them under *Kalyan mela* was that their movement and the note combination in *purvanga* and *uttaranga* showed the pattern of *Kalyan mela* rather than *Bilawal mela*. The writer of *Anupankush*, Bhavabhatta of 18th century, assigned *Bhupali*, *Shuddhakalyan* etc. under *Kalyan mela* only. Bhatkhande said that he found that the present day musicians accepted these *ragas* as belonging to *Kalyan mela* and their assigned time of singing as the first part of the night. In support of his argument he quoted from *Abhinava Raga Manjari* written by him.

This argument also could be given about *Deshkar* and *Vibhas*. Considering the movement of notes (*angas*) and the place of *vadi swara* which is at the *uttaranga* the singing time is assigned to the morning and these *ragas* are rightly attributed to the *Bilawal* and the *Bhairava thaat* respectively. Bhatkhande was aware of such criticism which was apparent from his writing. He says in his *Hindustani Sangeet Paddhati* (4th part, page 700) as follows: "I have distributed the current 150/125 *ragas* among ten *melas* according to their form and notes. If somebody asks why only ten *melas*? Then I would answer with all humility that I found it suitable to classify the existing *ragas* under ten *melas* only. If somebody insists on having more,

I have no objection. How many *melas* should be taken depends upon the author's convenience who formulates the theory." (Translation mine).

(C) Time Theory

Time theory or the practice of assigning times of the day or night for singing different *ragas* is one of the most distinguishing features of our music. There is evidence that our scholars and musicians adhered to this principle scrupulously right from the ancient period. Although no scientific explanation is possible for such division of *ragas* according to the scheduled singing time, Bhatkhande's analysis of the time and note relationship established the influence and impact of a particular note at a particular hour of the day and night. He also discovered a system in the use of *vadi swaras, teevra Madhyam* and *purvanga-uttaranga* *ragas* in relationship to time.

Bhatkhande has brought out this subtle relationship of notes and time by bringing out a systematic division of the time schedule of *ragas*. Firstly, he took 200 *ragas* which were generally practised and categorised them into broad melody types, namely,

1. *Bilawal* or *shuddha swara mela*,
2. *Bhairava mela*, and
3. *Kafi mela*.

In other words he divided the *ragas* under three broad groups:

1. *Ragas* which carry both *Re* and *Dha teevra* with *Ni teevra* or *Komal*
2. *Ragas* carrying *Re komal* and *Dha komal* or *teevra*.
3. *Ragas* carrying both *Ga* and *Ni komal* whatever the *Re* and *Dha* may be.

He further subdivided them by introducing *teevra Madhyam* in each of the three groups. Thus the revised groups were:

1. In case of *Bilawal*   --   (a) *Kalyan* and (b) *Khamaj*
2. In case of *Bhairava*   --   (a) *Purvi* and   (b) *Marwa*
3. In case of *Kafi*   --   (a) *Bhairavi* and (b) *Asavari*

All these, along with *Todi thaat*, which is a mixed variety, completed the 'Ten *thaats*' of the modern Hindustani music as stated earlier.

It was Bhatkhande's observation that the *ragas* (about 40 in number as practised today), coming under the fold of *Bhairava*, *Purvi* and *Marwa melas* (whose main feature is *komal Re*), were sung either in the early morning or evening and were categorised as *Sandhi Prakash ragas*, which literally means the junction of day and night. In his Sanskrit book *Lakshya Sangeet*, Chapter II, *Shloka*s 46-48, he mentioned and described the names of the *ragas* belonging to the *Bhairava mela.* Except for one *raga* named as *Gauri* belonging to the above-mentioned *mela*, all other *ragas* were assigned to sunrise and described as *Sandhi Prakash ragas*. Then again in *Lakshya Sangeet* (Chapter II, p. 53-57) he mentioned the names of the *ragas* belonging to *Purvi* and *Marwa melas*. These also came under the category of *Sandhi Prakash* -- either sung at sunrise or sunset, the period of which is taken as between 4 a.m. to 7 a.m. and 4 p.m. to 7 p.m. The deduction from their common feature was that such *ragas* employ *Re komal, Ga teevra* and either *teevra Dha* or *komal Dha*. Bhatkhande more categorically fixed the distinguishing note formation of *Sandhi Prakash ragas* as *ni, sā, re, ga*. In *Lakshya Sangeet* (Chapter II), after *Sandhi Prakash ragas* he discussed the *ragas* belonging to *Kalyan*, *Bilawal* and *Khamaj melas*, in which *teevra Re, teevra Dha* and *teevra Ga* were used. He next discussed *ragas* taking both *Ga* and *Ni komal* which fell under the *melas* of *Kafi, Asavari, Bhairavi* and *Todi*.

This principle applies both for the day and night. In other words, at sunrise when the morning *Sandhi Prakash ragas* are sung, the day *ragas* begin at 10 a.m. and go on up to 4 p.m., keeping the method of employing *komal* and *teevra* notes as mentioned above. The same process is followed after the evening *Sandhi Prakash ragas*, when the night *ragas* begin and which extend up to 4 a.m. when again the morning *Sandhi Prakash ragas* begin.

To be more precise, the whole cycle of twenty-four hours divided itself into two series -- morning and evening. Each series began with *Sandhi Prakash ragas*, with *Re komal*, to be followed by *ragas* with each *Re, Dha* and *Ga teevra*, and later by *ragas* with both *Ga* and *Ni komal*. Of course, there were some exceptions to this rule. Bhatkhande has elaborated the above-mentioned facts in *Hindustani Sangeet Paddhati*, part 4, pages 22 and 23.

(C-I)   Teevra Madhyam as the Time Indicator

Now Bhatkhande took up *teevra Madhyam swara* as indicative of
the time of singing. The presence of *teevra Madhyam* was usually
noted in the *raga*s sung at night. In fact, the evening *Sandhi Prakash*
*raga*s employ the *teevra Madhyam* while the morning counterparts
take mostly *shuddha Madhyam*. *Teevra Madhyam* was also used
abundantly in the *raga*s sung at night till the morning *Sandhi Prakash*
*raga*s begin. But as a general rule it did not appear in the *raga*s
having both *Ga* and *Ni komal*. However, Bhatkhande observed
that *raga*s taking *teevra Ma* and sung during the day were *Hindol,*
Todi, Gaudsarang and Multani. But there was difference of opinion
among the scholars about their singing time.   In this system
Madhyam is regarded as an important note as from its usage the
singing time of day and night is ascertained.

Bhatkhande also observed and noted that *teevra Madhyam* is
sometimes skillfully used in *raga*s like *Bihag, Shankara, Jhinjhoti*
and *Khamaj* without offending the musical susceptibilities of the
listener. The reason being that this note is indicative of night time
and when used sparingly and skillfully it is admissible as an
acceptable note in the four *raga*s assigned to the night. The note,
therefore, in Sanskrit *grantha*s is very expressively mentioned as
Adhvadarshak note. As an example we can quote that *Purvi raga*
changes into *Bhairava raga* with mere change of *teevra Madhyam*
to *shuddha.* Similarly, *Kalyan* can be converted into *Bilawal* type
by the mere substitution of *shuddha Ma* for *teevra Ma.*

Now Bhatkhande made a very interesting observation by putting
the entire time theory *vis-a-vis* the usage of *shuddha* and *komal*
notes by putting the entire group of *raga*s in two sets -- one on
either side of an imaginary line drawn from sunset to sunrise
dividing the whole day of 24 hours into the well-known two parts
of night and day. Each of these contains three groups of *raga*s
employing following characteristic notes:

(a)   *ni sa re ga.*

(b)   *ni sa re ga.*

(c)   *ni sa re ga.*

These three groups on either side of the dividing line may be
roughly described as the counterparts or reflexes of one another,
separated by an interval of twelve hours. The note *Madhyam* and
the *anga* which contains the *vadi* notes would be the unmistakable

sign of a *raga* falling under *purvanga* or *uttaranga* group. Thus the twelve different varieties of *Bilawal* are practically the counterparts of the *ragas* assigned to the night--each being mixture of the allied *ragas* with the definite *avaroha* or descension notes of *Bilawal*. For example:

		Night Raga		**Morning Raga**
Yamani Bilawal	is	*Yaman*	+	*Bilawal*
Sarparda	is	*Jhinjhoti*	+	*Bilawal*
Kukubh	is	*Jaijaiwanti*	+	*Bilawal*
Alhaiya Bilawal	is	*Hamir*	+	*Bilawal*
Devgiri	is	*Shuddhakalyan*	+	*Bilawal*
Chhaya Bilawal	is	*Chhayanat*	+	*Bilawal*

Similarly *Jait Bilawal, Madhav Bilawal* etc. It is noteworthy that the *Bilawals* are differentiated from their evening counterparts by the absence of *teevra Madhyam* and by the prominence given to the *uttaranga*.

In *Lakshya Sangeet*, Chapter II, Bhatkhande described another important feature under this system -- the presence of certain *ragas* in each *thaat* or *mela* called *Paramela Praveshak Raga*, indicative of the time at which transition from *ragas* of one *mela* to the following one takes place. Thus *Multani* is a *Paramela Praveshak Raga* for entering into *Purvi mela* (sung at sunset) from *Kafi*, having *teevra Madhyam* in use, and *Jaijaiwanti* ushers in the *ragas* belonging to the *Kanhara* group (sung at midnight) from the *Khamaj mela* and employs *komal Gandhar*.

In regard to the importance of *Madhyam* in our *raga* system he observes the following particulars or changing character of a *raga* by virtue of taking *teevra* or *shuddha Madhyam* or discarding it totally. Bhatkhande classified the *ragas* belonging to *Kalyan* group quoting such instance as follows:

1. *Ragas* containing no *Madhyam* or taking it only in the *avaroha* -- namely, *Bhupali, Shuddhakalyan, Jait* and *Chandrakant*.

2. *Ragas* taking only *teevra Madhyam* -- *Yaman, Hindol* and *Malashri*.

3. *Ragas* containing both *teevra* and *komal Madhyam* -- for example, *Hamir, Kedar, Chhayanat, Kamod, Shyamkalyan*.

Their singing time is the Ist part of the night and the *vadi swara* is placed in *purvanga*.

(C-II, and D) Position of Vadi Swara as the Time Indicator and Purvanga and Uttaranga

After classifying the *ragas* and their time schedule according to the *shuddha* and *komal swara* and *teevra Madhyam* as used therein Bhatkhande analysed their singing time accordiing to their *vadi* notes.

It will not be wrong to say that the most distinguishing feature of our music is the significance of the *vadi* note. It is considered as the life of a *raga* and hence is regarded as its most important feature. It was observed and analysed by Bhatkhande that in our music the place of the *vadi* note on the gamut is connected with the assigned time of its singing. The *ragas* which are sung between noon and midnight are called in common parlance as *purvanga* -- the *swaras* extending up to *sā re ga ma pa*. The *ragas* which are sung between midnight and noon have their *vadi* note placed in *uttaranga* indicating the notes *sā ni dha pa ma*.

It is obvious from the above statement that both *purvanga* and *uttaranga* have *Ma* and *Pa* as common notes. And hence the *ragas* having *Ma Pa* as *vadi* notes fall under both the *purvanga* and the *uttaranga ragas*.

If one changes the *vadi swara* from *uttaranga* to *purvanga*, one can change the time of singing from morning to evening. As for example, *Bhupali* and *Deshkar*. While both of them employ the same notes in ascension and descension, by virtue of the different placing of the *vadi swara* (*Ga* in case of *Bhupali* and *Dha* in case of *Deshkar*) their singing time differs from one another.

The *ragas* sung from midday to midnight have their *vadi swara* in *purvanga* (lower tetrachord) and are known as *Purva Ragas*, while those sung from midnight to midday have the *vadi swara* in the *uttaranga* (upper tetrachord) and are known as *Uttar Ragas*. In *Hindustani Sangeet Paddhati* (Ist part, page 20) Bhatkhande discussed *vadi*, *vivadi*, *samvadi* and *anuvadi swaras* emphasising and explaining their importance in a *raga*. The importance of a *vadi swara* is as follows:

1. *Vadi swara* is the main *swara* of a *raga* and is considered like a king. It is also called as *'Jiva'* *swara*, meaning the life-giving note.
2. Mere change of *vadi swara* can change a *raga* and also the singing time.
3. *Vadi swara* denotes a *raga*.
4. *Vadi swara* is uttered more than the others.
5. The pleasing quality of a *raga* depends on the *vadi swara*.

The form of *Purva Raga*, having the *vadi swara* in *purvanga* shows its characteristic in ascension, and the form of *Uttar Raga* shows its characteristic form in descension.

The *ragas* which are sung after midday or midnight usually emphasise the *swaras* Sā Ma Pa -- *Barwa, Bhimpalasi, Malkauns* etc. From every *thaat Purva* and *Uttar Ragas* can be evolved.

In every *raga* a *vadi swara* exists and there is a gap of 3/4 *swaras* between *vadi* and *samvadi*. Their place varies from *uttaranga* to *purvanga*.

He further discovered a system in the note combinations and note movements of different groups of *ragas* sung at different times of the day and night. This may be stated as follows:

1. The typical note combination indicative of the *Sandhi Prakash ragas* is *Ni Sa Re Ga*.
2. The morning *Sandhi Prakash ragas* mostly do not discard *Re* and *Dha*. Similarly the evening *Sandhi Prakash ragas* mostly do not discard *Ga* and *Ni*.
3. Usually *ragas* having *shuddha Re, Ga, Dha, Ni* are sung after both morning and evening *Sandhi Prakash ragas*.
4. *Ragas* employing *komal Ga Ni* are mostly sung either at midday or midnight.
5. The notes *Sa Ma* and *Pa* have special significance in the *ragas* sung during the third part of the day and the night.
6. After the evening *Sandhi Prakash ragas teevra Madhyam* is mostly used in the late night *ragas* unlike their day counter-parts.
7. *Ragas* have a special appeal sung at their assigned time but this rule is not applicable on the stage or in the court of the King.
8. *Ragas* assigned to the first part of the night, taking two *Madhyams (shuddha* and *teevra)* observe a general rule that *shuddha Madhyam* is used both in ascension and descen-

sion but *teevra Madhyam* is taken only in descension and used less than its *shuddha* counterpart (for example: *Bihag, Kedar, Chhayanat* etc.).

9. *Ragas* assigned to the first part of the night and taking two *Madhyams* observe the rule of using *Nishad* in a roundabout (*vakra*) way in ascension and using *Gandhar* in a roundabout way in descension. In these types of *ragas Nishad* appears as a weak note (*durbal*) in descension. For example: *Kedar, Kamod, Chhayanat, Hamir* etc.

10. *Sa Ma Pa* are an integral part of both *purvanga* and *uttaranga*. *Ragas* employing any one of the above-mentioned notes as *vadi swara* can be sung at any time of the day and night.

11. *Ragas* sung after 12 noon or 12 midnight gradually emphasise the *swaras Sa Ma Pa.* For example: *Barwa, Bhimpalasi, Malkauns* etc.

12. The morning *ragas* employ *komal Re* and counterpart *ragas* employ more of *teevra Ga* and *teevra Ni.*

13. The *ragas* which are sung exactly at midday show emphasis on *Re* and *Ni.* For example, all varieties of *Sarang.*

14. In every *raga* the *Sa* of *Madhya Saptak* is sung for a long time but not so with the *Sa* of *Tara Saptak.* If the *Sā* of *Tara Saptak* is sung more than its counterpart then the air of evening *ragas* takes place.

15. When *Dha* and *Pa* are emphasised it gives the impression of morning *raga*, but when *Re* and *Ga* are made pronounced it gives the impression of the evening.

16. If *Dha-Pa* or *komal Dha-Pa* are pronounced for a long time then the atmosphere of morning is created.

(E) Classification According to the Ragangas

The writers of the Middle age noted down the different varieties of *ragas* and classified them separately. For example, we can quote from *Anupa Sangeet Ratnakar,* written by Bhavabhatta, the names of the *ragas* belonging to the *Kanhara* variety: (1) *Shuddha Karnat* (2) *Nayaki* (3) *Bageshri* (4) *Adana* (5) *Sahana* (6) *Mudrik* (7) *Gara* (8) *Huseini* (9) *Kafi Kanhara* (10) *Sorati Kanhara* (11) *Khambavati Kanhara* etc. -- in all fourteen in number.

Bhavabhatta also grouped together eight varieties of *Gauri,* sixteen varieties of *Bilawal,* ten types of *Gaud,* twelve types of

Varati, thirteen types of *Kalyan* and seven types of *Puriya* in his famous work.

The present day *raga*s changed considerably since his time but there was enough scope for fresh classification. Bhatkhande identified a group of notes used characteristically in some types of *raga*s and named that common feature as *anga*.

According to the *anga* or particular character -- indicative note combination -- of *raga Kafi*, Bhatkhande classified the *raga*s evolved from the *Janak Mela* of *Kafi* into five groups:

(i)   Ragas having Kafi Anga
Kafi, *Sindhura* and *Pilu* etc.

(ii)   Ragas having Kanhara Anga
Bahar, *Bageshri*, *Suha*, *Sughrai*, *Nayaki*, *Sahana*, *Kaushi* etc.

(iii)   Ragas having Malhar Anga
Mian Ki Malhar, *Nat Malhar*, *Surdasi Malhar*, *Shuddha Malhar*, *Dhoolia Malhar*, *Ramdasi Malhar* etc.

(iv)   Ragas having Sarang Anga
Shuddha Sarang, *Madhmad*, *Vrindavani*, *Barahansa Sarang*, *Samanta Sarang*, *Mian Ki Sarang*, *Lankadahan Sarang*, *Patamanjari* etc.

(v)   Ragas having Dhanashri Anga
Dhanashri, *Dhani*, *Bhimpalasi*, *Hanskinkini*, *Pradipaki* etc.

These *Angas* are explained below as follows:

(i) Kafi Anga

Kafi is an important *raga* the notes of which are tallied with the *shuddha* scale of the middle age authors. In *Kafi mela Kafi* is the first *raga* which is regarded as *ashraya raga*. The indicative notes are *sa re re, ga ga, ma ma pa*.

The second *raga* nearest to it is *Sindhura*. Bhatkhande has done a scholarly discussion about its antiquity, origin and modern form in *Hindustani Sangeet Paddhati*, 4th part, page 62. Another important *raga* having *Kafi anga* is *raga Pilu*.

(ii) Kanhara Anga

Kanhara or Karnatak *ragas* are fairly old and were mentioned in
the books written by Hridayanarayan Dev, Lochan and Pundarik.
Bhatkhande mentioned in *Lakshya Sangeet* about the differences
of opinion about their number. In *Hindustani Sangeet Paddhati*,
4th part, pages 164 to 166, he discussed in detail this controversy.
However, he accepted that eighteen varieties of *Kanhara* were then
current, out of which he established eight as original. The rest
were combined *ragas*, meaning certain *ragas* on which the *Kanhara*
anga had been imposed and which were therefore included in the
Kanhara group. The names of the present *Kanhara* group of *ragas*
are: *Bageshri Kanhara, Nayaki Kanhara, Suha Kanhara, Kaushi
Kanhara, Sughrai Kanhara, Sahona Kanhara, Darbari Kanhara,
Adana Kanhara* etc. He fixed up the *Kanhara anga* or the typical
phrase of notes as *ga ma re sa, ni dha ni pa* and *ni pa ga ma*.
Except for one or two, the singing time of all the *Kanharas* is
midnight.

(iii) Malhar Anga

Bhatkhande mentioned (1) *Shuddha Malhar* (2) *Mian Ki Malhar*
(3) *Gaud Malhar* (4) *Nat Malhar* (5) *Surdasi Malhar* (6) *Dhoolia
Malhar* (7) *Ramdasi Malhar* (8) *Mirabai Ki Malhar* (9) *Charjoo Ki
Malhar* (10) *Jaijaiwanti Malhar* (11) *Rupamanjari Malhar* etc. and
classified them together having the common feature of notes, viz.,
ma re pa and *ma pa dha sa, dha pa ma*. Their singing time is
always at the rainy season or midnight. Bhatkhande's scholarly
discussion about them referring to their origin covered pages 328
to 407 of *Hindustani Sangeet Paddhati*, 4th part.

(iv) Sarang Anga

He fixed the common *anga* of *Sarang* group of *ragas* --
(1) *Vrindavani* (2) *Shuddha* (3) *Gaud* (4) *Lankadahan*
(5) *Barahansa* (6) *Mian Ki Sarang* (7) *Madhmad* (8) *Samanta* as
ni sa re ma re pa re. He has discussed this *raga* variety elaborately
quoting from his own books -- *Lakshya Sangeet, Abhinava Raga
Manjari* and *Hindustani Sangeet Paddhati*, 4th part, pages 243 to
327. The singing time is invariably the midday.

(v) Dhanashri Anga

The *ragas* having *Dhanashri anga* are *Dhani, Bhimpalasi, Hanskin-kini* and *Pradipaki*. *Dhanashri anga* he fixed as *pa pa ga, pa ga re sā, ni sā ga ma pa* either with *komal* or *teevra swara*.

He classified the varieties of *Bilawal* and identified the other *ragas* mixed with *Bilawal* creating different varieties. This we have discussed on page 149. The particular *Bilawal anga* he fixed as *ga pa dha, ma ga re ga* in *sthayi* and *ga pa ni dha ni sā* in *antara*.

Apart from these broad classifications he identified and isolated *Shri anga, Lalit anga, Gaud anga* etc. He fixed the note combination as *sa re re sa* for *Shri Anga* which is present in *Gauri, Malavi, Triveni* and *Tanki*. He fixed the *Lalit anga* as *ga ma ma ma ga* and identified this phrase in other *Samaprakritik Ragas*. Similarly he fixed the *Gaud anga* as *re ga re ma ga*.

Additional Rules of Ragas

The other rules which Bhatkhande observed and systematised about the movement and note formation of *ragas* are as follows:

(1) In any *raga Ma* and *Pa* together are never discarded as *varjit swaras*.

(2) *Sa* is never discarded in any *raga*.

(3) *Teevra Ma* is rarely connected with *komal Ni* in a *raga*.

(4) The *ragas* which take two *Madhyams* have some common features. The distinctive feature is noticeable in ascension. The *antara* parts often show the similarity. As for example: *Kedar, Kamod, Chhayanat* and *Hamir*. The *antara* in all these *ragas* is *pa pa su, re sa, sa dha ni pa* or *sā ni dha pa*.

(5) The *ragas* which freely use *komal Ni* -- for example, *ragas* belonging to *Kafi* and *Khamaj thaats* -- mostly use *teevra Ni* in ascension.

(6) In a *raga* two forms of a note, viz., *komal* and *teevra*, should not come one after the other. *Lalit* etc., however, are exceptions.

(7) In the Hindustani system of music *raga* is more important than *tala*. In the South Indian system it is just the reverse.

(F) Classification According to Rasa Expressed by the Notes

The purpose of music is to create an aesthetic mood which is termed in Sanskrit as *rasa*. In literature nine types of *rasas* -- viz., *Shringar, Hasya, Adbhut* etc. -- are accepted. Our ancient scholars referred to the following notes responsible for rousing the following *rasas* in the human mind:

Sa and *Re*	-	create *Veer, Raudra* and *Adbhut rasas.*
Dha	-	creates *Bibhatsa* and *Bhayanak rasas.*
Ga and *Ni*	-	create *Karuna rasa.*
Ma and *Pa*	-	create *Hasya* and *Shringar rasas.*

Although the ancient scholars attribute a particular *rasa* to a particular note, in actual practice it cannot be practicable for single notes to create the entire gamut of moods -- namely, *Karuna, Veer, Hasya* etc. For example, we can say that the ancient scholars have described *Sā* as indicative of *Veer rasa* and *Pancham* as indicative of *Shringar rasa.* As almost all our modern *ragas* have the usage of *Sā* and *Pa* one cannot say that all of them create *Veer* and *Shringar rasas.* In fact, a single *raga* by virtue of its note formation and *vadi* note can create different *rasas.*

Bhatkhande, keeping in view the ancient theory of *Rasa*, has accepted for music only four types of *rasas* -- viz., *Shringar, Veer, Karuna* and *Shanta* -- as the most important of all nine varieties of *rasas.*

Bhatkhande classified the existing *ragas* according to the *shuddha* and *komal swaras* they used and consequently the particular *rasas* or moods they were able to create. This may be stated as follows:

1. *Sandhi Prakash ragas* having *Re Dha komal* -- *Shanta* and *Karuna rasas.*
2. *Ragas* having *Re Dha teevra* -- *Shringar rasa.*
3. *Ragas* having *Ga Ni komal* -- *Veer rasa.*

As stated earlier this rule cannot be rigidly followed. This can be taken as a general rule only as the impact of other notes combining with these characteristic notes has always the possibility of leading to a deviation.

Bhatkhande in his *Hindustani Sangeet Paddhati* has stated that this theme has great scope for further research by future generations. For it will not be an easy proposition to establish the *rasa* and note relationship categorically.

South Indian Music

Bhatkhande was the first North Indian scholar to recognise South Indian music and throw light on its theory. The Sanskrit couplet in the beginning of *Shrimallakshya Sangeetam* mentioned two systems existing in our country, viz., Karnatak and Hindustani. Then in the same book, as he proceeded, he mentioned about the South Indian *Shuddha mela* as *Kanakangi*.

In fact, it was he who for the first time made it known to the public in the North that there were two distinct systems, the Karnatak and the Hindustani, and that the nomenclatures of the *shuddha* and *vikrit swaras* of these systems were different from one another. Even in South India itself these facts were little known and it was only after Bhatkhande's publication that the attention of the people in the South was drawn to them. It has been already mentioned that Bhatkhande edited the following books on South Indian theory and considered them valuable:

1. *Swaramelakalanidhi* by Ramamatya
2. *Chaturdandi Prakashika* by Venkatamakhi, and
3. *Raga Lakshana*

The Madras Music Academy, which has now taken up the editing and publishing of some of the old texts, was founded in 1927, at least 12 years after Bhatkhande published the texts determining the two systems. The late Shri M.S. Ramaswami Aiyer of Madura edited and published *Swaramelakalanidhi* by Ramamatya in 1932, i.e., about twenty years after the publication of the text by Bhatkhande.

It would not be wrong to surmise that in ancient India, only one system of music existed. As North India was subjected to repeated foreign invasions music changed invariably as a result of the fusion of cultures. After the Muslims occupied the country the rift between the North and South Indian music was complete. But it changed its form only on the surface and in the process of delineation whih the fundamentals remained the same. It was Bhatkhande's contribution to bring together the fundamentals, quoting them as counterparts.

He began with comparing the notes of South Indian and North Indian music. The theory of the 22 *shrutis* on the gamut and their division among the notes as *Chatushchatushchatushchaiva shadja-madhyama* etc. were the same but the placing of the notes on the gamut was different and also their nomenclatures.

In *Hindustani Sangeet Paddhati*, Ist part, page 31, he discussed the *swaras* of the South Indian music and compared them with those of the North Indian music:

North Indian Swaras   **South Indian Swaras**

1. *Sa*   *Sa*
2. *Komal Re*   *Shuddha Re*
3. *Shuddha Re*   *Panchashruti Re* or *Shuddha Ga*
4. *Komal Ga*   *Shatashruti Re* or *Sadharan Ga*
5. *Shuddha Ga*   *Antar Ga*
6. *Shuddha Ma*   *Shuddha Ma*
7. *Teevra Ma*   *Prati Ma*
8. *Pa*   *Pa*
9. *Komal Dha*   *Shuddha Dha*
10. *Shuddha Dha*   *Panchashruti Dha* or *Shuddha Ni*
11. *Komal Ni*   *Shatashruti Dha* or *Kaishik Ni*
12. *Shuddha Ni*   *Kakali Ni*

The nomenclatures differ slightly in the South Indian books *Raga Lakshana* and *Chaturdandi Prakashika*.

It is apparent from the above chart that except *Sa*, *shuddha Ma* and *Pa* the rest of the notes differ from their Hindustani counterparts of *shuddha* and *komal* form. It is noteworthy that unlike North Indian music, in South Indian music the lower form of a note is called *shuddha* and the higher form as *vikrit*.

After having compared the South Indian and the North Indian notes he endeavoured to compare the *shuddha* scale of both the systems. He found that the Southern music *granthas* had quite a different *shuddha* scale. This appeared from the recognised treatises on music of that part of the country, viz., *Swaramelakalanidhi*, *Raga Vibodha*, *Chaturdandi Prakashika*, *Sangeetsaramrit* and *Raga Lakshana*. The *shuddha* scale of these *granthas* was neither *Kafi* nor *Bilawal*. It was entirely a different scale. That scale had remained *shuddha* while with us *Kafi* of the old period had been changed to *Bilawal*.

Let us now turn to the *shuddha* scale of Southern music. Southerners tuned their *veena* just the same way as the Northerners did -- vide *Raga Vibodha* and *Swaramelakalanidhi*. These were the

Sanskrit *granthas* which adopted this new innovation of corrected form of *Panchashruti* and *Chatushruti Re* and *Ga* etc. The old scale was called *Mukhari*. The reformed one was called *Kanakangi*. In the *Kanakangi* scale the *shuddha Re* is of 2 *shruti* and the next note *shuddha Ga* is *Chatushruti Re*. The Sanskrit *grantha* adopting this new innovation was *Raga Lakshana*. The crux of the innovation is to fall in line with the ancient rule *Chatushchatushchatush-chaiva shadja* etc. It is noteworthy that a beginner in the North Indian music begins with the *Bilawal* scale while the Southerner begins with the *Maya Malva* scale which is the counterpart of our *Bhairava*.

In the third part of *Hindustani Sangeet Paddhati* Bhatkhande praised Venkatamakhi's scholarship and adopted his method of forming 10 *Janak Melas* of Hindustani music. He mentioned the South Indian counterparts of the 10 *thaats* adopted by him in *Lakshan Geets* composed by him. The counterparts are as follows:

Hindustani 10 Thaats	**South Indian Melas**
1. *Kalyan*	*Mechakalyani*
2. *Bilawal*	*Dhirashankarabharan*
3. *Khamaj*	*Harikambhoji*
4. *Bhairava*	*Mayamalavgoul*
5. *Purvi*	*Kamavardhini*
6. *Marwa*	*Gamanpriya*
7. *Kafi*	*Kharaharapriya*
8. *Asavari*	*Natbhairavi*
9. *Bhairavi*	*Hanumattori*
10. *Todi*	*Shuvapantubarali*

Apart from the *thaat raga* while discussing other *ragas* he mentioned also their counterparts in South Indian music with their points of deviation wherever possible.

Bhatkhande discovered that:

(i)   In Hindustani music system the *raga* is given more importance than the *tala* while in Karnatak music *tala* is regarded more important than *raga*.

(ii) The Northern musicians have their own way of using *vivadi* note.

(iii) The graces and flourishes and embellishments of the

Southern music are quite different from those of the Northern music.

(iv)   The *gamak*s are different.

(v)   In Northern music an artistic *raga* mixture is possible while in the South it is not so.

(vi)   The Northern *tala* system basically differs from the Southern.

He mentioned and described the complicated *tala* of the Southern system for the general knowledge of a student. It is interesting to note that there is hardly any book written by him where he did not write a few pages about the South Indian music either for comparison or for information. It shows his deep regard for the South Indian music which he recognised as the sister system.

In his book *A Comparative Study of the Music Systems of the 15th, 16th, 17th and 18th Centuries* (page 112) he said: "By a study of the works relating to the Southern system, we can compose songs for the Northern musicians in the *raga*s which are sung there but have not found a place in the Northern system and thus induce at some date, howsoever distant, a fusion of the two sister systems of music."

It was because of Bhatkhande's endeavours that the North Indian musicians came to know the rich repertoire of the South Indian music. It helped to break the isolation of the musical system of the South and of the North and proved that the basis of our Classical music was the same in our country.

3. Bhavi Sangeet   (Music of the Future Generations)

The theory of modern Hindustani music propounded by Bhatkhande marked the first step in the revival of music. But to put the subject of Music at par with other subjects of learning there were many steps yet to be taken. And in this regard Bhatkhande's thinking was much ahead of his time. As for example we can quote the aims and objects of future work which he read out at the All India Music Conference held at Baroda in 1916. These are:

1.   To take steps to protect and uplift our Indian music on national lines.

2.   To reduce the same to a regular system such as would be easily taught to and learnt by our educated countrymen and women.

3. To provide a fairly workable uniform system of *ragas* and *talas* (with special reference to the Northern system of music).

4. To effect if possible such a happy fusion of the Northern and Southern systems of music as would enrich both.

5. To provide a uniform system of notation for the whole country.

6. To arrange new *raga* productions on scientific and systematic lines.

7. To consider and take further steps towards the improvement of our musical instruments in the light of our knowledge of modern science, all the while taking care to preserve our national identity.

8. To take steps to correct and preserve permanently the great masterpieces of this sublime art now in the possession of our first class artists and others.

9. To collect all available literature (ancient as well as modern) on the subject of Indian Music and if necessary to publish them and render them available to our students of music.

10. To examine and fix the microtones of *shruti*s of Indian music with the help of our scientific instruments and the first class recognised artists of the day and to make an attempt, if possible, to distribute them among the *raga*s.

11. To start an 'Indian Men of Music' series.

12. To conduct a monthly journal of music on up-to-date lines.

13. To raise a permanent fund for carrying on the above-mentioned objectives.

14. To establish a National Academy of Music in a central place where first class instruction in music could be given on most up-to-date lines by eminent scholars and artists in music.

15. Using South Indian and North Indian music in such a way that the two systems reinforce each other and move towards ultimate integration.

16. Publishing and translating in Marathi the good ancient books on the theory of Music.

17. Establishing and ensuring efficient running of the music schools in one's own city by engaging qualified teachers in them.

18. Taking care for keeping alive the traditional art by opening special schools for the sons of the famous artists by engaging

       gharanedar ustads to teach therein.

19.   Keeping and preserving the records of ancient or rare *ragas* in the library and arranging for opportunity to listen to them by students and others.

20.   Ascertaining the points needing correction in *Natya Sangeet* after studying it thoroughly.

21.   Arranging and discussing in a meeting of scholars the *shruti* and *swaras* from the angle of the modern method of music, and the effect of *komal* and *teevratara swaras* in regard to the creation of *rasa*.[8]

These objectives are yet to be fully achieved except that some work in the direction of item nos. 8,9,11 and 14 has commenced.

His dream was that in a few years there would be an easy system of instruction in music which would lead to mass education. Then it could be utilised for the curricula of the universities and music instructions would become common and universal. He felt that once there was a regular system of music, the gates of instruction would be thrown open to all and compulsory musical education would immediately follow almost as a natural consequence and writing textbooks would be accompanied in a trice. The universities would have faculties of Music and thus the work of imparting education in music would spread far and wide. As we see today, this dream of his has been fulfilled. Music has been introduced in many universities and regular curricula have been evolved for imparting instruction. But among the large number of universities existing in our country, very few of them have taken up Music as a subject of study and instruction. Therefore we can say that his dream has yet been only partly fulfilled.

In *Hindustani Sangeet Paddhati*, 4th part, p.341, Bhatkhande prescribes the duty of the future generations of musicians as follows:

"A student must learn the past history of our music. If a student gets an opportunity of going out to a foreign land he should explore what type of music exists there.

We have dearth of good chorus singing. It should be explored and developed.

We do not have songs depicting *Veer rasa* and describing the beauty of God's creation. It could also be attempted. We have mostly songs depicting *Shringar rasa*. I have tried to present to you the music as it was in the past and also as it stands today to the best of my ability. The responsibility for future music, I leave it entirely to you. Now is the time to utilise the *ragas* with strong framework and compose new songs in them. The instrumental music needs lot of correction. Similarly the art form of dance also needs renovation."

His vision was that as there was a happy fusion of Hindu and Muslim art of music in the past, there should be complete fusion of the South and North Indian type of music so that the whole nation would sing with one voice. He welcomed the *ragas* of South India -- viz., *Shankarabharanam, Ahiri, Hansdhvani* -- being adopted in Hindustani music with the attitude that music would change in the evolutionary process. He visualised that contact with European countries would further influence our music with their music. He wrote in *Hindustani Sangeet Paddhati*, 4th part , p.335, as follows: "Within a few years the present form of *raga* will be subjected to gradual change and it is but natural. I welcome this change as artists will add new dimensions with new innovations and imagination. Our scholars and artists are visiting foreign lands and also we are importing hundreds of foreign records of music. It is but natural that European music will somewhat influence ours."

The last words of *Hindustani Sangeet Paddhati*, 4th part, p. 767, are a fervent appeal to the future generation for hard work and understanding:-- "I have something more to say. You are young and energetic. Therefore, it is my hope that you will think about these and avail of fame and name. To become successful in the above-mentioned work, you have to put in a great deal of effort, have to sacrifice your own self a lot and have to tolerate many adverse criticisms as well as good comments. If I am alive, I shall help you with all my might. But everything depends on God."

Scope of Further Research

In this age of science and technology anything irrational is discarded. In the advanced countries of the world, musical theory has been systematised and the position of the notes etc. scientifically established. Our music was also brought to the same scientific level by Bhatkhande's contribution in the field of theory and practice.

By careful study, analysis and recording of the Hindustani Classical music of his time and establishing as many linkages as possible with the ancient tradition Bhatkhande prepared the ground for historians and planners of the future development of music. For as Rafael Sabitini has said: "Where there is no knowledge of the past, there can be no vision of the future."

By evolving a scientific theory of the then current practice of music -- devising a notation system, fixing the *swaras* scientifically on the gamut, classifying the *ragas* under various heads -- Bhatkhande gave to our music a modern, scientific basis and made it a subject of serious study for today and tomorrow. The whole of India is strewn with his musical treatises, which are regarded as the authentic source of theory. Till today his books stand as the major source of reference for the analysis of a *raga*, its old form as well as the allied *ragas*.

Bhatkhande's work spreads over the entire spectrum of music and music education. He has set the ball rolling. Naturally there are many aspects on which further work would be needed by future scholars and educators. There are two aspects of further research:

(a) Those areas which Bhatkhande himself suggested, and

(b) Those that have emerged later in course of time.

As regards (a), Bhatkhande, in his *Hindustani Sangeet Paddhati*, 4th part, pages 766-767, recommended the scope of further research by future generations. His work was mainly connected with the systematisation of current music but as far as the ancient music was concerned there were many aspects which needed further elucidation. These are the following:

1. Comparing the *swaras* of *Samaveda* with those mentioned by the other authors of later centuries.

2. Elucidation of the *ragas* mentioned in the ancient *granthas* like *Sangeet Ratnakar* and trying to demonstrate them on the basis of the material contained therein.

3. Investigating whether it would be useful to adopt for current music the system of classification based on the family system of *ragas*, *raginis* etc. prevalent in ancient times.

4. Trying to re-establish the relationship between the *raga* and the *rasa* from the modern and the ancient view-point.

5. Analysing and establishing scientifically the ancient theory of *shruti* and *swaras* having their effect on the human body and animal world. For that purpose how far and in what proportion are the words of a song useful?

6. Establishing harmonious and logical relationship between the day and night *ragas*.

7. Ascertaining and presenting before society the origin of every *raga* and how it came into vogue in ancient music.

8. Finding out the method of improving the current form of dance after carefully studying its good and bad points.

9. Establishing a relationship between *rasa* and *swaras*. (Bhatkhande in his *Hindustani Sangeet Paddhati* has stated that this has a great scope for further research by the future generation. For, it will not be an easy task to establish the *rasa* and note relationship categorically).

10. To discover a method by which new *ragas* can be evolved on scientific and systematic lines.

11. To provide a uniform system of notation for the whole country.

12. To examine and fix the microtones of *shrutis* of Indian music with the help of scientific instruments and first class recognised artists of the day, and to make an attempt, if possible, to distribute them among the *ragas*.

In addition to the above, there is scope for further work on the writings of Bhatkhande himself. Some sugestions in this regard are offered as below:

1. He has given his views on various aspects of music in a question and answer form in the *Hindustani Sangeet Paddhati* series, covering the entire field of music. For easier understanding and study in depth, it would be useful to classify his ideas under significant heads.

2. The anecdotes based on his experience of meeting the *ustads* and *pandits* of that period can be culled out from the *Hindustani Sangeet Paddhati* and published separately to give comprehensive picture of the haphazard and arbitrary knowledge of the theory of music prevailing at the time.

3. The Sanskrit quotations from the *granthas*, which he mentioned in the *Hindustani Sangeet Paddhati* series to support his statements, can be translated for the students not conversant with that language for the purpose of better understanding.

4. The text of each composition published in *Kramik Pustak Malika* series can be written like a poem, before it is given

in notation form, for better understanding of its language, meaning and poetic beauty.

References

1. *Bhatkhande Smriti Grantha*, pp. 421-'2
2. Ratanjankar, Pandit S.N.: *Pandit Bhatkhande*, p. 54
3. Bhatkhande, Vishnu Narayan: *Hindustani Sangeet Paddhati*, Part II, pp. 23-38
4. *Bhatkhande Smriti Grantha*, op.cit., p.31
5. Bhatkhande, Vishnu Narayan: *Hindustani Sangeet Paddhati*, Part IV, p.6
6. Bhatkhande, Vishnu Narayan: *Shrimallakshya Sangeetam*
7. Venkatamakhi: *Chaturdandi Prakashika*
8. *Bhatkhande Smriti Grantha*, op.cit., pp. 417-'8

7
Training in Music : His Methodology

I

INTRODUCTION

The most significant contribution of Bhatkhande, in the realm of music, was to introduce a modern methodology of training in music. It was remarkably short, condensed, simple, scientific and systematic. Its implementation has proved that men, women, and children of average intelligence can learn and understand the grammar of Classical music within a short period. And only a person well versed in grammar can groom himself as a performer, a musicologist, a teacher and a critic.

Bhatkhande was, therefore, in favour of changing the method of teaching music and of introducing group education to spread its knowledge among the people quickly. Further, he noticed that in the advanced countries of the world musical theory had been systematised and the position of the notes etc. were scientifically established. He wanted to bring the learning and teaching of Hindustani music to the same level.

II

PREVAILING STATE OF MUSIC LEARNING AND TEACHING

The state of music and its training as was prevalent at the time of Bhatkhande has been discussed in Chapter II in detail. It would, however, be useful to sum it up here for the sake of clarity. The following points emerge:

(a)   Music was confined to a few families known as *gharana*s who preferred to rear up their own family members as the future musicians of the country.

(b)   Although they were expert musicians and by their individual styles enriched our Classical music for all time to come, they were extremely reluctant to teach anybody outside their family.

(c)   To extort music lessons, which were inevitably oral, from such musicians meant immense hardship and endless expenditure.

(d)   Even after spending much money and labour the knowledge a student used to get was irrational, unsystematic and incomplete as it largely depended on the whims of the *ustad*.

(e)   There were no books of theory to guide a student in either the theoretical or practical aspect of music.

Bhatkhande expressed these ideas in his paper read at the Music Conference held at first in Delhi and then at Lucknow. In this paper, entitled 'The Modern Hindustani Raga System and the Simplest Method of Studying the Same[1]', he advocated the cause of mass education in music. Till then this was unheard of and the introduction of this idea proved really a turning point in the annals of Hindustani music.

His speech, delivered on the same occasion, was remarkable for its modern outlook and imagination. The gist of his speech is as follows:

'The classical era was in full bloom. Classical art would, however, thrive only on the strong base of classical theory. The method he had evolved would help a learner -- whether a boy of tender age, or a grown up man or a woman of average intelligence. He also appealed to the educated class to accept music as an important subject of study like other important subjects, viz., History, Science, Language and Medicine. Music had a unique role to play to solve the economic and social problems of the country. The society which had interest in music became healthy, contented and happy. He also observed that for the last 15-20 years people had started disliking the *guru shishya parampara* method of teaching. People no longer liked to be announced as the pupil of any famous Khan Sahib. They did not like to surrender entirely and depend upon the whims of the *ustads*, ultimately to gain a haphazard knowledge of one or two *ragas* after wasting many years. These musicians, with incomplete training, when demonstrated their art, either displayed their own ignorance or showed impressionistic knowledge picked up only by listening to others. This type of slipshod and unsystematic teaching was unsuitable for satisfying one having intelligence, energy and curiosity. The old type of teaching was also unsuitable for giving lessons on a large scale. Music lessons should be easily available to all who wanted to learn. It was necessary that the public should be awakened to the need of music education and they should demand with one voice to make it a part of our education by introducing it in every college. It was a well-known fact that in the past music was patronised by the rulers of this country. If today music had to be firmly established in its proper place, it was possible only if the Government of the day took up the cause as a national one. Because through music only we could teach our countrymen tolerance and contentment and make them healthy and happy.'[2]

III

HIS METHOD OF TRAINING

Main Components

With the above-mentioned objective, Bhatkhande evolved a scientific and rationalistic method of teaching music where the rules and regulations of Classical music were clearly indicated and the salient points emphasised. The components of his method were:

(a) a notation system,

(b)   well-defined curricula and graded textbook ,
(c)   theory and practice taught side by side, and
(d)   well-defined easy stages of teaching and periodic, very
         carefully devised, evaluation.

The thrust of his method was to give quick *swaragyan* and *ragagyan*. The details of his methodology may now be spelt out.

Notation System

For *swaragyan* and *ragagyan* he used notations, as the medium of instruction, which he himself evolved. He insisted that the students should be imparted lessons written in notation and expected that the students should be able to read it from the first year itself. His notation system will be discussed in a later chapter.

Well-defined Curricula and Graded Textbooks

He devised a syllabus for the students of his first music school -- Madhav Sangeet Mahavidyalaya, Gwalior. Here he carefully watched the output and fixed the number of *ragas* and their types to be taught in a year after due experimentation. In the first year twenty-five *ragas* were prescribed to be taught.   Bhatkhande expected the teachers to teach at least two types of *sargam*, one *lakshan geet*, two *khayals* and one *dhrupad* in each *raga*.[3] It appears from his report which is published in the *Bhatkhande Smriti Grantha* that the teachers with maximum effort could teach only sixteen *ragas* with their prescribed songs.

In the second year twenty *ragas* were prescribed out of which fourteen *ragas* only were possible to teach.

In *Bhatkhande Smriti Grantha* (Page 106) a syllabus for the third year course is published. He named twenty *ragas* which should be taught in the class. He gave a lot of importance to the training in this year as by this time the students had got a foothold in the basic knowledge and were able to grasp intricate technicalities and *gayaki*. In this year a student was supposed to learn a number of *shlokas, sargams, dohas, lakshan geets, khayals* (*vilambit* and *drut*), *dhrupads, dhamars, saadras* etc.

Within four years 300 *khayals* and 150 *dhrupads* were expected to be learnt. In all twenty-five *ragas* were to be taught in the first year, twenty *ragas* each in the second and third year and up to the end of fifth year the knowledge of 100 or 125 *raga*s was expected to be given among which ninety *raga*s were to be taught with *gayaki*.

Carrying out this syllabus was not found practicable. As the Madhav Sangeet Mahavidyalaya was managed by the Government, therefore, the hours of the classes were fixed. The declared holidays and the vacation for teachers stood in the way of systematic lessons. Later seventy-five *raga*s were taken for coaching but it was felt that it also was too much. Therefore, ultimately only forty-five *raga*s were taken as the syllabus for the five years' course. Out of these ten *raga*s were taught in the first two years, another fifteen *raga*s were taught in the third year and during the fourth and fifth year another twenty *raga*s were taught. At the end of the fifth year a diploma was conferred on the successful candidates. Later Bhatkhande added two more years for studying advanced *raga*s after which he conferred another diploma. The schools established by Bhatkhande in the entire country are following this curricula at present.

Graded Textbooks

Bhatkhande wrote textbooks, namely, *Kramik Pustak Malika* series, which included *Swara Malika*, *lakshan geet*s and hundreds of traditional compositions in the form of *dhrupad*, *dhamar*, *chhota khayal*, *bara khayal*, *saaara*, *tarana* etc. The series also had introductory chapters dealing briefly with the theory of every *raga* and its salient features. At the end of each book *raga vistar* was included emphasising rest notes, *vadi* note and discarded notes of each *raga*. They were meant to cover the five years' course of study after which a diploma was given. The first, second and third part of the *Kramik Pustak Malika* series were expected to be covered each in one year. But the fourth part was scheduled to be completed in two years. Later he added two more books in the *Kramik Pustak Malika* series under the names of fifth and sixth parts to cover a course for seven year study.

The first book in this series, namely, *Kramik Pustak Malika*, (Part I), was published in 1920. It was originally written in Marathi and was later translated into Hindi. This is the most important book of the series as it lays strong foundations of knowledge for a beginner and prepares him thoroughly for advanced study. The content of this book was expected to be taught in the first year only. The opening chapters depict a series of instructions to the teachers about the method of imparting lessons. These instructions are minute and elaborate, being the result of profound thinking on the subject and vast experience. The purpose of these instructions is to give a student sound *swaragyan* and knowledge of basic *tala*, correct pronunciation, proper voice-production, knowledge of notation and practice of *alankar*. Like any primary reader it contains ten lessons consisting of simple and complicated note patterns. Each lesson carried a note for the teacher as to how to impart those lessons intelligently by permutation and combination. After proper coaching in these ten lessons a student was expected to have not only a comprehensive basic idea of *komal* and *vikrit swaras* but also a mobile and tuneful voice.

After this, ten *thaat ragas* or important *ragas* belonging to the ten basic parent scales were introduced with the *swaras* and a short note on each *raga* -- its *vadi swara*, *komal* and *vikrit swaras*, time of singing and *aroha* and *avaroha*. Unlike his later books he did not mention the catch notes *(pakad)* or *swaravistar* at the end, purposely keeping the lessons at the elementary level. It also contains a *sargam* set in *tala* and two or three compositions set in *drut trital* only in every *raga*.

In *Kramik Pustak Malika*, (Part II), again, ten *thaat ragas* were dealt with elaborately, each one having an introductory definition with *shlokas* and *dohas* mentioned in *Sangeetkalpadrumankur*, *Ragachandrikasar* and *Abhinava Raga Manjari*. After a short discussion -- comprising of its *komal* and *teevra swaras*, its brief history, and the ascending and descending notes *(aroha* and *avaroha)*, its catch notes *(pakad)* -- the compositions in notation are given. Each *raga* consists of a great variety of songs -- *sargam* set in *tala*, *chhota khayal*, *bara khayal*, *saadra*, *dhrupad*, *dhamar* etc. In the initial chapters short definitions are given of musical terms as mentioned in the *granthas*. At the end *swaravistar* of each *raga* is given where the comma has a special importance indicating the rest notes, pauses and *vadi swaras*. The idea of spreading the lessons of ten *thaat ragas* over two years was that the groundwork of a student should be profound and perfect. Therefore, when the third year coaching started it became easier for him to grasp the advanced lessons.

Bhatkhande's idea was that the study during the third year was very important because from this year -- in addition to compositions etc. -- *gayaki* was taught and creativity encouraged. He issued many valuable instructions to the teachers about the way of training the third year students.

The *Kramik Pustak Malika*, (Part III), begins with the description and definition of various *talas* which are used in different types of classical compositions. After this he describes elaborately the signs of the notations used by him. In fact, in all the parts of *Kramik Pustak Malika* he explained his method of recognising the notations. As already stated, he gave great importance to the notation system and insisted that the students should be able to read it from the very first year itself. Then he defines some classical terms mentioned in the *grantha*s. He also explains some basic theory about the classification of *raga*s etc. The book deals with fifteen common *raga*s and 512 songs in notation, covering all branches of Classical music. In the same way as in the 2nd part, he discusses the theory of each *raga* -- mentioning its *aroha* and *avaroha*, catch notes etc. -- and follows this up by a *ragavistar* at the end of the book. The study is prescribed for one year.

The *Kramik Pustak Malika*, (Part IV), is the most important of this series which is expected to be learnt in two years. It comprises of a more elaborate and intricate theory of *shruti* and *swarasthana* of both the ancient and the present day musicians followed by definitions of ancient terms. It also defines the different types of Classical music as existed in our country followed by a comparative study of the South and North Indian *swara*s.

This book deals with twenty *raga*s and 532 compositions covering all branches of Classical music. The *raga*s are of slightly complicated nature but are commonly heard and sung. Like the earlier books he gave elaborate *swaravistar* of each *raga* at the end.

While defining a *raga* he takes into account the following points:
1. Which *thaat* does it belong to?
2. Whether the *raga* belongs to the *Auduva*, *Shadava* or *Sampurna* group?
3. What is the proper time of singing it?
4. What are the discarded notes or which ones are weak or discarded either in ascension or descension?
5. What is a *vadi swara* of a *raga* and what is its *samvadi swara*?
6. How are the *anuvadi swaras* used in the development of a *raga*?

7. Whether the *raga* appears sweet when sung in the *uttaranga* or the *purvanga*?
8. What are the negative points in a *raga* which should be avoided?
9. Which *anga* is predominant?
10. What are its catch notes?
11. What are its particular note combinations?
12. If the *raga* is a mixed variety what are the *raga*s mixed and at what points?
13. The particular notes used in ascension and descension.
14. If the *raga* is *vakra*, at what point is it *vakra*?
15. Which are the rest notes?
16. Which notes are the beginning notes?
17. What is its ordinary movement?
18. Which notes would be typically expressive of *antara*?
19. The coinciding point of *avirbhava* and *tirobhava*.
20. Its form as mentioned in the ancient *grantha*s.
21. Its modern form and its base.

This modern and rationalistic method of studying and learning a *raga* helped the learner to have a quick grasp and a sound base of its rules and historical evolution. It is one of Bhatkhande's most original contributions in the realm of music.

A student getting through the fifth year examination had learnt forty-five *raga*s thoroughly and had access to 1,325 various classical compositions published in the four parts of the *Kramik Pustak Malika* series. In addition he had a broad idea about ancient music and the South Indian music.

It has already been stated that the Degree (*Sangeet Visharad*) was offered after this five-year course of studies.

Another two years of post-graduate study consisted of obsolete and uncommon *raga*s described in the same fashion. In the Vth part of the *Kramik Pustak Malika* series 68 *raga*s have been described, illustrated by 251 *Khandani* compositions in notation which fall under *Kalyan, Bilawal, Khamaj, Bhairava* and *Purvi thaat*s. In the 6th part, 68 *raga*s in notation have been included. They come under *Marwa, Kafi, Asavari, Todi* or *Bhairavi thaat*s. In these volumes also he included instructions to the teachers as to how to conduct the advanced study.

For such a condensed course he carefully devised a method for quick *swaragyan* and *ragagyan*. The five parts of graded textbooks, named as the *Kramik Pustak Malika* series, contain lessons gradually increasing in difficulty and complexity and by easy stages. In regard to the choice of *raga*s also he displayed the capacity for gradual initiation of difficult *raga*s. For example, the ten *thaat raga*s were prescribed to be taught during the two years. After this thorough groundwork, in the third year the *raga*s chosen were *Bhopali, Sohani, Kedar, Hamir, Vrindavani Sarang* etc. which have straight movement. The *raga*s which are prescribed for the fourth and the fifth years are of mixed variety, having *vakra* or roundabout movement. For example, *Jaijaiwanti, Darbari Kanhara, Chhayanat, Kamod* etc. The *raga*s to be taught in the sixth and the seventh year are of rare and complicated variety.

Teaching of Theory and Practice Side by Side

For providing a rational theory to music lovers he had already written the following books:

1. *Shrimallakshya Sangeetam,*
2. *Abhinava Raga Manjari,* and
3. *Hindustani Sangeet Paddhati* (In 4 parts).

There were other books on the same lines written under Bhatkhande's guidance:

1. *Ragachandrikasar,* and
2. *Sangeetkalpadrumankur.*

In these books he dealt with all the aspects of music from the ancient to the present times. He also presented an outline of South Indian music.

For teaching purposes he distributed the theoretical part into the beginning chapters of the *Kramik Pustak Malika* series, gradually initiating a student into the historical aspect of the *raga*s and the *swara*s. By the time a student completed the five-year study course, he had a clear idea about the *swara*s of the ancients and of the present day; of the development of *thaat*s or parent scales and their present position; of the development of *raga*s and their present form; of the detailed rules and regulations of the *raga*s as they are practised today and of the usage and meaning of the ancient and modern terms of music. He had carefully divided these theories among the different years of study so that a student could comprehend them easily.

It has already been mentioned that in all the books of his *Kramik*

Pustak Malika series while introducing a *raga* he discussed its historical evolution and its modern form. To make the students remember the rules and regulations of a *raga* he included the *shlokas* and *dohas* from *Abhinava Raga Manjari, Sangeetkalpadrumankur* and *Ragachandrikasar* for each raga and expected the students to memorise them from the third year. For practical lessons in each *raga*, he prescribed a *sargam* set in *tala* -- which depicted all its characteristic movements -- followed by a *lakshan geet* composed by himself. Then a number of *drut* or *chhota khayals* were to be taught in the same *raga*, followed by *vilambit khayal* or *bara khayal*. Later, *dhrupad* and *dhamar* were also taught in the same *raga*.

This way of teaching of theory and practice together and introducing them by stages was very effective and helped to give the students a thorough grounding in the grammar of music.

Carefully Devised Periodic Evaluation

Bhatkhande introduced the pattern of written examinations in music which was unknown to the music world till then. The practical examination was also used to judge the performing capacity of the students. He devised and introduced intelligent questions, both oral and written, to evaluate their knowledge. At the end of every academic year, one examination was held and the successful candidates were promoted to the next class. Before the final examination in the fifth year, he introduced a preliminary test examination after which the successful candidates only were allowed to sit for the Degree Examination.[4] The question paper was set by him in a fashion which could be equated and compared with papers in other modern subjects. The marking process was also as in other academic subjects, having 60% for first class and 50% for second class. 30% was marked as passed in the third class. A student securing below 30% was regarded as a failure. In the question paper, under one question, students were invariably asked to write a composition of the *Kramik Pustak Malika* from memory, in notation. Care was taken that they adhered to the original composition of the book to avoid distortion. Apart from the notation, questions were put about the history of Music and its evolution. Like other academic subjects students were asked to write an essay which carried the maximum marks in the question paper.

Each paper was to be answered in two hours. Only in the- fifth year was it expected to be answered in three hours. In the oral examination a team of teacher musicians used to hear the students sing the compositions of *khayal, dhrupad, dhamar* etc. from *Kramik Pustak Malika*. Emphasis was laid on the correct rendering of the compositions as written in the textbooks. Apart from listening to *gayaki* and the purity of *raga*'s form, the clarity of *tana*s was also taken into account. The examiners were not satisfied by listening to the demonstrations only. They also put many questions to test the groundwork of a student's knowledge.

Initially, he presented certificates to the students who completed the five-year course of study on the stamped paper of the King of Gwalior. The certificates were presented to the successful candidates by the King of Gwalior himself in a ceremony. The students who had done well were honoured with the presentation of gold and silver medals. Later, when the Marris College of Music was opened, the final Diploma of five-years' study was named as *Sangeet Visharad* and that of seven years' study was named as *Sangeet Nipun*. It was bestowed in the name of Bhatkhande Sangeet Vidyapeeth, a practice which even now continues. Bhatkhande tried his best to bring up the standard of *Sangeet Visharad* to graduation and of the *Sangeet Nipun* to the post-graduate level.

IV

BHATKHANDE AS A TEACHER

His Method of Selecting Students

It is interesting to note the method Bhatkhande adopted to select suitable students for the Music School of Gwalior. This has been related by Professor P.N. Chinchore in his article entitled 'Krantikari Shikshashastri Bhatkhande' in *Bhatkhande Smriti Grantha*:-- "He used to keep with him a long whistle which used to produce higher or lower notes when its length was decreased or increased respectively. First, all the boys were made to stand in a row and their voices were noted in a general way. Then Bhatkhande used to produce a sound by his whistle and asked a particular boy to reproduce the same note. This way each boy was asked to match his voice to two to three sounds of the whistle. Whoever was successful in the above-mentioned test was admitted to the Music School. On the first day, all the selected boys, numbering about 150, were called together in a hall. The first lesson was imparted to them by Bhatkhande himself. He used to sing a note and asked the boys to reproduce it. If somebody by mistake started singing along with him he immediately stopped him by putting up his two hands. The pitch of two or three notes was explained with the sign of different fingers. Later, within two to three days, half the *Saptak*, meaning from *Sa* to *Ma*, was introduced and explained, resorting to different methods -- sometimes along with fun and frolic so that the novices did not get bored with the lessons. At times he asked a student to sing with full-throated voice and asked another to name the notes. After imparting such lessons for five or six days he made the boys learn ten types of *alankar* and then he left for Bombay after proper instructions for further lessons to the other teachers." (Translation mine).

He did not agree to remain in Gwalior permanently. Most of the time he used to stay at Bombay and visited Gwalior as and when necessary. The school was run by the teachers trained by him.

How He handled His Classes

Bhatkhande was a shrewd judge of the capacity of his students and led them through carefully devised stages of instruction, keeping their capacity in view. In regard to teaching he introduced the following method. In the beginning the music students, who were beginners, were made to learn *sur* and *tala* -- the rudiments of the art -- for a week or ten days. After teaching them to sing in tune they were taught *Ardha Saptak* and *Saptak*. And then the *Dvadash Saptak*, belonging to ten *thaats* were taught. In this they took the help of their fingers to denote the patterns of note combinations. They were particularly taught to sing with the note names only and were also taught to read the notation from the blackboard, translating it in tune. Particular emphasis was laid on reproducing music in notation. And after the student had practised all this he was made to sing the seven notes having established each note as *Shadja*.

Care was taken that the students had a sound knowledge of *laya* and *tala* right from the beginning. They were taught the practical aspect of *tabala* so that they could become well versed within a short time, which would give them self-confidence in demonstration. They were made to learn by heart many *bol*s of *tabala* and *pakhavaj*. Bhatkhande insisted that as the lessons advanced the students should be taught to play the *theka* on the *tabala* and also short *bol*s and *paran*s. He was not in favour of practising *tala* and *matra* by counting fingers while singing. He favoured that every day at least 15 to 20 minutes' practice of singing should be done by listening to *theka* only so that the singer could learn to keep a mental note of the *tala* while demonstrating.

The beginner's class was initially called 'Infant Class' and was later named as 'Preparatory Class'. The purpose of this class was to give the *swaragyan*. Whoever attained this was sent to the first year class immediately even before the annual examination. Later the Preparatory Class was divided into two parts -- Prep. A and Prep. B. He insisted on making the beginners learn *Swara Malika* as described in the *Kramik Pustak Malika*, Ist part.

He kept a watchful eye on the effect of the lessons imparted to the beginners. For it was his idea that the students who came from an atmosphere of music, or the students who made rapid progress, should not be burdened by the elementary lessons of *sur* and *tala* for more than 2-3 months. They should be introduced to *raga*s straight away. He wanted the initial lessons to be attractive enough and did not want a student to exhaust his patience. He realised that the crucial period was the first one or two years when the teacher had to work hard to infuse a liking for real music in the students.

In this class the students were expected to reproduce any *swara* written in notation. How one should sing, fitting the composition into the division of *matra*s, Bhatkhande himself demonstrated in the presence of the students and the teachers. The variety of lessons he invented left an indelible mark on the mind of a student and made the groundwork of his knowledge sound and strong.

Teaching of Compositions

He had great regard for the traditional compositions which he collected with much pain and labour over the years. He considered these songs as the wealth of our *raga sangeet* which not only created a great variety but also enriched our classical art. Besides, a composition depicted the authentic movement of a *raga*.

To learn many compositions was regarded as a quality for a musician. For it helped him to get a broad idea of the movements of *raga*s. Therefore, Bhatkhande insisted on teaching the students many compositions strictly sticking to the note patterns as published in the *Kramik Pustak Malika* series. His emphasis on learning *dhrupad* arose from the fact that *khayal* is a product of *dhrupad* -- having restful air and serious mood -- which needed maturity in voice, faultless pronunciation and clear rendering. Without these qualities one could not be proficient in *khayal*. Therefore, Bhatkhande gave importance to both these classical varieties. It is a proof of his regard for the tradition of our music and is also a proof of his foresight.

Strong memory is a great qualification of a musician. It was regarded as an asset in the old days of oral training, when one had to keep the entire lesson in memory. Bhatkhande wanted to exploit this asset in a different way. He made the students memorise the *shloka*s of *Abhinava Raga Manjari* and *Shrimallakshya Sangeetam*, and also some *shloka*s from the *grantha*s.

Bhatkhande saw that the students developed respect for traditional music and developed self-confidence to learn and demonstrate independently.

In the Music School he organised a library of music literature and once a student was admitted there he had an access to plenty of books on music and thus could obtain precious knowledge without the trouble of having to search for it.

His Instructions to Teachers

To standardise his method of teaching and to put music education at the academic level he issued instructions to the teachers from time to time. The instructions are so detailed and comprehensive that they reveal his vast experience, deep concern and profound thinking on the subject.

It would be interesting to quote some of his instructions which he issued in 1920 to the teachers of the Madhav Sangeet Maha-vidyalaya, Gwalior:

1. While lecturing in the class the teacher should discuss the theory of music as, for example, the difference between the allied *raga*s, their catch notes, the important note combinations and their historical evolution. The student's desire

should be awakened to learn something new every day. The teacher should not discuss irrelevant subjects in the class.

2. While teaching a new *raga*, the teacher should read out its description from the *Hindustani Sangeet Paddhati* and demonstrate it vocally.

3. The teacher should give a full-fledged demonstration of his art in the presence of students once in a week and allow them to sit through the entire performance.

4. The teacher should take up a simple *raga* and sing its development in small note combinations and make the students repeat them.

5. While teaching a new song the teacher should write it on the board in notation and make the students reproduce it.

6. The teacher should sing short note patterns of a *raga* and ask the students to recognise them. Not only that, the teacher should also enquire the reason for the answer of each student. If there is a mistake the teacher should try to correct it and explain the mistake.

7. The teacher should expect the students to be able to sing well in the third year. The goal should be that the student should be able to sing one *raga* for about 15-20 minutes.

8. At the end of the second year the students should be taught 100 *khayal*s and 50 *dhrupad*s. It would be convenient for the students to learn by heart the *khayal*s and *dhrupad*s as published in the *Kramik Pustak Malika* series at home. The teacher should teach *tana*s and *alapa*s mentioned at the end of the second part of *Kramik Pustak Malika*.

9. The study course for the third year was very important and particularly in this year the teachers had an equally important role to play. Bhatkhande opined in this regard as follows:

(a) The teacher should sing many combinations of notes which the students should translate into note names. Sometimes one student should sing and another should translate it into note names.

(b) Without singing, the teacher should just utter the note names which a student should be able to sing.

(c) The teacher should endeavour to bring maturity to the student's singing. Proper pronunciation and *bol banana* were assets.

(d) The teacher should take quick *tana*s and should make

mistakes knowingly. After that he should get himself corrected by the students. The teacher should draw attention of the students to the characteristic *gayaki* of *khayal*.

(e) The teacher should mix the *ragas* and get them identified and separated by the students.

(f) The students should be made to listen to a good recital once a week.

(g) The students should be taught the method of practising *tana*. They should be made to sing with *akar*, *ekar* and *ukar*.

(h) Firstly, they should be taught *sampurna tana* and made to practise hard.

(i) Then it should be practised in parts.

(j) The students should be inspired to practise out of their own accord.

(k) *Sa Re Ga Ma Pa Dha Ni Sa* -- this combination should be practised in not less than four or five *thaats*, as for example, *Bhairava*, *Bhairavi*, *Bilawal*, *Kafi* etc. Then they should practise small pieces of *tanas* in them. After that one should learn short *tanas* and in them there should be one *swara* less each time.

These instructions are a proof of his scientific approach towards the teaching of *swara* and *raga* with emphasis on voice-culture and practice of faultless *tanas*.[5]

Bhatkhande kept a keen eye on the pattern of behaviour of teachers towards the students. His following instructions are self-revealing:

1. Teachers should not use harsh words when dealing with the students. The teacher should behave with affection and thus try to influence them. Attracting students towards music depends on the efficiency of the teachers. If any student falls ill the teacher should go to him to show his concern and sympathy. The student would certainly reciprocate and that would help increasing the tie of affection between them.

2. Every teacher should practise one hour daily. Teachers should also keep in mind that the students have to respect them always. They should also know how to handle the students to build up their self-confidence, develop their

aesthetic sense and inspire in them the spirit of *sadhana*.
3.   He asked the teachers to inspire the students in such a way that their practice becomes a matter of joy and not merely meaningless labour.[6]

It was Bhatkhande's firm idea that the future of a student depended on a good teacher and his relationship with his pupil.[7]

V

IMPLEMENTATION : HIS TWO-PRONGED STRATEGY

To implement his method of collective education in music it was necessary to train a team of teachers and also open several schools in different places. For this purpose he made two planned projects -- long-term, and short-term. Under the long-term project he took up the task of establishing music schools and colleges in all big cities to propagate Classical music. His main field of experimentation was to be at Gwalior and for further development and propagation of his educational ideas he was depending on its result.

Training His First Batch of Teachers

Under the short-term project a few good musicians were coaxed to go to Bhatkhande to learn his new scientific method of teaching which included the training of a group of students at one time with the help of notation. Bhatkhande taught them the novel and easy method of imparting lessons in *swaragyan* and *talagyan* to a beginner. The musicians had also to learn the art of administration for running a music institution. With the help of the Maharaja of Gwalior half a dozen musicians were selected to be sent to Bhatkhande. Their names were: Rajabhaiya Poochhwale, Krishnarao Date, Bhaskarrao Khandeparkar, Baburao Gokhale, Chunnilal Kathak and Vishnurao Deshpande.

The venue of teaching was fixed at Bombay as Bhatkhande did not agree to remain at Gwalior for long. The musicians selected were asked to stay at the Gwalior Palace at Bombay till their training was complete. As was the custom in those days, the musicians were unwilling to reveal their knowledge. How the reserve of those musicians was won over by Bhatkhande is narrated by Ratanjankar in his book *Pandit Bhatkhande*. For drawing up the course of studies Bhatkhande asked them to write their *dhrupad*s, *hori*s and *khayal*s in notation and sing them to him to enable him to make a selection out of these for teaching. They hesitated because they had learnt the compositions from their *guru,* Shankar Rao Pandit, the famous *khayal* singer of Gwalior, with great effort and these were then considered a treasure to be guarded and not exposed. But Bhatkhande placed before them a whole file of *khayal*s written in notation from their *guru*'s tradition which he had collected some years before from Eknath Pandit (known also as Maoo Pandit), the younger brother of Shankar Rao Pandit. He also sang some of the *khayal*s which he had learnt from Maoo Pandit. It was a revelation to these musicians to hear him sing compositions belonging to their *gharana*. This vanquished them. They wrote their *khayal*s and sang them without hesitation. There were, of course, slight differences here and there in the versions of the *khayal*s. This was but natural as they had learnt them, without the aid of notation, orally. Among them, Bhatkhande considered the versions sung by Shri Poochhwale to be the nearest to the original as taught by Shankar Rao Pandit. Pandit Bhatkhande selected some of the *khayal*s, *dhrupad*s, *saadra*s and *hori*s for the syllabi of the Gwalior Music School. Thus the musicians were thoroughly trained in the new method and sent back to Gwalior and soon after Madhav Sangeet Mahavidyalaya was opened there.

Starting of Music Schools

The first school of music to teach through his modern method was established in Gwalior in 1918 at the instance of Maharaja Madhavrao Scindia. Bhatkhande had already gained experience of introducing his method of teaching in the primary schools where music was introduced as a subject by the Bombay Municipality. Some musicians were appointed in these schools for the purpose of teaching. The Bombay Municipality requested Bhatkhande to train these music teachers and accordingly training classes were held in the Gayan Uttejak Mandali.

In the meantime his work of consolidating available information in regard to music and scrutinising and rearranging the same went on unhampered. The Maharaja of Gwalior, who had heard the commendable services of Bhatkhande to the cause of music, met him during one of his visits to Bombay and after a great deal of discussion understood and appreciated the view-point of Bhatkhande about his line of work and his method of teaching. To watch the modern type of lessons, invented and imparted by Bhatkhande, the Maharaja visited incognito the classes conducted by Bhatkhande at Bombay. Bhatkhande as usual wrote notations on the blackboard and asked the students to sing them. The students were also given some intelligence test questions which they readily answered. The Maharaja was highly pleased with the dexterity of the students and was thoroughly convinced about the success of Bhatkhande's modern approach to teaching.

Very soon the Maharaja invited Bhatkhande to open a similar school at Gwalior to which Bhatkhande agreed readily. On reaching Gwalior he drew up a scheme of a Music School with full details about the courses of studies, mode of training, examinations etc. Soon afterwards the Madhav Sangeet Mahavidyalaya was opened at Gwalior. The ruler of Gwalior also ordered that music classes be started in all the primary, pre-middle, middle and normal schools.

The Success of the First School and Establishment of other Schools

His first school of Music at Gwalior, imparting and propagating his new method of teaching, which was established in 1918, proved to be a great success. This certainly was a great revolutionary step towards modernising education of music and a breakthrough after centuries of the old method of narrow and dogmatically professional musicians. This not only provided a ray of hope to save music from further degeneration and extinction but also provided an effective step forward to elevate music as one of the modern academic subjects.

With the sincere work of the teachers under the able guidance of Bhatkhande, the Music School at Gwalior won the esteem of the public, in spite of the adverse propaganda of professional musicians. This Music College even today is running as a full-fledged Government Music College which is producing excellent performers and teachers. It was Bhatkhande's idea that after a student passed the final examination he should learn more and practise more to be able to emerge either as a skilled performer or as a teacher. He wrote as follows:

"After completing their music education, all students should go to the different cities and take up the role of music teachers. Their good work would win the faith of the people and that would be the real reward of learning by the new method. These students should be well versed in fifty *ragas* along with *gayaki*. Their singing should be mature, and should have flashes of sound training and artistic sensibility. The *tanas* should be solid and clear and the pronunciation and enunciation should be faultless. They should have the attractive quality of holding the listener's interest right from the beginning to the end of the recital. The entire country is watching the result of the new method experimented with the new school of Gwalior. If this method can successfully promote the glory and fame of Gwalior the entire country would certainly follow out of her own accord." (Translation mine)

These words proved prophetic as the Music School at Gwalior produced and sent out teachers and graduates in music to different centres like Indore, Jaipur, Bombay, Poona, Nagpur and Calcutta; thus develoing a series of similar institutions all over the country. Along with the school at Gwalior, the Baroda State Music School was also reorganised under Bhatkhande's directions. A noted instrumentalist, Hirjibhai Doctor, a Zamindar of the Baroda State, was appointed Principal of the institution. The school made good progress under his principalship. Later it was annexed to M. S. University of Baroda's Faculty of Fine Arts. Many renowned musicians of that time were on the teaching staff. Others came as Visiting Professors at the instance of Bhatkhande.

Among all the schools, established in the lifetime of Bhatkhande, Marris College of Music, established at Lucknow, was the most important. It was founded in July, 1926 in Topwali Kothi on Neel Road, near Kaisar Bagh. Madhav Rao Keshab Joshi was appointed as the Principal and Bhatkhande's favourite pupil and a renowned musician, S. N. Ratanjankar, was appointed as the Vice-Principal. Bhatkhande himself was in overall charge. The classes were opened in 1926 which immediately gained popularity. It was formally opened by Sir William Marris on 16th September, 1926 and was named as Marris College. A team of expert musicians was engaged which worked under the guidance of Bhatkhande. He stayed there for six months till the college could work independently. Some time after Madhav Rao Keshab Joshi retired and S.N. Ratanjankar was appointed as the Principal in his place. Soon the College expanded and the Government donated the Council Chamber in Kaisar Bagh for its classes. The popularity of this institution increased so much that for its added number of students the authorities had to take on rent the adjacent house called the Chandiwali Kothi. Later, this institution became the centre of Bhatkhande's new method of music education and was called as Bhatkhande Sangeet Vidyapeeth. Many similar institutions came up in different places in the country which were affiliated to the Bhatkhande Sangeet Vidyapeeth. Marris College sent teachers and examiners to the affiliated schools which followed its syllabus and teaching method.

It will be interesting to note that Bhatkhande's activity was not confined to the newly built schools for boys only. In Gwalior a school was opened, which was the first of its kind called the *Tavayaf School*. It meant the school for professional women. Bhatkhande took charge of it and sent teachers to teach the girls through his new method of teaching.

It was Bhatkhande's idea that music should purify the atmosphere in society and should inspire healthy thoughts. Therefore, music at the vice houses of the prostitutes should not be cheap and degraded which vitiated the atmosphere. So a school for them was opened at Gwalior where his new method of teaching became the medium of instruction. Some interesting facts are found about this school in his annual report of 1925:

"..........the teacher with permission of the Headmaster should go to the *Tavayaf School* and teach them *tanas* and *thumaris.*"[8]

The usual examination used to be held in this school also where Bhatkhande himself became the examiner. The following was his report:

"..........In this class two senior girls and two junior girls came for examination. The senior student sang well. ....We must say that the coaching is not up to the expectation. They should be taught on the lines of the new method following the syllabus. After this course, it would be good to teach them some other *geets* and *thumaris.*"[9]

However, in spite of a pious effort to run this institution, this had to be closed down due to various reasons. From the report of the annual examination in 1925 it appeared that the work and progress of this school was not satisfactory. The purpose of this school was to educate the women in the real sense not only in music, but also in academic subjects, so that they could stand on their own legs and support their own relatives through honourable earning. But after observing for years, it was found out that except the expenditure incurred on this project it had not made any progress in practice and theory. The inspectors gave many suggestions for improvement but nothing was implemented. Even after 7-8 years of coaching the girls could not show much result. One reason could be that the girls were not intelligent enough to learn through the new method.

VI

ADMINISTRATION   AND   SUPERVISION

Bhatkhande displayed the capacity of an able administrator in setting up and organising the insitutions for education in music. His three main activities were:

1.   training of the teachers,
2.   running of classes, and
3.   conducting examinations.

He designed and set up appropriate organisation for his several schools and ran them effectively by his knowledge of

(A)   man management,
(B)   detailed laying down of procedures,
(C)   effective supervision and coordination,
(D)   providing the necessary inputs, and
(E)   careful evaluation of the output.

(A) Man Management

He was a shrewd judge of men and had rare ability to pick up the right person for the right job. One such instance was his choice of Rajabhaiya Poochhwale as his righthand man to assist in his movement. Rajabhaiya proved his worth even though he had been branded by others as a mere harmonium player. Bhatkhande selected and trained up a team of musicians for teaching and entrusted the classes to them. They proved competent to run them. He also introduced an effective system of rewards and punishments to encourage the deserving and pull up the lazy and the incompetent among the teachers and the students.

(B) Detailed laying down of Procedures

In regard to the laying down of detailed procedures we can call him a master of detail. His instructions issued from time to time about the administration of the Music School at Gwalior will speak for themselves:

(i) The presence of a student in the class should be marked every day. In case of absence they should be asked to produce letters from their guardians.

(ii) Every month a report should be written and submitted to the Headmaster about the progress made in each class.

(iii) To point out the absence of the students sometimes the parents should be called in the classes.

(iv) There should be a meeting of the teachers on every Friday and suggestions to improve the lessons should be particularly placed there.

(v) The school should remain open till 8 p.m. every evening.

(vi) At times the art lovers, Sardars and Jagirdars should be invited to watch the work of the school and their opinions should be collected in writing.

(vii) The entire responsibility of the school lies on the Headmaster. He should watch the lessons imparted in every class, the number of students present and the time of the teachers' coming and leaving the class.

(viii) He wrote that he should get at least two letters in a month giving a full report of the school lessons. He further wrote: "I am not very eager about it, rather I would like to leave it to the wish of the teacher." But when he came to Gwalior, he instructed that all the reports of the past months should be presented to him. In short, his aspirations were to find it to be an ideal institution capable enough even in influencing the entire country.[10]

Apart from this his detailed instructions to the teachers as to how to make the lessons interesting and not allow them to be boring and stereotyped reveal his powerful imagination and vision.

(C) Effective Supervision and Coordination

He set up standards for each role in his institutions and watched the performance of each aspect very keenly. The overall supervision and coordination was done by him effectively. He was in overall charge of the different schools opened in Indore, Lucknow, Gwalior, Baroda, Nagpur etc. He went round and kept up the standard of lessons at a high level and conducted the examinations with great efficiency. He insisted on having periodic reports by the heads of the institutions.

(D) Providing the Necessary Inputs

While setting up an institution he saw to it that the same was provided with the necessary finance, curricula, guide-books etc. He knew how to involve moneyed people to make his project a success and effectively got financial help from the Rajas and Nawabs. As already stated, he designed workable and effective curricula after due experimentation and wrote graded textbooks. For practical lessons he continuously instructed the teachers to improve their manner of teaching.

(E) Careful Evaluation of the Output

Bhatkhande set very carefully devised question papers to evaluate the knowledge of the students. The oral questions devised by him were intelligent and razor sharp to test the students' knowledge.

In regard to the running of the institutions, his letters to the Secretary of the Madhav Sangeet Mahavidyalaya, Gwalior, are revealing. It will be relevant to mention one of them. This is one of the letters among many others written from the Noutalab Guest House, Gwalior and addressed to Rao Sahib G.V. Ambedkar. It is about the annual examination held in Gwalior on 11-11-1929. In this letter Bhatkhande observed with regret that the work of the primary classes was not satisfactory. In the Preparatory class there was not enough attempt to teach *swaras* to the students. He was told that frequent transfer of teachers and carelessness of students were the main reasons. He, however, felt that teaching must be improved at all cost.[11]

About the second year he found that a lot had been taught with *gayaki* but the progress of teaching of *dhrupad* was lagging behind. In addition to this, many students were found to be out of *swara* and *tala*. The students also could not sing the *vilambit khayal*s. Bhatkhande wanted the Headmaster to take note of these points.

*Raga*s were not taught at all to the third year students. The result was that 'they would have to be taught the missed lessons in the fourth year itself and as a result the advanced lessons would suffer.'

In the fourth year lessons were imparted properly but the students were found lacking in the capacity for all-round presentation of *raga*s.

Bhatkhande added in his letter a special message for the administrative authority. It was observed that the Headmaster remained out of station for 2 to 3 months along with the ruler of Gwalior. His advice, therefore, was to relieve the Headmaster of his duties and to appoint Rajabhaiya Poochhwale in his place. Bhatkhande pointed out in this regard the qualities of Rajabhaiya who would ably discharge the duties of the Headmaster. He also suggested that Rajabhaiya should be entrusted with the writing of the annual report. As his work would increase considerably after being appointed as the Headmaster he should be relieved of other duties. He also recommended an increase in his salary. He, however, suggested that the present Headmaster should not be dismissed from service entirely. He might be retained as a supervisor in the school who, when in Gwalior, would visit every class, watch the lessons imparted and give a full report to the new Headmaster. In addition to that he should supervise the teaching work of the other schools in the city and give a regular report to the Secretary.

Bhatkhande also noted that there was no textbook for teaching *tabala* and *sitar*. He directed that such books should be prepared by the respective teachers engaged for teaching those instruments.

He expressed unhappiness over the irregular attendance of the teachers in the class and their spending time in useless conversation. These facts he gathered from the students. He suggested a detailed procedure to prevent such practice.

He also suggested that a register should be kept ready and the remarks of the visitors who visited the school should be recorded in it on a regular basis.

VII

HIS METHOD : AN EVALUATION

His Success

The experiment of his method at the Gwalior school proved a great success. Within a month or a month and a half the music students were able to practise *sargam* and *palta*s. Within three to four months they were able to sing *dhrupad* and *dhamar*. They could pick up a new composition within 5 to 7 minutes.

This outstanding progress of music education agitated the professional musicians who were used to prolonging it to the maximum extent possible, much to the chagrin of the learner. For the purpose of imparting music lessons to a group of students, when Bhatkhande used to stand in front of the blackboard with a chalk in his hand writing notations and asking the students to reproduce them with voice the entire music society felt scandalised and stunned. The *gharanedar ustad*s, the torch-bearers of traditional music, were irritated. For it was an age when to translate a *tana* into *sargam* was regarded as difficult, writing music or music notation was considered as a sacrilege and accepting anyone or everyone into the fold of music was unthinkable and unbelievable. On the other hand, the general mass of the people rejoiced and welcomed the collective education in music under the guidance of Bhatkhande. His smallest order was obeyed with enthusiasm and respect. Such was the influence of his personality that the teacher and the students immersed themselves in the constant practice and study of music. Literally, this became their means of worship. The traditional compositions were memorised with the devotion of remembering the name of God. On religious festivals like *Ramnavami*, *Ganesh Chaturthi* etc. the students used to sing in temples or in public. In some houses the books on the theory of music written by Bhatkhande were read with religious fervour. After having bath and wearing silken clothes, the students used to chant in front of the deity *Shrimallakshya Sangeetam* and *Abhinava Raga Manjari*. The parents sometimes used to join them to give encouragement.[12]

This was the coveted influence of collective education which attracted more and more students every day.

Criticism of His Method

It is often said that Bhatkhande's new method of teaching and bookish knowledge do not make one an artist or a performer. According to Bhatkhande, the knowledge thus acquired by passing the Degree examination can be regarded as incomplete. The real benefit of attending this study course is that the student attains a standard of knowledge, which makes him capable of further study in the right direction of the different aspects of music. He must develop the capacity to judge what is good and bad in music and what is acceptable and what is not acceptable. It will not be easy to mislead him as he is no longer vulnerable. If he has an ideal to become proficient in the art of music he can pick up more knowledge from an ordinary musician or can learn by listening only. If he wants to go to a *khandani ustad* he can learn in one year the lessons of five years. In short, one can say that a degree holder gets the key to enter the realm of music but his days of further learning and practice are not yet over. The attitude should not be that by earning a degree one has achieved the goal of his life. Bhatkhande always gave importance to *gurumukh* type of training and advised his students to learn practical music with *gayaki* from a renowned musician after he had passed the course. He sent his favourite pupil S.N. Ratanjankar to Ustad Faiyaz Khan to learn *gayaki* and practical demonstration. Therefore, after a student obtains a degree, he should always try to keep his standard of performance high and learn more and practise more in order to establish himself as a full-fledged artist.

VIII

SCOPE FOR FURTHER RESEARCH

The first school teaching through the method of Bhatkhande was established at Gwalior in 1918. Since then other schools were established following the same pattern of teaching all over the North

and in other parts of the country. Although training the younger
generation through this method has evoked wide understanding
of and interest in Classical music as desired by him, it is observed
that these schools are not producing performers of high standard.
It may be due to the following reasons:

- (i)   Too many *raga*s and too much theoretical knowledge have
        to be learnt in a short span of time.
- (ii) Lack of adequate voice-culture.
- (iii) Lack of consideration of individual voice types, inevitable in
        group training.
- (iv) Tendency to learn the minimum and pass anyhow the ex-
        amination to get a diploma.

There is ample scope of research as to how the above deficiencies
can be removed. Some suggestions are given below:

1.   While introducing the *swara*s to a student through the
     notation system adequate importance should be given to
     voice-production. The need for simple but effective methods
     of voice-production opens up an interesting field of inves-
     tigation.

2.   Knowledge is so vast that one has to specialise after some
     time. It is suggested that students should specialise in either
     of the two broad categories of performers and musicologists,
     with much greater emphasis on voice-culture in the case of
     the former and on theoretical aspects in the case of the latter.
     It would be a matter of experimentation to determine the
     appropriate mix of the theoretical and practical components
     for the two types of specialisations. At what stage speciali-
     sation should be introduced would also merit investigation.

3.   In regard to the performers, further specialisation would
     be an advantage so that students can branch off into the
     singing of *dhrupad, khayal, thumari,* etc. in accordance with
     their voice and aptitude; and be taught proper voice-pro-
     duction and *gayaki* appropriate to each of these forms. How
     and at what stage should this further specialisation take place
     would require experimentation and research.

4.   Another problem that has arisen due to the use of the
     notation system in our schools and colleges has been a
     tendency to take the written text as the end-all of music.
     It would very much help matters if the *raga*s in their properly
     developed form, true to the notation, could be brought before

the students through the modern media -- electronic devices. The problems of using the modern media for purposes of music education opens up many interesting lines of investigation. Bhatkhande put the living music of his time in print. Now time has come when, with the help of modern gadgets, new life should be given to the printed material.

References

1. *Bhatkhande Smriti Grantha*, p. 79. Extract from Chinchore's article.
2. *Ibid.*
3. *Ibid.*, p.104
4. *Ibid.*, p.117
5. *Ibid.*, p.107
6. *Ibid.*, pp.106-'8
7. *Ibid.*, pp.109-'11
8. *Ibid.*, p.116
9. *Ibid.*, p.140
10. *Ibid.*, pp.106,107,108
11. *Ibid.*, p.150
12. *Ibid.*, p.85

8

As a Composer

I

INTRODUCTION

It is a well-known fact that the Mughals conquered and settled down in Northern India in the eleventh century. Their contribution in the domain of contemporary Classical music brought about a great change therein and enriched it with new types of artistic innovations. Prior to the Mughal occupation, scholars are of the opinion that, *Prabandha Geeti* was the main form of Classical music. The poetic content of the composition was rich in words as well as in melody. The words were clear, precise, well-integrated, fitting perfectly into tune and strictly in conformity with the *raga*'s basic structure.

As the centuries advanced *dhrupads* took the place of the above-mentioned types of songs and they were taught and kept in circulation on the *guru shishya parampara* basis, i.e., teaching only a very close relative or a privileged pupil. Even now we have in hand a rich collection of *dhrupads* which used to be practised and taught in the nineteenth century. Some of them have been handed down to us from the golden period of Akbar and the musicians of his time Mian Tansen and Swami Haridas of mythical fame. They are regarded as the models of the forms of the *ragas* in which they are set, depicting their salient melodic features. In regard to language, the *dhrupad*s retained the purity of the compositions of their predecessors.

In course of time *dhrupad* receded into the background and *khayal* took its place as the main form of Classical singing. Although there was some attempt to compose *khayals* earlier, the origin of most of the compositions is traced to Sadarang and Adarang, belonging to the court of the Mughal Emperor Muhammed Shah (1718-1748). The names of Niyamat Khan alias Sadarang, Feroze Khan alias Adarang, his nephew, and Manarang shine in the galaxy of *khayal* composers. In addition to these compositions the *ustad*s belonging to different *gharana*s composed many beautiful songs in *khayal* in later periods. These compositions -- some under a name and some anonymous -- developed around the personalities of the descendants and disciples of Sadarang and Adarang. Noteworthy schools of compositions flourished in Delhi, Punjab, Rajasthan and Gwalior. Some talented composers belonging to the towns of Atrauli, Agra, Sahaswan, Kairana, Lucknow, Varanasi and further east also added to the existing stock of *khayal*s. The beauty of these compositions was in the words embedded into notes and typically expressive of the *raga*'s form. In fact, these compositions mostly employed the typical note phrases of a *raga* indicating its movement, catch notes and rest notes. Melodically, they were superb and, in the absence of written music and notation system, were regarded as the basis for the note movements and note patterns of different *raga*s. The rhythm or *laya* part of these traditional compositions was intricate and intelligent, giving enough scope for pauses, which provided opportunities for extempore elaborations. *Khayal* compositions, however, as compared to the *dhrupad*, suffered in the poetic content and language structure.

To these traditional compositions were added, in the wake of the 20th century, the compositions of Bhatkhande. He made a very significant contribution in the field of compositions. A very conservative estimate would be 300 songs of different classical varieties, published in the *Kramik Pustak Malika* series alone. There are also a large number of songs either unpublished or published elsewhere. They are a proof of his versatile genius revealed in the contents pertaining to word, melody, form and *laya*.

II

LANGUAGE

The Language of Khayal

If we take into account the language of *khayal* we find that the traditional compositions are mostly written in Hindi except a few which are written in Punjabi. The Hindi in which the *khayal*s are written may not be understood as a modern version of this language. It is an admixture of Braj Bhasha, Rajasthani and the rural dialects of the suburbs of Lucknow, Awadh and the Eastern districts of Varanasi along with the Bhojpuri dialect. Some excellent compositions were also mixed with Khari Boli or the Arabic, Persian and Urdu vocabulary in large patches.

The Braj Bhasha, or the Braj vocabulary is in a class by itself. It is well-known for its suppleness and softness and has been extensively used in *vaishnava padavali* and other types of devotional songs. Its phonetic merit in poetry is unparalleled and has been eulogised by modern linguists. Even the modern composers are unable to free themselves from the impact of Braj Bhasha. The notable characater of Braj Bhasha is that while it is expressive, it hardly has any conjunct consonant. Therefore, it does not burden notes in songs with heavy pronunciation. As for example take this line: *sumiran karo re naam Hari ko.* Here the word *smaran* is applied as *sumiran* for the sake of its blending quality with the utterance of notes.

The *khayal*s written in Rajasthani also occupy an important position in the domain of music. The predominance of the language is evident in the compositions of the Manarang *gharana*, well-known as the Jaipur *gharana*. Bhatkhande collected from this *gharana* a good number of compositions and published them in the *Kramik Pustak Malika* series. It will be a mistake to take this language as Rajasthani in its pure form. For it is strewn with Gujarati, Awadhi, Khari Boli and Braj vocabulary. For example:

Bara khayal in *Shyam Kalyan—mhara rasiya baalam.*

Bara khayal in *Ahir Bhairava—rasiya mhara amalara.*

As stated earlier, a large number of *khayal*s are found written in a mixed language of the rural dialects of Lucknow, Awadh and Varanasi and the Bhojpuri dialect, but dominated by the Arabic,

Persian and Urdu vocabulary. Arabic and Persian vocabulary can be traced back to the songs composed by the *kavvals* at the tombs and the shrines of the Sufi saints. They had their impact on the *khayal* resulting in *Kavval Bani*. For example:

(Having Awadhi and Bhojpuri dialects)

Bara khayal in *Mian Ki Todi* -- *daiya vata.. dubara.*

Bara khayal in *Alhaiya Bilawal* -- *daiya kahan gaye log.*

Khari Boli (having Arabic, Persian and Urdu words)

Bara khayal in *Mian Ki Malhar* -- *Kareem naam tero.*

Bara khayal in *Basant* -- *Nabi ke darbar.*

Apart from this, the devotional songs composed by the poets belonging to the periods of *Bhakti* and *Reeti* of Hindi Literature influenced the world of *khayal*. Many compositions of Meera, Surdas etc. have been accepted as *khayal* compositions and successfully demonstrated by the present-day artists. Vishnu Digambar Paluskar made use of such compositions abundantly. For example, a popular *khayal* in *Darbari Kanhara* is a composition of Tulsidas (*Kramik Pustak Maiika,* 4th part, p.655, Marathi Edition):

और नहीं कछु काम के, मैं भरोसे अपने राम के ।
दोऊ अक्षर सब कुल तारे बारी जाऊँ उस नाम पे ।।

The Language of Bhatkhande's Compositions

In regard to language Bhatkhande's compositions mostly leaned towards Hindi with a touch of Braj Bhasha on the line of the poets of the *Bhakti* period. For example, we can take Bhatkhande's composition of *Chhota khayal* in *Raga Yaman (Trital)*; (*Kramik Pustak Malika,* 2nd part, p.37, Hindi Edition):

भज हरि नाम तू मोरे मनवा
सब सुखकारक भव भयहारक।
पूरन होत सकल तेरे काम।।

Khayal Gaudsarang (Trital); (*Kramik Pustak Malika,* 4th part, p.138, Marathi Edition):

भज मन राम नाम सुखदाई।

घरि घरि पल पल अवधि बितत सब फिर पाछे पछताई।।

भाइ बंधु सब कुटुम कबीला देखत जिय ललचाई।

अंत समै कोइ काम न आवत चतुर कहे समझाई।।

Chatur, Chaturi, Chatra, Chatara, Chat, Har, Hararang etc. were the pseudonyms of Bhatkhande which he used in all his compositions of songs. The idea and the manner of execution can well be compared to Meera's traditional *bhajan:*

भज मन चरण कमल अविनासी

or, Tulsidasa's *bhajan:*

भज मन राम चरण सुखदाई

Here is a composition of Bhatkhande in the same strain. It is a *Chhota khayal* in *Raga Kalingra; (Kramik Pustak Malika,* 3rd part, p.309, Hindi Edition.):

राम नाम भजन करो!

भव जलधी तुरत तरो।।

अनित जगत साँच समझ

नाहक तुम लोभ करो।।

चतुर कहत सुलभ जुगति

हररंग को ध्यान घरो।।

The only deviation from the traditional composition of the poets belonging to the *Bhakti* period is that, for the sake of the form of *khayal,* Bhatkhande's compositions are short, comprising of *sthayi* and *antara* only. His *Chhota khayal* in *Durga* and *Jaitkalyan* can very well be categorised as traditional devotional songs, both in spirit and language:

(1)   *Chhota khayal* in *Durga (Trital); (Kramik Pustak Malika,* 5th part, p.207, Hindi Edition):

देवी भजो दुरगा भवानी।

जगतजननी महिषासुर मरदनी।।

हिमनगनन्दिनि भवभयकंदिनि।

शरनागत चतुर अभयवरदानि।।

(2)   *Chhota khayal in Jaitkalyan (Jhaptal); (Kramik Pustak Malika,* 5th part, p.58, Hindi Edition):

जय जय भवानि पति जय पंचवदना।

नमन करे चतुर भाव धर सुघ अंतर जगत निस्तारना। ।

These are only a few illustrations picked up at random of the language and content of Bhatkhande's compositions.

Word Content -- Clear Words with Chaste Meaning -- of Musical Compositions

In the late nineteenth century and in the beginning of the twentieth century, the average musicians, by and large, neglected the poetic part of the compositions of *khayal* for the sake of the melodic structure. The few valuable compositions, having the beauty of content and melodic form, were in the hands of the few *gharanedar* musicians, who zealously guarded them and handed them over to the few close members of their families. It is also true that in the domain of Classical music there had always been a controversy raging between the poet and the musician. The musicians, by and large, felt that the literary aspect of songs, which were means to demonstrate *ragas,* was less important than their melodic structure. Driven by this idea the musicians of the nineteenth and the early twentieth century neglected the poetic and literary part of Classical songs. The illiteracy of the musicians no less contributed to such criminal neglect. In some cases of *Bara khayal* the composition shrank into a couple of words only which brought it up to the *sam* of the time measure. The rest was extempore elaboration of the note patterns, developed for the sake of the *raga.* The *Chhota khayal*s also met with the same fate. In many cases the composition had one line of *sthayi* and nothing else.

But in a musical composition the language part is as important as the melodic part. The language is the vehicle of poetry which, in conformity with the melodic form of a *raga,* is able to create *rasa* or the aesthetic experience of both the performer and the listener.

How the language was overlooked as the vehicle of sentiments portrayed, in correspondence with the tune, and how crude and disjointed was the manner of execution and interpretation -- with

no eye to the balance of words, tune and sentiment portrayed
-- was remarked upon by Capt. Willard in his *A Treatise on the
Music of Hindoostan:* "...But when we come to examine the sentiment which has been delivered in so delicate a strain, and which
we fancy will be in accordance with the beauty of the melody, we
find ourselves sadly disappointed for they contain odd sentences
awkwardly put together."

The traditional compositions -- though superbly balanced in
melodic content and *laya* (rhythmic) content, emphasising the salient
points of a *raga* -- mostly suffered in poetic idea and hence lacked
the quality for establishing the *rasa* or *bhava* in music.

If we go through the traditional *khayal*s we find that there are
very few compositions where the beauty of the word and the melody
coincide. Mostly the idea is drawn from every day life or the eternal
love-tale of a female -- jealous, frustrated and eager to meet the
beloved. The content is often finely sacrificed at the altar of the
melodic structure. Take, for instance, the widely sung traditional
khayal of *Jaijaiwanti* -- *vilambit khayal, raga Jaijaiwanti (Ektal);*
(*Kramik Pustak Malika,* 4th part, p.284, Marathi Edition):

पालना गढ़ ला रे बढ़ैया।

This first line has no poetic imagery, while it, as a *mukhra*, has
to be repeated a number of times to rest on the *sam*. The saving
factor of this prosaic composition, however, lies at the end of
the *antara* which saves the idea of this song from becoming
commonplace and mundane:

रतन जड़ाव को पालना बनावो
झूले   कृष्ण   कन्हैया।।

Let us take Bhatkhande's composition of *Bara khayal* in the same
raga; (*Kramik Pustak Malika,* 4th part, p.284, Hindi Edition):

गावो सखियाँ मंगल आज।
चतुर पिया घर आवन कीने मेलं करो खंमाज।
जयजयवंती गनि सुर जुगकर रिखबवादीनी कौ साध   ।।

It is a poem indicating the happy mood of a woman thrilled by
the coming of her lover, and the details of the *raga Jaijaiwanti* are

added to it cleverly.

Here is another example of a typical traditional composition having words of very poor poetic quality. *Khayal Darbari Kanhara* -- Agra School; (*Kramik Pustak Malika*, 4th part, p.679, Hindi Edition):

ए तब तो तुम कहते थे यूँ

अब तुम कैह्ने लागे यूँ।

Melodically, however, the composition is a beautiful one and the vowels and the rest notes mix up so well that the poor poetic aspect is overlooked.

Let us see Bhatkhande's composition in *Darbari* as against this:

समझत ना मन तू मेरा, समझत ना मन तू मेरा।

लाख बार समझावत हूँ मैं, काहे न तजत अँधेरा।।

झूठी माया झूठी काया, झूठा जगत बसेरा।

अंत समै कोई काम न आवत, चत्र प्रभू एक तेरा।।

The above song is from the Hindi edition of *Kramik Pustak Malika*, 4th part, page 659, in *khayal (Trital)*. The devotional and philosophical strain running through the song expressed in clear words is noteworthy.

One remarkable quality of Bhatkhande's compositions was that they contained words acceptable to respectable society. They avoided all that was base in ideas and vile in thoughts. Sometimes traditional compositions, while really superb, so far as the melodic structure was concerned, had very often vulgar ideas. Take for instance a traditional *khayal* in *Deshkar;* (*Kramik Pustak Malika*, 4th part, p.254, Marathi Edition):

मोरी अँगिया के बंद खुल गई ला

हे दइ मारे लंगरवा । हाँ हाँ रे मोरी ।।

अचरा पकर मोरि बैयाँ झिझके लीनि

औरे हाँ हाँ कर जोरि, मोरी ।।

It is a classic example of eve-teasing by a certain play-boy. Though the name of the amorous cowherd, Lord Krishna, as the mischief-maker is not mentioned in this song, the listeners usually connect their mind with the pranks of this boisterous God and hence exonerate the vulgar part of it.

Let us compare with this Bhatkhande's composition composed in the same *raga* and in the same *tala;* (*Kramik Pustak Malika,* 4th part, p.248,   Hindi Edition):

हरि को नाम उचार तू नर

निराकार निरविधि अति मंगल

तज मन को मल शुचि घर अंतर

भज करूणाकर निरगुण अघहर।

जो उपदेश करे हिरदे नर

गावत प्रात समै अति सुस्वर

एक भावघर प्रेम पुरस्सर

पाय चतुर उद्धार हि भू पर॥

The words are clear, well-chosen to express the devotional strain. The word composition of the *sthayi* has an air of expansion lent by the mention of God as the formless and all-pervading one. The last line of the *antara* bears Bhatkhande's pseudonym Chatur. The use of the words that "it should be sung in the morning" coincide with the temperament of *raga Deshkar,* the morning melody.

It is noteworthy that musically the first song starting with words '*Mori angiya...*' has to employ the words '*la*', '*he*', '*han*' to fill up the gaps in the division of 16 beats of *teental* while Bhatkhande's composition leaves no gap to add unnecessary syllables. It is a clear proof of his poetic capacity as a composer.

There is another *Bara khayal* in *Deshkar, trital vilambit,* in the traditional style. It is superb so far as the melodic structure is concerned. The words are:

खुमाभरे पी आइला रे दइ मारे लँगरवा

हा हा करत तोरे पैयाँ परिलवा

हमीसन माँगेइ पियलवा मा।।

हमरि नगरिया में मघवा लाईलवा

साँचि कहो तो मोरे सैयाँ

अनत जामे जहाँ रहीला लुभाये मा।।

(*Kramik Pustak Malika,* 4th part, p.256, Marathi Edition)

If we analyse the above song linguistically it appears to be a mixture of the rural language of eastern U.P. and Braj Bhasha. It is about a drunk play-boy who approaches his beloved. The utterances of the beloved, describing the condition of the drunk play-boy, are vulgar. The composition is inspired only by base thoughts. Compare this with Bhatkhande's composition of a *Bara khayal* in the same *raga* and *tala*:

भज ले महेश मनुजा पद को

सफल करें अपनी नर देह।

तज भव तृष्णा मोह जाल सब

इन सों मुधा चतुर जग मों नेह।।

(*Kramik Pustak Malika,* 4th part, p.258, Hindi Edition)

While musically it retains the beauty of the traditional composition the words are well-knit, clear in ideas, devotional in content and linguistically written in chaste Hindi with a tinge of Braj Bhasha.

We can draw another comparative illustration of similar *khayal* composition in *raga Darbari:*

Khayal Darbari Kanhara (Trital)

मधुवा भर लादे मीत मोरे हम से दें लुकाई

हम तुम भर भर पीवें।

भर्के दे लुकाई कहूँ कान न कान न जाने

जो जो देत मधुवा हमरा

तो तो हम तुम भर भर पीवें।

(*Kramik Pustak Malika,* 4th part, p.670, Hindi Edition)

This is a description of the hankering for wine by a drunkard. If a singer has to create the mood of this song, he can rouse only base feelings. It is only in the association of drunkards that this song can be successfully demonstrated. Moreover, these words cannot be the vehicle of expression of a sombre *raga* like *Darbari Kanhara.*

Let us compare this with a composition of Bhatkhande in

the same *tala* and the same *raga*:

सुमिरन कर मन पवीत्र निर्गुन पर ब्रह्म

फिर पछितावेगो तू मानि वृथा अभिमान।

जरा कही अरे अरे मन

जोबन् सरूप तन् हो जावे दहन्

नहिं साथ संगाथ कल्त्र पुत्र बतेन्

जो चाहे मुक्ति को चतुर तु जतन्।

(*Kramik Pustak Malika*, 4th part, p.660, Hindi Edition)

Contrary to the other song it produces a philosophical mood, a mood of renunciation. Bhatkhande, who composed innumerable songs in such devotional strain, had also collected and published in his *Kramik Pustak Malika* series some typical traditional compositions having mundane ideas for the sake of their melodic compositional beauty.   An example:

Darbari Kanhara (Trital)

घर जाने दे छाँड़ मोरि बैयाँ

हौं हौं करत तोरे पैयाँ परत हूँ

मोहन से झगरियाँ।

नगर बगर के लोगवा सुनत हैं, चर्चा करत ब्रज नारियाँ

जाओ जि जाओ जि तुम खाओगे गालियाँ।

मोहन से झगरियाँ।

(*Kramik Pustak Malika*, 4th part, p.665, Hindi Edition)

This is the utterance of a female, obviously of Braj, complaining against the playboyish behaviour of Lord Krishna. The words *khaoge gaaliyan, Mohan se jhagraiyan* are unpoetic and crude.   The whole composition does not inspire any sublime or deep emotion.

The Balance of Self-Explanatory Words and Tune

It is relevant to mention here that *khayal* unlike *dhrupad* is the most concise of the composed forms of Classical music. It has only two movements -- *Tuks* or *Dhatus*: the *sthayi* and the *antara*, which serve as the base for extempore elaboration. The innate structural quality of a *khayal* should be such that each part or patch fits into the *sthaya* or the musical phrases of *tanas* as they proceed. It is the development of these *sthayas* or phrases which leads to the development of both composed and improvised forms. Therefore, the ideal *khayal* composition should be such that its words should be able to fit into the tonal structure of the *sthaya*. The poem of a *khayal* cannot be highly literary at the cost of the *raga*. Nor can it be a fully developed melodic personality at the expense of poetry. Its beauty lies in the subtle balance between the two.

A *raga*, however, when demonstrated in the traditional way, even only with *alapa* (song with only vowels or meaningless sounds without words), is capable of establishing its own character as an individual personality. That is also apparent from the demonstration of instrumental music where there are no words at all.

When *Sahitya* is introduced in a *raga* then the first consideration is to keep the tonal structure of a *raga* intact. The words should not burden the notes and the rest notes of a *raga*, resulting in distortion of its form.

So, when we consider one of the best typical traditional compositions we find that melodically it is expressive of the *raga*'s form and in regard to word and meaning it does not have a complex idea which could take the listener's mind away from the *raga*'s form. For example, we can quote the traditional *Bara khayal* of *Desi Todi*:

Khayal Desi (Ektal Vilambit)

नैया मोरी भई पुरानी

खेवट सदा मतवार।

औघट घाट सूझत नाहीं

आन परी मझधार।।

(*Kramik Pustak Malika*, 6th part, p.317, Hindi Edition)

Melodically, it employs the characteristic feature of *raga Desi Todi* while the theme deals with a philosophic idea. The predominance of vowels in the word composition has a special importance. It is easier to develop the melodic pattern with the help of the vowels attached to the words. Meaningwise, the words are self-explanatory. Similarly, another instance is this *Bara khayal* of *Alhaiya Bilawal:*

दैया कहाँ गए लोग

ब्रज के बसैया।

Here also, the predominance of vowels is noteworthy. Bhatkhande's compositions also have the same quality. Let us take the example of the most widely sung *Bhairavi, Jhaptal (Madhya Laya); (Kramik Pustak Malika,* 2nd part, p.415, Hindi Edition):

STHAYI

(x)		(2)			(0)		(3)		
ध सां वा	– S	सां नी	– S	सां रें द	सां या	– S	नि घ नी	प S	ध भ प म
नि हा	– S	घ वा	– S	प कं	प बा	– S	म ग नी	– S	म सु
प र	प नि न	ध र	प मु	प नि	म ग ज	ग न	रें मां	– S	सा नि
सा ग स	ग कं	ग ल	रें बु	रें घ	सा ग्या	– S	नि घ नी	S,	नि भं

ANTARA

प ध ज ×	म ग	ध ज २	ध न	नि नि	सां ज ०	सां ग	सां जा ३	– S	सां नि
सां रें म ×	रें ही	रें षा २	– S	रें सु	ग र ०	रें म	रें र ३	सां द	सां नि
सां ग ज्वा ×	– S	रें ग ला २	– S	म मु	ग रें खी ०	– S	सां चं ३	– S	सां हि
प अ ×	घ म	नि र २	सां प	रें द	सां दा ०	– S	नि घ नी ३	– S,	मि म।

It is in praise of the all-powerful Mother Goddess, the Creator of the universe. The words are expressive, well-coined to be fitted into the 10 *matra* divisions of *jhaptal*.

The elongated vowels of *aa* and *ee* at the end of each line are capable of melodic development and are important for *firat* and *boltan*. The words *Bhavani, Dayani* and *Mahavakbani* are such that they suggest a whole gamut of ideas about attributes of the Goddess. Any one of these can be chosen for the development of the melodic structure and expression of emotion. The whole composition covers the upper octave and the *sam* is on the *tar su* which adds to the grandeur of the words and also creates a mood for prayer.

III

THE RAGA'S FORM

Importance of Raga's Form

Although in a musical composition both words and tune carry the same importance, yet on close scrutiny it appears that the melodic part carries more weight, especially when the composition belongs to the classical variety. The first condition of our classical composition is that it should adhere to the correct form of a *raga* -- its notes employed in ascension and descension, its employment of catch notes, typical melodic phrases and even its use of *vadi* and *vivadi swaras*. In fact the traditional compositions manifested all these qualities and were used as the model form of any *raga*.

Bhatkhande collected the traditional compositions from the stalwarts of Jaipur *gharana*, Rampur *gharana* and Gwalior *gharana*. He took lot of pains to scrutinise them, analyse them and translate them into note patterns *(sargam)*. He defined them as the *raga*'s form by taking into account the note pattern and their combinations. It is interesting to note that Bhatkhande composed some *khayals* keeping their melodic structures identical with those of the parallel traditional compositions. For example:

Traditional : *Gaudsarang (Trital)*

STHAYI

म		म													
ग	म	ध	प	ग	म	रे	सा	-	रे	सा	-	मप	मप	म	ग
मे	रो	म	न	न॑	S	द	ला	S	ल	सोँ	S	अS	टS	को	S
२				०				३				×			

-	-	-	-	सा	सा	म	ग	प	प	प	प	मप	धनि	मैं	ध
S	S	S	S	म	न	ब	स	ग	यो	अ	लि	श्याS	SS	म	सुं
२				० प				३ नि				×			

मैं	प	म	ग	म	-	प	प	ध	नि	सा	नि	घ	प	म	ग
द	र	के	S	मो	S	र	मु	क	ट	को	S	ल	ट	को	S।
२				०				३				×			

(Kramik Pustak Malika, 4th part, p.146, Hindi Edition)

Bhatkhande's similar composition : *Gaudsarang (Trital)*

STHAYI

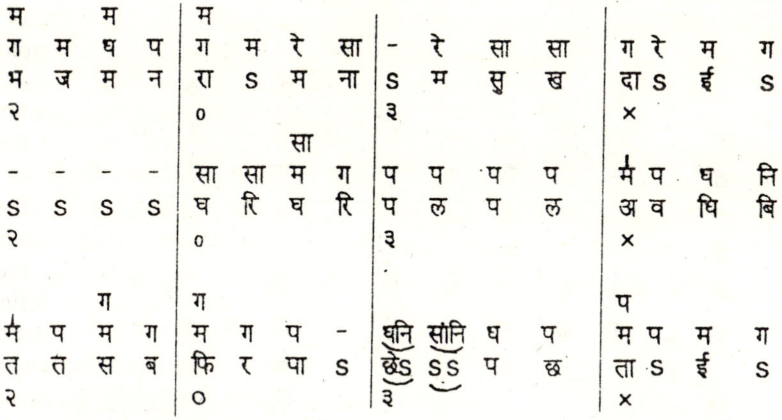

	म		म		म			—		ग	
ग	म	ध	प	ग	म	रे	सा	रे	सा सा	रे	म ग
भ ज	म न	रा S	म ना	S म	सु ख	दा S	ई S
२		0		३		×	
—	—	—	—	सा	सा	म	ग	प	प	प	प	मं	प	ध	नि
S	S	S	S	घ	रि	घ	रि	प प	ल	प	ल	अ व	धि	बि
२		0		३		×	
		ग		ग							प	
मं	प	म	ग	म	ग	प	—	(धनि)छेS	(सानि)SS	घ प	प छ	म	प	म	ग
त	त	स	ब	फि	र	पा	S	३		ता S	ई S
२		O		३		×	

(*Kramik Pustak Malika*, 4th part, p.145, Hindi Edition)

Another illustration of the same nature follows as under:

Traditional : *Surdasi Malhar (Trital)*

STHAYI

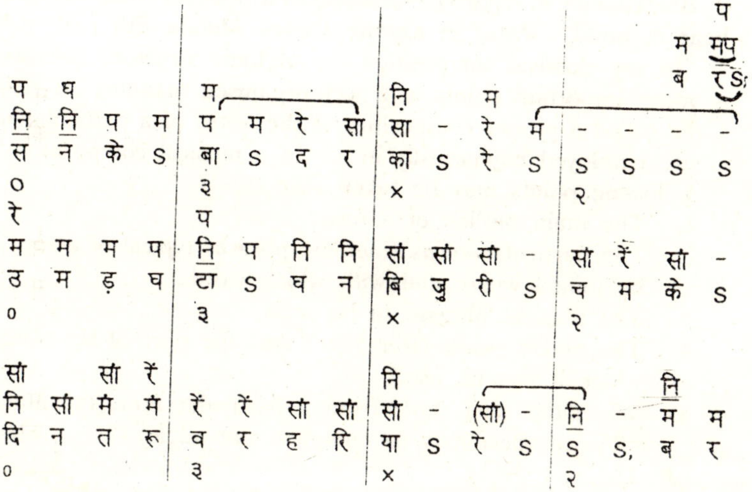

												प
												म	मप
प	ध		म	म प	म	रे	सा	नि	म	मं	—	—	—	ब	(रS)
निस	निन	प के	म S	बा S	द	र	सा का	S	रे रे	S	S	S	S
ओरे				३ प			×		२
म त	म ड़	म	प	निटा	प S	नि घ	नि न	सा बि	सा जु	सी री	— S	सां च	रें म	सी के	— S
0				३			×		२
सा	सा	रें						नि			नि		नि
निदि	सान	मत	मेरू	रेंव	रें र	साह	सारि	सा या	— S रे	(सा) S	निS	S,	मब	म र
0				३			×		२

(*Kramik Pustak Malika*, 6th part, p.266, Hindi Edition)

Bhatkhande's identical composition:

STHAYI

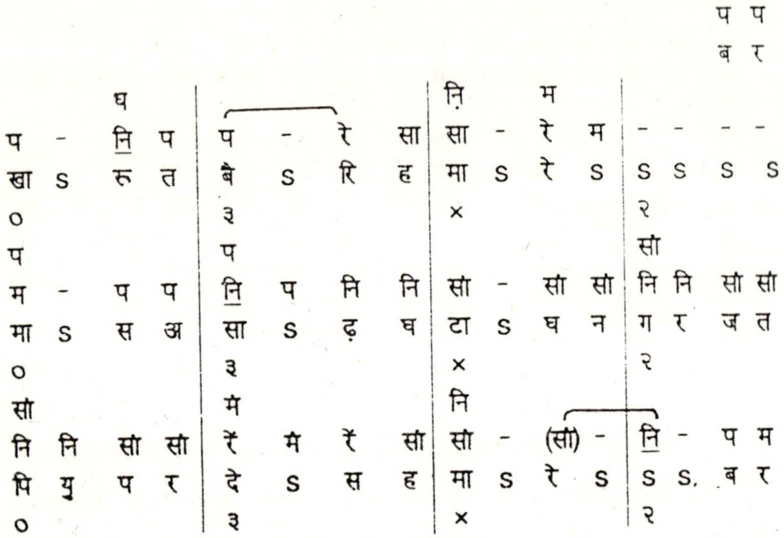

प - नि प | प - रे सा | सा - रे म | - - - -
खा S रू त | बै S रि ह | मा S रे S | S S S S
o | ३ | × | २
प | प | | सा
म - प प | नि प नि नि | सा - सा सा | नि नि सा सा
मा S स अ | सा S ढ़ घ | टा S घ न | ग र ज त
o | ३ | × | २
सा | म | नि |
नि नि सा सा | रें म रें सा | सा - (सा) - | नि - प म
पि यु प र | दे S स ह | मा S रे S | S S. ब र
o | ३ | × | २

(*Kramik Pustak Malika*, 6th part, p.265, Hindi Edition)

Bhatkhande, in regard to the important points a composer should bear in mind, writes in *Kramik Pustak Malika*, 5th part, p.49: "In any classical composition the melodic structure consists of many important points in a well-organised manner. It cannot be called a proper composition if the notes of a particular *raga* are employed haphazardly in it. In a musical composition the following points may be taken care of:

1. The main outline of a *raga*.
2. The particular *anga*s (melodic phrases typical of a *raga*) to be joined where and with which words?
3. The musical phrases to be used.
4. The *mukta swara* (free note) and the part of the song in which it can be used.
5. When the song starts from a particular note, the number of words necessary to complete one idea.
6. The rest notes.
7. The word to be prolonged for the sake of *raga*, *tala* and expression.

8. Which note should cover which note?
9. The relationship of the elongated word with the poetic effect of the composition or the *bandish*.
10. Which part of the song should be used in which part of the *tala?*"

These points are taken care of and successfully illustrated in his compositions. Here is a composition of Bhatkhande in *raga Todi* which follows all the above-mentioned rules.

Raga Todi (Trital)

नाहक पीतडि तोडि हमतें

ना कछु बोली ना कछु चाली, लाज शरम सब छोड़ी

याद आवत मोहे रागनि मूरत, मेल वरालो रोश मम विकरत

समवादी सुर रेखव धैवत, चांद सुरज की जोड़ी।

STHAYI

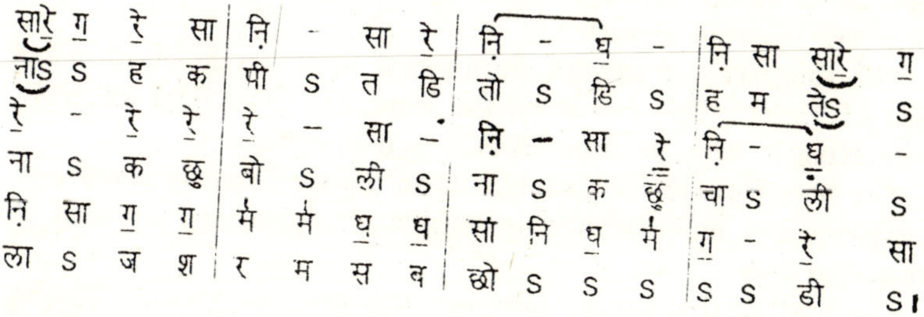

ANTARA

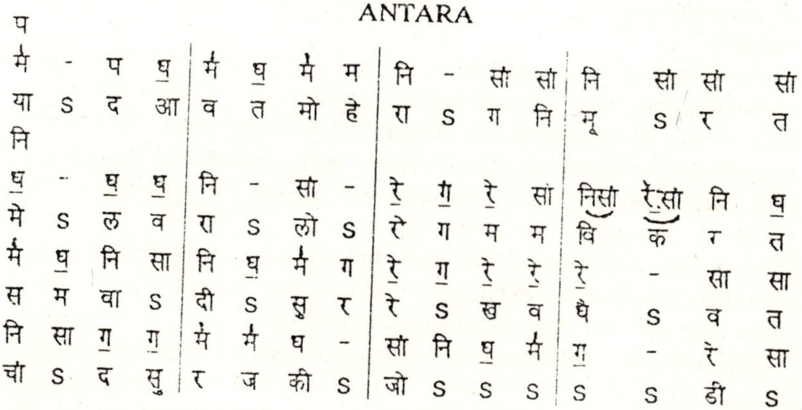

(From *Geet Malika*, 6th part, p.23. Reproduced in *Bhatkhande Smriti Grantha*, p.246)

The main outline of the *raga* is established in the first line of the composition.   The word *naahak* employs *raga Todi*'s catch notes *sa re ga re sa*.   By the time the first line is complete the entire picture of the *raga* is established by the note composition *sa re ga re sa, ni sa re ni dha ni sa su re ga*.   In the next line of *sthayi re* has been accentuated by its repeated use along with the word *na kachhu*.   Similarly in *antara*, apart from *Sa* which is the rest note *dha* is accentuated along with the word *mela*.   In *raga Todi* the notes *re* and *dha* have special significance which are *samvadi* and *vadi* respectively.   So by accentuating by repetition of *re* and *dha* the form of *raga* is correctly established in its purity.

The language bears the stamp of Bhatkhande's poetic genius. There is a pun on the word *todi* which also means *raga Todi*.   The words start with the emotional refrain in repentance,   love and anguish.   In *antara* this strain is followed by the beginning words *yaad aavat mohe* and then suddenly the particulars of the *raga*'s form are inserted cleverly.

The song starts from the ninth *matra* of the cycle of 16 *matra* beat of *Trital*.   The *sam* is on the word *todi*. The dual meaning, connecting it with the *raga Todi*,   is noteworthy.

The line, from the beginning,   up to the *sam naahak pitadi todi* completes one idea and also is capable of rousing the emotion of frustrated love.

The word *na* in the second line is elongated in notes. It is capable of accentuating the feeling of frustration and repentance mixed together.

At the end of the *sthayi* the word *chhodi* is prolonged to 8 *matras* employing the entire *avarohi* notes of *raga Todi*. Again,   with the help of this elongated word,   the mood of frustration,   love and repentance is expressed. Similarly the note pattern and the vowel *o* of *chhodi* leaves room for development of note patterns and short *tanas*.

It is also noteworthy that each line of *sthayi* and *antara* is a complete sentence by itself.   One line is not carried over to the other line for the sake of meaning or rhyme.

The last word *chhodi* easily rhymes with *todi*.   The word *hamten* at the end of the first line is a filler. The word *todi* has a pause after the *sam* which falls at *dha*. It is the   predominant note of *raga Todi*.

Let us take another example of Bhatkhande's composition:

Raga Tilak Kamod (Jhaptal)

सैंयाँ सन इतनी जाय कहो मोरि बिनति
तुम बिन कल न परत जुग सी बितत घरि।
नैनन कि नींद गई रजनी बैरन भई
सुनि सेज रि चतुर विरह तन अगन जरि ।।

(*Kramik Pustak Malika*, 3rd part, p.295, Hindi Edition)

STHAYI

	म.1	म.2	म.3	म.4	म.5	म.6	म.7	म.8	म.9	म.10
ताल	×		२			०		३		
स्वर	सा	–	प	नि	सां	प	ध	म	ग	रे
पद	सैं	S	S	याँ	S	स	न	इ	त	नी
स्वर	म	रे	रेप	गम	गरे	सा	रे	ग	नि	सा
पद	जा	S	य	क	होऽ	मो	रि	बि	न	ति
स्वर	नि॒	म	सा	सा	सा	गरे	रे	ग	नि	सा
पद	तु	म	बि	न	क	ल	न	प	र	त
स्वर	मरे	रे	रे	–	प	ध	प	ध	म	रे
पद	जु	ग	सी	S	बि	त	त	S	घ	रि

ANTARA

मॅ	-	प	नि	सॉं नि	सॉं नीं	-	नि	सॉं सॉं
नॅ	S	न	न	कि	S	द	ग	ई
×		२			०		३	
मॅ	गॅ				रॅ	गॅ	रॅ	
रॅ	रॅ	(गॅपॅ	मॅ	(गॅरॅं	सॉं रॅ	गॅ	नि	सॉं
रॅ	ज	नींऽ)	बॅ	SS)	रॅ न	S	मॅ	ई
×		२			०		३	
						प	प	
सॉं	-	नि	सॉं -	प	घ	मॅ	गॅ	रॅ
सुॅ	S	नि	से S	ज	रि	चॅ	तॅ	रॅ
×		२			०		३	
मॅ		रॅ	ग				रॅ	
रॅ	रॅ	प	मॅ	(गॅरॅ	सॉं	रॅ	गॅ	निॅ सॉं
बिॅ	रॅ	हॅ	तॅ	नऽ)	अ	ग	न	ज रि
×		२			०		३	

This is a poignant utterance of a female requesting the beloved not to leave her in anguish as the separation is unbearable for her. Poetically it creates a mood of love and anguish which goes well with the spirit of *Tilak Kamod*. It is a sweet melody, which is regarded not as sombre as *raga Darbari* and *Malkauns*, and is not to be demonstrated in a very slow tempo, having very slow exposition and elaboration. The main characteristic of *raga Tilak Kamod* is that, although it resembles *raga Desh*, its individuality is maintained by its particular phrases and note pattern. As, for example, in the opening line of the song the word *saiyaan* falls on the note pattern of *sa pa ni sa* which indicates a typical phrase of *raga Tilak Kamod* as opposed to the other *ragas* of allied nature. Again, *san itani* employs *pa dha ma ga re* which is again a significant phrase of *raga Tilak Kamod*. The rest note being *re* indicates the characteristic nature of *raga Tilak Kamod*. The second line *jaay kaho mori binati* again employs a typical phrase of *raga Tilak Kamod: re pa ma ga re, sa re ga ni sa*. The third line *tum bin kal na parat* takes the catch notes of *raga Tilak Kamod: ni pa ṇi sa sa re re ga ṇi sa.* These are a few instances to show how Bhatkhande's compositions are wonderfully balanced in words and classical *raga* structure.

IV

THE TALA CONTENT

There is a maxim '*Shruti Mata Layah Pita.*' The meaning of these words is that in a musical composition the notes have the position of a mother while the rhythm is regarded as the father. To explain it one can say that in a musical composition *swara* and *laya* have equal importance. If one analyses closely one finds that while a group of musical notes expresses the spirit and appeals of a musical composition, it is to a large extent the time duration and rhythm that determine its shape, emphasis and movement. From ancient times this subject had been treated at great length and as a result a very intricate and elaborate *tala* system developed in our music. It is only in the *tala* system of our music that we find not only a systematic study of time as an absolute factor but also as a function and a determinant of a musical structure. Both in Hindustani and Karnatak music an innumerable variety of *tala*s is conceived and practised which has no parallel in any other musical system of the world.

Structural forms based on these time measures or *tala*s have been cleverly utilised in applied forms. For our different types of music there is a variety of *tala*s in use for practical purposes. Bhatkhande's compositions employed all types of *tala*s in our Classical music, covering both common and uncommon ones.

When we analyse our Classical music, we feel that the *tala* has been magnificently conceived in *dhrupad*. In *dhrupad* the *tala* employed was elaborate, elastic and intricate. Usually the *dhrupad*s were composed in *chautal*--12 *matra* beat--and also in 10 *matra* beat, known as *sultal* and *jhaptal*. *Dhrupad* is also composed in *teevra* (7 *matra* beat) and in other uncommon *tala*s as *Brahmatal* etc.

Bhatkhande has a number of *dhrupad* compositions to his credit. His *dhrupad*s retain the pristine purity of the form and content of the traditional compositions. His *dhrupad* in *Multani* composed in *chautal* bears this out:

स्थायी – नित्य शुद्ध बुद्ध मुक्त सच्चिदानंद रूप
          जा को न कछु उपाधि पार ब्रह्म अति अनूप।
अंतरा – सकल जगत उपादान मूल प्रकृति है निदान
          जाके संयोग जनित व्यक्त होत नाम रूप।।
संचारी – माया संगत ईश्वर एक हू अनेक होत
          भोगत आदृष्टज फल जाको जैसोहि करम।
आभोग – स्वप्नावस्थित रहे जिव हेम पूर्व होत गर्भ
          जाग्रत वैश्वान्र नित हरंग बरनत सरूप।।

The idea is in praise of the Formless, Omnipotent and Omniscient God. The language is pure Hindi, rather Sanskritised, and the melodic part is in strict conformity with the *raga*'s form, complete with four parts of song *(sthayi, antara, sanchari* and *abhog)*. Rhythmwise he set it magnificently in 12 *matra* beat.

Multani Dhrupad (Chautal)

STHAYI

Sthayi

प	–	प	ग	म̇	प	ग	–	रे	सा	–	सा
नि	S	त्य	शु	S	द	बु	S	द	मु	S	क्त
×		0		२		0		३		४	

नि	–	सा	म̇	ग	म̇	प	–	प	ध	–	प
स	S	च्चि	दा	S	S	नें	S	द	रू	S	प
×		0		२		0		३		४	

प	–	–	ग	–	म̇	प	नि	नि	नि	सा	सा
जा	S	S	को	S	न	क	छु	उ	पा	S	धि
×		0		२		0		३		४	

नि	सा	नि	ध	प	ग	प	ग	रे	सा	–	सा
पा	S	र	ब्र	S	ह्म	अ	ति	अ	नू	S	प
×		0		२		0		३		४	

(Kramik Pustak Malika, 4th part, p.778, Hindi Edition)

It will be noticed that the first vowel of each word is systematically prolonged to 1 *matra* right up to the end. Each line is complete within 12 *matra*s. The precision of the self-explanatory words gives it a balance of tune and rhythm, providing scope for making the rhythm double, treble and of other intricate patterns which is the usual technique of *dhrupad* singing.

Here is another instance of his composition in *chautal*. It is set in *raga Bhimpalasi*.

स्थायी – नाद सागर अप्रपार
किन हूँ न पायो पार।
सरसती अजहूँ डरत
करत तूँब के आधार ।।

अंतरा – सारंग देव भरत
राम सोम पुंडरीक।
व्यंकटमखि अहोबल
चत्र थाके कर विचार ।।

(*Kramik Pustak Malika*, 3rd part, pp.547-'8, Hindi Edition)

It is a beautiful composition in praise of the cosmic sound which took the form of musical notes. In the second part of the song the well-known musicologists Bharata, Sharngadeva, Venkatamakhi, Ahobal etc. -- from the ancient age to the present day--are named. In the end the name 'Chatra' is indicative of Bhatkhande himself. Here also the first vowel of each word is prolonged to 1 *matra* and each line is complete within 12 *matra*s. The *sam* starts from the first *matra* so that after the development of the intricacy of rhythm it can easily come back to the beginning of *chautal*, synchronising it with the beginning of the song:

सा नि॒ंसा (नं॑S)	ग S	रे द	सा सा	– S	नि॑ं ध॑ं ग	प॑ म॑ र	प॑ म॒ अ	प॑ प्रं॑ ३	नि॑ं पा	सा S	सा र
×	०	२				०		३		४	
सा नि॒ंकि॑	सा नि॒ंन	सा S	म हूँ	(सा ग॒ S	म न	प पा	– S	म॒ग॒ योंS) ३	म॒ग॒ पाS)	रे S	सा र
×	०	२				०				४	
सा नि॒ंसं	सा नि॒ंर॑	सा S	ग॒ म स	म ग॒ ती	म S	म प अ	प प ज	प नि॒ हूँ ३	प नि॒ ड	घ र॒	प त
×	०		२			०				४	
प नि॒ क	प र	प त	म तूँ	(म ग॒ S	म ब	प पा के	प ग॒ आ	– S धा	रे ३	– S	सा र
×	०	२				०		३		४	

He has *dhrupad* compositions in *sultal* also.   We are quoting here a composition in *raga Shri* (*Bhatkhande Smriti Grantha*, p. 225):

तमोगुण राजस गुण सत्व गुण तृतीय रे
मूल प्रकृती सुभाय जिन व्याप्यो जग रे
राजस तामस गुण जीव करव जब बस
पावत परब्रह्म सत्व गुणि चतुर रे।

By virtue of the word meaning it has been elevated to the *dhrupad* style. The words express the basic doctrine of our religious scriptures about the qualities of human nature which are responsible both for our downfall and for attaining God. The idea is clear and fitted into the 10 *matra* beat, completing each line in 10 *matras* only. It is also noteworthy that in three consecutive lines the *sam* is on the *komal Re* which is the *vadi swara* of *raga Shri*.

His *dhamar* compositions are not many. Here is one instance:

Raga Surdasi Malhar

STHAYI

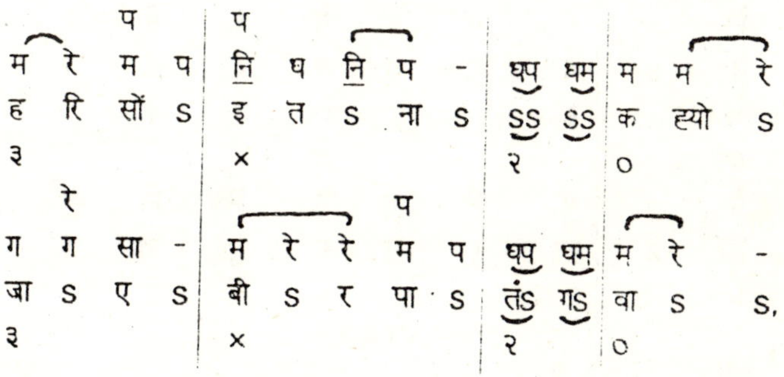

म	रे	म	प	नि	घ	नि	प	–	धुप	धम	म	म	रे
ह	रि	सों	S	इ	त	S	ना	S	SS	SS	क	ह्यो	S
३				×					र		०		

	रे					प							
ग	ग	सा	–	म	रे	रे	म	प	धुप	धम	म	रे	–
जा	S	ए	S	बी	S	र	पा	S	तंड	गड	वा	S	S,
३				×					र		०		

(*Kramik Pustak Malika*, 6th part, p.274, Hindi Edition)

Here the composition is in a lighter vein, as *dhamar* denotes the lighter mood, often depicting the *Hori* festival. Therefore, it has been mentioned as *Hori* also.

He has a rich repertoire of *saadras* which are set in *jhaptal*, 10 *matra* beat, both as songs and also as *lakshan geets*. His *saadras* in words retain the grandeur and purity of *dhrupad* and can be sung either as a *dhrupad* or a *khayal*. Musically they are well-balanced in strict conformity with the *raga*'s form. Take for instance the *saadra* in *Puriya Dhanashri* (*Jhaptal*):

STHAYI

प				म॑	ध॒		ध॒		
ध॒	-	प	-	प	म॑	ग	म॑	रे॒	ग
ते	S	रे	S	द	र	स	की	S	S
×		२			०		३		
ध॒					रे॒				
म॑	म॑ध॒	म॑	ग	रे॒	म॑	ग	रे॒	सा	सा
ला	SS	ल	सा	S	क	र	त	स	ब
×		२			०		३		
सा					ग				
नि़	-	रे॒	ग	-	म॑	रे॒	ग	प	प
दे	S	व	ग	S	ध	र	व	ग	न
×		२			०		३		
ध॒					ध॒				
म॑	-	ध॒	नि	ध॒	रें॒	निध॒	नि	ध॒	प
कि	S	न्न	र	न	र	मुS	नी	S	S।
×		२			०		३		

ANTARA

ध॒		ध॒			ध॒				
म॑	ग	म॑	प	ध॒	सां	-	सां	-	सां
आ	S	रा	S	ध	ना	S	ते	S	रे
×		२			०		३		
नि					सां				
सां	-	निध॒	नि	ध॒	नि	निरें॒	नि	ध॒	प
ना	S	मS	की	S	जो	SS	क	रे	S
×		२			०		३		
ध॒		ध॒							
म॑	म॑ध॒	म॑	म॑	गरे॒	म॑	ग	रे॒	-	सा
पा	SS	व	त	सS	क	ल	सि	S	द्वि
×		२			०		३		
सां	सां						ध॒		
नि	निरें॒	नि	ध॒	नि	ध॒	प	म॑ग	म॑रे॒	ग
ह	रS	र	ग	क	ह	त	गुS	नीS	S।
×		२			०		३		

(*Kramik Pustak Malika*, 4th part, pp.352-'3, Hindi Edition)

By virtue of the word meaning it should be sung in *dhrupad* style.

His composition in *jhaptal* of *raga Khambavati* has a different air. It should be developed in the form of a *khayal*:

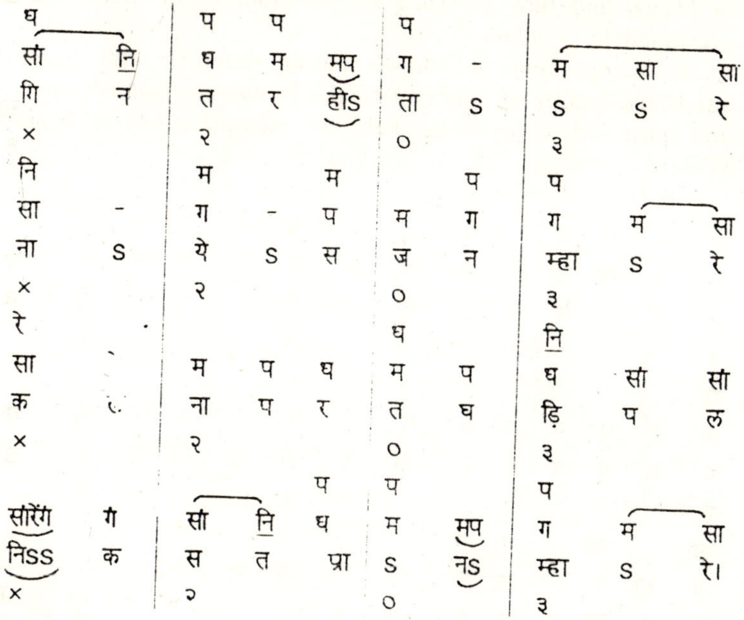

घ
सी   नि   प   प   प
गि   न   ध   म   मप   पग   -   म   सा   सां
×   त   र   हींऽ)   ता   S   S   S   रे
नि   २   ०   ३
सा   -   म   म   म   प   प   म   सां
ना   S   ग   प   स   ग   ग   मां   सा   रे
×   ये   S   स   ज   न   S   रे
रे   २   ०   नि
           ४   घ   ध
सा   .   म   प   घ   म   प   घ   सां   सां
क   ः   ना   प   र   त   घ   ड़ि   प   ल
×   २   ०   ३
                 प   प   प
सोरेंग ग   सी   नि   घ   मप   ग   म   सां
निऽऽ) क   स   त   प्रा   नऽ)   म्हा   S   रे।
×   २   ०   ३

(*Kramik Pustak Malika*, 5th part, pp.252-'3, Hindi Edition)

Employment of Tala in His Khayal Composition

If we discuss about the origin of the *khayal* compositions we find that *khayal*, as composed at the time of Sadarang and Adarang, was a loose type of *dhrupad* which employed simpler time measures and with less discipline in tempo, variation and mood.

As centuries passed, *khayal* developed its own type of *bandish* and time measure. *Khayals* were mainly in three speeds : *Vilambit*, *Madhya* and *Drut*. The commonly used *talas* were and even now are in *vilambit ektal* (12 *matras*), *trital* (16 *matras*), *jhoomra* and *ara chautal* (14 *matras*). In *madhya laya* there are mainly *trital* (16 *matras*), *ektal* (12 *matras*) and *jhaptal* (10 *matras*). In *drut laya* the *madhya laya* variety is employed with faster speed. There are a few other uncommon types of *tala*s having 9 *matra*, 17 *matra* and 18 *matra* beats etc. which are not popular.

Bhatkhande's compositions cover all types of *tala*s in the domain of *khayal* and they are sung by the students of today and are acclaimed by scholars.

His compositions in *khayal*s having different *tala*s have the admirable quality of adhering to the traditional *bandish* in tune and spirit with clear words. Take for example a *khayal* in *Hamir* (*Trital*):

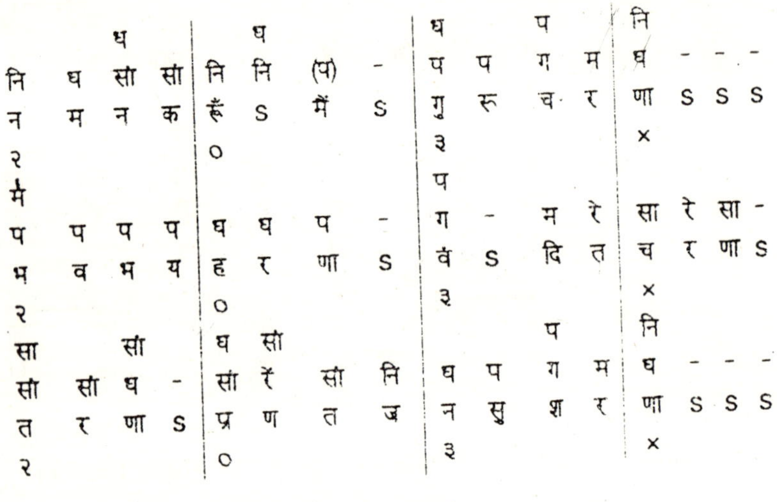

	Vibhāg (२)	Vibhāg (०)	Vibhāg (३)	Vibhāg (×)
upper svara	— ध — —	— घ — —	ध — प —	नि — — —
svara	नि घ सा सा	नि नि (प) –	प प ग म	घ – – –
sāhitya	न म न क	हुँ S मैं S	गु रू च र	णा S S S
upper svara	मैं — — —		प — — —	नि — — —
svara	प प प प	घ घ प –	ग – म रे	सा रे सा –
sāhitya	भ व म य	ह र णा S	वं S दि त	च र णा S
upper svara	सा — सा —	घ सा — —		नि — — —
svara	सा सा घ –	सां रैं सा नि	घ प ग म	घ – – –
sāhitya	त र णा S	प्र ण त ज	न सु श र	णा S S S

(Kramik Pustak Malika, 3rd part, p. 73 Hindi Edition)

It is apparent from the above composition that the *vadi swara* *dha* is accentuated on the *sam* at the end of the first line. The composition starts with each word covering almost one *matra*. The gap of 3 *matra*s after the word *charana*, which has the *sam* on the last letter, indicates the end of the line and the end of one complete idea.

In a musical composition (*bandish*) it is important to know which word should be prolonged for the sake of *tala*. It is also important to know which part of the song should be used in which part of the *tala*.

If we go through the traditional compositions we come across some beautiful compositions which manifest the above-mentioned points. Take for instance a beautiful traditional composition of Sadarang in *raga Kamod* in *trital* (16 *matra* beat) :

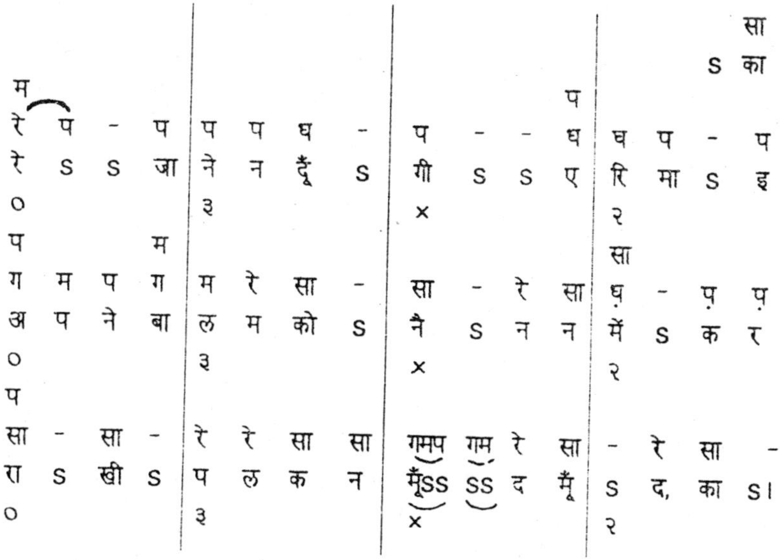

															सा
														S	का
म											प				
रे	प	–	प	प	प	ध	–	प	–	–	ध	ध	प	–	प
रे	S	S	जा	ने	न	दूँ	S	गी	S	S	ए	रि	मा	S	इ
o			३					x				२			
प			म									सा			
ग	म	प	ग	म	रे	सा	–	सा	–	रे	सा	ध॒	–	प॒	प॒
अ	प	ने	बा	ल	म	को	S	नै	S	न	न	में	S	क	र
o			३					x				२			
प															
सा	–	सा	–	रे	रे	सा	सा	गम॑प	गम॑	रे	सा	–	रे	सा	–
रा	S	खी	S	प	ल	क	न	मूँ)SS	)SS	द	मूँ	S	द,	का	S।
o			३					x				२			

(*Kramik Pustak Malika*, 4th part, p.102, Hindi Edition)

It starts from the eighth *matra* and has the *sam* on the last letter of the last word which completes the sentence expressing the idea of determination, anxiety and love mixed together. The *sam* on the word *doongi* falls on the note *pancham* which depicts the agonised state of mind. The pause of 3 *matras* after the first line depicting determination *eri mai* is treated as a filler of 4 *matras* starting from the fifth *matra*. *Apane baalam ko* again starts from the *khali* and the words *nainan mein kar rakhi palkan* starts from *sam* or the first *matra*, thus emphasising it and alerting the listeners about projecting the idea as it starts from *sam*.

We can compare these with Bhatkhande's compositions which have similar qualities. Here is a composition in *raga Kamod* in *Ektal:*

मैंपध काSS) 0	मैंप हेS)	ग म सो ३ ग म ┐ ३	रे S	सा च ४	सा त	म रे ┐ प तू S ×	प मो 0 सा घ॰ ह Ö रे प 0	प रे	घ धनि घS)	घ म २ प॰ र २ घ॰ त २	प न
मैंपध जSS) 0	मैंप नS)	म सो म न ३	रे र ४	सा न	सा दे ×	– S					प॰ म
प सा अ 0	सा वि	रे क ३	रे ल	सा अ ४	सा ज	सा म रे प प र ×	– S 0				प म।

(*Kramik Pustak Malika*, 4th part, p.98, Hindi Edition)

The idea is to alert one's mind about the short-lived nature of
human life. Here the human mind is personified and addressed as
tu. To assert the idea the *sam* falls on the word *tu* which expresses
exclamation -- (Why not O, human mind). The word *more mana*
starts from *khali* and is a filler. It is noteworthy that one line
completes one sentence in 12 *matra* beat. Nowhere is the word
broken for the *tala* nor is it unnecessarily prolonged.

Tala for Accentuating the Salient Feature of a Raga

Sometimes in the traditional compositions *tala* is used to emphasise
the main feature of a *raga*. We had discussed earlier that a *raga*
had several notes which were rest notes and accent notes -- *vadi*
and *samvadi swaras*. In traditional compositions *sam* or the
predominant *tala* comes on the *vadi swara*, thus accentuating the
main feature of a *raga*. As for example the *khayal Mubarak badiyan*
in *raga Darbari* has the *sam* on *komal Gandhar* which is peculiar
and characteristic feature in the *raga Darbari* (see *Kramik Pustak*

Malika, 4th part). Another example is *Peer na jani re* in *raga Malkauns* (see *Kramik Pustak Malika*, 3rd part). Here is a composition by Bhatkhande having similar qualities. It is in *raga Lalit* (Trital):

	मात्रा 1–4 (०)	मात्रा 5–8 (३)	मात्रा 9–12 (×)	मात्रा 13–16 (२)
स्वर	(सा) नि रे ग रे	सा – ग म	(ग) म – (ग) म म	– मॅ म (ग) ग
साहित्य	ब लि ब लि	जा S तॅ मु	खा S र बि	S द के S
स्वर	– घ मॅ घ	(सा) सा – सा सा	सा सा (रॅ)नि घ	(घ)मॅ घ सा सा
साहित्य	S सुँ द र	की S छ बि	मो रे म न	ब स ग इ
स्वर	सा – सा सा	(सा) रॅ नि घ घ	(घ)मॅ – घ म	(घ) घ मॅ – मग
साहित्य	का S क हुँ	अ प ने अ	न S द को	S पा S (ऽ)

(*Kramik Pustak Malika*, 4th part, p. 494, Hindi Edition)

Here the sam falls on the *vadi swara* of *raga Lalit* which is *shuddha ma*.

To quote another similar instance let us take the *lakshan geet* of *raga Mian Ki Malhar* (Trital):

	मात्रा 1–4 (०)	मात्रा 5–8 (३)	मात्रा 9–12 (×)	मात्रा 13–16 (२)
स्वर	(निं सा) सा म रे सा	(घ) निं निं रॅ सं	निं – घ निं	सा – सा सा
साहित्य	गा S व त	रे S स म	ला S S गुॅ	नी S ज न
स्वर	(निं) सा – सा –	रे – सं S	निं सा प म	गं मेॅ म रे सा
साहित्य	मी S याँ S	रे S स म	ह रि प्रि य	मे S ल न
स्वर	(सा) म – म प	प॰ प म (ऽ)	प गं गं म	रे – सा सा
साहित्य	अं S ग ल	स त द	बा S S गुॅ	नी S ज न।

(*Kramik Pustak Malika*, 4th part, p.565, Hindi Edition)

Here, within the four *matras* of the *sam* the *swaras* are employed which is a peculiar and significant note combination of *Mian Ki Malhar.*

Compositions in Uncommon Talas

It would be relevant to quote some of Bhatkhande's compositions in uncommon *talas*. Here is a composition in *Brahmatal* which interestingly defines *Brahmatal* in its content. It says that it has 28 *matras*, 10 *talas*, and the rest are *khalis*. In the second line it includes the *bol* of *Brahmatal:*

Line 1

Swar	सा नि	–	सा	सा	सा नि	–	प सा	नि	–	प	नि म	–	प	प	प नि	–	प	–
Bol	गा	S	व	त	ब्र	S	ह्व	ता	S	ल	चौ	S	द	स	मा	S	त्रा	S
Matra	1	2	3	4	5	6	7	8	9	10	11	12	13	14	15	16	17	18
Tala	×		०		२		३		०		४		५		६		०	

Line 2

Swar	म	प	सा	–	नि	प	म	रे	सा	सा
Bol	द	श	धा	S	त	गु	नि	क	ह	त
Matra	19	20	21	22	23	24	25	26	27	28
Tala	७		८		९		१०		०	

Line 3

Swar	सा नि	सा	सा	सा	रे	रे	म	म	रे	रे	म	–	प	–	नि	प	म	रे
Bol	धा	S	धि	न	न	क	धि	न	न	क	धि	S	द्वि	S	द्वि	न	न	क
Tala	×		०		२		३		०		४		५		६		०	

Line 4

Swar	रे सा	–	नि	प	प	म	म	रे	सा	सा
Bol	धि	S	द्वि	न	न	धि	न	न	त	क
Tala	७		८		९		१०		०	

(*Kramik Pustak Malika*, 3rd part, pp. 458-'9, Hindi Edition)

Here is another illustration of his composition in a rare *tala* called *Matta tala*. It is in *raga Shankara* and has 18 *matras*:

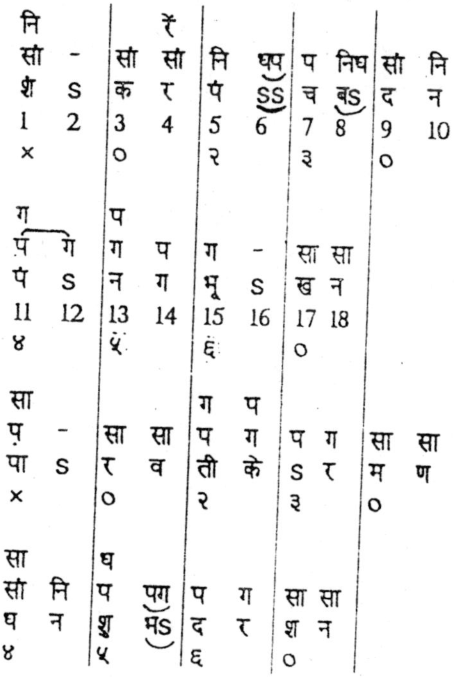

नि सॉ श्र 1 ×	- S 2	सॉ क 3 ०	रँ सॉ र 4	नि प 5 २	ध्प SS 6	प च 7 ३	निघ बS 8	सॉ द 9 ०	नि न 10
ग प्‍प पे 11 ४	ग S 12	प ग न 13 पॅ	प ग 14	ग भू 15 हॅ	- S 16	सॉ ख 17 ०	सॉ न 18		
सॉ प पा ×	- S	सॉ र ०	सॉ व	गप पती २	पग गके	प S ३	गर र	सॉ म ०	सॉ ण
सॉसॉ घ ४	नि न	धपश्‍ ५	पुग्‍MS)	पद ६	गर	सॉसॉ श ०	सॉन न		

(*Kramik Pustak Malika*, 4th part, p.211, Hindi Edition)

It is in praise of Lord Shankar whose name synchronises with *raga Shankara*. It is noteworthy how in 18 *matras* of *Matta tala* Bhatkhande has composed this song with appropriate words which are not broken, overlapped or prolonged for the sake of rhythm.

Lastly, here is another illustration of his composition in an uncommon *tala* called *Vasant tala* (18 *matra* beat):

निᵇ
सा	–	नि	प	प	नि	धसा	–	नि	प	पप	ग	ग	प
ना	S	च	त	स	ब	ता	S	ल	ब	सं	S	त	जु
1	2	3	4	5	6	7	8	9	10	11	12	13	14
×		२		३		४				५			

ग	सा	सा	सा
व	ति	ग	ण
15	16	17	18
६			

निसां	सा	ग	प	ग	सा	सासां	सा	नि	प	प	ग	ग	प
त्र	य	ग	त	ल	घु	त्र	य	क	र	ल	य	को	S
×		२		३		४				५			

ग	–	सा	सा
म	S	ध्य	म
६			

(*Kramik Pustak Malika*, 4th part, p.212, Hindi Edition)

This is a poetic imagery of the beautiful and young women dancing round, of course, in the rhythm of *Vasant tala*. The name *Vasant* is connected with the spring and gaiety, most suitable to be described in this *tala*.

We may now easily conclude that the rhythmic designs in his compositions are perfect which hold together the words, classical tune and emotion in a subtle balance.

V

LAKSHAN GEETS

The Sanskrit word *lakshan* means sign. *Lakshan geets* can be literally translated as songs describing signs to recognise all *rugas*.

In other words, a *lakshan geet* is a song which describes the rules and regulations of a particular *raga*.

Bhatkhande's *lakshan geet*s are in a class by themselves. They cover all types of *raga*s--common and uncommon. The quality of choosing the right type of word, portraying the *raga*'s technicality and mood and at the same time in the musical part of it depicting correctly the notation of a particular *raga* with the catch notes etc., is the sign of his genius. The ingenuity and beauty of his compositions are that wordwise they describe the rules and regulations, including the salient points, of a *raga*, even when it is complicated or *vakra*, wonderfully set and expressed in the short compositions of *sthayi* and *antara* and also bearing the name of its counterpart *raga* in South Indian music. The compositions are so well-set and balanced in note patterns that they can be sung and developed as *Chhota khayal*, *Bara khayal* or *Saadra* independently. The purpose of *lakshan geet*s is invariably to give a comprehensive picture of a *raga*, in a nutshell, to the learner.

The beauty of these compositions is that the melodic part starts with such combination of notes that the edifice of a *raga* is established immediately.

Bhatkhande's *lakshan geet*s, published in the *Kramik Pustak Malika*, reveal musical knowledge in such an amazingly clear, easy and poetic form that once having learnt them by heart the student or a lover of music would never forget the salient points of various *raga*s. The *gharanedar ustad*s used to hold this technical knowledge as a secret treasure and thought it a sacrilege to part with it.

Let us take some examples at random from his huge compositions of *lakshan geet*s. This is an illustration of a *lakshan geet* in *raga* *Bhupali:*

मनि बरज गाय रागनि कर जब भोपाली

अंग कहत गुनी   सब

शुद कल्याण बिलुम न तजत।

गा वादी अरु धा समवादी

देशिकार में अंश सुधैवत

राग विभास सज्जत कोमल घर

शास्त्र भेद समझाय चतुर ।।

(*Kramik Pustak Malika*, 3rd part, pp. 24-'5, Hindi Edition)

In the first line Bhatkhande describes the main feature of the *raga Bhupali* that the notes *ma* and *ni* are always dropped. Then he explains the difference between *raga Shuddha Kalyan* and *Bhupali* which are very much alike.. He says that in descension *ma* and *ni* will not be dropped in the case of *raga Shuddha Kalyan*. In fact this is the main point of difference between *Bhupali* and *Shuddha Kalyan*.

In *antara* he says that the *vadi swara* or the predominant note will be *ga* and the second predominant and *samvadi* note will be *dha* in the case of *raga Bhupali*. Then he takes up another very similar *raga Deshkar* where the predominant note is *dha* as against *Bhupali*'s *ga*. In fact, *Deshkar* and *Bhupali* are so much alike in all aspects that the only difference is the predominant note (*vadi swara*). Then in the last line he mentions about another allied *raga Vibhas* which drops *ma* and *ni* like *Bhupali* but employs *komal re* and *komal dha* in place of *Bhupali*'s *shuddha* notes of the same kind.

The most noteworthy point here is how in a song of 6-7 lines, while fitting it into the 16 *matra* beat of *teental* and the *raga Bhupali*'s note pattern, Bhatkhande has not only explained the main feature of the *raga Bhupali* but also has taken three more allied *ragas* and explained their points of difference with *Bhupali*. It shows his amazing quality of creativity and ingenuity combined with a keen sense of poetic imagery and musical knowledge. A learner, while learning *Bhupali*, is thus able to visualise three more *ragas* and the knowledge is impressed upon him in such a way that he can never be confused about the development of *Bhupali, Shuddha Kalyan, Deshkar* and *Vibhas*.

Let us take another instance of a *lakshan geet* of *raga Bageshri* (*Jhaptal*):

गावो बागेसरी मृदु लगत सुर गनां
खरहर प्रिय ठाठ तीवर करत घरी।
मध्यम करे जान समवादि सामान
पंचम करे अल्प

रे सा नि ध नि सा S म म ग
म ध नि ध मं प ग रे रे सा

(*Kramik Pustak Malika*, 3rd part, pp. 407-'8, Hindi Edition)

In this short composition, in 10 *matra* beat, Bhatkhande explains all the peculiarities of *raga Bageshri*. It mentions that the *raga* belongs to *Kharaharapriya Thaat*--the South Indian counterpart of *raga Kafi* of Hindustani music which hints that the *komal swara* of *ga* and *ni* should be employed. Then he says that *ga* and *ni* should be sung in a soft way which hints that a delicate hue of *komal ga* and *komal ni* was the characteristic of the *raga*. Then he says that *dha* and *re* should be *teevra*.

In *antara* he says that *ma* should be the predominant note. Next predominant note should be *sa*. *Pa* is used in flashes and he gives an outline of the *raga* in note patterns.

The rhyme part of this concise song is noteworthy. While keeping the technical points well-expressed he rhymes *sari* of *Bagesari* with the last word of the last line of *sthayi*. Then in the *antara* he rhymes *jaan* with *maan* in the first line. The note part is strictly in conformity with the *raga's* form:

STHAYI

	×	२	०	३
swara	सां म ग	रे सा –	ध नि गे ध	सा सा –
sahitya	गा S	वो बा S	गे S	स री S
swara	नि सा	सां म म	म म	म प ग म ग नी –
sahitya	सृ द	म ग त	सु र	प ग नी S
swara	ग म म	म नि ध	सां सां	रें सा सा
sahitya	म ख	ह S र	प्रि य	ठा S ठ
swara	घ सां	नि घ ध	नि घ घ	म प ध म ग री –
sahitya	ती	व र	र क	म र त प ध री S

ANTARA

म ग॒ म ×	म S	ध नि॒ ध्य २	ध म	नि॒ क	सा रे॒ o	– S	सा जा ३ – S सा न
नि॒ सा स ×	सा म	रे॒ वा २	– S	सां दि	नि॒ सा o	सा S	नि॒ मा ३ – S ध न
– ध प ×	– S	नि॒ च म २ नि॒ २	नि॒ म	ध क	म ग॒ रे॒ o	– S	रे॒ अ ३ – S सा ल्प
रे॒ × म ×	सा ध	नि॒ २ नि॒ २	घ॒	नि॒ ़	सा o प o	नॽ S	म ३ रे॒ ३ म रे॒ ग॒ सा

P.N. Chinchore in his article in *Bhatkhande Smriti Grantha* narrates an incident from which one can deduce how popular his *lakshan geet*s became, even with the *ustad*s of his time: "The famous *sarangi* player Ustad Bundu Khan learnt by heart all the *lakshan geet*s of Bhatkhande and played their tunes in musical soirees. Mostly, he used to play the *lakshan geet*s of *raga Bageshri*. While playing it, repeatedly, he used to explain to the listeners how with the particular note patterns the spirit of *Bageshri* became alive. Again, when Ustad Bundu Khan played the *lakshan geet* of *Bhupali* on *sarangi*, he sang the words with it. As soon as he reached the last line *raga bhed samajhaye Chatur* his eyes became heavy with tears. He used to remark about Bhatkhande: 'Such clear-headed man was never born in India before.'" (Translation mine).

Let us take another example of a *lakshan geet* in *raga Sohani* (*Ektal*):

मारवा को ठाठ करे पचम सुर छाँडिये
सोहनी सरूप चतुर सोच करे जानिये।
तार स्थान सोहत अति वादि धा को मानिये
मध्यम सुध परसत कोऊ रागनि पहिचानिये।।

(Kramik Pustak Malika, 3rd part, pp.371-'3, Hindi Edition)

Apart from its technical description, complete with its *thaat raga*, dropped off notes, predominant note and his pseudonym Chatur, the composition is so concise in rhythm and well-balanced in words that it is readable as a piece of poetry.

Here is another illustration of a *lakshan geet* in *raga Puriya*. It is fitted into 16 *matra* beat called *Trital:*

पूरी आस सखी मोरे मन की
चत्र पिया मोहे राग सुनायो
मेल गमनसिरि पंचम विरहित
वादि गंधार सुखद बतलायो।
पूरब अंग प्रबल मनि संगत
मंद्र निधनि अति चित्र दिखायो
संधि प्रकाश समय नित समुचित
मो मन अद्भुत रस उपजायो।।

(*Kramik Pustak Malika*, 4th part, pp.451-'2, Hindi Edition)

The literal translation of the song would be: "O friend, today my desire is fulfilled, the clever beloved (*Chatur*) is demonstrating a *raga* for me. The *raga* belongs to the 'Mela Gaman Shri' which drops *pa*, the fifth note. The predominant note is *gandhar* (*ga*, the third note) which is pleasing. The lower octave is important and also important is the combination of *ma* and *ni*. The *ni* and *dha* in the lower octave complete the picture. The time should always be the sunset. This has filled my mind with peculiar ecstasy."

Poetically, it is a superb illustration of his genius. The rhyme is uniformly present at the end of the 2nd, 4th, 6th and 8th lines. The word *puriya* is broken and turned into *puri aas* which, in singing, gives the full name of *puriya* with long drawn vowel. The pun on the word *Puriya* has been aptly fitted in with the poetic theme of the entire song. In the third line he mentions about *Mela Gaman Shri* which is the South Indian counterpart of *thaat Marwa* of Hindustani scale which employs *komal re* and *teevra ma* among other *shuddha* notes.

The second part of the song relates to the distinct features of the song which separate it from its other sister *raga*s from the same *thaat*--that is, it should be sung in the middle and lower octave with *ma* and *ni* combination. The picture of the *raga* is fully established if the note combination of *'ni dha'* is taken and the time of singing is sunset. So here is a complete picture of the *raga*'s salient features--its notes, scale, singing time, predominant note and important note combinations--amazingly squeezed into a verse of eight lines having a poetic theme as opposed to a dry verse of theory. Now let us examine it from the point of music:

STHAYI

ग ग ग रे॒ | नि सा ग॒ रे॒ | धे म॒ ग॒ धे॒ | ध॒ म॒ घ॒ सा सा सा -
म॒ म॒ री S सा नि॒ (सऽ) नि॒ | म॒ खी ग॒S मो रे॒ | म॒ मो रे॒ म न की S
प॒ S ... (notation)

(STHAYI और ANTARA की स्वरलिपि — सरगम नोटेशन)

ANTARA

(स्वरलिपि — सरगम नोटेशन)

According to his theory that *Puriya* should be sung in the lower octave, the first line moves to the lower octave with its *sam* on the *teevra ma*. In the last line of the first part of the song he states that the predominant note should be *ga*. In his notation of *sthayi* he has used the note *ga* in abundance, sometimes using a double note indicating a pause and hence prominence. The second part of the song takes the typical note pattern of the *antara* of *Puriya-- ma ga ga ma, dha ma dha sā*. Then in the second line when he says *nidhani ati chitra dikhayo* he actually employs the notes *ni dha ni* synchronising them with the words. So, poetically as well as musically this composition is a superb combination for manifesting the *raga Puriya*.

Use of Predominant Feature (Anga) of Ragas

It is true that musically all his *lakshan geet*s manifest all the typical musical phrases of the concerned *ragas*. Let us take for instance the *lakshan geet* of *raga Lalit* in *Teevratal*:

STHAYI

```
सा          ग           ग
नि  -  रे   म  -  म  -   म  -  म   म म  म म
मा  S  र    वा S  को S   ठा S ठ   ज ब  क र
 ×          २     ३       ×         र     ३
ग                          ग
म  ग  म    मैं -  म  म    ग  म  मैं  म म म  ग ग
क  र  त    प  S  च  म    ब  र  ज   गु नि व र
 ×          २     ३       ×       रुर    ३
ग          घ              सो       गं      सो सो
म  ग  ग    मैं -  घ  घ    सा -  सांनि रैंसुं - सा र
ल  लि त    रा S  ग  स    रू S  (पS) २  S  द र
 ×          २     ३       ×       रुर२    ३
नि         रैं          घ
सा  - सांनि नि  -  घ  घ    मैं घ  मैं  म म  ग ग
शा  S (त्रिS) सं S  म  त   हो S  त  म न  ह रा।
 ×          २     ३       ×       र२      ३
```

ANTARA

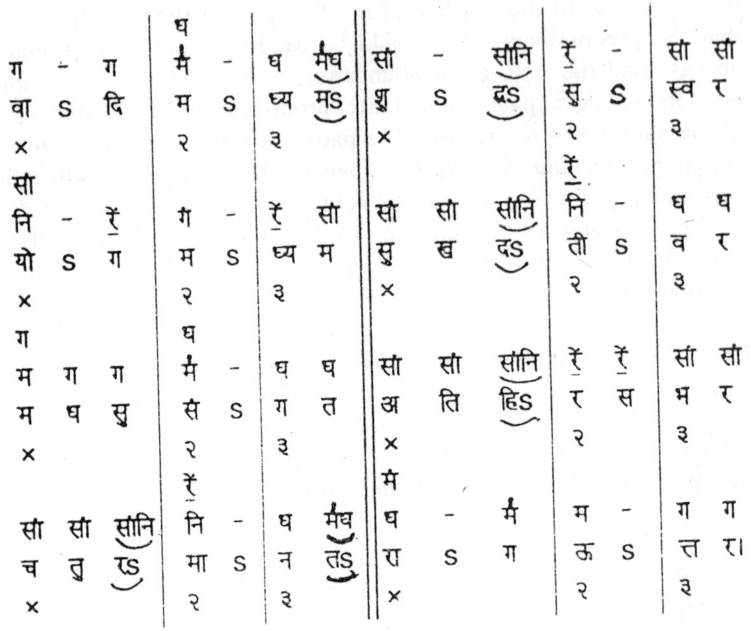

ग	-	ग		घ मैं	-		घ घ्य	मैंघ मॅS		सां श्रु	-		सानि दS	रें सु		सां सां स्व र
वा	S	दि		म	S		३	)		×	S		)	२		३
×				२				×						रें रें		
सी नि	-	रें		ग	-		रें घ्य	सा म		सा सु	सा ख		सानि दS	नि ती		घ घ व र
यो	S	ग		म	S		३			×			)	२		३
×				२												
ग म	ग घ	ग सु		घ मैं स	-		घ ग	घ त		सा अ	सा ति		सानि हिS	रें र र	रें स		सां सां म र
म				२	S		३			×			)	२		३
×				रें						मैं						
सी च	सा तु	सानि ङS		नि मा	-		घ न	मैंघ तS		घ रा	-		मैं ग	म ऊ	-		ग ग त रा।
×		)		२	S		३		)	×	S			२	S		३

(Kramik Pustak Malika, 4th part, pp.491-'2, Hindi Edition)

The composition starts from the catch phrase *ni re ga ma ma ma* and makes *ma* the predominant (*vadi*) note by using it abundantly. The movement of the *antara* also starts from its typical phrase *ga ga ma dha ma dha sā*. The catch phrase or *pakad* is very important for learning a *raga*. For a catch phrase is the particular note pattern which is the most distinguishing and characteristic feature of a *raga* like the facial character of a human being. It is a great contribution of Bhatkhande in the modern world of music to bring out and illustrate them in the form of *lakshan geets*. It shows his depth of knowledge and observation and his power of expression in the world of tune and word.

Let us take another illustration of a *lakshan geet* of *raga Shri* in *Jhaptal:*

STHAYI

ANTARA

(Kramik Pustak Malika, 3rd part, pp.333-'4, Hindi Edition)

Here he determines the catch notes as *pa ma ga re, ga re re sā*. In the first two lines he has established the catch notes musically.

These *lakshan geet*s can be developed and sung as *Chhota khayal* with proper development etc.

It is amazing that even when a *raga* has a complicated or *vakra* form Bhatkhande composes a *lakshan geet* with rare ingenuity. We can quote here the *lakshan geet* of *raga Khambavati*, in *jhaptal*, for instance. *Khambavati* is a charming *raga* having all the moods and sweetness of *raga Khamaj*. It is a mixed *raga* having a proportionate mixture of allied *raga*s, namely, *Tilang*, *Khamaj* and *Durga*.

STHAYI

म रे च × नि घ के × ग म सु × नि सी बा × सी घ च ×

म रे. तु प S म घ – S सी घ तु

म र २ घ प सु २ म बु २ रें व २ घ सी घ र २

प S घ S प घ गि रि नि S

घ खं म र सां निह सा ब प खं

घ प बा ० प ग गा ० सी नि रा ० नि सी ना ०

घ S – S सी S – S

सां S ३ म ग ३ नि य ३ घ नि ग ३

सा व सा यो सा स घ यो

नि ति – S सा ब – S

ANTARA

<table>
<tr><td>ग</td><td></td><td></td><td>सां</td><td></td><td>सां</td><td>नि</td><td>सां</td><td>-</td><td>सां</td></tr>
<tr><td>म</td><td>-</td><td>प</td><td>नि</td><td></td><td>ग</td><td>ख</td><td>म्मा</td><td>S</td><td>ज</td></tr>
<tr><td>ना</td><td>S</td><td>ति</td><td>ल</td><td></td><td>०</td><td></td><td>३</td><td></td><td></td></tr>
<tr><td>×</td><td></td><td>२</td><td></td><td></td><td>सां</td><td>-</td><td>नि</td><td>-</td><td>घ</td></tr>
<tr><td>नि</td><td></td><td>रैं</td><td>-</td><td>गे</td><td>दी</td><td>S</td><td>स</td><td>S</td><td>त</td></tr>
<tr><td>सां</td><td>सां</td><td>गा</td><td>S</td><td>न</td><td>०</td><td></td><td>३</td><td></td><td></td></tr>
<tr><td>दु</td><td>र</td><td>२</td><td></td><td></td><td>घ</td><td>घ</td><td>सां</td><td>सां</td><td>नि</td></tr>
<tr><td>×</td><td></td><td>सां</td><td>नि</td><td>प</td><td>प</td><td></td><td>त्र</td><td>मो</td><td>हे</td></tr>
<tr><td>सां</td><td>सां</td><td>घ</td><td>व</td><td>वि</td><td>ची</td><td>S</td><td>३</td><td></td><td></td></tr>
<tr><td>ध</td><td>ध</td><td>न</td><td></td><td></td><td>०</td><td></td><td>म</td><td>सां</td><td>-</td></tr>
<tr><td>अ</td><td>भि</td><td>२</td><td></td><td></td><td>प</td><td>-</td><td>ग</td><td>यो</td><td>S।</td></tr>
<tr><td>×</td><td></td><td>घ</td><td></td><td></td><td>ग</td><td></td><td>३</td><td></td><td></td></tr>
<tr><td>नि</td><td></td><td>प</td><td>ध</td><td>म</td><td>खो</td><td>S</td><td></td><td></td><td></td></tr>
<tr><td>घ</td><td>प</td><td>प</td><td>S</td><td>दि</td><td>०</td><td></td><td></td><td></td><td></td></tr>
<tr><td>रू</td><td>S</td><td>२</td><td></td><td></td><td></td><td></td><td></td><td></td><td></td></tr>
<tr><td>×</td><td></td><td></td><td></td><td></td><td></td><td></td><td></td><td></td><td></td></tr>
</table>

(*Kramik Pustak Malika*, 5th part, pp.249-'50, Hindi Edition)

The words of *sthayi* bear his pseudonym and describe the sweet mood of the *raga*. The words of *antara* denote that *raga Khambavati* borrows some shades of *Tilang*, *Khamaj* and *Durga*. These shades should be used in such proportions that they do not take the form and shape of their original self. In other words, in demonstration while weaving and developing the note pattern of *raga Khambavati* the artist will have to be alert to save *Khambavati* becoming completely *Tilang*, *Khamaj* or *Durga* by bringing up again the catch notes of *Khambavati*.

The lines of the *antara* have not only originality in the poetic content, they also express the salient points of the *raga* as well as alert the artist in two lines about the secret of the proper treatment of the melodic part. In a most concise manner the song defines and picturises the movements of the *raga* and gives a glimpse of its form. The result is poetic as well as informative--both qualities having blended in a manner unprecedented in musical history.

Unless the *raga* is explained in this way, the learner has no chance of grasping it without a lifetime of listening and practice.

Sometimes Bhatkhande takes some traditional compositions which have a typical melodic framework denoting the particular movement of a *raga* and replaces the words by his own, depicting the *lakshan* of that *raga*. Melodically, the identical *jugalbandi* compositions serve the purpose of establishing the original form and movement of a *raga* as one is a traditional one and the other one a copy thereof. Wordwise the new composition establishes Bhatkhande's genius how he deciphers the particular character of a *raga* from the traditional composition and how he replaces its words by clear and expressive words of his own, defining a *raga*'s character within the traditional melodic framework. Take for instance, the *lakshan geet* of *raga* Chhayanat. Melodically it is based on the popular *khayal* (*Trital*):

```
                                                          ग
                                                      म   ग
                                                      प्या  रि

      म
म    नि   ध   प  |  -   रे  (गम)  प  |  म   ग   म   रे  |  सा  -   -   -
न    वे   लि  ला |  S   इ  (लीS)  S  |  र   S   S   थि  |  का  S   S   S
०                |         ३        |  ×              |  २

      नि̣                           |  ग       म      |  ग           म
सा   -    सा  रे |  ग   -   म   -  |  म   नि  ध   प  |  म   ग   रे  सा
ला   S    ड   क  |  री  S   लो  S  |  ल   ल   न   सु  |  त   न   हैं  स
०                |         ३        |  ×              |  २

                 |                  |  ग   ग      ग  |  ग           ग
रे   रे   ग   -  |  म   म   प   -  |  म   म   रे  म  |  म   रे  म   ग
र    स    की  S  |  ब   ति  यैं  S  |  क   र   त   प्या| S   रि  प्या रि।
०                |         ३        |  ×              |  २
```

(*Kramik Pustak Malika*, 4th part, p. 122, Hindi Edition)

Here is Bhatkhande's *lakshan geet* of the same *raga* in identical melodic composition:

(Kramik Pustak Malika, 4th part, p.117, Hindi-Edition)

Among many others we can quote another instance of a similar identical composition in *raga Shukla Bilawal (Jhaptal)*:

Traditional composition:

(Kramik Pustak Malika, 5th part, p.146, Hindi Edition)

Bhatkhande's *lakshan geet* in identical melodic composition:

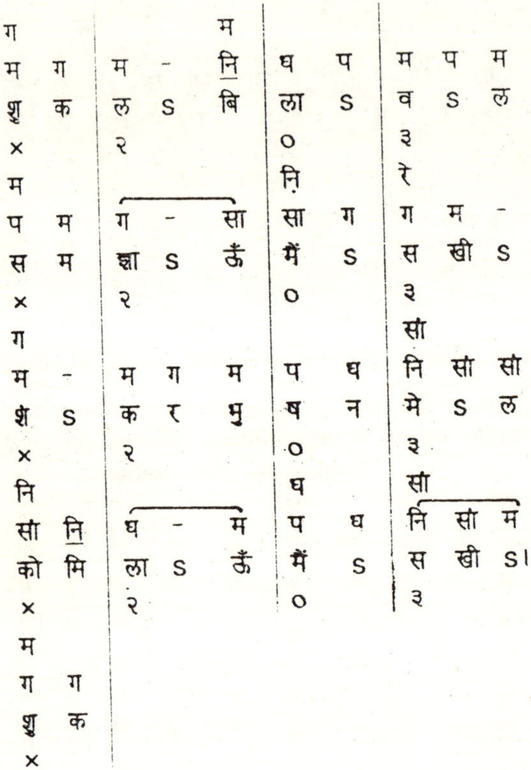

```
ग
म   ग      म   –      म        घ   प      म   प   म
श्र  क      ल   S      नि        ल   S      व   S   ल
×         २      बि       ०         ३
म                              नि        र
प   म      ग   –   सा           सा       ग   म   –
स   म      झा  S   ऊँ       मैं  S      स   खी  S
×         २                 ०         ३
ग                              सा
म   –      म   ग   म        प   घ      नि  सा  सा
श्र  S      क   र   मु       ष   न      मे  S   ल
×         २                 ०         ३
नि                              सा
सा  नि     घ   –   म        घ   प      नि  सा  म
को  मि     ला  S   ऊँ       मैं  S      स   खी  S।
×         २                 ०         ३
म
ग   ग
श्र  क
×
```

(*Kramik Pustak Malika*, 5th part, p.145, Hindi Edition)

His poetic capacity was so powerful and precise that sometimes he composed songs indicating the entire theory of *thaats*, ten in number, the principal ten *ragas* under each and mentioning the singing time of each *raga*.

Take for instance the following in *raga Darbari Kanhara* in *Trital*:

दशमित ठाठ चतुर गुनि माने

यमन बिलावल और खमाजी

भैरव पूरवि मारुव काफी

आसा भैरवि टोडि बखाने।

रि ध तीवर तीवर ग प्रथम त्रय

संधिप्रकाश अपर त्रय जाने

ग नि कोमल त्रय मिश्रित अंतिम

जनक सकल यह शास्त्र बखाने।।

(*Kramik Pustak Malika,* 4th part, pp. 667-'8, Hindi Edition)

Another illustration, in *raga Darbari (Jhoomra),* we can quote to the same effect:

राग अलाप लच्छन   माने

राग अलाप चतुर गुनि माने।

ग्रह अपन्यास न्यास   सों अंश

मंदर तार ओढव खाडो

अल्प बहुत्त साच पछाने।।

(*Bhatkhande Smriti Grantha,* p. 233)

The words *graha, apanyasa, nyasa* and *ansha* are the technical terms indicating the important and rest notes of a *raga* which a musician should be conversant with. The last line of the *antara* also mentions two technical terms--*alpa* and *bahuta.* These also express a method of developing a particular note in a *raga.* His ingenuity in putting the dry technical terms in the form of a verse and a song has immensely helped the later generation to study the technique of Classical music in a simpler way.

Here is another instance of Bhatkhande's capacity for including the theory of music in the form of a classical song. In the following *khayal* he indicates the number and the names of *shruti* and their division among the notes *sa re ga ma* respectively. This is composed in *raga Bihag (Trital):*

तीब्रा कुमुदवती मंदा अरु छन्दोवति

श्रुति चतुर खरज की

दयावती रंजनि रक्तिका त्रय

मानत सब गुनि रीखब की श्रुति।

रौद्री क्रोधि गंधार गहत नित, वज्रि प्रसारनि मार्जनि प्रीती

मध्यम की ख्रिति रक्ता संदीपनी आलापनि पंचम की श्रुति

मंदति रोहिणि रम्भा धैवत, राखत उग्रा क्षाभिणिकी

रतनाकर दरपन मन समव चतुर कहे सब नाम यथामति।।

(*Bhatkhande Smriti Grantha*, p. 206)

It is interesting to note how he squeezed the names of twenty-two *shruti*s and their division among the notes serially, aptly fitted into the note pattern of *raga Bihag* and in the framework of *trital.* In the last line, with his natural ingenuity, he mentions the names of the two books of ancient times--*Ratnakar,* which indicates *Sangeet Ratnakar,* written by Sharngadeva of the 13th century, and *Darpan,* indicating *Sangeet Darpan,* written by Pandit Damodar of the 17th century. By the words *Chatur kahe sab naam* he says that he is only repeating all these names as written by the above-mentioned scholars. It is obvious that a mere learning of the song will help a learner to memorise twenty-two Sanskrit names of the *shruti* and their division among the notes.

Here is an interesting composition:

भैरव बिभास परभात गुनकरि गवरि

सौराष्ट आहेरी शिव जोगि रामकरी

आनंद बंगाल पंचम ललत पूरब

चतुर कहे मेघ रंजनि मेल रागनि।

(*Bhatkhande Smriti Grantha*, p. 219)

In four lines Bhatkhande has mentioned the names of all the *raga*s belonging to the *thaat* of *Bhairava,* numbering fifteen, set in the notes of *raga Bhairava* and in 10 *matra* beat (*Jhaptal*).

Let us mention another composition of the same nature:

गुनी गाय अष्टभेद रागनि बिलावल
सकल सुर शुद्ध जामे प्रथम प्रहर काल है।
अलैया शुक्ल नाट और इमनि लच्छासाग
कोकभ सरपरदा पुनि देवगिरि जाति है।।

(*Bhatkhande Smriti Grantha*, p. 203)

In the first part of the song he has described the nature of notes employed *sakal soor shuddha* and also the singing time *pratham prahar*. In the second part of the song he mentions the names of eight types of *Bilawal--Alhaiya, Shukla, Nat* etc. set in 12 *matra* beat *(Chautal)* and in *raga Alhaiya Bilawal*.

Bhatkhande's way of describing the definitions of Classical music in rhymes and tunes was not confined to the rules of the *ragas* only. He also defined *tala* in rhymes and set them in classical tune. For example, *raga Kedar (Trital)*:

क्षिन लव काण्टा निमिष कला   त्रुटि
बिन्दु अणूद्रुत द्रुत लघु गुरू प्लुत
तीन मार्ग ग्रह चार तीन लय
द्रुत मध बिलमित अंग लघुन सों
मारग देशी भेद ताल के
चतर करत प्रस्तार त्रिविध जति!

(*Bhatkhande Smriti Grantha*, p. 191)

This is about the concept of rhythm in our music as expressed in our ancient *granthas*. Here, by the words *anoodrut drut laghu guru plut* he indicates the system of the division and variety of the time measure (*tala*) which stands for 1 beat, 2 beats, 4 beats, 8 beats and 12 beats consecutively. He also says in the last three lines that in Classical and prevalent local music three types of tempo (*laya*) are employed, namely *drut, madhya* and *vilambit*.

Here is another *lakshan geet* by Bhatkhande where he defines a rare *tala* called *Malla tala* having 13 *matra* beat. It is in *raga*

***Kedar*, set in *Malla tala* (13 *matra* beat):**

गावत नाम प्रभु को जब

मानव पावत सुख विशद

मृत्यु लोक विषय तजता

मिथ्या ज्ञान सु जनित सब ।

गाय केदार गुण सुनियम

लघु द्वय द्रुत द्वय एक विरम

संतोषित मन प्रभु चतर

बकसत वांछित अमर पद ।

(*Bhatkhande Smriti Grantha*, p.193)

In the first part of the song, in a devotional mood, he asks mankind to remember God, by virture of which he can enjoy real eternal happiness. In the second line of the second part he introduces the definition of *Malla tala* as *laghu dvaya drut dvaya eka viram*. In musical terminology *laghu* means four beats. Therefore, *laghu dvaya* literally means 'twice four', meaning eight. Then comes *drut dvaya* which indicates 2 beats, twice of which makes four. Lastly, *viram* means one. Therefore, 8+4+1 makes thirteen beats, which make *Malla tala*. Invariably, the *bol* of *Malla tala* is also divided according to the above definition:

laghu dvaya	=	4+4
drut dvaya	=	2+2
viram	=	1

मात्रा –	1	2	3	4	5	6	7	8	9	10	11	12	13
ठेका –	धि	धि	धागे	त्रक	धि	S	धा	त्रक	तू	ना	कत्	S-त्रा	त्रक
	x				२				३		४		५

Here is another instance of the same nature. This *lakshan geet* describes *tala Chandrakrida*, an uncommon *tala* having nine *matra* beat. This song is set in *raga Bihag* and in *tala Chandrakrida*:

द्रुत द्वय विरम लघु

ताल धुनि विचरत

संगीत दरपन।

ग्रह संख्या मात्रा

जामे अत सोहत

चंद्र क्रीड़ा कहे

अनुसरन कर मन।

(*Bhatkhande Smriti Grantha*, p.207)

In the first part of the song it stands thus:

drut dvaya	=	2+2
viram	=	1
laghu	=	4

All in all it becomes 9. The division and *bol* of *Chandrakrida tala* are also in similar order:

मात्रा -	1	2	3	4	5	6	7	8	9
ठेका -	धि	त्रक	धी	ना	त्रक	घा	धी	धी	ना
	×		२		३	४			

In the last line of the first part of the song he tells us that in *Sangeet Darpan*, by Pandit Damodar of the 17th century, the reference to this *tala* can be found.

These examples not only show Bhatkhande's unique power of composition with right coinage of words in classical tune, they also bear testimony to a precise and analytic mind which created a rich treasure in the domain of Classical music. The dry grammar and theory of music are made interesting by being set in poetical compositions.

His *lakshan geet*s in various *raga*s and *tala*s were highly acclaimed by the musicians in his lifetime itself. Nazir Khan, who was an employee of the Mandali in Bombay which was under the charge of Bhatkhande, taught the *lakshan geet*s to professional singers, who, in turn, because of their uniqueness, made them a part of their demonstrations. So, right from the beginning to the present day, his *lakshan geets* are enjoying the same height of popularity.

VI

BLENDING OF POETRY AND MELODY

His Power of Imagination Depicted in His Poetry and Capacity to Blend it with Classical Melody

Fertility of imagination is one of the greatest qualities of a poet and it is most obvious in all of Bhatkhande's poems meant to be sung as *khayals*, *dhrupads* and *saadras*. He was born with a poetic power which enabled him to compose verses even out of dry legal definitions when as a young man he studied law and aspired to be a lawyer.

Fertility of imagination enables him to choose his words with rare insight. Perhaps no composer of songs has words so numerous, incisive or beautiful in meaning. Take for instance this poignant song in *raga Paraj (Ektal)* from *Bhatkhande Smriti Grantha*, p.227:

काहे मदन इतनो श्रम

बिरथा मो मन के हरन

कोकिल बस करो निस्फल

कलरव अपनो मनरम।

मुग्धा तुमरे कटाच्छ

लोल मधुर स्निग्ध परम

हमते क्यों डारो तुम

हरसों अब लागि लगन।।

This is an utterance, full of despair, of a maiden, who, in anguish, addresses Cupid -- the God of Love -- not to waste the grandeur of spring to attract her attention, for she, in disgust, has diverted her attachment to *Hara* and, therefore, has become indifferent to all this. Now the word *Hara* in this poem means God--Lord Shiva -- who is known for his non-attachment to worldly objects. *Hara* also stands for the pseudonym of Bhatkhande as a composer. In this poem, the God of Love, Cupid, is personified and the utterance depicts a vivid picture of spring, the season of love. It also describes the feeling of a woman's heart who loved someone and lost him. The dwelling strains of despair and love which emanate from these four lines of composition are noteworthy. Here, the beauty of nature in spring and the pangs of the lovelorn heart are intermingled.

Let us take another composition in same strain. It is in *raga Surdasi Malhar (Trital)*:

बरखा रूत बैरि हमारे

मास असाढ़ घटा घन गरजत पियु परदेस हमारे।

दादुर मोर पपैया चात्रक पियु पियु करत पुकारे

अब न सहत सखि चतुर बिरह दुख निकसत प्रान हमारे ।।

(*Kramik Pustak Malika*, 6th part, pp.265-'6, Hindi Edition)

Here the pangs of separation from the beloved and the description of nature in the rainy season are blended together in beautiful harmony. Nature in its gorgeous beauty of the rainy season only inspires sadness in the heart of a young woman whose beloved is away. The poem speaks of the rainy season which has appeared with its thundering clouds, pouring rains, chorus of frogs and other seasonal birds. A lovelorn heart cannot bear the sad feelings for the beloved who is away in a distant land. In the first line, the use of the metaphor *barkha rut bairi hamare* has given the entire picture of separation from the beloved in its full intensity.

Bhatkhande's poetic genius included his powerful art of suggestion also. See his composition in *raga Desh (Chitratal)* from *Bhatkhande Smriti Grantha*, p.214:

जा रे जा जा रे पतंगवा इतनो संदेस

अब रहो न जाय मोसे छाँड़ी परदेस।

बिरहानल तन सब करत दहन

तुम चतुर जाय कहो इतनो संदेस।।

Here again the poem bears the utterance of a lovelorn maiden tormented by the pangs of separation from the beloved who is away in a foreign land. She, in anguish, is asking the flying insects to carry her message to the beloved, which is simple, yet deep: "I cannot remain without you." The simple suggestion of carrying the message by the flying insects has the power of intensifying the heart-breaking pain of separation from the beloved.

His art of suggestion is again manifested in the following *khayal* composition of *Darbari Kanhara (Trital)*:

इनमें कौन राधिका रानी
सब मेला में ढूँढ़न जाऊँ जानूँ प्रेम रस खानी।
रुक्मनि पूछत चलि सखियन सों प्रेम चतुर मृदु बानि
जिस पर प्रभु जी प्रेम रखत हैं यहि क्या पुरन कमानी।।

(*Kramik Pustak Malika*, 4th part, pp. 663-'4, Hindi Edition)

In Vaishnava literature, Radha, the beloved of Lord Krishna and the heroine of his *leela* in Vrindavan, is the epitome of all female charm, grace and beauty. She is also regarded as the epitome of love, affection and devotion for Krishna. The love of Krishna and Radha is legendary and has figured in abundance in our music, art, literature, dance etc. This song is the utterance of Rukmani, the queen of Dwarika, who comes to Vrindavan to have a glimpse of Radha who has won the heart of her Master--Lord Krishna, the King of Dwarika. In this poem the supremacy of Radha as a woman and conqueror of Krishna's affection is fully established by the art of suggestion through Rukmani's action and query.

In every language the description of beautiful women occupies a predominant place in poetry. Here is a poem by Bhatkhande on the above subject in *raga Hanskankani (Jhaptal)*:

नये नये सिंगार सखि कामिनी रचाये।
हाथ में कंकनि हंसगत सोहे अत
गौर तन सिंह कटि चतुर मन भाये।।

(*Bhatkhande Smriti Grantha*, p.231)

This is a description of a beautiful woman who is decorated with ornaments. Here the poem avoids sensuality but uses metaphor *simha kati* to vivify the picture. In fact to a poet like Bhatkhande, who is possessed by an imagination so fertile, metaphor becomes the common mode of expression. See the following composition:

देखहि मन लजत चंद्रमा
सुंदर सुरत वाकी अतहि सलोनी।
का बरनु सखी मो मन की गत
निरखि निरखि सुघ बुध बिसरानी ।।

(*Bhatkhande Smriti Grantha*, p.216)

It is the description by a woman, of her beloved, who has fallen in love with him at first sight. Here it is noteworthy that these utterances do not betray any sensuality. "After seeing him my reason and intelligence have failed," -- this description in the last line very intelligently depicts the intensity of her feeling. The use of the metaphor *lajat chandrama* indicates the poetic power of suggestion.

Here is another illustration in *raga Sarparda (Trital):*

जब से सजन परदेस सिधारे

तब तें बिपत भइ जिया में हमारें आलि।

रैन दिन मोहे जुग सी बितत सब

कब आवेंगी हर रंग हमारें आलि।।

(Bhatkhande Smriti Grantha, p.203)

The grandeur of the tragic feeling and the wealth of the poetical power and imagination contribute most to the effect of the whole.

It is the characteristic quality of Bhatkhande as a composer that poetical inspiration and intellectual power are developed in him, each to the same degree. In most composers one is the handmaid of the other. But in Bhatkhande they unite on equal terms. It is partly because his compositions have these two cardinal functions, instead of one, that his songs have such variety. Here is an instance of such a composition in *raga Paraj* where the definition of a rare *tala Gajaleela* and poetic imagery blend together:

नाचत गजलीला मिल जुवतिजन

जमुना तट पर खेलत मन मोहन।

अगणित भाव करत लय नवपरन

चतर हसत लघु लघु लघु विरम।।

(Bhatkhande Smriti Grantha, p.226)

The song mainly indicates the composition of *tala Gajaleela,* the *matra'* of which is 17. The name of the *tala Gajaleela* is introduced in the first line and poetic imagery is drawn in by depicting the dance scene of Krishna and young Gopis on the bank of the river Yamuna. The dance is performed in *tala Gajaleela.* In the last line the *matras* of the *tala* are introduced intelligently by the words *laghu laghu laghu viram.* In South Indian musical terminology *laghu* can for 4 *matras* and *viram* stands for 1 *matra*. Therefore, the repetition of four *laghus* stands for 16 *matras* whereas *viram* stands for 1 *matra*, the total number of which becomes 17.

In traditional compositions, to our dismay, we find that the beauty of words, phrases and meaning are readily sacrificed for the sake of musical ideas. But Bhatkhande in his works flings the reigns on to the necks of a headlong inspiration and a galloping intellect.

The main characteristic of his style is his power to haunt the memory and imagination with a phrase or a line or a passage. His seasonal songs bear ample proof of his genius. For instance, his composition in *raga Gaud Malhar (Ektal)*:

गाजे राजे घन गरजत अति बरसत

द्रुम बेली सब हरषत

चातक शिखि करत शोर

घन घन घन राजे।

इंद्रधनुष सोहत नभ

दामिनि दमकत चमकत

राग मलारी उपजत

हर रंग गुनी आजे ।।

(*Kramik Pustak Malika*, 4th part, pp.532-'3, Hindi Edition)

The majesty and grandeur of the rainy season are portrayed here in lyrical beauty.

Bhatkhande has within him the power to haunt the imagination with phrases that can never be expelled, and thereby setting up before one's mind's eye images of power and beauty. Let us take another composition in *raga Megha Malhar (Jhaptal)*:

प्रबल दल साज जग जूमजा भूम पर

उमँड़ घन घोर जल इंद्र लायो है।

बरसत मूसलघार होत पहाड़ छार

कृष्ण कर घर गिरिवर बचायो है॥

(*Kramik Pustak Malika*, 6th part, pp. 251-'2, Hindi Edition)

Here is another illustration which is a beautiful *lakshan geet* of *Megha Malhar* composed by him:

उमँड़ घुमँड़ मेघ गगन चढ़ि आये
विविध बरन सकल विबुध मन हरषाये।

(*Kramik Pustak Malika*, 6th part, p.243, Hindi Edition)

The coinage of words are such that the picture of the rainy season with its thunder, lightning and rainbow becomes vividly alive. Here is another composition in *raga Vasant (Trital)*:

सरस सुगंध नई बन बेली
फूल रही सब बेला चमेली।
पवन सुगंधित बहत चहुँ ओर
गाय बसंत चतुर अलबेली।।

(*Kramik Pustak Malika*, 4th part, p.376, Hindi Edition)

Within the framework of a classical melody and in the 16 *matra* beat this song is capable of creating a picturesque effectiveness of spring with its sweet smelling flowers, refreshing breeze and greenery of the forest that captures the imagination and lives on in the memory.

He translated in *dhrupad* form the description of the rainy season from Kalidasa's Sanskrit Classic *Ritusamhara*. He set this in the tune of *raga Megha Malhar*. It was a unique attempt to translate Classical literature in Classical *raga*. It is still more unique because, while translating it, he adhered closely to the essence of Kalidasa's original poem '*sasikarambhodharamatta-kunjarastaditpatakoshanishadvamardalah*' etc.:

STHAYI

आयो अब बरखा रुत
उत्कट कांति नरेश, अम्बाधर नग प्रमत्त
कामीजन सब हरखत।।

ANTARA

चमकत दामिनी पताक डंका भयो असनीरव
कृष्ण वरण मधुर मेघ गगन भयो समतान्त।।

SANCHARI

बहुधार घन बरसत तोय भार भन्द चलत
अत मनहर नाद करत चातक कुल सब हुलसत॥

(*Bhatkhande Smriti Grantha*, p. 73)

VII

EMOTIONAL CONTENT (RASA)

According to our Sanskrit scholars the ultimate object of Art is to create *rasa*. *Rasa* is ineffable and inexpressible. It has to be tasted to be experienced and to be realised. That results from an elevated state of mind, inspired by the object of art and poetry. The art critics (*Alankarikas*), belonging to the Classical age of Sanskrit Literature, equated the feeling of *rasa* with bliss -- the experience of the ultimate reality. However, they indentified 8 or 9 *rasas* according to the specific emotion portrayed in art and literature. These are: *Shringar, Hasya, Karuna, Bhayanak, Raudra, Bibhatsa, Adbhuta* and *Veer*. Some add the ninth *Shanta* to these. For rousing and culminating a particular emotional state in the experience of *rasa*, a certain specific condition of mental state in a certain direction is necessary. Stimulated by an object of art the mind has to pass through many stages of temporary and transitory feelings which ultimately crystallise into a particular deep emotion and its consequence which can be identified as a particular *rasa*. The different fluid stages of emotion are named by the Sanskrit scholars as *Alambana* and *Uddipana vibhava* and their consequents as *Anubhava*. The transitory stages are named *Sanchari* or *Vyabhichari bhavas*. We can mention some of the *Sanchari bhavas* for the sake of giving example -- (1) Discouragement (*Nirveda*), (2) Joy (*Harsha*), (3) Despair (*Vishad*), (4) Recollection (*Smriti*), (5) Inconstancy (*Chapalata*), (6) Sleep (*Nidra*), (7) Dreaming (*Supta*), (8) Awakening (*Vibodh*), (9) Anxiety (*Chinta*), (10) Envy (*Irshya*), (11) Intoxication (*Mada*), (12) Epilepsy (*Apasmara*), (13) Deliberation (*Vitarka*), (14) Apprehension (*Shanka*), (15) Distraction (*Moha*) etc. It is with these organised units of emotion that one of the nine dominant states (*rasa* or *sthayi bhava*) like Love, Heroism, Pathos, Wonder, Fear, etc. is awakened and carried to consummation.

Nayaka-Nayika Bhed

The domain of poetics in Classical literature is also dominated by *nayaka-nayika bhed*. The hero and the heroine as the objects of love and adoration were elaborated and categorised according to the emotional state and included into the fold of *bhava*s. The idea of *nayaka-nayika bhed* needs elucidation. The idea of *nayaka* and *nayika* came from the concept of hero and heroine in Dramatics. In fact in ancient India the qualities of heroes and heroines and other dramatic personages were much stressed upon in the Dramaturgy and in the subsequent poetry. This idea was elaborately developed by the saint poets of the Vaishnava cult depicting Radha as the heroine or *nayika* of the different types.

In ancient times the following scholars defined and classified *nayaka*s and *nayika*s in the following subjects:

(1) Bharata and Dhananjaya in Dramaturgy,
(2) Rudrata and Vishvanatha in Poetics,
(3) Vatsyayana and Koke in The Science of Love.

Some illustrations of *nayaka*s and *nayika*s can be obtained from the pictures painted by the artists, belonging to the reign of Maharaja Kishan Singh of Baghal of the Himachal Pradesh.

Here are the names of the main *ashta nayika*s or eight types of heroine:

(1) Proshitapriya
(2) Svadhinabhartrika
(3) Khandita
(4) Abhisarika
(5) Vipralabdha
(6) Kalahantarita
(7) Vasakasajjita
(8) Virahotkanthita

We have already stated that the *rasa* theory and *nayaka-nayika bhed* originally applied to Poetics and Dramaturgy and later travelled into the domain of music. The ancient scholars of music defined the 12 notes in terms of the 9 *rasa*s:

Sā and *Re* -- *Veer* and *Raudra* (Heroic and Furious).
Dha -- *Bibhatsa* and *Bhayanak* (Odious and Terrible).
Ga and *Ni* -- *Karuna* (Pathetic).
Ma and *Pa* -- *Hasya* (Comic).
Komal Re &

Komal Dha -- *Shanta* and *Karuna* (Quietistic and Pathetic).
Komal Ga &
Komal Ni -- *Veer* (Heroic).
Re and *Dha* -- *Shringar* (Erotic).

What is possible in the most concise text of the *khayal*, in its pure literary aspect, is to arouse merely one *bhava* or some of the thirty-three *vyabhichari* or *sanchari bhavas*. It is noteworthy that the *vyabhichari bhavas* are established not by the effect of the poetical composition alone. The combination of the note formation of a *raga* with its practical manifestation of modulation, intonation and voice-production of a singer adds to the enhancement of the above-mentioned *bhavas*. In fact for achieving and rousing a particular *rasa* the tone and tune of a *raga* play a major role rather than the words of a song.

Yet a well-knit composition with expressive words is necessary to produce *bhava* for the purpose of producing the transitory emotions and having them consummated into *rasa*. For example, let us take the following *Chhota khayal* of *Puriya raga* in *Trital*, very widely sung, composed by Sadarang:

सपने में आये जब तें मोरी मा

सुख चैन की कल बिगर गई।

(*Kramik Pustak Malika*, 4th part, p. 455, Hindi Edition)

This has its own inimitable charm portraying the *vyabhichari bhavas* known as *Nidra* (sleeping), *Supta* (dreaming) and *Vibodh* (awakening) in the form of the illusive romance of the dreamland brought to an abrupt end to the *Vishad* (despair) of the beloved. It conveys the passing chain and phase of the four *vyabhichari bhavas* -- *Nidra, Supta, Vibodh* and *Vishad* -- which reach their culmination in the 'treachery of the eyelids' created by the power of suggestion. The artist can raise the full mansion of the *Vipralabdha Shringar* (Love in Separation) with the help of the *raga* in which the song is set.

Another composition of similar strain can be mentioned here. It is a *Bara khayal* in *Bihaga*, composed by Sadarang in *Ektal*:

कैसे सुख सोवे नींदरिया

श्याम मुरत चित चढ़ी।

(*Kramik Pustak Malika*, 3rd part, pp. 201-'2, Hindi Edition)

Another illustration is in *raga Khambavati* composed in *Trital:*

पिया बिन नैना नींद न आवे।

सगरि रैन तरफ तरफ बीती

भोर भये जियरा घबरावे ।।

(*Kramik Pustak Malika*, 5th part, p. 252, Hindi Edition)

Or in *Shyamkalyan* composed in *Trital:*

नींद न आवत पिया बिन देखे

कैसे   परे   अब   चैन ।

(*Kramik Pustak Malika*, 5th part, p. 69, Hindi Edition)

These beautiful compositions are capable of being the vehicle of *vyabhichari bhava*s as mentioned above and with the help of the tonal beauty of the *raga* certain *rasa* of love or pathos can be created. The words and the *raga* balance each other in achieving this result. But when the words are meaningless jargon, the tonal beauty of a *raga* is nothing but a cry in the wilderness. Take, for example, a composition of *Puriya Dhanashri* -- a *Bara khayal* in meaningless jargon:

आशिक मरा पड़ा वे जालिम

तेरी गरम् निगाह की अदा का।

छिता बेखबर लेती पर मेरी

पूछत नाहीं या सुना

जाता है हाल   अदारंग गदा का।

(*Kramik Pustak Malika*, 4th part, pp. 360-'1, Hindi Edition)

Let us take Bhatkhande's composition vis-a-vis the composition mentioned above. This composition also is in *Puriya Dhanashri* with *Vilambit Ektal:*

मुरलि बजाय मेरो मन लीनो

श्याम सुंदर सखि

धन सिरि चत्र कन्हाई।

मेलन पूरबि पंचम

वादी म रि सुर संगत

अति मन भाई ।।

(*Kramik Pustak Malika*, 4th part, pp. 345-'6, Hindi Edition)

This composition not only speaks of the sweet melody of Krishna's flute but also defines the *raga* with its *thaat, Purvi; vadi swara, Pa;* and the note combination of *Ma Re;* typical of the *raga*. The suggestion of the melody of *Puriya Dhanashri* being played on Krishna's flute is not only intelligent but also sweet and sublime. It is noteworthy that his pseudonym Chatur is used as an adjective to the word 'Kanhai'-- the name of Krishna -- who in Indian mythology is known for his mischief and cleverness. The sentiment of love and pathos as *vyabhichari bhavas* can be portrayed here. The sentiment of longing for the beloved is lingered on and can rightly be attuned to the note combination of *Puriya Dhanashri* -- *komal Re* and *komal Dha*.

There is no denying the fact that the structure of the *khayal* has in its wake disorganised the literary part of most of the *Bara* and *Chhota khayals* and led to the neglect of the aspect of sentiment being projected through words.

Bhatkhande's opinion was that the sentiment of the words should be projected to portray the sentiment of the *raga*. Let us examine what he says in his *Hindustani Sangeet Paddhati* about it: "The tune has to be rendered in correspondence with the sentiment portrayed. But we have seen singers who do not know the meaning of their compositions. How can they have the key to the emotions? Now, further, can they adjust their intonations in the desired proportion?"

It was indeed more than half a century ago when he made this remark and complained of music having been monopolised by the uneducated ones with their odd handling and its repercussions.

How strongly he felt about the words of the song as a vehicle of the sentiment is apparent from another writing of his. Here he expresses the opinion that the interpretation of the *raga*'s tonal form should be in conformity with the spirit of the poetic content. He illustrates this by the following song:

'आज राधे तोरे बदन पर

श्याम मिले की चोरी ।

"The slow and the medium improvisations can proceed in this beautiful *khayal* of *Ramkali* in tune with the sentiment. But when an artist starts very fast with crude *tanas* to display his vocal power the entire spirit of this delicate song is totally ruined."

So he strongly pleaded for the text and its interpretation in creating a *bhava* or sentiment enhanced by the spirit of the *raga*.

It was natural, therefore, that at the time of composing *khayal* he would be specially careful about the literary content along with the musical structure. Let us quote Bhatkhande's composition in *raga Khambavati (Jhaptal):*

गिनत रही तारे ना ये सजन म्हारे
कल ना परत घड़ि पल निकसत प्राण हमारे।
नींद न आवत नैन बिरह बिथा तन जारे
हररंग पिया के बिन कवन दुख टारे ।।

(*Kramik Pustak Malika*, 5th part, pp.252-'3, Hindi Edition)

This is a poignant song depicting the longing for the beloved in the form of sleeplessness and restlessness which culminate in frustration and sadness. From the point of *vyabhichari bhava*s we can define them as *Anidra* (Sleeplessness), *Akshepa* (Frustration), *Smriti* (Recollection) and *Vishad* (Despair). These passing phases of emotion can be harnessed to create the dominant state of emotion *(sthayi bhava)* as, *Shringar rasa* or *Karuna rasa*. The impact of the entire note patterns of the *raga* has no less contribution in creating the above *rasa*s.

Here is another illustration of the same nature in *raga Sindhura*:

कौन हरे दुख मो मन को सखी
चतुर पिया बिन तरसत जिया नित।
घायल की गति घायल जाने
का सें कहूँ सब या तन की गति ।।

(*Kramik Pustak Malika*, 6th part, p.104, Hindi Edition)

The pangs of separation and the injured feelings of a tender lovelorn heart, conveyed by the powerful art of suggestion, have a special appeal when they are demonstrated in *raga Sindhura*. Here also the feeling of despair (*Vishad*) can be successfully culminated in *Karuna rasa*.

Here is another example of Bhatkhande's composition which can rouse a number of *vyabhichari bhava*s:

कौन सौतन में दिरमाये प्यारे मोरे
अजहुँ न आवत कैसे रहे जिया धीर।
जावो चतर सखी पियु सों लगी लगन
छिन छिन ठठ तजिय पीर ।।

(Bhatkhande Smriti Grantha, pp. 241-'2)

Here the utterance is by a female who is torn by the feeling
of love, jealousy and suspicion. She cannot bear the absence of the
beloved who is callous and unkind. Here a number of *vyabhichari
bhavas* are evoked: Inconstancy *(Chapalata)*, Anxiety *(Chinta)*,
Suspicion *(Sandeha)*, Envy *(Irshya)* and Expectation *(Asha)*. Here
the artist can raise the full mansion of the *Vipralabdha Shringar*
with the help of the musical medium.

Many compositions of Bhatkhande can be categorised as having
Shanta as *rasa* (Quietistic sentiment). For example take the following composition in *Shri raga* in *Jhaptal:*

प्रभु के चरण कमल निसं दिन सुमिर रे
भाव घर सुध भीतर भव जलधि तर रे।
जोइ जोइ धरत ध्यान पावत समाधान
हररंग कहे ज्ञान अबहु चित धर रे ।।

(Kramik Pustak Malika, 3rd part, pp. 343-'4, Hindi Edition)

The *raga* itself has a great contribution to make in creating *Shanta
rasa* as it employs *komal Re* and *komal Dha*. As stated earlier
these two notes are responsible for evoking *Shanta rasa*.

The portrayal of *nayakas* and *nayikas* is also present in
Bhatkhande's compositions. For example, refer to the following song
quoted in *Bhatkhande Smriti Grantha*, p.69:

जाओ मोहन मोरे फाँद परोना
कपटि कुटिल हम आप भले हो
गुन निघान और श्याम सलोना।
मन्दमति हम कान चतुर तुम
बिरह बिथा भले हमको सतावत
मंदिर में अब देर परेगी
क्यों पूछो तुम हमरो रोना ।।

In this the heroine utters to her beloved, who is none other than the mischievous Lord Krishna, in a sarcastic tone about her difficulties in having a meeting with him. This utterance qualifies the heroine as *Khandita* according to the theory of *Nayika Bhed*.

That Bhatkhande was aware of the *Nayika Bhed* theory in some of his compositions is apparent from the following song composed in *raga Bhairavi* in *Trital:*

सखी आज प्रमाद भईला साजन आप तजीला।

चाटु वचन कछु श्रवन न कीने अर्पित हार तजीला

बोध सखीजन के अवमाने पच्छाताप भईला।।

चरनन ते गिर पर्यो चतुर सखि तबहुँ न हाथ गहीला

कलहान्तरिता कहत नायिका जिया में दाग रहीला।।

(*Kramik Pustak Malika,* 2nd part, pp. 402-'3, Hindi Edition)

This is a poignant utterance of a female who out of jealousy and assumed anger has refused the love and cajoling of the beloved. She, later, repents of her action and tries to find a way for a reunion. This situation and the repenting words qualify the heroine as *Kalahantarita* which Bhatkhande himself has indicated in the last line of this poem.

His numerous compositions, having a wide variety of subjects and ideas, can rouse a number of fleeting emotions culminating in dominant states or *sthayi bhavas*. With the help of the melodic medium and proper intonation these beautiful compositions can be the vehicle of establishing *rasa* -- the ultimate goal of all the arts.

VIII

PHILOSOPHIC IDEAS REFLECTED IN HIS COMPOSITIONS

Bhatkhande's religion, philosophy and ethics, which inspire and illumine his compositions, are expressed fully in his poems. For example, take the following in *Darbari Kanhara (Trital):*

समझत ना मन तूँ मेरा।

लाख बार समझावत हूँ मैं

काहे न तजत अंधेरा।।

झूठी माया झूठी काया

झूठा जगत बसेरा।

अंत समै कोई काम न आवत

चत्र प्रभू एक तेरा।।

(*Kramik Pustak Malika*, 4th part, pp. 659-'60, Hindi Edition)

Here, in a deep philosophical mood he mentions about the transiency of the world. Bhatkhande reminds the soul that it would have no use for anything when it departs from the body and merges with the Infinite One.

The following *antara* under *khayal* '*Bhaj Hari naam tu more manava*' in *raga Yaman* is composed in the same strain:

यह संसार घड़ी का सपना

साँच एक चतुर कौ नाम।

(*Kramik Pustak Malika*, 2nd part, p. 38, Hindi Edition)

The variegated beauty of nature around us and the worldly ties are only short-lived. They with their beauty and variety enchant the human mind and make it forget their inherent nature. They exist as long as man exists. But a man is born to die. Death looms large round him and can snatch him away any time even with a moment's notice.

Again, he says in *khayal Gauri (Trital):*

भटकत काहे फिरे बावरे।

नश्वर तन को कौन भरोसो

खटपट यूँ हि करे।।

(*Kramik Pustak Malika*, 5th part, pp. 376-'7, Hindi Edition)

"O man! Why do you tire yourself quarrelling and in search of worldly happiness? This body of yours is prone to disease and death and, therefore, cannot be relied upon."

Although the shortness of human life infuses his writings with a spirit of renunciation, he believes in the doctrine of *Karma* as explained and elaborated in our Shastras. In the *antara* of the said *khayal* of *Gauri* he again says:

करम लिखो उतनो हि मिलेगो लाखों जतन करे।

चतुर कृपा बिन कछु नहिं साधत काहे को सोच करें॥

The theory of *Karma* says that we are destined to enjoy happiness or to suffer sorrows according to our good or bad deeds in our previous birth. Virtue is rewarded while misdeeds are punished. Inspired by this idea Bhatkhande says that it is useless to be agitated about the good or bad events in life. A man has to go through them and experience them as he has deserved them by his own action. But Bhatkhande is not a pessimist, though his view of this life is dismal. His solution to all this is expressed in the following lines composed in *raga Kalingra (Dadra)*:

राम नाम भजन करो भव जलधी तुरत तरो।

अनित जगत साँच समझ नाहक तुम लोभ करो

चतुर कहत सुलभ जुगति हररंग को ध्यान घरो।।

(*Kramik Pustak Malika*, 3rd part, p. 309, Hindi Edition)

The mere repetition of the Lord's name enables one to conquer the attachments of this world. This burning faith in God has saved his compositions from pessimism. He says that whoever has devotion for *Guru* and takes shelter in him can shake off the shackles of worldly attachments. This is composed in *raga Bhairavi (Trital)*:

जा ए तु मन गुरू चरन शरन

एक भाव घर अंतर मोघन।

जोइ जावत जन सद्‌गुरू के शरन

वाको हरत चतुर भवबंधन ।।

(*Kramik Pustak Malika*, 2nd part, p. 394, Hindi Edition)

His deep spiritualism is reflected in most of his compositions. The remedy of the false lure of the world as suggested by him is to worship the Eternal Being and surrender one's ego. In a prayerful mood he writes in *raga Chhayanat (Trital)*:

अब के राखो भगवान कान मोरि
हौं अनाथ तुम नाथ जगत के
आपहि तात करुणा निधान।
विपत विदारन अघ निस्तारन
तुमरो नाम सकल जगजान
हरंग के पूरो मन काम।

(*Kramik Pustak Malika*, 4th part, p. 120-'1, Hindi Edition)

Prayer is the highest function of the soul, the source of life to it and the fountain-head of conduct. It also grants the worldly aspirations of man. See in this respect the following composition in *raga Kedar (Teevra):*

शरन कर तु गोविंद मेरे मन
त्रिविध ताप हरत ततच्छिन
हर बिना सब व्यर्थ जीवन।
जोग जाग रू ताप तीरथ
भक्ति बिन सब निष्फल करम
एक नाम करत भवतरन
का न समझत मूढ मेरे मन ।।

(*Kramik Pustak Malika*, 3rd part, pp. 147-'8, Hindi Edition)

It is the self-surrender to God which rescues the devotee from all his miseries and helps him to attain immortality. This is interpreted in the following composition in *raga Bhupali (Trital):*

जाऊँ तोरे चरन कमल पर वारि
हे गोपाल गोबिंद मुरारि
शरनागत हूँ द्वार तिहारे।
अनगिन दुरित भर्यो हूँ जड़मत
किस विधि पाऊँ चतुर तुमरे पद
तुम ही जग के एक अधार।।

(*Kramik Pustak Malika*, 3rd part, pp. 25-'6, Hindi Edition)

Composing this poem in *raga Hamir (Teevra)* he says again:

हे जगदीश चतुर मुरार
भव भय हार दुःख निवार।
सबको अधार नाम तुम्हार
कीजे पार बेड़ो हमार।।

(*Kramik Pustak Malika*, 3rd part, pp. 90-'1, Hindi Edition)

But what is the form of God and what are His attributes? In the following composition in *raga Multani (Chautal)* Bhatkhande makes a mention of His inseparable qualities:

नित्य शुद्ध बुद्ध मुक्त
सच्चिदानंद रूप
जा को न कछु उपाधि
पार ब्रह्म अति अनूप।

(*Kramik Pustak Malika*, 4th part, p. 778, Hindi Edition)

God is birthless, eternal, undecaying and ancient. He is all-pervading, he is omnipotent, omnipresent and omniscient. He is Truth, Consciousness and Bliss. He is the Formless One. This conception of God, as the Supreme Being, has emerged from Bhatkhande's deep knowledge of our philosophy given to us by the Vedas and the Upanishads. His attitude to life is one of renunciation and dedication to the Inner Being who is the Creator of this Universe. Although he loves to look at this world in its beauty and diversity, he never forgets its short-lived nature and he has an eye to reach the unity underlying this diversity. His conception of the Universe is the manifestation of the Eternal Formless One.

In *antara, sanchari* and *abhog* parts of the above-mentioned composition he says:

सकल जगत उपादान
मूल प्रकृति है निदान
जाके संयोग जनित
व्यक्त होत नाम रूप ।।
माया संगत ईश्वर
एक हू अनेक होत
भोगत आदृष्टज फल
जाको जैसो हि करम ।।
स्वप्नावस्थित रहे जिव
हेम पूर्व होत गर्भ
जाग्रत वैश्वानर नित
हररंग बरनत सरूप।।

(*Kramik Pustak Malika*, 4th part, pp. 778-'80, Hindi Edition)

Here he explains God as the ultimate cause of the Universe from whom everything is born, through whom we live and unto whom we return and in whom we merge. The cause of manifestation of the Formless One in numerous forms, with different shapes and names, is that He covers himself with the great 'Illusion' and hence appears to be many. In these few lines Bhatkhande has expressed the essence of our philosophy as delineated in the Vedas and Upanishads. The words of the Vedas *'Eko ' ham bahusyam'* have found way in Bhatkhande's poem.

Here is another composition in *raga Kamod (Ektal)* which expresses the philosophical idea about death and rebirth as delineated in the *Gita*, the Gospel of the Hindu religion:

काहे सोचत तू मोरे मन
जनम मरन देह धरम   अविकल अज परमातम।
जैसे नित छाँड जीरन अंबर नव पहेरत जन
तैसे यह धारत तन हररंग नित परमातम ।।

(*Kramik Pustak Malika*, 4th part, pp. 98-'9, Hindi Edition)

In these lines Bhatkhande has admirably expressed the idea of the 22nd verse belonging to the Second Discourse of The *Gita:* "Just as a man casts off worn out clothes and puts on new ones, so also the embodied self casts off worn out bodies and enters others which are new."

This shows how deep was Bhatkhande's knowledge of our philosophy, how he was saturated with it and how it inspired his musical compositions. We get his mental picture -- his ethics and his spiritual ideas -- in the following poem composed in *raga Lalit (Ektal)*:

मनुष जनम अतुल पायो
हरिगुन कबहूँ न गायो
धिक धिक जीवन निष्फल
मानव देही कहायो।
अजहूँ तू चेत मंद
कहाँ लों अब रहेगो अंध
दो दिन की साँस चतुर
माया बस यूँ लुभायो।।

(*Kramik Pustak Malika*, 4th part, pp. 495-'6, Hindi Edition)

Bhatkhande painfully addresses that we, though being the best of God's creation, do not care to sing the praise of the Creator. Under the spell of illusion we forget the transiency of life and indulge in wrong doings of the world. "O man ! even now wake up, shun the mundane and realise the futility of all these."

It is interesting to mention here that even when he composed *dhamar* -- a lighter composition in *dhrupad* style -- the philosophic ideas dominated his poems. Usually the content of *dhamar* is connected with the *Holi* festival. As the central theme is usually borrowed from the love-episode of Radha and Krishna, it invariably has an air of love and gaiety. Here is an instance of Bhatkhande's *dhamar* which deals with the subject of *Holi:*

होरी खेले संत सुज्ञाने री
आतमा राम सो।
जोगी जो खेले जोग जुगति सों
साधू खेले हरिनाम सों।।

(*Kramik Pustak Malika*, 6th part, pp. 110-'11, Hindi Edition)

This composition in *raga Sindhura* enters into the deeper meaning of '*Holi*' -- the colourful *leela* -- exchange of thoughts and ideas by a saint with the Innermost Being. It is the subtle communication of the human soul and the Eternal Soul when a devotee becomes conscious of the cosmic existence within himself. Here the word *hori* stands for such communication. Bhatkhande, with his stunning ingenuity, has elevated *Holi* from its ordinary meaning of joyful festival and given it a status of the height of spirituality which man can aspire for.

Bhatkhande's deep study of our philosophy and his spiritualism combined into a unified whole and was reflected in his total personality as well as in his compositions.

IX

CONCLUSION

His compositions -- so varied, covering almost all the branches of Classical music -- are marked by certain qualities peculiarly his very own. They are lyrical in nature and endowed with a deep spiritual insight into the world and creation. His ethical and philosophical ideas, the appeal to the intellect and aesthetics, the wealth of imagination and the torrent of chosen words illuminated by flashes of exquisite beauty of phrases and poetic ideas -- all are different aspects of one integrated personality. Both his imagination and his intellect are richly productive and his work is noble in design and faultless in results. He has left a treasure for posterity most remarkable in quality and quantity.

9

Music Conference as a Tool and Strategy

Right from the time of Tansen at the Court of Emperor Akbar in the sixteenth century our musicians were primarily court musicians, patronised and sheltered by the ruling kings. Their music was meant primarily to entertain the king, and they were expected to enter into contests etc. as desired by the king. The listeners were the few fortunate ones who had access to the king's court or could otherwise come close to him. The ordinary people, even with aptitude or curiosity about Classical music, therefore, had no opportunity of listening to the stalwarts, leave alone learning from them.

During the eighteenth and the nineteenth century, on the advent of British rule, the celebrated artists took shelter in the courts of petty kings, rulers and Jagirdars. They were retained by their respective masters for their personal entertainment in return for which they were provided with material comfort and gain. The musicians thus, confined to the different courts, lost contact with the masses and lack of travel and absence of exchange of knowledge with other musicians bred narrowness, egoism and false vanity. This led to the birth of the *gharana* system, which, while it enriched the art of music by very attractive stylised forms of singing, bred conservative ideas in teaching and constant rivalry among the various *gharana*s.

Bhatkhande realised that these factors were hampering the progress of this noble art and the art of music would soon face extinction unless the public took interest in it and the educated class started learning it.

It was, therefore, necessary to take action to spread the message of music far and wide, thereby building a rapport between the musicians and the people and to give it a respectable and academic status. So Bhatkhande planned an All India Music Conference where the living stalwarts from all the *gharanas* were to be invited to perform in the presence of the public. The Nawab of Rampur, Chhamman Sahib and Thakur Nawab Ali, his close associates and well-wishers, supported him whole-heartedly in this proposal. But for such a big venture the greatest need was money which he did not have. As in those days the rulers of the native States patronised musicians and the cause of music and they could also afford to spend money if they were sufficiently interested, he started contacting State after State for monetary help. But all the rulers were not keen to spend money on his project. A letter written to Rai Umanath Bali, a close associate in his work, on 26th May, 1922 shows his worry in this regard:

"My dear Umanath Sahib,

We have given up all hope about Indore now. It is said that the State wants to save as much money as possible and won't now spend on the Music Conference. Poor Music! I really do not know what sins Music has committed. No protector comes forward to champion its cause. Nobody appreciates its great utility. People will have certainly to repent some day. The next decade will kill most of the leading artists and scholars and by the time the people wake up there will be only fifth class musicians left to please them. My friend, Mr. Kaul, is trying to induce the Calcutta gentry to invite a conference and let us hope his efforts succeed... A conference at Lucknow is a good idea too. I shall try to help you as far as I can. I believe Baroda, Gwalior and Indore would certainly send their artists. I can't say they will come at State expense... Lucknow can, with its great Rajas and Talukdars, easily put together Rs.10,000/- if she has a mind to do it. The guests will come at their own expense...

Yours sincerely,

Anna."[1]

This letter clearly speaks how dire was his financial need to follow up his project. His only asset was his sincerity of purpose and endless effort for the fulfilment of his noble task.

First All India Music Conference

Ultimately, by his continuous effort, along with that of his few close associates, he was able to organise the first All India Music Conference at Baroda under the patronage of the ruler of Baroda in the year of 1916. It was the first of its kind which enabled the public to listen to the celebrated musicians, whose performance was hither-to confined to the four walls of the Darbar Halls of the princes and the nobility. It was a real achievement to put the artists from different *gharana*s on one platform for the purpose of demonstration.

The first All India Music Conference was such a novel and revolutionary event that a month before the event took place a column was published in the weekly paper *Jayaji Pratap* from Gwalior praising the worthy cause. It would be relevant to quote a portion of it:

जहाँ भारत की अन्य विद्याएँ हीन दशा को प्राप्त हैं वहाँ संगीत की भी यही दशा है। उन सज्जनों को धन्यवाद है जो इसे पुनः जीवित करने में कार्यबद्ध हैं। विद्या-प्रचार के लिये महाराजा बड़ौदा प्रशंसनीय हैं। श्रीमान् की प्रेरणा से तथा उनके प्रधानत्व में २० मार्च तथा आगामी दिवसों में बड़ौदा में एक भारतीय संगीत परिषद् होने वाली है।[2]

The conference was a complete success as many well-known theoreticians and practical musicians took part in it. It set the ball rolling for other subsequent conferences. It would be interesting to read the account of this conference in the words of S.N. Ratanjankar: "Papers on different topics of music were read by scholars of music that came to the conference from all over India, including South India. K.B. Deval and E. Clements, I.C.S., read their papers, the main gist of which was that the Major Tone, Minor Tone and Semitone were the same respectively as the four *shruti*, three *shruti* and two *shruti* intervals of the ancient musicologists and accordingly the *Shuddha Rishabh* and *Shuddha Dhaivat*, which were at three *shruti* intervals from *Su* and *Pa* respectively, according to the ancients, were Minor Tones and therefore the *Shuddha*

Rishabh should be considered to be at a degree lower by one *shruti*, i.e., 10/9 (Minor Tone) than that of *Sa*. Similarly, *Shuddha Dhaivat* too should not be considered to be the 9/8 of *Pancham* but at a degree lower by one *shruti*. This proposition was vehemently opposed by many musicologists including the learned Subram Panditar. It was tested also by a practical demonstration by Mr. E.Clements on his *Shruti* harmonium on the one hand and, on the other, by reproduction of the correct pitch of *Shuddha Rishabh* in Hindustani music by no less a person than Ustad Zakiruddin Khan of Udaipur. Ultimately, Messrs. Clements' and Dewal's theory was not accepted. Besides these discussions and debates at the Baroda College held during the day time, practical demonstrations of music by eminent artists deputed by the Indian States were held in the evening at the Darbar Hall of the Laxmi Vilas Palace of Baroda. Thakur (afterwards known as Raja) Nawab Ali Khan Sahib of Lucknow presided at this conference. A permanent body by name All India Music Conference Working Committee was established with Pandit Bhatkhande as its General Secretary."[3]

In this session Bhatkhande read a paper in English entitled 'A Short Historical Survey of the Music of Upper India.' This paper was a unique contribution of its kind, which had no precedence. Studying music from the historical point of view and exploring its facts from the writings in the Sanskrit language of scholars belonging to different periods was a unique achievement. This brochure is even now regarded as a valuable document on the history of music for its originality, clarity and simplicity.

Another achievement of this conference was to compare and fix the notes of *Shuddha Rishabh* and *Shuddha Dhaivat* by practical demonstration, which later found its way into the theory formulated by Bhatkhande.

This conference, under the guidance of Bhatkhande, laid down the following lines of further action to preserve and develop Indian music:

1. "To take steps to protect and uplift our Indian music on national lines.
2. To reduce the same to a regular system such as would be easily taught to and learnt by our educated countrymen and women.
3. To provide a fairly workable uniform system of *ragas* and

*tala*s (with special reference to the Northern system of music).

4. To effect if possible such a happy fusion of the Northern and Southern systems of music as would enrich both.

5. To provide a uniform system of notation for the whole country.

6. To arrange new *raga* productions on scientific and systematic lines.

7. To consider and take further steps towards the improvement of our musical instruments in the light of our knowledge of modern science, all the while taking care to preserve our national identity.

8. To take steps to correct and preserve permanently the great masterpieces of this sublime art now in the possession of our first class artists and others.

9. To collect in a great central library all available literature (ancient and modern) on the subject of Indian music and if necessary to publish and render it available to our students of music.

10. To examine and fix the microtones of *shruti*s of Indian music with the help of our scientific instruments and the first class recognised artists of the day and to make an attempt if possible to distribute them among the *raga*s.

11. To start *Indian Men of Music* series.

12. To conduct a monthly journal of Music on up-to-date lines.

13. To raise a permanent fund for carrying on the above-mentioned objects

14. To establish a National Academy of Music in a central place where first class instruction in music could be given on most up-to-date lines by eminent scholars and artists in music."[4]

The above-mentioned items of the future programme show Bhatkhande's amazing power of thinking ahead of time. Never before was music given thought and discussed as a modern academic subject. The movement of Bhatkhande for the revival of music got momentum with this conference at Baroda and, being encouraged by its success, Bhatkhande called for the Second All Indian Music Conference at Delhi and issued an appeal through the weekly newspaper *Jayaji Pratap* in the name of the following members: Prof.V.N. Bhatkhande, Rai Bahadur Lala Sultan Singh, Rai Bahadur Damodar Das and Nawab Ahmed Sayeed Khan of Loharu. It was again a fervent appeal to the educated society to come forward and save this sublime art from extinction. It ran as follows:

"...Exchange of views on knotty points will be another great advantage secured, and it will lead to our introducing a uniform system of notation for the whole country for the adequate expression of the soul of music. Our immediate needs are:-

1. A good workable uniform *raga* system such as would enable us to learn and teach music without difficulty.
2. A good simple uniform notation system for the whole country.
3. A perfectly reliable history of Indian music and musicians.
4. The determination of *shrutis* and their uses in the *ragas.*
5. Impressing on people the educational value of music and necessity of introducing graded courses in schools and colleges.
6. A modern central academy of music where first class music could be taught according to the most up-to-date methods.

With these objects in view we beg to approach your kind and noble self with the request that you will come forward and help us so that the conference may be a great success. Any donations and promise of service will be looked upon with a deep sense of gratitude by us and the permanent body of the All India Music Conference Committee."[5]

Interim Conference

Before holding the Second All India Music Conference there was an Interim Conference held at Rampur as a special session on the 7th September, 1918 and the following resolutions were adopted:

1. "That the dates of the Delhi Conference be fixed as 7th to 10th December.
2. That the *raga* system advocated by Prof. V.N.Bhatkhande of Bombay is suitable for mass-education in music.
3. That a central music college should be established in Delhi.
4. That rupees ten lakhs be collected for establishing this college and special deputations should wait on various ruling chiefs for funds.
5. That detailed scheme be drafted by a body of experts like Prof. V.N.Bhatkhande, Thakur M. Nawab Ali, Taluqdar of Akbarpur, Mr. S.N. Karnad, Prof. S.L. Joshi of Baroda,

Prof. P.B. Joshi of Ajmer, etc. within one month.

6.   That the foundation-stone should be laid at the time of the conference if promises for rupees five lakhs are secured within the next three months."[6]

From this it appears that though Bhatkhande was only one of the members of the Standing Committee, his scholarship was universally acknowledged. It also appears that his theory of Hindustani music as propounded from his research and analysis also gained approval of the knowledgeable persons of that time.

Second All India Music Conference

The second All India Music Conference was held in December, 1918 at Delhi under the Presidentship of the Nawab of Rampur. While Bhatkhande was the guiding spirit behind it, Brij Kishan Kaul acted as the Secretary of the Conference. In the Delhi Conference all the expert musicians of All India fame participated and demonstrated their art. Bhatkhande called all the important musicians together to discuss certain differences of opinion regarding some *ragas*. A common understanding was reached and the rules of these *ragas* were laid down definitely. Pandit Bhatkhande incorporated these agreed rules in the fourth part of the *Hindustani Sangeet Paddhati*. The controversial forms of the following *ragas* were discussed and standardised forms were evolved with common consensus: *Malhar Ke Prakar, Sarang Ke Prakar, Todi Ke Prakar, Kanhara Ke Prakar* etc. For the future students and lovers of music this was a great step forward taken to end the *gharanedar* differences which caused confusion among the learners.

Normally the professional musicians were unwilling to attend such meetings, fearing, on the one hand, that they would have to demonstrate in the presence of other fellow musicians their traditional compositions which they had jealously guarded as precious jewels; and on the other hand, perhaps, they were afraid of being challenged by other musicians. But with Bhatkhande's inspiration and persuasion all their objections were dropped and the ice was broken. Bhatkhande always aimed at such academic meetings of practising musicians in the All India Music Conferences.

Chhamman Sahib and Thakur Nawab Ali were also among the organisers and participants of the second All India Music Conference. Proposed by all of them, it was decided for the first time that a Central Training Institution in the form of a Music Academy should be established in Delhi. The Nawab of Rampur promised monetary help in this regard but later, on account of some unavoidable circumstances, it did not come through.

At the concluding session of the second All India Music Conference, Bhatkhande moved a resolution about establishing a National Academy of Music at Delhi and also narrated a brief history of Classical music, highlighting the causes of its downfall and its present degenerated state. He said: "It is true that some of our learned scholars are directing their attention to this state of things and there have been some praiseworthy attempts to improve the unsatisfactory condition, but, in a matter of such national importance, stray and isolated attempts on the part of a few scholars could never be expected to yield permanent beneficial results. The whole nation must take up the cause, and make a grand and organised effort.[7] The best way to begin the work of regeneration is to recognise the present Hindustani practice of music and to establish the same on a scientific and sound basis, that is, to support it by a good, well-reasoned and easily intelligible theory. Theory is rightly described as the backbone of practice, and when that perishes, the practice gradually begins to degenerate. This means that the time has now arrived when the educated classes should take up the subject in hand earnestly and proceed to give it its due position and importance. They can do this by supplying the following essentials:

1. A good workable *raga* system embodying all the *raga*s now sung in Northern India.
2. A plentiful supply of valuable up-to-date literature on music.
3. A fair supply of well-equipped professors.
4. A faithful record of all the available masterpieces of our first class experts for future guidance,
5. And a public institution where music could be taught on the most scientific and up-to-date lines."[8]

Third All India Music Conference

All these programmes were taken up enthusiastically in the third All India Music Conference which was held at Banaras in November, 1919. The Secretary was the late Shibendra Nath Basu alias Santu Babu. He was a rich resident of Banaras and was a great lover of music. The Permanent Secretary of All India Music Conference was Bhatkhande himself and, needless to say, all the plans and proposals were drawn up by him. All the top vocal musicians and instrumentalists of our country participated and demonstrated their art. The names of some of the stalwarts who were present are: Ustad Faiyaz Khan, Zakiruddin Khan, Nasiruddin Khan, Allah Bande Khan, Musharraf Khan Beenkar, Imdad Khan and his sons Sadiq Ali Khan and Inayat Khan, Fida Hussain Khan (*Sarod* player), Mushtaq Hussain Khan, Hafiz Ali Khan (*Sarod* player), Barkatullah and Pandit Vishnu Digambar Paluskar. Apart from the demonstration, the usual discussions, reading of pap
debates with illustrations etc. were also held.

As of the earlier conferences, the objective of this confere. also was to compromise the quarrels of the *gharanedar ustad*s and bring about a consensus regarding the controversial *raga*s through discussion. This consensus was brought about under the leadership of Bhatkhande and it led him to formulate the theory after proper analysis which he later published in his books *Kramik Pustak Malika* series and *Hindustani Sangeet Paddhati*. The *raga*s *Bilawal Ke Prakar, Sarang Ke Prakar, Malhar Ke Prakar, Todi Ke Prakar*, and *Kanhara Ke Prakar* were discussed. After a lot of debate the final decision was taken about their forms and uniform rules and regulations emerged. There was lot of discussion about forming a notation system, *thaat raga* or the Parent Scale, fixing the main features of *raga*s and their classification. All the musicians present sincerely and enthusiastically praised the endeavours and work done by Bhatkhande in this field. It is noteworthy that even though being a scholar, having practical experience of music as well, he did not force his own opinion about the contorversial *raga*s without arranging for discussion with and the approval of the recognised musicians of his time.

At this conference the proposal for creating a Central Academy of Music in Delhi came up for consideration once again. Mrs. Atiya Begum Faizee Rahim submitted a scheme. But as this scheme was rather ambitious, involving an expenditure of ten to fifteen lakhs of rupees, it could not be considered as practicable.

The success of the third All India Music Conference was described in the weekly journal of Gwalior *Jayaji Pratap* of 25th December, 1918, as follows: "...In this function many renowned musicians from the United Provinces, Deccan, Punjab and

Gujarat took part. These artists took part in the demonstrations and discussions and established the highly cultured refined mode of the art of music. Many proposals were passed about the progress and uplift of music. The Nawab of Rampur has donated Rs. 50,000/- for the purpose of expanding and spreading this great art and also to arrange for its scientific training."

Fourth All India Music Conference

The fourth All India Music Conference was held at Lucknow in December, 1924, under the guidance of Pandit Bhatkhande. There was an awakening among the people as a result of first three conferences and more and more people were coming forward to serve the cause of music. This time no less a person than Rai Umanath Bali, a leading Talukdar of U.P., Daryabad (Barabanki), came forward to join hands with Bhatkhande. His influence also drew Raja Rai Rajeshwar Bali, who was the Minister of Education in the Govt. of United Provinces, and a close friend of Thakur Nawab Ali. The Balis of Daryabad were not only lovers of music but learnt music from the musicians in their employ. Rai Umanath Bali was in search of a standardised systematic and scientific form of lessons in music as he possessed an analytical mind along with his aptitude for music. He was impressed by Bhatkhande's pioneering work in this direction and also corresponded with him with a desire to take an active part in his movement.

In the Delhi All India Music Conference a proposal was taken up to establish a Central Academy of Music with a training institution on modern scientific lines which never materialised. Rai Umanath Bali also prepared a scheme for establishing a Music Association at Lucknow with facilities of teaching to which Bhatkhande readily agreed. It was sheer luck that the administrative authorities of Lucknow showed interest in the success of this scheme. The then Governor of U.P., Sir William Marris, was interested in Sanskrit literature, Classical music and studied Indian art and Unani literature. His interest in these subjects brought him close to the Taluqdar of Daryabad. The most important factor was the co-operation of Raja Rai Rajeshwar Bali who was the Minister of Education of U.P. at that time. In fact, he was instrumental in getting the consent of Governor Marris to establish a music institution at Lucknow. Rai Umnath Bali invited Bhatkhande to

Daryabad for his approval of the scheme. Bhatkhande obliged him by reaching there in the month of December, 1923. Raja Rai Rajeshwar Bali, Rai Umnath Bali and Bhatkhande formulated a scheme together according to which the fourth All India Music Conference was held at Kaiser Bagh, Baradari, in the month of December, 1924. In response to Bhatkhande's invitation, the renowned musicians from all over India took part in it.

In this conference Bhatkhande again arranged debates and discussions about the uncommon *raga*s in the presence of the participants. But due to the obstructive attitude of some of the musicians he had to abandon the idea. Efforts were made again in this regard in the Music Conferences held in later years at Kanpur and Ajmer but the above-mentioned reasons worked again to make the endeavour unsuccessful. Already there was a scheme ready to open a music institution at Lucknow, but the organisers desisted from it as enough funds had not been collected. However, the fourth Music Conference could spread the message of music throughout the length and breadth of Upper India.

Fifth All India Music Conference

The last Music Conference held during the lifetime of Bhatkhande was the fifth All India Music Conference. It took place in the same Kaiser Bagh Palace at Lucknow, in the month of December, 1925. It was a big event in the history of the United Provinces. The people of U.P. were artistically inclined, and they were thrilled to hear the demonstration of such expert musicians whose art had been hidden within the courts of the different States. About five thousand listeners turned up to listen to the celebrated musicians. Apart from the propagation of music the main object of this conference was to pass a resolution to establish an institution of musical training at Lucknow itself. The resolution was welcomed by all and enough money was collected to start this noble project. Accordingly in July, 1926 music classes were opened at Topwali Kothi, Neel Road, near Kaiser Bagh. In fact that was the beginning of the celebrated Marris College of Music which later developed into the Bhatkhande University with branches affiliated to it spread over North and Eastern India. Needless to say, in this College Bhatkhande experimented with his new and modern method of teaching music with graded textbooks and it proved to be a great success. Since then it has been training hundreds of students of music every year.

The Achievements

The achievements of these conferences may be summed up as follows:

1. The Conferences were first of their kind which enabled the public to listen to the celebrated musicians.

2. This was a great step to end the isolation in which Hindustani Classical music was imprisoned by the fanatics.

3. The greatest achievement of these conferences was to put the practising stalwarts of different *gharana*s on one platform and enable them to perform for the enlightenment of the general public. It had the salutary effect of unfolding the rich treasure of our Classical art to the people who were educated and interested in understanding it.

4. It helped a great deal in minimising the *gharanedar* quarrels and also settled the disputes about the different versions of a single *raga* as practised in the different pockets of Northern India.

5. It brought a virtual revolution by putting Hindu and Muslim musicians on one platform thus uplifting music above the barriers of caste, creed and religion.

6. It enabled the musicians and the public to think about the various problems connected with music and turned their attention towards the fruitful consolidation of the available knowledge and current practice of Hindustani music.

7. Discussions among the musicians helped to bring about a common consensus about some controversial *raga*s which was incorporated in the music books written by Bhatkhande.

8. Through discussions and demonstrations of the musicians the positions of the notes, *Shuddha Dha* and *Shuddha Re*, were fixed for the benefit of the music learners of posterity.

9. It also paved the way for establishing music institutions and collective education, thereby raising its status to the academic level.

10. Through discussions and debates universal and standardised forms of many *raga*s were evolved for the purpose of learning in the future.

References

1. *Bhatkhande Smriti Grantha,* p.377
2. Ibid., p.359
3. Ratanjankar, Pandit S.N. : *Pandit Bhatkhande,* pp.32-'3
4. *Bhatkhande Smriti Grantha,op.cit.,* pp.417-'8
5. Ibid., p.419
6. Ibid., p.360
7. Ibid., p.421
8. Ibid., pp.421-'2

10

Forming a Notation System

The Early Evidence

In the Vedas, the earliest holy scriptures in human history, a type of sign system about different pitch and notes of the *Sama* music was introduced in the following manner. The different notes of a *Saptak* were indicated by the different fingers of the right hand and as the human body became the medium of denoting the different *swaras*, it was called *Gatra* (body) *Veena*. *Veena* was a genetic term to denote any instrument. This type of sign indication of various notes was not abandoned in later periods and was named as Cheironomic notation. Thus, *Samaveda* was the inventor of the earliest system of music notation.

In ancient India of the time of Panini, the great grammarian, there is found an evidence of some sort of a notation system for indicating music in writing. Sir William Wilson Hunter, the historian, has explained, in his *Imperial Gazetteer of India*, Vol.VI, that for the musical notes a system of notation was prevalent even earlier than the time of Panini. But the system of notation of that time was rather sketchy and obviously quite different from what is understood by it at present. There was no system of writing songs or music in *tala* and *matra* along with the *komal* and *teevra swaras*. Consequently, the musicians of the later periods could not be benefited by the notation system of the ancients.

In fact, right from ancient times, in our music system there was no method of recording it in notation in the strict sense of the term. Consequently many valuable compositions and treasures were lost. On the contrary, Western musicians invented a notation system quite early which was highly accurate and successful for mass orchestration and other types of music. But their music demonstration does not allow variations whereas our music offers many opportunities to an artist to introduce numerous variations each time he sings the same songs. This is a unique quality of our Classical music which is able to create a new appeal in every performance. Perhaps for this reason there was no emphasis placed on a notation system by our old masters. Additional reasons for the absence of a notation system may be as follows:

1. In ancient times importance was given to practical music. The pupil used to learn by listening and copying the demonstration of his *guru*.
2. The system demanded that the *raga*s be learnt by heart.
3. The custom was that the *guru* made the pupil learn all lessons orally and the pupil in his turn did the same, thus keeping the knowledge of music as *guru parampara vidya* handed down from generation to generation.
4. The musicians of olden times never used to write music even for their own sons. They preferred to make them sit in front of them and learn directly which was called *guru shishya parampara*.
5. The artists and the musicians, by and large, could not read or write and the facilities, if there were any, were very poor for writing and printing in those days.

However, as centuries advanced, some attempts were made by Sharngadeva of the thirteenth century in his *Sangeet Ratnakar*. He invented signs for *laghu*, *guru*, *plut* and *drut*--a first step towards the present day notation system. We also come across signs for different types of *gamak*s in *Raga Vibodha* written by Somnath.

But our music changed from theirs due to the Muslim influence from the eleventh century onwards and, therefore, could not be expressed further by the signs of *Sangeet Ratnakara* and *Raga Vibodha*.

In the early twentieth century when Bhatkhande started his movement to recast and reconstruct the theory of music on scientific lines, he thought of introducing a notation system in Hindustani music as an integral part of his new method of music education.

His idea was to form a simple and uniform notation system throughout the country so that the same way of instruction could be provided and assimilation ensured in a uniform way. Therefore, he put forward several proposals on this necessity in the music conferences that he arranged to focus the attention of the learned scholars, who assembled there from all parts of India. He also felt that the forming of a notation system was absolutely necessary for an easy and effective instruction in music which was needed for mass education. Therefore, in the Second Music Conference which was held in Delhi in 1918, he placed on the agenda the following as one of the items:

"A good simple uniform notation system for the whole country."[1]

Advantage of Notation System

The advantages of a notation system, according to Bhatkhande, were as follows:

1. Music is a dynamic art. It changes by a natural evolutionary process through the centuries. To keep a record of the existing music in notation is the only method of handing down our real heritage to the next generation.

2. The only authentic and fool-proof method of learning a composition or the development of a *raga* is possible through the medium of notation.

3. It helps a learner to have a clear-cut idea of the movement of a *raga* as he can visualise the whole movement in the note names like a picture.

4. It also helps a learner to remember and understand the subtle shades of difference between allied *ragas*.

5. The basis of real training should be to enable a pupil to recognise notation and develop in him the ability to translate it into voice.

6. Dependence on the oral system of training means the invariable distortion of note formation and languages which can be prevented by learning through notation.

7. The quick understanding of the salient points of a *raga*, its characteristic note patterns and exact points of *tala* and *matra* as delineated in the compositions, can best be attained and learnt from notation.

The notation system is the most useful and easy method to learn a *raga* from the grammatical point of view. If necessary one can at least give a correct rendering of the form of a *raga* from the structural aspect. It is absolutely necessary for the collective system of music education, which means teaching a group of students the grammatically   correct form of a *raga*.

The Limitations

It is, however, a fact that the notation by which compositions are recorded -- indicating *swara*, *tala* and *matra* or which can write *sa ra ga ma* and grace notes -- is useful up to a degree only. The finer nuances and graces of a full-fledged performance cannot be recorded in notation. It is true that the quality of voice and the style of voice-production, the method of clear pronunciation of the text, the subtle relationship between the notes, the resting points and the prolonged gliding *swara*s, which is an integral part of the spirit of a *raga*, can never be expressed by the lifeless notations. Nor is it possible to record the feeble and loud voice-production for expression through them. In this regard Bhatkhande remarked as follows in the *Hindustani Sangeet Paddhati*: "It is true that some points of music can never be written in notation. But it is my conviction that no knowledgeable person would argue that because of the drawbacks in using them as mentioned above the notations should not be used at all. My opinion in this regard is , that a notation system is a must and music would be easily understood if there could be uniform system of notation throughout the country. It would certainly help in the progress of the art. The Western countries have realised this fact and have accepted a uniform notation system which has benefited all alike." (Second Part, page 205).

It is true that in our system of music a fool-proof notation is not possible. Even with the best attempts there is always something which cannot be covered by notation. For example, the subtle balance of rendering note combinations which becomes responsible for differentiating one *raga* from the other as in *Jogia* and *Gunkali*, *Bhairava* and *Ramkali*. The balance *ma re sa* of each of these *raga*s at the time of descension is different, but when they are written in notation they would appear as the same combination of notes.

Again, today, with the advancement of science and technology, the masterly demonstrations of the present day artists are recorded and stored in tapes and discs to be played by modern machines. They are playing a significant role in the preservation of music with all its finer graces. They undoubtedly reproduce a finished performance by the artist with well-modulated voice and well-practised *tana*s and *vistar*. But it is difficult for a student to learn and understand the movement of a *raga* from such finished performances. For that he needs the help of notation.

The Various Experiments by other Scholars

In the latter half of the nineteenth century, when Bhatkhande's movement gained some momentum, the necessity of a notation system was felt by many scholar musicians and some experiments were also made in this field by them.

When Bhatkhande took over the charge of the Sayajirao School of Music, Baroda, he came across a musician who was formerly in charge of that school, named Maula Bux Ghisse Khan, who invented a notation system for imparting lessons.

Bhatkhande mentioned in his book called *A Historical Survey of the Music of Upper India* that Krishna Dhan Banerji in his *Gita Sutrasar* had written hundreds of *dhrupad*s and *khayal*s after the European notation system in very clever manner. There were also others who made continuous efforts to invent a form of notation, each one of which differed from the other. It is interesting to note that each one claimed his method as the most authentic and faultless. Bhatkhande studied the different types of notations prevalent at his time from the angle of simplicity, universality and utility for the group education system and gave his comments in the second part of his *Hindustani Sangeet Paddhati*, which are summarised as below:

"I have gone through them and found out that none is free from the Western influence. Some scholar has taken the staff from the European system to show the place of *swara*, some has used the Bar from the European system and some has adopted the Western sign of repetition. It is obvious that the Western style of notation cannot express the embellishments (*meend, moorchhana, gamak* etc.) and grace notes. One argument can be that if Western method is accepted it should be accepted totally as this method is well-advanced and well-tried. What is the use of adding or subtracting something from it? It is a fact that we cannot adopt the signs of *Sangeet Ratnakar* of Sharngadeva or *Raga Vibodha* of Somnath, as our music has far deviated from their music. The scholars and musicians who ridicule the system of notation should take into account the fact that in the absence of a notation system the oral training produced so much of distortion that it was difficult to recognise the *guru*'s *gayaki* in that of the pupil's. One can well imagine what would be the condition of practical music after a few generations.

"It is not proper for me to criticise and find fault with some points of each method of notation in vogue. This will not be in the interest of the progress of music in general. On the other hand, I have composed some *lakshan geets* and recorded them in notation. You can learn them and find out for yourself their utility as I have made use of notations therein."

With the full knowledge of its merits and demerits, Bhatkhande championed the cause of a notation system from the beginning and he invented an easy form of it from the early stage of his training. He had an uncanny sense of *swaras* and when he used to learn from the *ustads* of the Gayan Uttejak Mandali he used to record them in notation and could reproduce them instantly. He always recorded his collection of compositions in notation. When others found him doing so they took it as a wastage of time but the day he published these compositions with notations the astonishment of the music world knew no bounds. Later, from 1915 onwards, he started publishing the old traditional compositions of music in notation in series of monthly pamphlets, known as *Geet Malika* series, at the nominal price of four annas (equivalent to twenty-five paisas of the present day) per copy.

The Notation System of Bhatkhande

While he started his new method of teaching at the Madhav Sangeet Mahavidyalaya, Gwalior, he imparted the lessons in notation, writing it on the blackboard. It created a commotion in the music world as in those days writing music was considered as sacrilege and to translate a *tana* in note names *sa re ga ma* was considered difficult.

The following are the signs of notation invented by Bhatkhande for use in his notation system:

1. The notes which do not have any signs, either at the bottom or the top, are called *shuddha swaras*, as for example: *sa re ga ma*.

2. The *komal swaras* are marked with a line underneath, as for example: *re ga dha ni*.

3. To indicate *teevra ma* a vertical line is drawn above the note *ma*, as for example: *ma*.

4. The *swaras* belonging to the *Mandra Saptak* (lower octave) are indicated by putting dots at the bottom, as for example: *ma pa dha*.

5. The *swaras* indicated by putting dots on the top belong to the *Tara Saptak* (higher octave), as for example: *re ga ma pa*.

6. The *swaras* having no dots either at the bottom or the top are regarded as belonging to the *Madhya Saptak* (middle octave), as for example: *re ga ma pa*.

7. Each of the ऽ sign when used against any letter (part of a word) means one *matra* pause, as for example: *sa ऽ ऽ khi* (4 *matras*).

8. Similarly when a line is used after a note name it is considered as one *matra*, the number of which has to increase with the number of *matras*. As for example: *ga – –* (3 *matras*).

9. When two or more *swaras* are intended to be sung in one *matra*, the following sign is used: *pa ma ga* (one *matra*) or *re ga ma pa* (one *matra*).

10. The *meend* is indicated with a sign as in the following example: *ma pa dha ni*. The sign indicates that there should be *meend* from *ma* to *ni*.

11. If one *swara* is written above the other it indicates a *kan swara*. For example *ma pa*. It means that just after touching the *swara ma* sing or play the *swara pa*.

12. The *swara* which is hidden as an embellishment should be sung like this: First the *swara* succeeding the ornamental note, then coming back to the original note, then again singing the preceding note and return to the original note, as for example *(pa)* meaning *dha pa ma pa* (one *matra*).

13. The sign for indicating the main *tala* or *sam* is **✕**.

14. For indicating *khali* o is used.

15. The *sam* is regarded as the first *tala*, the rest are counted after it.

At the time of Bhatkhande's work, Vishnu Digambar Paluskar, well-known as the founder of the chain of music schools, named as Gandharva Mahavidyalayas, invented a type of notation to spread music education. Paluskar was a contemporary of Bhatkhande and was greatly responsible for reviving and purifying the practical music of his time. His notation system was greatly influenced by the European notation system, as the following example will show.

This is a well-known *Chhota khayal:*

Jab Se Tumi San Laagli

(Bhupali, Teental)

ग रि ग रि रि सा सा	सा सा रि रि ग Ψ Ψ
0 0 0 0 0 0 0	ꡳ 0 - 0 -
घ 0	

जब से ओ तु मि स न   ला · · ग ली · ·

One can see that to express the three registers *(mandra, madhya* and *tara)* he used the staff of the European notations. The signs he coined to express *shuddha* and *komal swaras* as well as their pauses and their utterances in relation to their *matras* in songs were as follows:

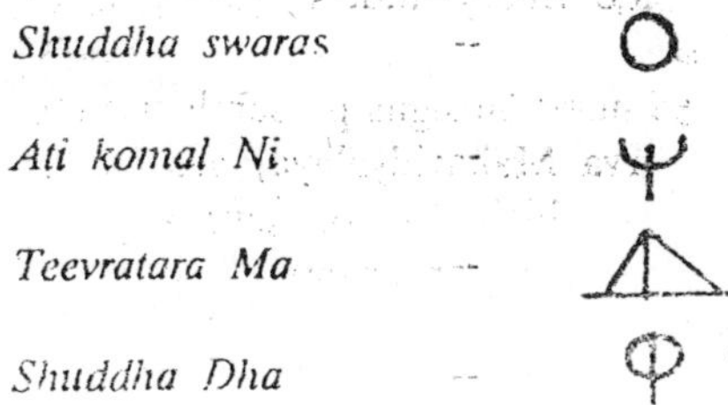

Shuddha swaras	--	O
Ati komal Ni	--	Ψ
Teevratara Ma	--	△
Shuddha Dha	--	Φ

In regard to the *swara*'s division in *matra* in songs his signs were as follows:

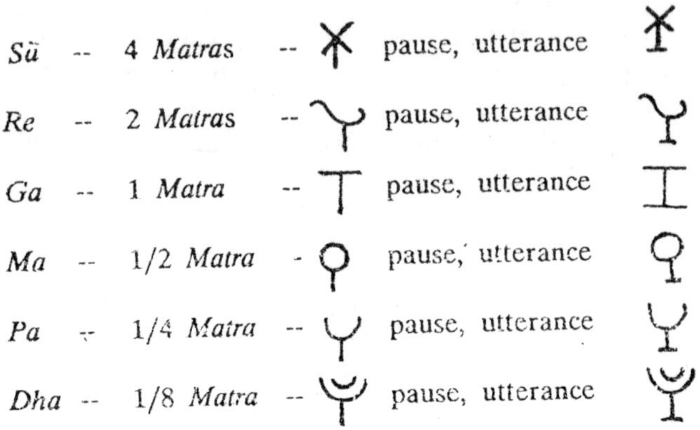

Sä	-- 4 Matras	-- ✗ pause, utterance	
Re	-- 2 Matras	-- ∨ pause, utterance	
Ga	-- 1 Matra	-- ⊤ pause, utterance	
Ma	-- 1/2 Matra	- ♀ pause, utterance	
Pa	-- 1/4 Matra	-- ∪ pause, utterance	
Dha	-- 1/8 Matra	-- ∪ pause, utterance	

For writing songs in *Tisra Jati* he coined the following signs:

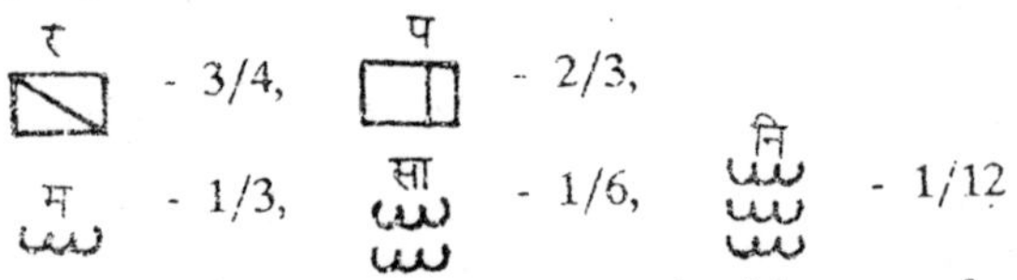

र ▱ - 3/4, प ▭ - 2/3,

म - 1/3, सा - 1/6, नि - 1/12

He wrote songs and their *raga vistar* in this type of notation in *Raga Pravesh* series.

Later, some of the main disciples of Vishnu Digambar Paluskar discarded this type of notation for its complicated nature and invented simpler ones. However, even now the modified notation system is accepted and practised by the Gandharva Mahavidyalaya and in all its branches all over the country.

It will be relevant for the purpose of comparison to illustrate the current notation system of the *Vishnu Digambar Paluskar Paddhati*, alongside Bhatkhande's system as it is widely popular even at present.

The renovated notation signs presently used by Vishnu Digambar Schools (Gandharva Mahavidyalaya) are as follows:

1. The *swaras* which do not have any sign are regarded as *shuddha swaras*. For example: *re ga ma pa*.
2. Where a verticle line is attached below a *swara*, it is regarded as a *komal swara*. For example: *re ga dha ni*.

3. *Teevra Madhyam* is indicated with a vertical line turned to the opposite side. For example: *ma/* .

4. The *Mandra Saptak* (lower octave) is indicated by a dot on the top of the *swara*. For example: *pa dha ni*.

5. The *Tara Saptak* (higher octave) is indicated by a vertical line on the top of the swaras: *sa re ga ma*.

6. For the purpose of indicating the number of *matra* + is used for 4 *swaras*. For example: *sa* (four *matras*)

7. For indicating two *matras* on a swara ∽ is used. For example: *sa* (two *matras*).

8. For indicating one *matra* __ is used. For example: *sa* (to be sung in 1 *matra*).

9. For indicating half *matra* o is used. For example: *sa* (to be sung in 1/2 *matra*).

10. Similarly, 1/4 *matra* is indicated by the sign of ∪ . For example: *pa* and,

11. 1/8 *matra* is indicated by ∪. For example: *ma*.

12. While prolonging a *swara* ऽ sign is used, one for each *matra*. For example: *ga* ऽ ऽ *pa* (4 *matras*).

13. For prolonging a word dots are used one for each *matra*. For example: *re . . ma* (4 *matras*).

14. While the *swaras* bear 1/3 or 1/6 at the bottom, it means 3 or 6 notes uttered in one *matra*.

15. If some note is written above another it indicates the grace note *kan swara*. For example: *re ga^{ma} ga^{ma}*.

16. For indicating *tala* in notation, 1 is used for *sam*, for *khali* + is used, for other *talas* 2,3,4 numbers are used.

17. Pauses are indicated by commas.

On close scrutiny of the Paluskar's and Bhatkhande's notation systems one finds that apart from differences in signs the main approach to the sign method is the same in the two systems. But while Bhatkhande endeavoured to express the embellishments with special signs, Paluskar did nothing of the sort. Whereas Paluskar has invented signs for uttering the *swaras* in 1/2, 1/4, 1/6 and 1/8 *matra*, Bhatkhande has done nothing in that direction. Rather he squeezed several notes in one *matra* with ∪ sign at the bottom to cover them in one *matra*.

The sign of *meend* ⌐⌐⌐ covering the concerned notes depicted by Bhatkhande has a special significance in his method of notation system which is lacking in Paluskar's. The *raga*s which have *meend* as a special characteristic can be very well expressed by Bhatkhande's method. For example, *raga Desh*. Its characteristic feature is *meend* from *ma* to *re* and *ni dha pa*. At least with Bhatkhande's system it can be expressed as *ma re, ni-dha pa* but in Paluskar's system it cannot be expressed. However, one argument could be that if notes are uttered in the balance of 1/4, 1/6 or 1/8 *matra*s (which are indicated by signs in the Paluskar system) automatically the function of *meend* would be discharged. But then the learner of the notation would not be conscious of the *meend*, which is a characteristic feature of some *raga*s.

Again, Bhatkhande has used the sign of brackets indicating the embellishment, as for example (*pa*), while Paluskar has squeezed in 3 or 4 notes together with 1/4 or 1/8 *matra* sign.

From the above facts it will not be wrong to deduce that the remarkable feature of Bhatkhande's notation system is its simple yet expressive coinage of signs which could adhere successfully to the *raga*'s form, expressing some of its grace notes, *meend* and embellishments. The commas and particular indication of prolonging *matra*s in regard to words and *swara*s express vital pauses which are an essential part of the delineation of a *raga*.

In the early twentieth century alongside Bhatkhande's movement, Rabindranath Tagore, the famous poet, composed hundreds of songs, set them in tune and wrote them down in notation. His system of notation is known as '*Akar Matrik Swaralipi*'. It was originally expounded by Dwijendra Nath Tagore and at a later stage was improved upon by his younger brother Jyotirindra Nath Tagore.

This notation system has been standardised and published from which thousands of musicians of Bengal learn the songs of Tagore even today. This notation system is somewhat different from the above-mentioned system for its complicated nature. The particular feature of this notation is that it does not use any sign for *komal* or *teevra swara*s. Instead it uses different letters from the Bengali alphabet having identical sound. It also uses grace notes extensively and does not indicate any other embellishments as *meend, moorchhana* etc. It will be relevant to illustrate this type of notation:

Rabindra Sangeet

अयि भूवनमनोमोहिनी मा

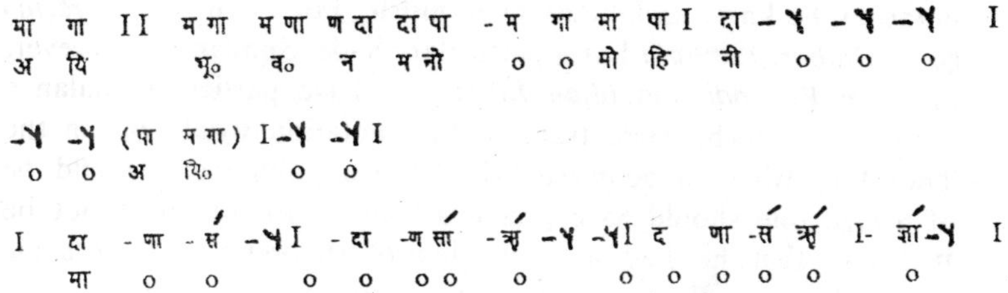

मा गा II म गा म णा ण दा दा पा – म गा मा पा I दा – ४ – ४ – ४ I
अ यि   भू० व० न म नो ० ० मो हि नी ० ० ०

– ४ – ४ (पा म गा) I – ४ – ४ I
० ० अ यि० ० o

I दा – णा – सं – ४ I – दा – ण सां – ऋं – ४ – ४ I द णा – सं ऋं I – ज्ञां – ४ I
मा ० ० ० ० ० ० ० ० ० ० ० ०

There is another type of notation still prevalent in Bengal which is called *Danda Matrik*. Here is an illustration:

Bhairava Chautal

लाल अलसाने भोरहि आये

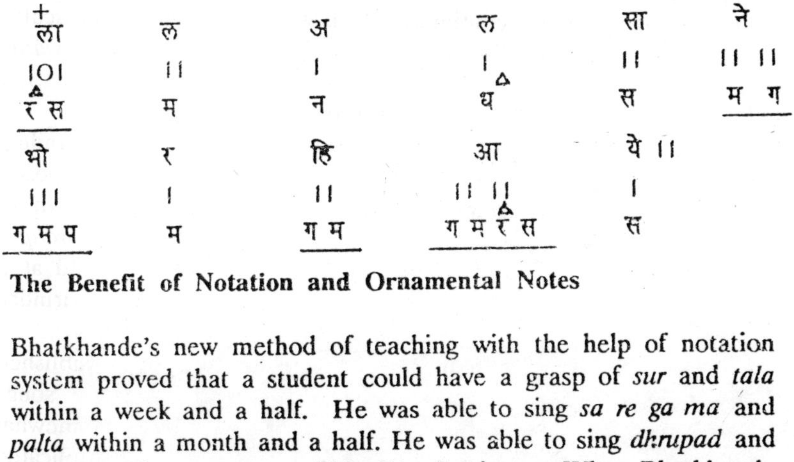

+ ला	ल	अ	ल	सा	ने
IOI	II	I	I △	II	II II
रे स	म	न	ध	स	म ग

भो	र	हि	आ	ये II
III	I	II	II II △	I
ग म प	म	ग म	ग म रे स	स

The Benefit of Notation and Ornamental Notes

Bhatkhande's new method of teaching with the help of notation system proved that a student could have a grasp of *sur* and *tala* within a week and a half. He was able to sing *sa re ga ma* and *palta* within a month and a half. He was able to sing *dhrupad* and *dhamar* and a new song within 5 to 7 minutes. When Bhatkhande with his tall stature and imposing personality used to stand in front of a blackboard with a chalk in hand to teach and write music in notation the traditional *ustad*s were scandalised.[2]

It is also noticed that a student who learns through this method, understands and grasps better and quicker the *gayaki* and *gharana* lessons from an expert musician, having a good *swaragyan* and *ra-*

gagyan as a base than those who were not trained through this method.

Although Bhatkhande noted down all his collections and compositions in notation emphasising the need for learning through notation, he knew its limitations in music. For example, the *komal ga* of *Darbari Kanhara* has a particular shade. Similarly, the *gandhar* of *Mian Ki Todi* and *Mian Ki Malhar* have particular shades of their own, which, while translated in notation would be *ga* only. Therefore, Bhatkhande insisted that after learning the basic skeleton of a *raga* one should have practical training for perfect rendering. It shows that he had a clear idea of theoretical and practical knowledge and their respective place in training. His notation system expressed the outline or the basic structure of a *raga* which he called *Nayaki*. He felt that the *Gayaki* part should be added and learnt later. The value of his contribution in forming a notation system is explained by Ratanjankar in the following words:

"His theory and notations were a basic skeleton which made it a great deal easier for a student of music to understand and pick up the music that he heard from his teacher or from an artist. It also gave a basic continuity which would help in preserving the music from undue distortion."[3]

References

1. *Bhatkhande Smriti Grantha,* p.419
2. Ibid., p.81
3. Ratanjankar, Pandit S.N. : *Pandit Bhatkhande,* p.52

11

Overcoming Social Taboos

A reformer's uphill journey is full of thorns. A pioneer, who set out to put music in its dignified position and to make it available to all music lovers had to face obstacles in overcoming the social censorship on learning and teaching of music, collecting of compositions and even on listening to and mixing with musicians.

The General State of Music

For, as stated earlier, music, at the time of Bhatkhande, was utilised to please the rich -- the princes, the Sardars, the Zamindars, the Seths and the Sahukars. Bhatkhande was oppressed by the thought that music was being used for such frivolous purposes. It had consequently deviated from its path of progress and was stagnating. The educated people cried it down, branding it as a subject fit only for the idlers and loafers. Any one, other than the hereditary musicians, who tried to learn it and pursue it invited moral censure from all quarters. Bhatkhande could not escape facing many obstacles in the form of social taboos, right from his childhood, not to speak of the obstacles he faced at later stages of his work for the revival of music. How he overcame them is revealed by many interesting episodes.

Censorship in His Early Life

Bhatkhande's talent for music was revealed from his childhood when he won prizes in school for singing nursery rhymes in a tuneful voice. As he grew, he became popular as a flute player and a *bhajan* singer. Although he was regular and serious about his studies his passion for music made his parents worried for his future. As music in those days was regarded as a degenerate art and its propagators were far from a respectable lot, the elders of Bhatkhande feared that he might turn out to be a vagabond, the synonym for a musician, and at times warned him sternly. But the inborn musician in him could not be suppressed. He took to *sitar* playing and became a pupil of a blind *sitar* player, Vallabhdas Damulji while studying in college. But to avoid opposition from his family members he had to go stealthily at night for his training. However, he could not hold his secret for long. One day in a private *mandali* he came face to face with his father where he was a performer and his father a listener. After this he did not have to face violent opposition to music from his elders as he was proficient in studies and he remained so till he became a full-fledged lawyer. Thus by following up his academic studies creditably he overcame the opposition of his elders to his life of music.

Listening

His passion for music continued and in his youth he became a member of the Gayan Uttejak Mandali, a music association of Bombay. Here he came into contact with experts in music and also had an opportunity to listen to the stalwarts. So strong was his desire to listen to good music that he did not mind brushing shoulders with the illiterate musicians and even visiting places which were known as dens of vice. It is difficult to imagine today what it meant for a high caste educated Brahmin of Bhatkhande's rank to remain day and night in the company of the illiterate musicians. He braved the social stigma undaunted. Thus he listened to celebrated musicians which inspired him to formulate the theory of the current practice of music and give it a theoretical base.

Collecting and Learning

In pursuit of this ambition, he started learning and collecting information and musical compositions simultaneously. But the obstacles he faced were difficult and varied. The musicians of his time were narrow-minded and reluctant to part with their knowledge. They considered music as a treasure which should be preserved as a family tradition and should not be shared with a stranger. Bhatkhande, not being born in a musician's family, was considered by them as having no claim to learn music. To overcome this taboo he had to resort to many tactics.

Initially, he started learning *bandish* form the *ustad*s who were connected with the Mandali in exchange for money. That was possible as on the advent of the British rule many princely kingdoms were annexed by them and their protege musicians came to Bombay to earn a living. His method of learning was novel according to the standard of those days. Not being satisfied with oral training he used to write down his lessons in notation in which he was already an adept.

Among the few musicians who appreciated his spirit of research and cooperated with him whole-heartedly was Nazir Khan, a leading *sarangi* player of those days, who was in the service of the Mandali. Through him Bhatkhande got acquainted with Ashiq Ali Khan, the son of Muhammed Ali Khan of Jaipur. They were the retainers of authentic *raga*-revealing compositions of *khayal*s in abundance. Bhatkhande started learning from Ashiq Ali the priceless compositions of his *gharana* (Jaipur) in exchange for money and in his unique way put them down in notation. It was disapproved by his illustrious father Munammed Ali, who chided Ashiq Ali for parting with their own wealth of knowledge. Bhatkhande pacified the old *Ustad* by falling at his feet and surrendering himself. By his sincere appeal the old *Ustad* was pacified and accepted Bhatkhande as his pupil--a fact which Bhatkhande acknowledged in his compositions and also in the *Hindustani Sangeet Paddhati*.

Study Tours

Later, when he started collecting information about both theoretical and practical music from every conceivable quarters, he had to face and overcome many more obstacles. For this purpose he proceeded on a study tour, covering almost the entire country when he listened to all the living stalwarts and met and discussed with anyone he found knowledgeable. After landing in a place he wasted no time and did not hesitate to visit the member of any community for collecting information. But the stumbling blocks were many. Most of the time he had to fight against prejudice, hypocrisy and arrogance, not to speak of ignorance.

In the second part of the *Hindustani Sangeet Paddhati* Bhatkhande recalls his conversation with a Pandit, somewhere in Eastern India, about the theory of music. The Pandit began his conversation with the following words: "I hope you are a *Brahmin* -- only then you will be able to understand the spiritual implications of the *swara*s in music."

The Pandit was assured that Bhatkhande belonged to the highest caste. Bhatkhande, however, was disappointed with his explanation of the origin of the *swara*s and the forms of *jati, moorchhana* etc.

In the same part of the *Hindustani Sangeet Paddhati* he again records the conversation he had with another Pandit, from South India. The Pandit, though well-known for his knowledge of music, both theoretical and practical, and having a good following, distorted the meaning to impress Bhatkhande of the Sanskrit couplets of Ahobal's *Sangeet Parijat* and tried to establish that the note *sā* was obtained from the sound of peacock, *re* from the bull, *ga* from the goat and so on. His entire approach was this type of quaint explanation of the *swara*s and *raga*s. Not only that, when he learnt that Bhatkhande had come to him with the desire for gathering knowledge, he said haughtily: "If you have dared to enter this city (a place of scholars like me), you will have to accept the formal ritual of becoming my pupil before you go out from here."

In the same part of the book as said above he quotes another incident cast in the same mould. He visited a place known for teaching and propagating music and owned by a petty king, known as a knowledgeable person. Bhatkhande heard that he possessed a valuable manuscript about the theory of music. When Bhatkhande with all humility requested him to show that manuscript, his answer was: "If I show my manuscript to anybody and everybody, then there would be Pandits in every nook and corner. The treasure of knowledge which was carefully stored by our predecessors would become available to everybody. If ever this book is printed then nobody would look to us in quest of knowledge. Who would then care for the learned and the wise?"

Obviously, Bhatkhande had to return without any success. These incidents are enough to indicate the ignorance, pride, prejudice, narrow-mindedness and possessiveness of the custodians of the great traditions of Hindustani music which their intellectual puritanism had brought in. These put up serious barriers which Bhatkhande met with when he began to collect information and check his personal experiences and impressions about the knowledge he had derived from the ancient books on Hindustani music.

The Muslim *ustads* were no better. Although they were excellent performers, they had lost touch completely with the *grantha*s and claimed that modern Classical music had originated from Sadarang and Adarang only. Further, they kept their knowledge of music confined to the members of their family only.

His Method of Overcoming Difficulties

The way he cleared these stumbling blocks is revealing of the important traits of his character--tact, patience and humility. While meeting the performers and so called musicologists of that period he was always careful not to give the impression that he was a professional musician or a showman theoretician. While he never degraded himself by unnecessarily praising or scandalising anybody, he at the same time carefully avoided insulting others or running down their ignorance, and tried not to make others feel small before his own superior knowledge. He never used to lose his patience in any situation or circumstance, nor did he ever use any rude words. He used to start and guide the question and answer process in such a way that out of it some useful material emerged to enrich his knowledge.

Overcoming Difficulties in Collection from Gharanedar Ustads

On his return from his study tours he aspired to collect compositions from *gharanedar ustad*s. The opposition he faced in this was not only stiff but also humiliating. The *gharanedar* musicians in those days were mostly sheltered by the small kings and petty jagirdars. Although their practical music had deviated from the ancient *grantha*s, still they were the torch-bearers of the tradition and consequently were arrogant and egoistic. They were pampered by their patron kings and moneyed people to a degree that made them vain, orthodox and narrow-minded. They were choosy and whimsical in selecting their pupils and in their method of teaching.

There were perhaps very good reasons why the old *gharanedar* musicians were reluctant to part with their long treasured compositions and style of singing. They were to some extent justified in protecting their art from the profanity of the irresponsible, immature, amateur or the commercial person. But Bhatkhande felt that time had come when the treasures must be fully revealed and must be fully shared by all without any barriers.

To give a new shape to music lessons and training he endeavoured to collect the *gharanedar bandish* and *gayaki* and through the introduction of some common friends reached the State of Rampur. Rampur was the seat of pure Classical music, having Ustad Wazir Khan, the descendant of Tansen, as the court-musician. The Nawab of Rampur, himself a pupil of Wazir Khan, was also well versed in Classical music. Naturally, Wazir Khan, according to the custom of those days, was averse to part with his knowledge to an outsider like Bhatkhande. But Bhatkhande, having known the reality of the situation, acted shrewdly to reach his goal. He convinced a sophisticated musician like Nawab about his view-point and sincerity of purpose and ceremoniously became his pupil. The Nawab also thought it to be a privilege, as by that time Bhatkhande's fame had already spread far and wide as a scholar musician. Within a short time Bhatkhande requested the Nawab to ask Wazir Khan, who was in his employ and could not dare to disregard his request, to teach him his *gharanedar bandish*, to which the Nawab readily agreed.

Thus to overcome this obstacle Bhatkhande's shrewdness worked and he enriched his knowledge by collecting the invaluable compositions of Tansen *gharana* which he later published in the *Kramik Pustak Malika* series to make them known to all the music lovers of the country. Similarly he collected valuable compositions also from Gwalior *gharana* and Jaipur *gharana*, overcoming the difficulties of prejudices, being sometimes comical and sometimes humourous.

Music Conferences

The obstacles he faced during the music conferences organised by him were not negligible. The purpose of organising such conferences was not only to hear demonstrations but also to solve differences through academic discussions. The first Music Conference was held at Baroda in the year of 1916. It was very creditable that he could put both Hindu and Muslim artists on one platform for the purpose of demonstrations. For social ostracism and their own personal prejudices drove the performing musicians into such narrowness of outlook that every artist created a wall of vanity around himself, having his own following and propagating his own rules and regulations of Classical music. In those days it was unthinkable that the stalwarts of different *gharana*s would sit on the same platform and perform for the same audience. One can imagine the amount of persuasion and influence he must have used to achieve his objective. During the first Music Conference E. Clements came up with the theory of Major Tone, Minor Tone and Semitone of European music as equivalent to four *shruti*, three *shruti* and two *shruti* intervals. This was vehemently opposed by the scholars and musicians present there and was not accepted by Bhatkhande. He fixed up his *swara*s on the gamut according to the demonstration of the eminent vocalists. This act also came under sharp attack by some scholars.

E. Clements, in an article, vehemently protested against Bhatkhande's theory of evolving *raga*s from the gamut of 12 notes only. He also disagreed with Bhatkhande's theory of *shruti*s having equal intervals. This article is mentioned in *Encyclopaedia of Indian Music with Special Reference to Ragas*.

In those days Philharmonic Society was engaged in explaining and discovering the ancient *raga*s and for this purpose its members evolved their own theories for comparing and showing resemblance between Indian and European music. Another strong criticism of the same nature appeared in the same book by G.S. Khare. Referring to the second part of the *Hindustani Sangeet Paddhati* he wrote: "Anybody who reads this book will see that Mr. Bhatkhande is not sure of his own scale."

At the second Music Conference at Delhi, Bhatkhande called all the important musicians together to discuss certain differences of opinion regarding some *raga*s. A common agreement was reached and the rules of the *raga*s were laid down definitely. These rules were incorporated by Bhatkhande in the fourth part of the *Hindustani Sangeet Paddhati*. This was a great step taken to make the rules of Classical music standardised, resulting in the emergence of an integrated eclectic style of rendering. "But academic meetings," writes Ratanjankar, "by the musicians in subsequent conferences were not possible as the professional musicians were unwilling to attend such meetings, fearing that they would have to demonstrate in the presence of other fellow musicians their traditional compositions of music which they jealously guarded as precious jewels through generations. And also perhaps they had the fear of being challenged by other artists."[1]

Although Bhatkhande attempted to hold similar discussions in the subsequent conferences, it was foiled by the strong resistance of one or the other section of musicians.

Music Institutions

The maximum resistance he had to face in the pursuit of his mission was when he first set up a music institution with his new and modern method of teaching in order to make music lessons available to all. The first school of music was established at Gwalior in the year of 1919. The Baroda State Music School was soon thereafter reorganised to teach by the new method under the direction of Bhatkhande.

In this regard he had to face persistent opposition from a large number of old-fashioned professional musicians. Due to the tradition of oral training for generations, they had contempt for texts and for learning music from books. They were highly suspicious of the new form of systematised and rational type of theory of music. On top of everything they were afraid of losing the claim of the superiority of their *gharana*s which they used to exploit in the old days. Many claimed that Bhatkhande's entire system was quite different from the one which they had learnt from their *guru*s.

As the work of the music schools continued uninterrupted and more and more students joined the classes, the enraged professional musicians devised a method to prevent the boys from attending these classes by composing a poem to ridicule this system of training. It was sung in open streets to put to shame anyone who joined these classes. The couplet expressed intense contempt, utter disbelief and biting hatred for the new system: *"Dakshin se aya Bhatkhande aur diye saat ande, ek Poochhwale baki bande."*[2] ["One person named Bhatkhande has come from the South (Bombay). He has hatched seven eggs. One of them is Poochhwale and others are barren."]

But Bhatkhande and the few teachers, trained by him, were undaunted, working tirelessly and braving this hostile atmosphere. How the wagging tongues came to a stop and the jealous ones were won over is narrated by Acharya Balabhau Umrekar: "It was the effect of his (Bhatkhande's) personality that goaded us (the students) to practise rigourously to defeat the opposition by showing our skill in music. After the coaching of one and a half year Bhatkhande invited the well-known musicians and scholars of the town, in whose presence the students demonstrated their art."[3]

The distinguished audience praised their performance and acknowledged whole-heartedly that what could be learnt by the old method in ten years had been imparted in one and a half year only.

But in spite of this he had to face often harsh words, sharp criticism and severe taunts. Even his book of theory, *Shrimallakshya Sangeetam,*written in Sanskrit, came under scathing attack by G. J. Agashe, then a retired Education Inspector. He criticised the verses of *Shrimallakshya Sangeetam* (43-58) and wrote: "The verses are grammatically inaccurate in some places and more often than not transgress the rules of metrical compositions..."

Again the same writer criticised his work as said using almost abusive language which runs as follows:

"The work is ill conceived and worse executed... If it is a work by someone who is now living, the audacious fraud, for it is nothing less of palming off on an uncritical and gullible public a stupid work, deserves severe condemnation."[4]

Acharya Balabhau Umrekar has narrated another incident telling us jealous musicians virtually abusing him on one occasion. Bhatkhande tolerated all this with his usual patience but at last retorted by saying: "A day will come when my students will take your place in the world of music."

His prediction came true. Within a few years all the products of his training centres occupied coveted places in the world of music education in the entire country. Thus Bhatkhande overcame all obstacles which came in his way by his devotion, persuasive tenacity and tact. It was his greatest triumph that the professional music world, which used to tease and taunt him in annoyance, later, in admiration, called him *Panditji* and acclaimed his works.

References

1. Ratanjankar, Pandit S.N. : *Pandit Bhatkhande*, p.44
2. 'Poochhwale' refers to Bhatkhande's pupil and friend Rajabhaiya Poochhwale.
3. *Bhatkhande Smriti Grantha*, p.320
4. *Encyclopaedia of Indian Music with Special Reference to Ragas.*

PART III

THE PARTING MILIEU

12

His Contemporaries

I

INTRODUCTION

The work started by any great man cannot be accomplished by him alone. For, his initiative and inspiration influence like-minded people who take up his cause and thus a movement starts and spreads. Bhatkhande, while working for the noble task of reviving, systematising and reconstructing music, also attracted patrons who supported his cause, friends and colleagues who developed and implemented his projects, and pupils who put his ideas into practice.

II

HIS PATRONS

The following were the important patrons of Bhatkhande's movement who appreciated, encouraged and financed his different activities for the revival of music:

NOTE: This Chapter is largely based on *Bhatkhande Smriti Grantha*.

His Highness Maharaja Madhav Rao Scindia of Gwalior

He heard about Bhatkhande's movement and called him to discuss about establishing a music school at Gwalior, teaching through his new method. He visited Bombay and watched incognito the music classes run by Bhatkhande. He immensely liked his new method of teaching and requested him to establish a music school for propagating his theory and method of learning. Accordingly, Madhav Rao School of Music was founded at Gwalior in 1918.

Bhatkhande trained up a team of musicians to impart lessons in the newly founded school, but he declined to stay himself permanently at Gwalior. The Maharaja accepted his plea and extended to him the maximum hospitality by placing Nautal Guest House at his disposal and keeping a Victoria carriage ready to carry him wherever he went as long as he stayed there. He was a great admirer of Bhatkhande and through his generous cooperation Bhatkhande was able to experiment with his new method of teaching which proved to be a great success.

His Highness Maharaja Sayaji Rao Gaekwad of Baroda

He was responsible for making Baroda a progressive State. He was introduced to Bhatkhande by Prof. S. L. Joshi, a teacher at Baroda. The Maharaja became interested in Bhatkhande's movement and arranged for the first Music Conference in 1916. Later, a School of Music, on the lines of the Gwalior School, was opened at Baroda under Bhatkhande's guidance. The Maharaja spent liberally for this School and also for propagating Bhatkhande's movement.

Nawab Hamid Ali Khan of Rampur

Hamid Ali, the Nawab of Rampur, was a learned musician and a great patron of music. He was the pupil of his employee Ustad Wazir Khan, descendant of Tansen of mythical fame, who was in his employ. Bhatkhande aspired to collect the valuable compositions belonging to the *gharana* of Tansen and, therefore, he became formally a pupil of the Nawab Sahib. It was through the Nawab Sahib that he could collect the priceless compositions of Rampur. The Nawab was a great admirer of Bhatkhande's work for establishing a rational theory of music and publishing the compositions in the form of textbooks. Later, he financed and permitted an Interim Conference of music to be held at Rampur on 7th September, 1918, under his presidentship.

Shrimant Sardar Balwantrao Shinde

He was one of the sons of His Highness Jiyaji Rao Scindia who was in touch with the famous musicians of his days. He was well versed in Persian, English, Hindi and Marathi. He had a religious temperament and he composed hundreds of devotional songs in Hindi and Marathi. Acharya Bhaskar Rao Khandeparkar mentioned to him about Bhatkhande and his movement, by which he was much influenced.

Later, he actively participated in the movement and took the charge of organising the first Music Conference at Baroda. He helped in solving some differences among the musicians. He acted as a bridge between the Maharaja and Bhatkhande and was responsible for introducing him to the Maharaja.

Rai Rajeshwar Bali

He was the Talukdar of Daryabad, U.P. He was also the Education Minister of the United Provinces. He was a cultured man who was a lover of art, equally fond of both music and painting. He took interest in Bhatkhande's work and sought the help of the then Government of U.P. through its Governor, Sir William Marris, in organising an association and establishing the Marris College of Music at Lucknow. Shri Bali took active interest in this college of Music and was on its Executive Board till his death.

Sir William Marris

In the year 1924-'25, when the 4th and 5th sessions of the All India Music Conference were held, he was posted at Lucknow as the Governor of U.P. He was greatly interested in Eastern literature and music.

Sir William Marris cooperated and helped a great deal in forming the music association sponsored by Bhatkhande and establishing the training college at Lucknow. He inaugurated the fourth Music Conference in 1924. In this connection he got acquainted with

Bhatkhande. The famous training centre of music at Lucknow--
Marris College of Music -- is named after him.

III

HIS TEACHERS

The following are the names of Bhatkhande's teachers from whom
he learnt music and collected compositions in his formative period.
In fact, he remained a student of music throughout his life so
that he could become a great teacher -- always increasing his store
of knowledge, always eager to add to his information and always
seeking to classify the knowledge he gathered.

Vallabhdas Damulji

He was a blind gentleman of the Bhatia community of Bombay.
He was a *beenkar* and also a *sitar* player. He himself learnt *sitar*
from the well-known Jeevanlal Maharaj, the religious head of one
of the Vaishnavite temples of Bhuleshwar in Bombay.

Young Bhatkhande, while he was studying in college,
was introduced to Vallabhdas by Gopal Giri. Vallabhdas was
not a professional musician and charged no fees. In the
beginning, Bhatkhande had to go to him stealthily to avoid the
objection of his parents. He had to serve his *guru,* now and
then, as was the custom of those days. Bhatkhande was much
impressed by his music and kept on listening to it regularly.
Vallabhdas did not give him any lesson for two to three
months. Perhaps he was trying his patience. But the impres-
sionable mind of Bhatkhande took note of every fingering, during
the playing of *sitar* by his *guru,* and after securing a *sitar* he
tried to play it all by himself under the guidance of Gopal
Giri. In the meantime, Vallabhdas started giving him lessons and
was surprised by his progress. The reason was that Bhatkhande,
having been a songster and a flute player, had already acquired
a good *swaragyan* and, therefore, could reproduce his lessons
quickly and faultlessly. Vallabhdas started teaching him with
enthusiasm and Bhatkhande flowered forth as a concert artist very
quickly.

Raoji Buwa Belbaugkar

After Bhatkhande passed his LL.B.examination in 1887, he joined the Gayan Uttejak Mandali, a music club founded by some wealthy members of the Parsee community of Bombay. Here he came into contact with Raoji Buwa who was in the employ of the Gayan Uttejak Mandali. Bhatkhande learnt about 300 *dhrupad*s from Raoji Buwa.

Ali Hussain Khayalia and (his uncle) Vilayat Hussain Khan

These two *ustad*s were also in the employ of the Gayan Uttejak Mandali. Bhatkhande learnt about 100 to 125 *khayals* from them. He considered these compositions as very valuable from the point of having a correct idea of a *raga*'s form.

Ashiq Ali Khan

He was the son of Muhammed Ali Khan of Jaipur. The family was known as *Kothiwal*s due to the fact that they had a store-house of songs belonging to an old *gharana*. Bhatkhande was introduced to him through Wadilal, who, in his turn, knew him through Muhammed Khan, the son of Naththan Khan.

In the mean time, Bhatkhande's idea about systematising music crystallised and he was engaged in collecting authentic compositions to formulate the theory of *raga*. Ashiq Ali was passing through financial difficulty and was introduced to Bhatkhande through Wadilal and Nazir Khan. Bhatkhande heard a few *khayals* from him and realised their value and, therefore, engaged him to teach him on payment of money. The arrangement was that Ashiq Ali would sing his *khayals* and Bhatkhande would take them down with notation and *tala* marks and reproduce them from the notations by voice. In this fashion within 2 or 3 months 250 *khayals* were learnt and recorded with notation.

Muhammed Ali Khan of Jaipur

He was the father of Ashiq Ali Khan from whom Bhatkhande learnt *khayal*. He was known as *Kothiwal*, meaning the owner of a store-house of compositions. He came down to Bombay and met

Bhatkhande to test how much he had learnt, from his son, the treasured compositions of his *gharana*. In good faith, when Bhatkhande took out his notebook and sang the *khayal*s from the notations, the old *ustad* got into an uncontrollable fit of anger and started abusing his son Ashiq Ali Khan for such abundant generosity. At this Bhatkhande, with tears in his eyes, fell at his feet and pacified him by assuring him that he would never misuse his *gharanedar* compositions and would always acknowledge his obligation. Accordingly, he considered himself as Muhammed Ali Khan's pupil and acknowledged him as his *guru* in the book *Hindustani Sangeet Paddhati*. In all, Bhatkhande learnt from him about 300 *khayal*s and *saadra*s of Manarang *gharana* to which the *ustad* belonged.

Nawab Hamid Ali Khan and Ustad Wazir Khan of Rampur

The Nawab of Rampur was a very good musician and a disciple of Wazir Khan, who was in his employ. Ustad Wazir Khan was a descendant and also the torch-bearer of the *gharana* of Tansen. Bhatkhande decided to collect the priceless compositions belonging to Tansen *gharana* and to overcome the narrow-mindedness of the *gharanedar ustad*s became the pupil of the Nawab Sahib. The Nawab considered it an honour as Bhatkhande's reputation as a scholar-musician had already spread far and wide. Very soon he made the Nawab ask Wazir Khan to teach him the compositions belonging to the Tansen *gharana* and the *ustad* had no other way but to agree. Thus Bhatkhande learnt from Wazir Khan many compositions belonging to the Tansen *gharana*.

Ganapati Buwa Milbarikar

He was a well-known musician. He took his music training from Bare Balkrishna Buwa, Krishna Shastri Shukla, Vasudev Buwa Joshi etc. He not only sang well but also had a good collection of compositions of different *gharana*s. He was introduced to Bhatkhande through one of his pupils. Bhatkhande was impressed by his knowledge and engaged him in the Gayan Uttejak Mandali. From 1910 till the end of his life he taught classical compositions to Bhatkhande at times.

After leaving Bombay in his old age he settled at Sangli and there he opened a music school, Chatur Sangeet Vidyalaya, in the name of Bhatkhande. He was a teacher of Bhatkhande but the gesture of opening a school in his name showed his affection and respect for his pupil. He died in 1927 at a ripe old age.

Eknath Pandit (alias Maoo Pandit)

He was the younger brother of the famous singer Shankar Rao Pandit. Both he and his brother received music training from Ustad Nissar Hussain Khan of Gwalior *gharana*. He used to play on *been* and *sitar* very well and also learnt by heart all the compositions of the Gwalior *gharana*. Once Bhatkhande engaged him on monthly salary and he came to Bombay to teach him compositions belonging to the Gwalior *gharana*. Bhatkhande learnt from him about 350 compositions.

Muhammed Ali Khan of Giddhaur

A resident of Rampur, he was a knowledgeable musician belonging to the family of Tansen. He was a reputed *rabab* player. He had a good stock of *dhrupad*s and *dhamar*s of Tansen tradition. Bhatkhande learnt a good number of compositions from him which he valued as having the basic notes of a *raga*'s form. Bhatkhande considered him as his *guru* and his training was made possible through the introduction of Nawab Hamid Ali, Chhamman Sahib and Thakur Nawab Ali.

Jiwanji Maharaj

He was a Mahant in a Temple of Bombay belonging to the Vaishnava Sect. He was a reputed *been* player. He was well-known for the demonstration of the following *raga*s: *Kedara*, *Darbari Kanhara*, *Bageshri*, *Malkauns* etc. His pupil was Vallabhdas Damulji from whom Bhatkhande learnt *sitar* at a young age. Jiwanji Maharaj collected many *grantha*s of theory which Bhatkhande had an opportunity to study. He encouraged Bhatkhande to take up the research work in music.

IV

CLOSE ASSOCIATES

The following were some of Bhatkhande's close associates, admirers and friends who were responsible for popularising his new method of teaching and propagating his movements:

Saadat Ali Khan (Chhamman Sahib)

Bhatkhande had a great friendship and a sweet relationship with the Prince of Bilsi -- Saadat Ali Khan Bahadur -- popularly known as Chhamman Sahib. He was related to the Nawab of Rampur and helped Bhatkhande to avail of music coaching from Ustad Wazir Khan. Bhatkhande came very close to the Nawab and was accepted in his household as a family member.

Both Chhamman Sahib and Bhatkhande discovered in each other a great love for music and an unbiased and analytical mind. Chhamman Sahib enrolled himself in Bhatkhande's movement for the revival of music and rendered him all help.

Bhatkhande's and Chhamman Sahib's opinions about the theory and practice of modern Classical music were so much alike that their concept of music appeared to be uttered by one and the same person. Their friendship was unique in nature and the common point of unity was pure music. Bhatkhande took his assistance and advice in formulating the theory from the compositions he collected. A consensus was worked out regarding the controversial forms of *Malhar, Sarang, Todi, Bilawal* and *Kanhara* in the All India Music Conference and a standard form was established with the help of Chhamman Sahib in consultation with other stalwarts.

Thakur Nawab Ali

Raja Nawab Ali was one of the foremost among the torch-bearers of Bhatkhande's movement. He was the Talukdar of Akbarpur and a reputed musician. He was responsible for introducing Bhatkhande to the Nawab of Rampur. He was an admirer and follower of Bhatkhande. Raja Nawab Ali will always be remembered for his book on music written in Urdu, the first of its kind in that period. He was inspired by Bhatkhande in writing this book in a series called *Marif-un-Naghmat*. He took an active part in the fourth and fifth Music Conferences held under the guidance of Bhatkhande.

Kashinath Sastry Appa Tulsi

One of Bhatkhande's most important and active supporters in his theoretical work was Appa Tulsi. While Bhatkhande was on his study tour he met Kashinath Sastry Appa Tulsi in Deccan. He explained to him the outline of the theory of music he had formulated, on the basis of the practice in vogue, and Appa Tulsi at once took up his ideas with enthusiasm. When Bhatkhande sent his *Shrimallakshya Sangeetam* to him, Appa Tulsi composed his own couplets of the definitions of the various *ragas* explained by Bhatkhande in his work. He wrote three pamphlets in Sanskrit, namely, *Sangeet Sudhakar*, *Sangeet Kalpadrumankur* and *Raga Chandrika* and one in Hindi, namely, *Raga Chandrikasar*, all on the basis of the definitions of *ragas* given by Bhatkhande, which he later quoted in his *Kramik Pustak Malika* series.

Shankar Rao Karnad

He was a Kanarese Brahmin and a lawyer at the Bombay High Court. He learnt music initially from a pupil of Maulabux of Gwalior. Later, he got acquainted with Bhatkhande and was much influenced by his work. He learnt the compositions of Bhatkhande and regarded himself as his pupil. He assisted Bhatkhande in all his Music Conferences at Baroda, Gwalior, Rampur etc.

Brijkishan Kaul

He was a Kashmiri Brahmin, residing in Delhi. He became the Secretary of the All India Music Conference held in Delhi. He had an intimate relationship with Bhatkhande which remained steady to the last. He took keen interest in the work of the Conferences and the proposed Music Academy.

Prof. S.L. Joshi

He was a Christian and worked as a Professor of English at Baroda

College. Dr. Bhalchandra Sitaram Sukthankar, who was a ward of Bhatkhande in childhood, was responsible for introducing him to Bhatkhande. He was much impressed by his movement and books and influenced the Maharaja of Baroda to arrange the All India Music Conference in the year 1916. Prof. Joshi worked hard to make this Conference a success.

Acharya Shri Bhaskar Rao Khandeparkar

A resident of Gwalior, he was a pupil of the famous singer Shankar Rao Pandit. He was well-acquainted with the work of Bhatkhande and a great admirer of him. He was responsible for Bhatkhande's introduction to the Royal family and the other renowned musicians of Gwalior. When the Music School of Gwalior was opened to implement the new method of teaching he was chosen as a teacher and he carried on with his work with much sincerity and labour.

Rai Umanath Bali

He was the uncle of Rai Rajeshwar Bali, the Talukdar of Daryabad, Uttar Pradesh. The planning of the fourth and fifth sessions of the All India Music Conference held in December, 1924 and December, 1925 was done by him which took place under Bhatkhande's guidance. It was proposed to have an Academy of Music in Delhi, which was abandoned later for some reasons. Thereupon Umanath Bali prepared a scheme to organise a music institution at Lucknow and to open an Academy there itself.

Accordingly, Music Conferences were arranged at Lucknow and the Marris College of Hindustani music was established. He was connected with this college till 1935. Bhatkhande passed away in the year 1936. Thereupon, to keep his memory alive, Umanath Bali started another institution called Bhatkhande Sangeet Vidyapeeth. Rai Umanath Bali took lot of pains to run this institution and looked after it throughout his life.

Dr. Bhalchandra Sitaram Sukthankar

He was working as a solicitor at Bombay. His father was well-known to Bhatkhande after whose death Bhatkhande agreed to look after the estate of the deceased and his young children. Bhalchandra was a ward of Bhatkhande from the tender age of seven. Bhatkhande lived at their house and had started his work for revival of music while residing there.

Bhalchandra was well-acquainted with Bhatkhande's movement and had accompanied him on his study tours. Bhatkhande considered him as his godson. He assisted Bhatkhande a great deal in publishing his books, the task he continued even after Bhatkhande's death. Unfortunately, he died at a young age in the year of 1940.

Premballav Joshi

He was a Brahmin from Kumaon and a great lover of music. He was very much impressed by Bhatkhande's movement and the literature on music published by him. He started corresponding with Bhatkhande and was always respectful to him. He worked as the Principal of the Government College, Ajmer and arranged for a Music Conference at Ajmer. He was an intelligent and learned man, well-known in the entire region of Rajasthan. As an active worker in Bhatkhande's movement, he used to be present at all the Music Conferences sponsored by him.

Dattatreya Keshav Joshi

He was a resident of Pune and possessed a great liking for music. He learnt music from Pandwa and Ganapati Buwa Milbarikar. He read the book published by Bhatkhande and was much influenced by them. Later, an affectionate relationship developed between him and Bhatkhande. He also helped him in publishing his books. He was working as a teacher in a Marathi school and was known as Dada Sahib. He used to visit Rampur, Gwalior and Baroda along with Bhatkhande and used to be present in the Music Conferences at Delhi, Banaras and Lucknow. After the Marris College of Music was founded, he came to Lucknow and stayed there for two years. He had several books to his credit.

Nazir Khan

After the death of Raoji Buwa, Nazir Khan joined the service of the Gayan Uttejak Mandali of Bombay. He was a leading *sarangi* player and a knowledgeable and experienced man in music. He got interested in Bhatkhande's work on theory and the rules of the *ragas* as framed by him. Bhatkhande composed the definitions of *ragas* in songs *(Lakshan Geets)* and he taught some of them to Nazir Khan. Nazir Khan himself taught them to his pupils, namely, Anjanibai Malpekar, Achchhanbai of Lucknow and others.

Kale Nazir Khan

Kale Nazir Khan was a well-known vocalist and a knowledgeable person in the theory of music. He was employed as a court musician in Rampur Darbar. He had training in *alapa* and *dhrupad*, singing under Ustad Zakiruddin Khan, at Udaipur. Prior to his coming to Rampur he was in the employ of the Talukdar of Akbarpur, Raja Nawab Ali. Raja Nawab Ali heard the reputation of Bhatkhande and to satisfy his curiosity deputed Kale Nazir Khan to assess his knowledge by sending him down to Bombay. Kale Nazir Khan was much impressed by Bhatkhande's deep study of music and systematic work, which he reported to Raja Nawab Ali. This greatly helped to develop a friendly relationship between the Raja Sahib and Bhatkhande. Kale Nazir Khan was responsible for introducing Bhatkhande to the Nawab of Rampur.

Anjanibai Malpekar

She was a famous singer of Bombay. She received her music training from Ustad Nazir Khan Sahib. As has been stated in the paragraph prior to the preceding one, Ustad Nazir Khan was a teacher in the Gayan Uttejak Mandali. Bhatkhande was a member of this club where he used to give lectures on the theory of music as formulated by him. Nazir Khan learnt many *lakshan geets* and the *shlokas* of *Shrimallakshya Sangeetam* composed by Bhatkhande and taught them to Anjanibai Malpekar. She used to sing them in the music concerts and was responsible for popularising them.

Dhaklibai Sukthankar

Dhaklibai was the daughter of M. Shantaram Narayan Patkar, a wealthy lawyer of Bombay. She became a widow at a young age while her children were minor. She was not able to look after her property which was given to her by her father. Therefore, Shantaram Patkar, who knew Bhatkhande and his family well and was much impressed by Bhatkhande's intelligence and honesty, engaged him as a trustee of the large estate of lands and buildings which he had gifted to his daughter. Bhatkhande carried on with this responsibility with efficiency and accompanied Dhaklibai Sukthankar in her pilgrimage to all corners of the country where he studied the *granthas* in different libraries and had the opportunity of discussing the problems of music with the scholars and musicians. Later, it was her son who took up the responsibility of publishing Bhatkhande's books.

B.V. Keskar

B.V. Keskar was a lecturer in the Sanskrit Vidyapeeth, Banaras. Later, he became the Information and Broadcasting Minister in Delhi. He learnt *dhrupad* from Hari Narayan Mukerji of Banaras and was well-acquainted with Bhatkhande's movement. It was he who translated in Hindi from Marathi the theoretical part of *Kramik Pustak Malika* series.

Maharaja Vijay Devji of Dharampur

The writer of *Sangeet Bhava* was Vijay Devji, the ruler of Dharampur. He came in contact with Bhatkhande and was inspired by him. He appreciated and supported Bhatkhande's movement and rendered great help in popularising it.

In addition to these Rai Bahadur Lala Sultan Singh, Rai Bahadur Damodar Das, Nawab Ahmed Sayeed Khan of Loharu and Prof. P. B. Joshi were also Bhatkhande's close associates who were helpful to him in spreading his new concept of music teaching and making various Music Conferences a success.

V

THE SCHOLARS HE MET

During his study tours and on other occasions Bhatkhande met and discussed music with a large number of scholars. Below are given a few names:

Shrikrishna Joshi

Shrikrishna Joshi was a scholar and a knowledgeable person residing in Allahabad. During his study tours Bhatkhande met him and discussed his theory with him.

Dhurjati Prasad Mukherji

He was a professor at the University of Lucknow and a great lover of music. He used to come and meet Bhatkhande and spend his time with him in lively discussions on music.

Raja Sir Sourindra Mohan Tagore

Popularly known as Raja Sahib, Sir Sourindra Mohan Tagore was a well-known landlord of Bengal. He was highly respected as a musicologist and a writer of many books on music. Bhatkhande read his books and visited him during his study tours. He discussed many problems of music with the Raja Sahib. Tagore became an admirer of Bhatkhande and kept on writing to him on this subject.

VI

HIS PUPILS

The following are the names of some of his important pupils who learnt directly from him and entertained deep devotion for him throughout their lives:

Wadilal Shivram

He worked as a composer of music and music director in a Gujarati drama company. Nazir Khan, the *sarangi* player in the employment of the Mandali and a great admirer of Bhatkhande, was the *guru* of Wadilal Shivram. He brought him to Bhatkhande to study the Sangeet Shastra under his guidance. Wadilal was also a learned person in Sanskrit literature. He found that Bhatkhande was not only a theorist but had in his possession quite a good stock of the traditional compositions which he sang perfectly in a tuneful voice.

Wadilal was greatly impressed with his knowledge and practical ability in music, his great culture and high educational attainments. An attachment grew in him for his *guru* and it was so deep that he continued his zeal even after Bhatkhande's death. Wadilal studied all old Sanskrit texts on music then available under Bhatkhande's instructions and learnt hundreds of traditional compositions.

Dr. Shrikrishna Narayan Ratanjankar

He was the most important among his pupils. He came in contact with Bhatkhande in the year 1911 and received training from him till his death. He passed B.A. from the Bombay University in the year 1926 and was appointed as a professor of vocal music at Marris College of Music at Lucknow. In 1928, he was selected as the Principal of the College. He retained that post for 28 years and propagated the new method of training introduced by Bhatkhande. In 1957, he was selected to function as the first Vice-Chancellor of the Indira Kala Sangeet Vishvavidyalaya, Khairagarh. He retired after serving there for three years. He received music training from Ustad Faiyaz Khan also.

Dr. Ratanjankar had written many articles on all aspects of music. He was well versed in Sanskrit, English, Gujarati, Hindi and Marathi which he learnt in the interest of the theory of music. He trained hundreds of students who became well-known in this field. He composed hundreds of classical songs, under the pseudonym of 'Sujan' and also composed new *ragas* which were acclaimed by the scholars. Some of his books are *Tana Sangraha, Abhinava Sangeet Shiksha* and *Abhinava Geet Manjari*. He can rightly be called an institution and not an individual. His place is in the forefront among the music scholars of today.

Acharya Rajabhaiya Poochhwale

His real name was Balkrishna Ashtekar. His predecessors came from the South and settled in a village called Poochh at Jhansi. They had landed property there. Later they settled in Gwalior. He

was working as a typist in an office at Gwalior. He had a great
love for music and had his music training from the renowned
musician Shankar Rao Pandit of Gwalior. He learnt *dhrupad* and
dhamar from Vamanrao Deshpande. After Bhatkhande came to
Gwalior at the invitation of the ruler of Gwalior, Rajabhaiya got
the opportunity to meet him. He was then an accompanist on the
harmonium and played with Madhav Rao Scindia, when he sang
bhajans. He was one of the teachers of the Music School who
was selected to be trained in Bhatkhande's new method of training
music. Accordingly, he was sent to Bhatkhande at Bombay for
his special training.

Rajabhaiya was so deeply influenced by Bhatkhande's scholarship
and affectionate behaviour that he started respecting him as his *guru*.
This regard he entertained throughout his life. He was an eminent
khayal singer. In addition to that he had a good collection of *thumari*s and *tappa*s. Bhatkhande held him in great esteem for his
authentic knowledge and his adherence to the traditional form.
Bhatkhande collected many compositions from him belonging to the
Gwalior *gharana* and later depended on him for the correction of
the defective traditional compositions.

In the beginning, Rajabhaiya was engaged as a Senior Professor
in the Madhav Music College, Gwalior. After some years he was
engaged as the Principal of that College. He trained hundreds of
pupils who even now sing and play following the method introduced
by Bhatkhande. Rajabhaiya had a successful career and received
the award from Rashtrapati towards the end of his life.

Rabindra Lal Roy and Hemendra Lal Roy

These two educated Bengali youths enrolled themselves as students
at Lucknow Marris College. Rabindra Lal Roy wrote a book *Raga
Nirnaya* in Bengali and later he was appointed as the Dean of the
Faculty of Music at the University of Delhi.

Sachindra Kumar Datta

He was a graduate from Calcutta University. His brother, Himanshu
Kumar Datta, was a renowned poet and composer of music in
Bengal. After studying for five years at Lucknow, he became a pupil
of Ustad Alauddin Khan of Maihar and made a name as a *sitar*

player and a teacher.

Narayan Lakshman Gupte

He was the first Graduate who passed from the Madhav Sangeet Mahavidyalaya, Gwalior. Bhatkhande was very fond of him and mentioned about him in his notes. He worked as an ordinary teacher at Gwalior School where he was appointed as the Principal later.

Balaji Shridhar Pathak

He was a resident of Sagar, Madhya Pradesh. He enrolled himself as a student at the Music School, Gwalior, in 1920. He was a favourite student of Bhatkhande who appointed him as a teacher at the Lucknow College of Music.

Hirjibhai Doctor

He was one of the many Parsee pupils of Bhatkhande. He was appointed as the Principal of Baroda Sangeet Mahavidyalaya. He was an expert player of *dilruba* and *vichitra veena*. He started learning from Bhatkhande from the year 1925 and became a skilful musician.

Then there were the musicians who were specially selected by Bhatkhande to be trained in his new method of teaching and then to act as teachers in different music schools. Some of them were: Krishnarao Date, Bhaskar Rao Khandeparkar, Vishnurao Deshpande, Baburao Gokhale, Balwant Rao Sable and Chunnilal Kathak.

VII

MUSICIANS WHO IMPRESSED BHATKHANDE

There were some eminent musicians whose performance always deeply impressed Bhatkhande and he held them in great esteem. He also depended on their demonstration for formulating his theory of music. Some of them were:

Zakiruddin Khan and Alabande Khan

These two brothers were the grandsons of the famous Behram Khan. They were experts in *alapa*. They were also able to form hundreds of combinations with the relevant notes of a *raga*. They used to sing *dhrupad*s with well-cultivated sweet and deep voice. They were introduced to Bhatkhande by Wadilal, his pupil. Bhatkhande, as he was a great admirer of these two brothers, invited them to attend the All India Music Conference in 1916. Practical demonstration by them proved that the notes of harmonium were not suitable for practising *swara*s of *Ragadari* Music. Their successors are still keeping their tradition alive in the name of *Dagar*.

Ustad Faiyaz Khan

At the time of Bhatkhande Faiyaz Khan was acclaimed as an ideal singer with a novel style. He was a court musician of Baroda. He introduced a new style in *khayal* with the help of the style of *dhrupad* of which he had a good repertoire. He was an expert demonstrator of *dhrupad, dhamar, tappa, thumari, ghazal, Kavvali* etc. Bhatkhande met him at Baroda and appreciated his art. Faiyaz Khan composed many *khayal*s using his pseudonym as Premapia. Some compositions he did on his own and some he did at the request of Bhatkhande which the latter published in the *Kramik Pustak Malika* series. Mutual admiration and friendship developed between him and Bhatkhande and the latter deputed his favourite pupil, Shrikrishna Ratanjankar, to learn from him.

Bundu Khan Saranginawaz

He was introduced to Bhatkhande through Nazir Khan. He was an eminent *sarangi* player of his time who supported and appreciated Bhatkhande's movement for the revival of music. He learnt hundreds of *lakshan geet*s composed by Bhatkhande which he used to demonstrate on his *sarangi*. He approved Bhatkhande's theory of music and helped to propagate it.

Alauddin Khan Maihar

He was one of the torch-bearers of the Rampur *gharana* of music with which Bhatkhande was also associated. He was a reputed *sarod* player and also well versed in other instruments such as violin, *pakhavaj*, clarionet, *sursingar* etc. He was a trend setter of the modern style of playing on the plucked string instruments and successfully trained many pupils. He was employed as the Principal of the Maihar Royal School of Music. Bhatkhande had great admiration for him and had a great friendship with him.

Vishnu Digambar Paluskar

The most important person among Bhatkhande's contemporaries was Vishnu Digambar Paluskar who was a noted musician and a musicologist who launched a similar movement to that of Bhatkhande's. In fact, a student of musicology cannot make a beginning without studying their lives and their immense work done in this field.

Paluskar hailed from Maharashtra and received his training in music from Pandit Balkrishna Buwa. He had an attractive sweet voice by which he used to charm the listeners. His demonstration helped to rouse the desire for learning sublime music among the public. As a result Gandharva Mahavidyalaya was established which opened branches all over India. These are still running with credit in many cities. He devised a notation system which was somewhat different from Bhatkhande's. He was the author of many books on music. Some of the important books are: *Sangeet Balbodh*, *Sangeet Balprakash*, *Sangeet Tattvadarshak*, *Raga Pravesh* etc. He trained many pupils who became famous musicians. His son, D.V. Paluskar, was one of them.

Though both Bhatkhande and Paluskar were contemporaries, the work that each undertook, in the field of music, was rather different in nature. Whereas Bhatkhande dedicated his whole life to research in ancient and contemporary Indian music and endeavoured to give a systematic shape to it, Paluskar endeavoured to spread music practically and to gain for it a respectable place in society. As has been stated earlier, till that time the musicians were considered as belonging to the lower strata of society and respectable persons shunned them though they appreciated their art. The modern generation would perhaps find it difficult to conceive the plight of the Indian musicians and the art of music in those days. These two stalwarts worked for the uplift of music and their propagators with undaunted courage and tenacity. They worked throughout their lives to attain this goal.

13

Conclusion

I

INTRODUCTION

On August 10, 1860 was born a child at Bombay whom his father
-- a Brahmin, working as a *munim* to a rich *seth* -- named Gajanan.
When he grew up under the name of Vishnu Narayan Bhatkhande,
he was destined to bring about a revolution in the world of music
and give it a scientific basis. Within 30 years he established its
credentials as an academic subject and created a country-wide
movement to establish education of music on modern lines, thereby
ensuring its easier and wider propagation. The purpose of the
present study has been to get an integrated and objective view of
this extraordinary man and his phenomenal work in an historical
perspective.

II

AIMS AND OBJECTIVES OF PRESENT STUDY

The above broad aim may be spelt out as follows:
  A. To consolidate, classify and analyse his contributions and
      assess objectively the herculean task he performed to resus-

citate, revive and systematise Hindustani Classical music.
B. To establish the linkages between his work, his life and
    personality and his environment.
C. To give an analysis in depth of every important aspect of
    his contribution. In the available literature references to
    different aspects of Bhatkhande are scattered.
D. To study his work from the historical, social and cultural
    points of view.

III

BHATKHANDE AND HIS AGE

He lived, grew up and worked in an age when there was an upsurge
of political and patriotic consciousness and an all-out effort was
launched by the thinkers, leaders, seers and path-finders to recognise
and re-establish India's glorious past in all spheres of life. In fact,
out of the ashes of the 1857 uprising were born the path-finders
of the new India. The heralds of the new dawn paved the way
for a great awakening in the mass consciousness of the people of
this country. In the last half of the 19th century India witnessed
a great renaissance in every walk of life -- religion, politics, social
structure, literature, art, music etc. It was a period that saw the
end of mere imitation of Western modes on the one hand and
revival of India's own values on the other -- a period of reaffirmation
of all that was best in the past of India and readjustment of the
past to the new realities. Bhatkhande was born in this great age
and imbibed all its inspiration, imagination and creativity. He was
the man destined to bring together in a grand synthesis our rich
heritage in the field of music, rescue it from current degeneration
due to the various adverse influences of foreign rule and neglect
of the educated class and give it a new strength and vigour.

The Current State of Music

In the beginning of the nineteenth century, music -- like the other
branches of art, culture and education -- also reached a stage of
degeneration and stagnation. The disappearance of the Mughal
Court and the other big principalities, where the musicians had

earlier congregated, led to the scattering of talent to the courts of the petty chieftains. The musicians developed their art in isolation from one another, giving rise to the *gharana* system. While the system produced many eminent performers and led to the emergence of different styles, it also bred narrow-mindedness and resulted in factional quarrels. The musicians adopted the degraded life-style of their masters and brought down their art to cater to their cheap tastes. On the top of it their orthodox temperament, conservative ideas and arrogant air alienated the educated class which branded music as fit only for the loafers and vagabonds.

Although there were some performing musicians of high calibre, they were illiterate, ignorant and contemptuous of the Sanskrit *granthas* and the theory written therein. There was no coherent theory to back current practice. Instead, fanciful stories occupied the place of the rules and regulations of the *ragas*. The condition of the training of music was deplorable. The musicians were conservative and did not want to part with their knowledge. A student had to do physical labour for years or spend a fortune to have music lessons. The absence of theory as a guiding force and the system of whimsical oral teaching -- not to speak of any notation system or textbooks -- led to incomplete and haphazard knowledge, much to the dismay of the educated music lovers.

IV

MENTAL MAKE-UP AND PERIOD OF PREPARATION

Bhatkhande had an inborn aptitude and taste for music. Nature endowed him with sharp intellect, poetic quality and aesthetic sense. On top of it he had the cool, analytical capacity of a scientific mind. Like all others belonging to the high castes of the period he also joined school and college and finally qualified as a lawyer. But the musician in him sought self-expression and he started learning from various teachers from an early age. Because of the taboo on the learning of music, he learnt *sitar* stealthily in his college days and showed proficiency in it. As it was the common belief in those days that music was not fit for respectable people, his elders were worried about his future. But he dispelled everybody's fears by passing in the law examination and starting its practice. Like every other common man, he also married and settled down to earn through practising law but his love for music remained undiminished.

He continued his contact with music by becoming a member of the Gayan Uttejak Mandali -- a private association run by the Parsees -- to promote and propagate Classical music. Here he came in contact with many knowledgeable musicians from some of whom he learnt compositions and others he only listened to. From then onwards the picture of the real state of music as it existed in that period revealed itself before his eyes. An important point that Bhatkhande, with his mind well-trained in modern methodology, noted was that although the musicians were incapable of any coherent explanation about the salient features and other important points of a *raga*, there was a system, a method in their rendering and enough material existed even then for research and systematising the theory underlying the practice of current music.

His contact with the Gayan Uttejak Mandali proved a boon as he came in intimate contact with some of the cream of musicians of those days who were employed by the Mandali. Bhatkhande started learning from them *khayal*s and *dhrupad*s, and kept a diary noting down the movements of the note patterns etc. He started collecting compositions of the old masters to have a correct idea of the forms of the various *raga*s from the combination of their note patterns. He had an uncanny sense of *swara* and could record any song in notation instantly. He deduced the system behind the forms of the *raga*s from the compositions he collected and prepared short articles on that which he read out among his friends from time to time. Some of his musician friends encouraged him and he plunged himself into the work of discovering and elucidating the theory underlying the practice of contemporary music.

In the meantime his only infant daughter and wife died as if God wished him to be wedded to music alone, denying him any other distraction. With this, he renounced all worldly life and devoted his entire energy, time and intellect to the cause of music. He took a vow not to accept a single penny from his dedicated work and through his legal practice he earned just enough to sustain himself. Later he gave up even his legal practice and led a life of self-imposed poverty, always learning, collecting and increasing his store of knowledge, always dreaming and planning and working to serve more and more the cause of music.

At this time he was appointed a trustee of a large estate of lands and buildings left by a successful and wealthy lawyer of Bombay to his widowed daughter, Dhaklibai Sukthankar, who had minor children. It was her son, when he grew up, who became the publisher of Bhatkhande's books. Dhaklibai Sukthankar went on pilgrimage all over India and Bhatkhande accompanied her. His interest in the tours was not religious but to dig out our past heritage of music from the *granthas* available in all corners of our country. He visited all the libraries of the principal cities of the country and studied hundreds of *granthas* available there. He made a note of the relevant points, translated the facts that were clear for future reference and on the anomalous parts he prepared a series of questionnaires. He went to different *ustads*, *pandits*, musicologists and scholars for understanding the difficult portions of the *granthas* at all the places he visited. It was amazing how he studied hundreds of Sanskrit *granthas*, digested them, analysed them and discussed them in his books written in Marathi and English; thus greatly minimising the labour of a future student of music. Before writing his books, he approached the *gharanedar ustads*, the touch-bearers of the heritage of Classical music, and learnt from them. He took care to collect the priceless compositions belonging to the *gharanedar ustads*, for he realised that those were the basic source for understanding the form of the present day *ragas*. He spent a life of 30 years of most intensive research work which saw the light of the day in the form of several significant contributions.

V

HIS CONTRIBUTION

The Main Thrust of His Effort

The main thrust of Bhatkhande's effort was to understand and elucidate the system underlying the rendering of the various *ragas*. This would facilitate the understanding, learning and teaching of music. He felt that the fundamental characteristics of a *raga* should be clearly indicated to establish its identity and individuality. He also wanted to put Classical music at par with other academic subjects, having enough written material for study and research. Again, he wanted to introduce collective education, necessary for its wide propagation. His aim was to free music from dogmatism and conservatism, elevating it above the barriers of caste, creed and religion. He wanted to provide the sound base of theory, which would save music from distortions, unavoidable in an exclusively oral training. In short, his purpose was to create expert performers, discerning listeners, competent critics, devoted pupils, dedicated teachers and interested patrons.

His Conviction

Music is a dynamic art. It changed during the centuries like human habits, customs and society through a natural evolutionary process. He realised that the present form of Classical music was different from that of the ancient period. It was important from the historical point of view to study this process and the ancient *grantha*s and the theory embedded therein. In view, however, of the many changes that had taken place during the centuries, the highest priority at the moment was to elucidate the system underlying current practice so that the listeners and learners both could be benefited by it. He felt that the present age had developed interaction with the ideas of the outside world because of the easy communication system. Native States, which had sheltered the musicians were abolished. On top of that there was a movement by the path-finders of modern India to remove the barriers dividing man and man. Under all these circumstances it was Bhatkhande's conviction that the modern generation of musicians could not remain isolated and tied to different *gharana*s. The musicians of today should have opportunities of listening to and learning the different styles of Classical music.

Collecting the Scattered Treasure

For the purpose of reconstructing music on scientific lines, the first step he took was to collect traditional compositions from all available quarters. It was obvious that the *raga*s, that were played and sung in his time, had developed forms which were much changed from what they had been described in the *grantha*s. Therefore, to learn and understand the changed new forms of the *raga*s one had to depend on the practical demonstration of the traditional compositions. His collections started from the *ustad*s belonging to the Gayan Uttejak Mandali and then he went on to other *ustad*s of the *gharana*s of Jaipur, Gwalior and Rampur. To rescue the compositions from the orthodox *ustad*s he had to suffer humiliation and resort to many ingenious ways to acquire his objective. He also collected disc recordings of the compositions sung by some reputed musicians. He compared, analysed and scrutinised these compositions again and again to bring out a clear picture of a *raga* and its salient features. He discussed his findings with his friends who were knowledgeable before arriving at his conclusions. Later he published these compositions in the textbooks written by him, i.e., the *Kramik Pustak Malika* series. Like an honest scholar and a sincere artist he gratefully acknowledged his obligation to the musicians from whom he learnt and collected compositions.

His endeavour to collect and publish the compositions proved a great step forward in making music available to all the music lovers. Nobody had ever dreamt at that time that the *gharanedar* musical compositions which were imprisoned in the *doodh-khoon ke rishte* (blood relations) tradition would ever be available for learning at any price by outsiders. Another reason for publishing these compositions was that he believed that if the *khayal*s of Jaipur were accepted in Gwalior, or vice versa, the consciousness for national unity would be developed. In those days of British rule which fostered sectarianism, Bhatkhande was responsible for establishing the triumph of the spirit of unity on the national and secular front through the vehicle of music.

As a Composer

One of his greatest contributions in the field of music is the hundreds of songs he composed in all types of Classical music. He wrote them in notation and published them in the *Kramik Pustak Malika* series to be learnt freely by any lover of music.

These compositions, varied in nature, are marked by certain qualities peculiarly his very own. They are lyrical and endowed with a deep spiritual insight into the world and creation. Another characteristic of Bhatkhande is that he avoided vulgar words, common place ideas and cheap thoughts which tarnished many a traditional composition. His rich and apt imagery, combined with the balanced and beautiful blending of words and the appropriate classical melody -- all establishing and enhancing the proper mood of the *raga* -- give his creation a unique character. These compositions are a proof of his versatile genius and a singer can draw upon them in case he finds the word content of traditional compositions incoherent and vulgar or their musicality inadequate and incorrect.

His compositions are written in chaste language, embodying coherent thoughts -- devotional and sublime. While he gave them the colour of the traditional compositions, they are rich in poetic imagery, luminous in ideas and well-balanced within the *raga*'s framework -- with its *vadi*, *samvadi* and catch notes. Unlike some traditional compositions they are pleasantly readable as poems.

The store-house of *lakshan geets*--which he composed in the form of *dhrupad*, *saadra*, *chhota khayal* and *bara khayal* bear testimony to his poetic genius and creative ability. They indicate and describe the rules and regulations of a *raga*, wonderfully balanced in words and tune. They also mention its counterpart in Karnatak music. The *lakshan geets* can be sung independently as *chhota khayals* and, in fact, that is often done by the artists. It is an easy and effective method to teach his theory and analysis of a *raga* to a student of music through the *lakshan geet*.

He observed that the ancient *granthas* did not throw any light on the principles which should guide the compositions of tune and song, so that every one had to fall back on a limited stock of *ustadi* songs, the correctness of which no one could be sure of, as they had never been recorded in notation and had only been handed down orally from generation to generation. If these principles could be determined and standardised, incorrect versions of the *ustadi* compositions could be corrected while new compositions could be created.

With the idea of providing a wider choice of compositions, he, therefore, evolved a principle to guide and up to the end of his life he composed songs and reached these priceless compositions to every home -- at least two for one paise through his *Geet Malika* series. In this way he left a vast treasure for posterity.

Providing the Theoretical Framework

His greatest contribution, however, was to formulate and establish a well-reasoned and easily intelligible, systematic theory of the current practice of music. In this regard, firstly, he explored the old *granthas*. He translated some of them which he thought would be useful in the present context. He wrote annotated editions of some others. His books on the theory of current music are invaluable and are the result of long years of research.

His main finding about the old theory was that the *shrutis* and *swaras* as expounded by the old masters could not be pinpointed on the gamut due to the absence of any measurement of the gaps between the *shrutis*. He also found that due to various factors the forms of the *ragas* had changed a great deal from their old forms though they might have still retained the old names. He defined clearly *ragas* and *thaats* and formed their rules which deviated from their ancient definitions. He fixed the present day *swaras* on the gamut scientifically, by counting the vibrations per second. He placed the position of *re* and *dha* on the gamut with the help of the practical demonstrations of the stalwarts of music. In fixing the *swaras* on the gamut he also took into account the traditional theory of the 'Cycle of the Fifth'.

In this process of formulating the theory of current music he connected the present day music with the ancient theory wherever possible. He evolved 10 *thaats* or the parent scales and distributed the existing *ragas* among them, thus ending the centuries old experimentation of the old scholars about the number of *thaats*.

He accepted the *Bilawal* scale as the *Shuddha* scale. He systematised the time theory and established the connection of different notes with different times of the day and night. He classified the existing *ragas*:

1. according to the *komal* and *shuddha swaras* they use,
2. under the ten parent scales,
3. according to the time of singing,
4. according to *vadi swaras* -- the governing or the expressive note of a *raga*,
5. according to the *purvanga* (lower tetrachord) and *uttaranga* (higher tetrachord), and
6. according to the *ragangas* such as *Kanhara anga, Malhar anga, Sarang anga* etc.

It was Bhatkhande, who, for the first time, made it known to the public in the North that there were two distinct systems -- the Karnatak and the Hindustani and that the nomenclature of the *shuddha* and *vikrit swaras* of these systems were different from one another. Even in South India itself these facts were little known and it was after Bhatkhande's publications that the attention of people in the South was drawn to them.

His exploration of the ancient theory from the *grantha*s helped to solve diverse, mysterious and baffling theories of music as expounded by the old scholars. But for his efforts the music of the past centuries would have passed into oblivion. His formulation of the present day theory bore the stamp of his genius -- an imaginative mind, balanced with rationalism and sanity -- which made the study of music easy for the future generations.

Establishing Academic Status and Methodology of Music

One of his most important contributions was to modernise the method of teaching music and introduce it for group education in schools and colleges, thus elevating music to the status of an academic subject. While bringing about a virtual revolution in the teaching method of music, he was fully conscious of our great heritage and never failed to remind the public of its glorious traditions.

The first school, Madhav Sangeet Mahavidyalaya, imparting and propagating his new method of teaching, was established in 1918 at Gwalior, which proved to be a great success. Sayajirao College of Music in the State of Baroda followed. Later a series of similar institutions were opened at Indore, Jaipur, Bombay, Poona, Nagpur and Calcutta. In 1926 the Lucknow Marris College was established and examinations were being conducted under the name of Bhatkhande Sangeet Vidyapeeth.

After due experimentation, a syllabus was fixed for the five-year study course, having 45 *raga*s. Out of these 25 *raga*s were taught during the first three years and 20 *raga*s in the course of the last two years. During this period, a student had to learn *dhrupad, dhamar, bara khayal, chhota khayal, saadra, lakshan geet, chaturang, tarana,* etc.

Bhatkhande had always issued elaborate written instructions to the teachers about the implementation of his new method of teaching. These instructions bear testimony to his powerful vision and administrative ability.

For the purpose of collective education in music he wrote textbooks, namely, the *Kramik Pustak Malika* series, which included hundreds of traditional compositions along with his own. They included a brief comparative study of the modern and ancient theory in regard to *swara*s and *raga*s as well as an introductory chapter of present day theory, preceding each of the *raga*s discussed therein. They also contained *raga vistar* of each *raga* in note names at the back of each book. The first four books of the *Kramik Pustak Malika* series were scheduled to be taught within five years. He wrote two more books under this series which contained less common *raga*s and prescribed them to be studied during a further period of two years. In all, seven years of study was fixed under this scheme. He also wrote *Hindustani Sangeet Paddhati*, a treatise in four parts, discussing elaborately each *raga* from the historical angle. This treatise deals with the subject of music in all its aspects.

Bhatkhande was also the one to start written examinations in music, which was unknown to the music world so far. He set the question papers in a fashion which could be equated and compared with those in other academic subjects. The marking process also followed the same principle. The music examination comprised of both practical and written examinations. At the end of the fifth year the successful candidates were conferred upon a diploma called *Sangeet Visharad*. Similarly, *Sangeet Nipun* was conferred at the end of seven years of study.

It was only through Bhatkhande's efforts that music could be introduced as a modern subject in the academic field taking it as a part of our education and culture. He was the saint, the seer and the artist whose toil paved the way for a new era.

Music Conference as a Tool and Strategy

For the purpose of spreading the message of music far and wide among the masses, to build up a rapport between the musicians and the public and to give music a respectable and academic shape Bhatkhande arranged Music Conferences. Five All India Conferences were held at five different places -- Baroda, Delhi, Banaras and lastly, twice at Lucknow. He was a permanent member of the association which organised these conferences and he was the nucleus around which all the activities pertaining to them revolved. In India, these conferences, for the first time, brought to light the different musical styles of the North and the South. Almost all the stalwarts of music (both vocal and instrumental) belonging to the different *gharanas*, came together on such occasions. The result was that, apart from the mutual discussions and differences, some common points could emerge, thereby reducing the area of controversy about the forms of the various *ragas*. In the conferences several schemes to rebuild the future of Hindustani music were also put forth by Bhatkhande.

The greatest achievement of these conferences was to put the practising stalwarts of different *gharanas* on one platform and enable them to perform for the general public. They had the salutary effect of unfolding the rich treasure of our Classical art to the educated and the enlightened. They also helped a great deal in minimising the *gharanedar* quarrels and also settled some disputes about the different versions of a *raga* as practised in different pockets of Northern India. These conferences laid the foundation stone for a great movement and focussed the nation's eyes on music and its problems. Through these conferences he put the Hindus and the Muslims on one platform, thus elevating music above caste, creed and religion. The institution of conferences, which was started by Bhatkhande, has now become a part of the cultural life of the country.

Forming a Notation System

To propagate his new method of collective education in music Bhatkhande invented and formulated a notation system and recorded in it all the compositions he could get hold of. All his textbooks have the *raga*'s movement and salient points written in notation with an introduction to its signs in the beginning. The signs coined by him are crisp, simple and expressive and clearly indicate a *raga*'s form. He insisted on training in music being conducted with the help of notations right from the beginning and trained a team of teachers to implement his ideas. He experimented with his method of teaching through notation in his first school, established at Gwalior, which proved highly successful. For, it gave a quick grasp of *swaragyan*, a quick understanding of a *raga*'s characteristic movement and the immediate picking up ability of different types of classical compositions. Bhatkhande strongly advocated the cause of a universal notation system for the reason that it would create a common understanding in the artistic field and would build up emotional integration among musicians and music lovers. It would prevent distortions which inevitably result from an exclusively oral method of teaching. It would also keep a correct record of present day music for posterity. There were many experiments in regard to notations -- signs and forms -- by contemporary scholars, which Bhatkhande was aware of. He studied them and found them unsuitable for his purpose. He finalised his own system of notation after due experimentation.

He accepted the fact that all the subtle nuances of music and all the balances of rendering could not be expressed and recorded through notations. Nor was it possible to express through notation a characteristic particular shade of a note in a particular *raga*. Bhatkhande was of the opinion that his notation system was a basic skeleton which helped a learner to be well versed in the grammar of Classical music and only a sound knowledge of the grammar could create well-qualified performers, teachers, critics and listeners.

Having formulated an easy notation system and introduced it as a medium of instruction in music, Bhatkhande brought to an end the age old system of exclusively oral training and establishing a scientific method which was largely responsible for giving music a well-defined shape.

By his deep research and analysis over many years Bhatkhande opened up new vista for further research for the future generation. The scope of further research has been mentioned at proper place of this treatise.

VI

ORGANISATIONAL AND ADMINISTRATIVE ABILITY

The mighty movement he launched for the revival and reform of Hindustani Classical music and carried to a grand success would not have been possible but for his great organisational and administrative ability. He was a leader of men who inspired many a stalwart to join and serve his movement. He was also a master of detail in manpower-management, laying down of detailed procedures and carefully ensuring the necessary inputs as well as the anticipated results.

Overcoming Social Taboos

A picture of the state of music of his time has already been presented. When he worked for uplifting Hindustani music from its decadent state he had to face social, intellectual and, finally, professional prejudices. These were not merely at the academic or abstract level. These were prejudices taking the shape of positive obstacles to the development of music. To overcome them, he had to adopt various methods. His many-splendoured personality became an asset in winning over the hostile forces.

His movement removed the social stigma attached to music. It gave young people the opportunity to give free vent to their natural instinct for rhythm and tune, having relieved them from repression, censorship and ban.

He elevated music to the high pedestal of glory and popularity by weeding out the vices, dogmatism and vulgarity which had become a part and parcel of the life and character of most of the musicians of the time. Himself a picture of manliness, grace, simplicity and honour, rich in knowledge and humour, he lifted up the image of musicians in the public mind. He carried this image everywhere -- from the huts to the palaces.

VII

THE END

Bhatkhande's contribution is so varied, so profound and so vast that it is difficult to comprehend its magnitude at one glance. He acted and worked tirelessly for the revival of a glorious art, by listening and writing. His insatiable thirst for information and knowledge and manifold activities helped to establish a musical heritage which was comprehensive, non-sectarian and scientific. He was always eager to add to the already achieved, to more information and knowledge, looking after the publication of his books, arranging Conferences, planning and working always to give more and more to inspire and help the students and lovers of music.

His life was a saga of sacrifice and a melody of renunciation.

The rulers of Baroda and Gwalior wanted to keep Bhatkhande in their respective states with lucrative remuneration and other amenities. But he refused and, like a roaming apostle, preferred to go round from place to place looking after the different schools at Baroda, Gwalior, Lucknow etc. holding examinations, preparing reports and issuing instructions to the teachers for the betterment of performance. Life flowed swiftly for this intellectual giant and in the year 1933 his myriad activities came to a sudden halt when he was struck by paralysis at Bombay. He was suffering from high blood pressure and the premonition of death had been haunting him for some time.

A letter written by him to his dear pupil Shrikrishna Narayan Ratanjankar and reproduced on page 483 of the *Bhatkhande Smriti Grantha* is indicative of such premonitions:

Dated: 16th Feb., 1933

"My dear Babu,

I feel that my life has reached the end of its journey... I have done whatever I deemed my duty. Whatever material I could collect I have recorded and protected it. I have full faith that in future there will be worthy people to use it suitably. While writing, sometimes with over-enthusiasm I have used sharp words in discussing the theory of music. But believe me, it was not intended to hurt anybody's feelings... I am greateful to my countrymen for the appreciation of my work.

At the end I would like to say that I bow to the God Almighty who helped me even in my declining years to fulfil my dream and enabled me to complete my work. Jai Jagdish!

-- Bhatkhande."

He was bedridden for two and a half years but his indomitable spirit and energy showed no decline. He used to write and discuss with his friends lying down in bed. In those days the fourth part of the *Hindustani Sangeet Paddhati* had just been published and the 5th and 6th parts of the *Kramik Pustak Malika* series were on the way to be published. On the 19th September, 1936, on the festive religious occasion of *Ganesh Chaturthi* day, this epoch-making figure of Indian music departed to the other world forever, leaving his name to be symbolised by a lifetime of devotion, dedication and sacrifice. For, in his lifetime he worked armed with nothing else but unsoiled integrity and utter surrender to a noble and great cause. Thus ended the eventful life of a person who remoulded and reshaped music into modernity and lifted it, from the degenerate state into which this great heritage had fallen, to its present position of pristine glory.

Bibliography

Ahobal, *Sangeet Parijat*, Sangeet Karyalaya, Hathras

Ali, Raja Nawab, *Marif-un-Naghmat*, 2 Parts, Sangeet Karyalaya, Hathras

Arthur, Sir, G., *Life of Lord Kitchener*

Basu, Raj Narayan, *Sakal and Ekal*, published by Prabhulal Garg

Bhatkhande, Pandit V.N., *A Comparative Study of the Music Systems of the 15th, 16th, 17th and 18th Centuries*

Bhatkhande, Pandit V.N., *A Historical Survey of the Music of Upper India*, published by Karkhore Manekji Minocha of 'Bombay Samachar,' 1917

Bhatkhande, Pandit V.N., *Abhinava Raga Manjari*, Sangeet Karyalaya, Hathras

Bhatkhande, Pandit V.N., *Abhinava Tala Manjari*, Sangeet Karyalaya, Hathras

Bhatkhande, Pandit V.N., *Hindustani Sangeet Paddhati*, 4 Volumes, Sangeet Karyalaya, Hathras

Bhatkhande, Pandit V.N., *Kramik Pustak Malika*, 6 Volumes, Sangeet Karyalaya, Hathras

Bhatkhande, Pandit V.N., *Shrimallakshya Sangeetam*, Sangeet Karyalaya, Hathras

Blassemera, *Theory of Sound in its Relation to Music*

Bolts, William, *Considerations on Indian Affairs*, London, 1972

Briggs, John, *The Present Land Tax in India*, London, 1830

Chappill, *History of Music*

Chinchore, P.N., *Bhatkhande Smriti Grantha*, Indira Kala Sangeet Vishvavidyalaya, Khairagarh

Clements, E., *Introduction to the Study of Indian Music*, Longman, Green and Co.

Damodar, *Sangeet Darpan*, Sangeet Karyalaya, Hathras

Dattil, *Dattilam*, Sangeet Karyalaya, Hathras

Dibelius, Wilhelm, *England*, Jonathan Cape, London, 1930 (Translated from the original German Edition, 1922)

Durant, Will, *The Case for India*, Simon and Shuster, New York, 1930

Durant, Will, *The Story of Civilization*, Simon and Shuster, New York, 1930

Dutt, Romesh, Burke's Speech, quoted from *The Economic History of India under Early British Rule*, Kegan Paul, Trench Trubner and Co. Ltd., London

East India Papers, Vol. II, London, 1820

Encyclopaedia of Indian Music with Special Reference to Ragas

Forest, Selections from *The Minutes and other Official Writings of the Hon. Mount Stuart Elphinstone*, 1885

Gandhi, M.K., 'Brahmo Samaj's Contribution to Hinduism,' *Young India*, August 30, 1928

Graham, G.F.I., *Life and Work of Sir Syed Ahmed Khan*, 22nd Edition

Joshi and Lobo, *Introducing Indian Music*, Sangeet Karyalaya, Hathras

Kaye, *Life of Metcalfe*

Lochan, *Raga Tarangini*

Marshall, Sir John, 'The Prehistoric Civilization of India,' *Illustrated London News*, Jan. 7, 1928

Mehta, R.S., *Psychology of Music*, Sangeet Karyalaya, Hathras

Nanyabhupal, *Bharat Bhashyam*, Sangeet Karyalaya, Hathras

Narad, *Sangeet Makarand*, Sangeet Karyalaya, Hathras

Paluskar, Pandit Vishnu Digambar, *Sangeet Balprakash*, 3 Parts

Paluskar, Pandit Vishnu Digambar, *Sangeet Balbodh*, 4 Parts, Vishnu Digambar Sangeet Prakashan, Pune

Patvardhan, Vinayak Rao, *Raga Vigyan*, Sangeet Gaurav Grantha Mala, Pune

Poplay, Herbert, A., *Music of India*, Association Press, Calcutta

Projnanananda, Swami, *Historical Development of Indian Music,* Firma K.L. Mukhopadhyaya, Calcutta

Ramamatya, *Swaramelakalanidhi*, Sangeet Karyalaya, Hathras

Ramji, Firoz, *Hindustani Sangeet Ki Encyclopaedia* (Hindi), Sangeet Karyalaya, Hathras

Rao, H.P. Krishna, *The Psychology of Music*, Western Mission Press, Mysore, 1916

Ratanjankar, Pandit S.N., *Pandit Bhatkhande*, National Book Trust, New Delhi

Report of First Indian Music Conference Held at Baroda-1916, Baroda Printing Works, Baroda

Ritter, *Student's History of Music*

Ronaldsay, Earl of, The, *The Heart of Aryavarta,* Constable and Co. Ltd., London, 1927

Sharma, D.S., 'Ancient Wisdom', quoted in *Studies in the Renaissance of Hinduism*, Banaras Hindu University, Varanasi

Sharngadeva, *Sangeet Ratnakar*, Sangeet Karyalaya, Hathras

Shrikantha, *Rasa Kaumudi*, Sangeet Karyalaya, Hathras

Singh, Thakur Jaidev, 'Guru Shishya Parampara', *Lipika*, Vol. II, Sonis and Rajam Printers, New Delhi

Smith, Wilfred Cantwell, quoted in *The Causes of the Indian Revolt in Modern Islam in India*, Minerva Book Depot, Lahore, 1943

Strangway, A.H. Fox, *The Hindu Scale*, Clarendon Press, Oxford

Strangway, A.H. Fox, *The Music of Hindoostan*, Clarendon Press, Oxford, 1914

Tagore, S.M., *Hindu Music*, published by Babu Panchanan Mukherji, Calcutta, 1875

Tagore, S.M., *The Six Principal Ragas*, Calcutta Central Press Co. Ltd.

Tagore, S.M., *Universal History of Music*, Sangeet Karyalaya, Hathras

Thompson, E. and Garatt, G.T., *Rise and Fulfilment of British Rule in India*, Macmillan and Co. Ltd., London, 1935

Vishnu Digambar, Sangeet Prakashan, Pune

Glossary

Alapa	:	Melodic elaboration of a *raga* without the rhythmic accompaniment preceding a demonstration.
Alpatva	:	A technical term of ancient music denoting the usage of a note in a *raga*.
Anga	:	Melodic phrase integral to a particular *raga*.
Ansha	:	A term used in ancient music denoting the most important note of a *raga*.
Antara	:	Second part of a musical composition which moves to the upper octave.
Anuvadi	:	Notes other than the *vadi* and *samvadi* in a *raga*, subordinate in importance to the other two.
Apanyasa	:	A term used in ancient music denoting the rule of a pause in a *raga*.
Aroha	:	Ascension of notes.
Ashraya Raga	:	An important *raga* of a certain scale with particular note combinations which accommodates other *raga*s having the same notes.
Auduva	:	Pentatonic *raga*s.
Avaroha	:	Descension of notes.
Bahutva	:	An ancient term of note movement in a *raga*.
Bandish	:	A classical composition in words.
Bhava	:	Emotion.
Bol	:	Words in music or the rhythmic sound of a per-

	:	cussion.
Bol (Tabala)	:	Sounds of a percussion instrument to produce set music designs.
Boltan	:	Melodic textual variations.
Cheej	:	Music composition with words.
Dhamar	:	It is similar to *dhrupad* but less grave in melodic progression and denotes the festival of colours (see also *Hori*).
Dhrupad	:	Types of classical song set in a *raga* having intricate rhythmic patterns which flourished in the 15th and 16th centuries.
Drut Laya	:	Fast tempo.
Gamak	:	The grace that pleases the mind of the listener. Produced by reiteration of notes giving the effect of forceful shake or trill.
Gayaki	:	State of singing with graces, trills and glides.
Gharana	:	Houses or families specialised in the technicalities of classical music each with its own specific style.
Graha	:	The note characteristically commencing a section of the melody.
Grama	:	Two standard scales (*Shadja* & *Madhyam*) of the ancients.
Hori	:	The colour festival celebrated in Spring. Denotes classical and semi-classical music connected with it.
Jati	:	Melodic type of the ancient music.
Kan	:	A grace note within the periphery of the main note, slightly below or above it, used as an embellishment.
Kayada	:	An arrangement of *bol*s with definite indication of the *tala* sections.
Khali	:	A softer beat of a *tala* preceding the *sam*.
Khayal	:	It is accepted at present as the highest form of classical art in North India. It allows melodic variation and improvisation within the framework of a *raga* and is more free and flowery compared to *dhrupad*.
Komal Swara	:	Distorted or intermediate note.
Lakshan Geet	:	Classical song describing the rules of a *raga* and

		set in that particular *raga*.
Laya	:	Tempo.
Madhya Laya	:	Medium tempo.
Madhya Saptak	:	The middle octave.
Mandra Saptak	:	The lower octave.
Marga	:	Classical type of ancient music.
Matra	:	Smallest unit in time measure having equal gaps.
Mela	:	Sanskrit name for a parent scale.
Moorchhana	:	Later development of *grama* as the musical scale of the ancients.
Mukhra	:	First line of a musical composition.
Nayaki	:	Broad framework of a classical composition without any embellishment.
Nyasa	:	Notes on which one can pause according to the prescribed rules of a *raga*.
Pakad	:	Typical musical catch phrase to identify a *raga*.
Prabandha Geeti	:	A classical composition having four parts which was sung before the advent of *dhrupad*.
Purvanga	:	Lower tetrachord.
Raga	:	A melodic scheme having traditionally accepted rules with the possibility of improvisations.
Rasa	:	Aesthetic emotion.
Saadra	:	Compositions in 10 *matra* beat called *Jhaptal*.
Sam	:	The first beat of the *tala*.
Sampurna	:	Heptatonic *ragas*.
Samvadi	:	The second important note in a *raga* which has a relation of fourth to fifth note to the *vadi*.
Saptak	:	Group of seven notes in an order of increasing pitch to form a scale equivalent to an octave.
Sarana	:	A kind of string instrument without frets.
Sargam	:	Note name *(Sol-fa)*.
Shadava	:	Hexatonic *ragas*.
Shadja Pancham Bhava	:	The cycle of the fifth note.
Shruti	:	Microtones.
Shuddha Swara	:	Natural notes.
Sthayi	:	First part of a classical composition.
Sur	:	Melody
Swara	:	Basic major musical notes.

Tala	:	Rhythm used in music having various patterns with equally divided gaps. The essential characteristic is its cyclic or repetitive nature.
Tana	:	Very fast musical note rendered in rhythm usually with vowels.
Tappa	:	The songs of camel-drivers of North-West have been made refined in classical *tappa*. It is recognised by very quick turns of phrase with no slower elaborations.
Tara Saptak	:	The upper octave.
Tarana	:	Meaningless syllables woven into a rhythmic piece in a *raga*.
Teevra Swara	:	Sharp note.
Thaat	:	Musical scale capable of producing *raga*s.
Theka	:	The assigned basic set of *bol*s in musical compositions by which a *tala* is identified.
Thumari	:	It is a lyrical variety of light classical music, romantic in mood and less rigid as a *raga*.
Uttaranga	:	Upper tetrachord.
Vadi	:	The note most significant in a *raga*.
Varjit Swara	:	Discarded note.
Vikrit Swara	:	Distorted from natural notes or intermediate notes.
Vilambit Laya	:	Slow tempo.
Vivadi	:	A dissonant note but sometimes used in a restricted fashion to enhance the beauty of a *raga*.

Index